COMPETING DISCOURSES

ORTHODOXY, AUTHENTICITY, AND ENGENDERED MEANINGS IN LATE IMPERIAL CHINESE FICTION

Harvard East Asian Monographs 197

Competing Discourses

Orthodoxy, Authenticity, and Engendered Meanings in Late Imperial Chinese Fiction

Maram Epstein

Published by the Harvard University Asia Center
and distributed by Harvard University Press
Cambridge (Massachusetts) and London, 2001

Printed in the United States of America

The Harvard University Asia Center publishes a monograph series and, in coordination with the Fairbank Center for East Asian Research, the Korea Institute, the Reischauer Institute of Japanese Studies, and other faculties and institutes, administers research projects designed to further scholarly understanding of China, Japan, Vietnam, Korea, and other Asian countries. The Center also sponsors projects addressing multidisciplinary and regional issues in Asia.

Library of Congress Cataloging-in-Publication Data
Epstein, Maram.

Competing discourses : orthodoxy, authenticity, and engendered meanings in late Imperial Chinese fiction / Maram Epstein

p. cm. -- (Harvard East Asian monographs ; 197)

Includes bibliographical references and index.

ISBN 0-674-00512-0 (alk. paper)

1. Chinese fiction--Ming dynasty, 1368–1644--History and criticism. 2. Chinese fiction--Ch'ing dynasty, 1644–1912--History and criticism. 3. Women in literature. I. Title. II. Series.

PL2436.E67 2001
895.1'34609--dc21

00-050598

Index by the author

Printed on acid-free paper

Last figure below indicates year of this printing

10 09 08 07 06 05 04 03 02 01

To Barbara and Leo and Amos,

for seeing me through the last millennium and into the new

Acknowledgments

The research for this book began over fifteen years ago as an attempt to fill in some of the silences of my graduate training. Many of the details in the novels we read for seminars were so odd, and sometimes even disturbing, that none of us, including myself, felt comfortable discussing the implications of what was so clearly laid out before us. I have been fortunate that the fields of Chinese gender studies and late imperial fiction have come into maturity as I continued to wrestle with these long and unruly novels, for recent scholarship in both fields has provided me with the vocabulary to explain why I believe gender (what I naïvely called "women" back then) is so central to the study of Chinese fiction.

My intellectual and scholarly debts exceed what can be expressed in the notes. I remain grateful to my dissertation committee, Andrew H. Plaks, Yu-kung Kao, and Willard Peterson, for insisting on the primacy of the text and for setting such high standards of scholarship. I hope to challenge my own students with these same humanistic goals. I could not have finished my dissertation without the support and critical insights of Thamora Fishel; she helped me to understand that people and texts can speak their truths in many voices and that being a good listener, or reader, requires listening for the contradictions and points of conflict.

I would like to express my gratitude to the many people who have read all or portions of the manuscript: Barbara Altmann, Katy Carlitz, Elise Hansen, Wilt Idema, Andrea Goldman, Wendy Larson, Hongwei Liu, Cathy Silber, Rui Shen, Ellen Widmer, and Shiyi Yu. I owe a special thanks to Waiyee Li and David Rolston, who went beyond the call of friendship in providing me with their generous criticism and corrections, and to the two anonymous readers for the press, who went beyond the call of collegial duty in pointing out an embarrassment of necessary corrections. It has been a delight to work with John R. Ziemer of the Harvard University Asia Center;

throughout the process, he has treated the manuscript with as much care as any author could hope. This book is much stronger for the contributions of all these readers. For my own reading, I would like to thank Bob Felsing of Knight Library at the University of Oregon, who always manages to do the impossible during this period of budget cuts, and the staff, especially Martin Heijdra, of Gest Library at Princeton University. Those who taught me how to read the Chinese novel deserve my greatest thanks because I still remember the bewilderment I felt as an undergraduate after my first attempt. Andrew Plaks and David Rolston showed me the importance of commentaries; Naifei Ding and Pat Sieber modeled the necessity of reading against received traditions; the work of Katherine Carlitz and Keith McMahon, always seeming to appear just as I am noticing a certain textual issue, has opened up many new texts and methodologies to me.

Over the years, I have been fortunate to receive support from Princeton University, the Gest Library at Princeton, the University of Oregon, and the American Council of Learned Societies. I would also like to thank my chairs from the Department of East Asian Languages and Literatures at the University of Oregon, Wendy Larson and Mike Fishlen, for allowing me to engineer several terms off for writing. The most precious support comes from one's family. My greatest thanks go to Barbara Altmann and her sons, Leo and Amos, for opening their hearts and home to me; and to Susan Sygall and Tom Broeker for their contagious joy in celebrating all of life.

M.E.

Contents

REFERENCE MATTER

Abbreviations

The following abbreviations are used in the text and the notes. For complete citations, see the Bibliography, pp. 315–39.

A History	Fung Yu-lan, *A History of Chinese Philosophy*
Cambridge History	Frederick W. Mote and Denis Twitchett, eds., *The Cambridge History of China*, vol. 7, pt. I, *The Ming Dynasty, 1368–1644*
CQFL	Dong Zhongshu, *Chunqiu fanlu zhuzi suoyin*
DMB	L. Carrington Goodrich and Chao-ying Fang, eds., *Dictionary of Ming Biography*
ECCP	Arthur W. Hummel, ed., *Eminent Chinese of the Ch'ing Period*
EN	Wen Kang, *Huandu woshu shi zhuren ping Ernü yingxiong zhuan*
HLM	Cao Xueqin and Gao E, *Honglou meng bashihui jiaoben*
HLMJ	Yisu, *"Honglou meng" juan*
JHY	Li Ruzhen, *Huitu Jinghua yuan*
JPM	Wang Rumei et al., *Zhang Zhupo piping Jin Ping Mei*
JSL	Zhu Xi and Lü Zuqian, *Jinsi lu jizhu*
MDT	Tang Xianzu, *Mudan ting*
MRXA	Huang Zongxi, *Mingru xue'an*
Orthodoxy	Kwang-ching Liu, ed., *Orthodoxy in Late Imperial China*
Records	Julia Ching, trans., *Records of Ming Scholars*

Reflections	Wing-tsit Chan, trans., *Reflections on Things at Hand, by Chu Hsi and Lü Tsu-ch'ien*
SG	Chen Xizhong et al., *Sanguo yanyi huiping ben*
SHZ	Chen Xizhong et al., *Shuihu zhuan huiping ben*
SJPB	*"Honglou meng" sanjia pingben*
Source Book	Wing-tsit Chan, *A Source Book in Chinese Philosophy*
XS	*Xingshi yinyuan zhuan* (1993)
YSPY	Xia Jingqu, *Yesou puyan* (1881, 152-chapter edition)
ZYZ	Chen Qinghao, *Xinbian Shitou ji Zhiyan Zhai pingyu jijiao zengding ben*

COMPETING DISCOURSES

ORTHODOXY, AUTHENTICITY, AND ENGENDERED MEANINGS IN LATE IMPERIAL CHINESE FICTION

Introduction

In the traditional Chinese symbolic vocabulary, the construction of gender roles was never far from philosophical debates about ritual propriety, desire, and even cosmic harmony. This study of Ming-Qing fiction attempts to map out the ideological and aesthetic meanings invoked by the use of gender in five *xiaoshuo* 小說 novels that span the mid-seventeenth century to the mid-nineteenth century. Recent Western scholarship has made great contributions in mapping out the poetics of Ming and Qing *xiaoshuo* fiction by shedding light on how long narratives are organized and derive meaning from a number of symbolic structures, including five-element 五行 correlative symbolic systems, *yinyang* 陰陽 bipolarity, and karmic retribution, as well as specifically Buddhist, Daoist, and syncretist Neo-Confucian enlightenment narratives.[1] However, since sexual difference was not included in traditional commentaries as a substantial category of analysis, modern scholars have tended to overlook its importance. My discussions of the poetics of gender are meant to complement these other structural approaches to traditional Chinese fiction by adding gendered differences as another tool of analysis. In addition to showing how gender complementarity, as a form of bipolarity, was exploited by writers of fiction and drama as a compositional feature, this book also considers the cultural meanings implicit in gendered tropes, of which traditional writers may not have been consciously aware.

Within the past decade, there has been a veritable explosion of published research on women's lives and the status of women in late imperial China. Although I began with the hope that my readings in *xiaoshuo* fiction would

1. See, e.g., Plaks, *Archetype and Allegory*; idem, *Four Masterworks*; Roy, "Translator's Commentary" and "Introduction," in *The Plum in the Golden Vase*, pp. xxxii–xlviii; Carlitz, *Rhetoric*; Martinson, "Pao, Order, and Redemption"; and A. Yu, "Introduction," in *The Journey to the West*, 1: 36–62.

shed light on developments in social history, this project took me in a very different direction when I realized how little attention has been paid to the way literary convention informs fictional depictions of gender. To the social historian of China who faces a dearth of sources on domestic life, novels contain a trove of information on women. The novel does open a precious window onto the past, but it is a window that distorts our view in ways that are as yet little understood. Before we can read fiction as a reliable source for history, we need to learn to read it as a fictional construct that may shed more light on the historical imaginary than on historical practices. Some readers of this book may be dismayed by how seldom I take note of recent scholarship on the lives of actual women and my seeming refusal to connect the changing fictional depictions of women to social changes. For now, however, I have felt it important to limit this book to the intermediate stage of identifying and analyzing the fictional conventions of gender. Entering a traditional novel is sometimes like walking into the Fun House at the local carnival; the mirrors tweak reality in ways that are entertaining and often highly predictable. Many of the depictions of women in traditional fiction, the shrews especially, read as if they were some weird parodic refraction of the Confucian ideal. Even though the most extreme fictional stereotypes may derive from social reality, they can take on a life of their own and may come, in turn, to influence social practice. The question of the relationship between the fictional worlds mirrored in the traditional Chinese novel and social reality is a complex one and beyond the scope of my research here. Yet it is the issue that motivates my interest in the poetics of the novel.

Even though it is clear that gendered terms are important to structure and meaning, it is largely impossible to pin down their exact meanings in *xiaoshuo* novels. However, since the manipulation of gendered terms is crucial to the meanings produced by the texts discussed in this book, I attempt to map out the range of meanings implied by each of them. This hermeneutic process is complicated not only by the rich ambiguity of many of the symbolic terms employed in Chinese fiction but also by the fact that traditional Chinese novels are less unified than their European cousins and frequently resist unifying readings. The "episodic" nature of the Chinese novel, long taken to be a weakness of the genre by critics steeped in Western aesthetics, can also be seen as adding a heteroglossic breadth by allowing a variety of voices to speak with equal authority. From a deconstructionist perspective, the full meaning of these texts can be found precisely in the unresolved tensions between the parts. Commentators on and editors and writers of traditional fiction were aware of the repetitive and somewhat loose narrative development of many longer narratives and took great pains to argue for narrative intentionality, even for those texts that were based on oral story cycles and were clearly accretive in composition. These defenders of fiction, the most influential of whom was the great commentator Jin Shengtan 金聖歎 (1608–61), devised an aesthetic and interpretive system based on structural and rhetorical patterns that gave a sense of unity to these sprawling texts. However, despite their best efforts to convince readers of the narrative integrity of the great novels, the inconsistencies remain. In this study, I show how gendered terms are used as a compositional device to give these novels structural coherence; I then argue that these neat structural patterns are frequently at odds with other gendered meanings raised in the texts.

Although the organization of this study is loosely chronological, my interests and arguments are more thematic than historical. The progression of intellectual and aesthetic trends is not linear, for changes in cultural taste both incorporate and react against what came before. By arranging the texts chronologically, I risk implying lines of influence where there may be none. Thus, even though *Yesou puyan* 野叟曝言 (A country codger's words of exposure) reads convincingly as a response to *Honglou meng* 紅樓夢 (Dream of the red chamber; also known as *Shitou ji* 石頭記, The story of the stone), there is no evidence that Xia Jingqu 夏敬渠 (1705–87), the author of *Yesou puyan*, knew of the *Honglou meng*. It is more likely that he wrote his novel as a reaction against those same aesthetic trends that inspired Cao Xueqin 曹雪芹 (ca. 1715–ca. 1763). Moreover, even though I argue that the construction of gender associated with the discourse of authenticity derived from orthodox rhetoric, the two discourses existed in a dialectical, not a sequential relationship. Indeed, *Xingshi yinyuan zhuan* 醒世姻緣傳 (Marriage bonds to awaken the world), my primary example of orthodox fiction, was not published until half a century after *Mudan ting* 牡丹亭 (Peony pavilion), an enormously influential drama that epitomizes the aesthetics of authenticity. Moreover, rather than attempt an exhaustive study, I have limited my focus to five novels; the primary criterion in choosing them was that they do interesting things with gender. As I have read more broadly in Ming-Qing fiction, I have been reassured to discover that the gendered patterns of meaning I see in these works are representative.

Despite my reluctance to frame my readings of fiction historically, there is no doubt that a profound shift in *xiaoshuo* aesthetics occurred during the seventeenth century. Only 150 years separate the earliest circulation of manuscripts of the two greatest traditional novels of manners, *Jin Ping Mei* 金瓶梅 (The golden lotus) and *Honglou meng*, yet the depictions of desire in each novel could not be more different. *Jin Ping Mei* depicts a ruthless society in which the main characters, especially the central male protagonist, Ximen Qing 西門慶, are driven by crude impulses, which stimulate their senses in ever more extreme forms, and a will to power through the acquisition of wealth and social status and the domination of others. Relations between the characters are so embattled that it seems the only route to peace of mind is to withdraw from the corrupt sexual, economic, and political economies depicted in the 100-chapter novel. Although *Honglou meng* draws upon *Jin Ping Mei* structurally and thematically, the relations between the male protagonist, Jia Baoyu 賈寶玉, and the many girls who surround him are of a different order than those between Ximen Qing and his six wives. The Grand Prospect Garden in *Honglou meng* provides the setting for a celebration of sensuality in minute detail; this utopic feminine microcosm seems to offer the promise of spiritual redemption. The dystopic *Jin Ping Mei* reduces humanity to a series of brute and frequently sadistic desires; the narrative has been so successful that Ximen Qing's fifth wife, the murderous Pan Jinlian 潘金蓮, has become an icon in Chinese culture of the dangers associated with female sexuality. The two most important girls in *Honglou meng*, Lin Daiyu 林黛玉 and Xue Baochai 薛寶釵, quickly came to represent two modes of feminine desirability. Although the proponents of these two beauties may be engaged in a debate whether Lin Daiyu's emotive and quick self-expressive wit or Baochai's steady but reliable reserve represents femininity in its fullest perfection, both sides could agree that the feminine in *Honglou meng* had taken on more positive meanings than those in *Jin Ping Mei*. This book attempts to make sense of this radical shift in attitude toward women and the feminine during this crucial period in the development of fiction aesthetics.

It was not just in fiction that the status of women had become a subject of discussion. By the seventeenth century and continuing into the Qing, despite, or perhaps because of, the vast socioeconomic changes that were reorganizing urban society, the Confucian dictum that the sexes needed to be segregated and hierarchically separated in order to maintain social order was voiced from all quarters: household instructions compiled by clan elders, school primers such as the *Xiaoxue* 小學 (Elementary learning), the *Nü xiaojing* 女孝經 (The classic of filial piety for women), and non-Confucian sources such as popular precious scrolls (*baojuan* 寶卷) printed by Buddhist communities for lay members all repeated similar messages about women's position in society.[2] Yet, even as the volume of conservative writings about women increased, the fiction of the period flirts with and celebrates images of women and girls who transcend the limits of ritual in their roles as lovers, creative talents, and knights-errant. Clearly, the status of women was being contested in a number of arenas. However, as I will argue, the construction of gender in fiction is different from that found in other kinds of writings. Within the literary context, both the feminine and the masculine, as signs within the cultural imaginary, took on meanings that went beyond the social debate about the status of women.

Rather than explaining the changing gender depictions, especially those of women, as somehow reflective of social practice, a task better left to social historians,[3] or as a form of political allegory in which the sympathetic depictions of women in many Qing novels are read as expressive of Han loyalism under the alien Manchu regime,[4] this study reads the various, and frequently conflicting, images of women and the feminine within the context of the sixteenth-century debate about the place of desire (*yu* 欲) and the emotions (*qing* 情) in human nature. A number of influential figures, including the controversial Li Zhi 李贄 (1527–1602), a thinker closely associated with the early production of commentaries to vernacular fiction, attacked institutionalized Neo-Confucian ritualism as inimical to a true expression of each individual's nature and as having transformed moral self-cultivation into a spiritually empty, if not hypocritical, performance. These revisionists questioned the moral integrity and intellectual validity of the basic metaphysical

2. For Confucian sources, see Furth, "The Patriarch's Legacy"; Kelleher, "Back to Basics"; Pei-yi Wu, "Education of Children"; Birge, "Chu Hsi and Women's Education"; and Mann, "Grooming a Daughter for Marriage." For popular Buddhist materials, see Overmyer, "Values in Chinese Sectarian Literature"; and idem, *Precious Volumes*. See Despeux, *Immortelles de la Chine*, for a discussion of the adoption of Confucian values into Daoist regulations for nuns instructing them to be filial, respectful, yielding, reasonable, and without jealousy.

3. For studies of elite women's lives in late imperial China, see Ko, *Teachers of the Inner Chambers*; and Mann, *Precious Records*.

4. Both *Honglou meng* and *Jinghua yuan* have been read in this light. See, e.g., Cai Yuanpei 蔡元培 (1868–1940), *"Shitou ji" suoyin* 石頭記索引; and You, *"Jinghua yuan* de zhuzhi."

premises of Neo-Confucianism and began imagining possibilities of a more humanist and activist moral order. Their critiques of Neo-Confucian philosophy and practices, which they often exaggerated for polemical ends, helped fuel the rise of the cult of sentiment (or affect, *qing*) during the latter half of the sixteenth century. As discussed in Chapter 2, although their number was small, these iconoclastic figures had a disproportionate influence on the development of cultural and literary aesthetics.

This book breaks into two halves: the first two chapters provide the background to the sixteenth-century "culture wars," which were so crucial to the late Ming appropriation of the feminine as a positive counterbalance to the perceived excesses of institutionalized Neo-Confucianism. In this section, I define the two dominant discursive systems that I see as informing the poetics of gender in late imperial fiction. The two poles of the ideological continuum that frame my readings are a broadly defined Neo-Confucian orthodoxy and the late Ming cult of sentiment. Chapter 1 argues that a number of common gendered tropes were derived from orthodox discourse. In my definition, "orthodoxy" (*zheng* 正), a broad concept historically invoked by those who wished to strengthen their claims to political, moral, and intellectual legitimacy, literally meaning "the upright," "the correct," is best understood in its gerundive sense as the process of regulating or bringing order—"making orthodox" or "correcting"—rather than as a rigid and unchanging set of beliefs. A number of cultural tools were available to Neo-Confucian literati to regulate their world: first and most important was the performance of ritual, the complementary practice of introspective self-cultivation and the externally oriented governance of family and state; a second and related, but less obvious, tool was the spreading of Confucian values by reproducing patterns of order (*wen* 文) through cultural production (also *wen*), especially literature. Although the details of ritual performance and the process of ritual mastery were hotly debated during the late imperial period, evidence points to a near-universal acceptance of the necessity of the fundamental principles of Confucian ritual as a means to maintain social order.

In the first chapter, I build on the work of cultural anthropologists to suggest that hierarchically differentiated gender roles were an essential component of Confucian ritual theory because of their role in naturalizing and anchoring the system of abstract *yinyang* correspondences that informed natural, social, and metaphysical epistemologies. Although the Confucian system of binary gender roles was not rooted in an essentialized biology, as it has been in the European West, by the late imperial period the maintenance of distinctions between male and female was widely treated as foundational to the social order. As shown in the associative symbolic logic of correlative thinking, tampering with this naturalized social order was thought to disrupt the cosmological balance. The primacy of hierarchical gender differentiation, in which the male is dominant and the female subordinate, may explain why so many of the orthodox narratives directed at men about the necessity of self-cultivation are framed as fantasies about embattled relations between the sexes.[5] The figure of the shrew, particularly the licentious *yinfu* 淫婦, who is emblematic of female transgression, is crucial to these depictions of the inversion of the social and moral order.

The other component I identify as integral to orthodox discourse is formalism. Highly patterned and regular structures were quickly adopted as an important aspect of fiction aesthetics as fiction commentators began to equate a text's formal aesthetics (*wen*) with the author's ethical vision. As I hope to show, the manipulation of *yinyang* symbolism in fictional texts is a central node where formalism and orthodox values intersect: orthodox narratives make use of a broad range of associatively linked *yinyang* symbolism to construct metanarratives about the loss and reinstatement of normative Confucian order. Within these narratives, *yin* is loosely associated with loss of order and *yang* with order.

Chapter 2 discusses the idealization of the feminine and the fascination with gender fluidity in late sixteenth-century fiction within the context of the late Ming critique of the Neo-Confucian bias against desire. This philosophic reformulation of the desires and emotions as a positive and authentic expression of self gave rise to an aesthetic movement that made use of a counterhegemonic vocabulary derived from orthodox norms. At the core of the aesthetic movement was the development of an iconography of *qing*, a system of *yin*-associated values that promoted the feminine and the natural as markers of moral and spiritual authenticity (*zhen* 眞) in contrast to a mechanical, even false (*jia* 假) ritualism.

To be sure, I am uncertain whether the thinkers or writers discussed throughout this study would recognize or accept the terms I use to name the two framing ideological stances of orthodoxy and authenticity. Yet these English terms, which impose an artificial clarity and polarization on a

5. For self-cultivation as a central theme of late sixteenth- and seventeenth-century vernacular fiction, see Plaks, *Four Masterworks*; and McMahon, *Causality and Containment*.

densely tangled web of ideological and aesthetic ideas and values, get at a very real intellectual schism that peaked during the latter half of the sixteenth century. No reader of Li Zhi's writings can fail to appreciate his anger; equally powerful was Huang Zongxi's 黃宗羲 (1610–95) decision to exclude Li Zhi from his anthology of Ming intellectual history, the *Mingru xue'an* 明儒學案 (Records of Ming scholars). The orthodox position is easier to define; it takes as its basis the teachings and practices of Cheng-Zhu Neo-Confucianism and its bias against the subjective self.

The authentic is more amorphous; it was the result of a frustration with the rigidity and prescriptive nature of institutionalized Neo-Confucian practices and teachings, and it sought to create a greater tolerance for self-expression. Because the defenders of *qing* defined the "authentic" against conventional orthodoxy, the marker of authenticity became the unconventional, even the eccentric. Despite the often polemical discursive strategies adopted, however, the goals of many of those who promoted *qing* were not all that different from those of more orthodox thinkers, who also sought to reinvest ritualism with deep personal significance. Two of the most beloved examples of authentic behavior in fiction and drama, Du Liniang 杜麗娘 of *Mudan ting* and Jia Baoyu of *Honglou meng*, create distinct, even if temporary, worlds of self-expressive passion that resist orthodox norms. Most other authors did not create so radical an opposition between authenticity and orthodoxy; in fact, in most writers' hands, unconventional behavior, emblematic of authenticity, became a necessary stage in reclaiming the conventional orthodox values of filiality and loyalty as authentic rather than rote. The appropriation of a highly sentimentalized femininity was one of these unconventional expressions of authenticity. The imaginings of a reinvigorated literati culture based on the subjective and dynamic qualities of *qing* animate much of late Ming and Qing fiction and drama; yet, even in fiction, the tensions between the desire for the benefits of community-centered orthodoxy and individualistic authenticity were never fully resolved. The underlying contradictions between the two value systems give rise to the competing discursive constructions of gender from which this study takes its name. My labeling of these two rhetorical strategies as discourses is a heuristic means to distinguish certain narrative features in fictional works rather than to categorize their content. Because the terms are descriptive rather than prescriptive, I adapt them to each text I analyze here. Although this tweaking may undermine the stability of the terms, my emphasis is on finding language to make sense of certain dynamic tensions within these fictional texts.

The second half of the book is made up of readings of five novels in which gender plays important semantic and aesthetic roles. In these close readings, I analyze how gendered patterns give structural coherence to texts that otherwise seem loosely episodic. Central to my formalist readings is the presence of numerological puns based primarily on the *yin* number six and to a lesser extent the *yang* number nine in "six" or "nine" chapters. Frequently, however, the structural use of gender, in which *yin* terms are associated with chaos in Chapters 6 or 66, is at odds with the novel's larger sympathy for women or the feminine.

Chapter 3 considers the late Ming, early Qing novel *Xingshi yinyuan zhuan* as an example of orthodox narrative. Much in this 100-chapter novel will be familiar to readers of *Jin Ping Mei*; it is a story of failed self-cultivation in which the male protagonist and his family are almost destroyed by his shrewish wife. Although the prologue briefly points to the husband's inability to control himself as the root of the problem, his culpability is quickly overshadowed by the outrageous behavior of Sujie 素姐, who becomes a nightmarish inversion of the sequestered and subordinate Confucian wife. Although the treatment of transgressive sexual desire in *Xingshi* is relatively muted compared to that in *Jin Ping Mei*, the novel is nonetheless filled with oblique references to its threat. The figure of the shrew is associatively linked to a number of other *yin* motifs, including floods and political upheavals, that threaten the normative Confucian order. The negative *yin* motifs that dominate *Xingshi* continue to evoke the stern moral logic of Confucian orthodoxy even when they appear in abbreviated form in more sentimental texts that generally take a more positive view of women.

No work of vernacular fiction expresses the values and aesthetics of authenticity more fully than the mid-eighteenth-century *Honglou meng*. Yet woven into its celebration of the unorthodox values associated with *qing* is a narrative strand that counters the novel's dominant lyric values. Chapter 4 explores these two faces of the novel, which the nineteenth-century commentator Zhang Xinzhi 張新之 (1828–50) referred to as its alluring "surface aspect" (*zhengmian* 正面) and its true "flip side" (*fanmian* 反面).[6] In *Honglou meng*, the construction of Grand Prospect Garden as a "naturalistic" space

6. For Zhang's use of these terms, see his prefatory "How to Read" (*dufa* 讀法) essay in the *SJPB*, p. 2; for a translation, see Plaks, "How to Read," p. 323.

apart from the demands of conventional society, Baoyu's appropriation of the feminine, and other playful inversions of gender, as well as the primacy of emotions over ritual, are all emblematic of the authentic. In contrast to the intricate and constantly shifting aesthetic patterns of the *zhengmian* is the blunt didacticism of the "Precious Mirror" chapters. I argue that these chapters, which most critics of the novel have dismissed as awkward vestiges of an early version of the text, form a coherent sequence based on *yinyang* numerology. The "Precious Mirror" narrative makes up one face of the two-sided mirror presented to Jia Rui 賈瑞; this orthodox narrative strand, parallel to the side of the mirror the unfortunate Jia Rui ignores, is integral to the full meaning of the novel. The interweaving of these two discourses leads to the use of two, if not more, gender codes in the novel: one that associates the feminine positively with authentic self-expression, and the other in which a series of shrews almost succeeds in destroying the Jia line.

Chapter 5 takes up *Yesou puyan*, a sprawling novel written at about the same time as *Honglou meng*. Although it is impossible to determine whether its author was aware of *Honglou meng*, it is clear he was reacting against the sensualism that is at the heart of Baoyu's world. The novel features a rare depiction of a virile and impassioned hero who eradicates heterodoxy from the known world and establishes a reinvigorated Confucian orthodoxy in its place. Instead of privileging the feminine as the site of cultural redemption, *Yesou puyan* develops an extended masculinist fantasy of Confucian imperialism. Although Wen Suchen 文素臣, the protagonist, is described as passionate (*duoqing* 多情), his unconventional authenticity is expressed through his choice of maverick expedient actions (*quan* 權), which are contrasted with the moderated orthodoxy (*zheng*) of his mother. The recuperation of the poetics of authenticity into the novel's masculinist Confucian vision results in the topos of the garden being reconfigured into a setting where the women of the household engage in martial competitions rather than the more usual poetry competitions. One of the most unusual aspects of the way *yinyang* iconography is deployed in *Yesou puyan* is its rare development of extended *yang* symbolism when the hero travels to China's southwestern regions.

Chapter 6 returns to the legacy of *Honglou meng* to discuss Li Ruzhen's 李汝珍 (ca. 1763–1830) *Jinghua yuan* 鏡花緣 (Flowers in the mirror), written during the early nineteenth century, and Wen Kang's 文康 (fl. 1821–50) late nineteenth-century *Ernü yingxiong zhuan* 兒女英雄傳 (A tale of heroic lovers). Reading *Jinghua yuan* and *Ernü yingxiong zhuan* as responses to *Honglou meng* can deepen our understanding of how these two nineteenth-century authors reacted to certain aspects of Cao Xueqin's masterpiece, particularly its use of gender. Although the sensuality in *Honglou meng* seemed to trouble these later writers as self-indulgent, the expansions of that novel's use of gender inversions suggest that by the nineteenth century gender inversions were largely an aesthetic gesture rather than a transgressive challenge to normative Confucianism. Both novels are notable for their idealized portrayals of female protagonists who displace men from their traditional "outer" (*wai* 外) roles as rulers, scholars, and warriors, and both conclude with reinstatements of a revitalized male-dominated orthodox order. However, unlike the female protagonists and their young husbands who easily attain the goals of examination success and meaningful public service, the older, more mature male characters are never able to resolve their troubled and problematic relationship to these traditional literati ideals. Although on one level the inversions of gender roles in these two works add narrative interest to what would otherwise be highly conventional plots and characterizations, the inability or unwillingness of many of the most positively depicted male characters to accommodate themselves to these institutionalized roles points to a certain pessimism underlying the superficial celebration of late Qing literati culture.

Although the meanings associated with specific gendered terms shift from novel to novel, the manipulation of symbolic gender pairings is a consistent feature of each text. These gendered terms, rather than reflecting an essential biological phenomenon, are discursively derived. This study attempts to map out some of the aesthetic and semantic meanings associated with these gendered patterns. Much of my analyses of fiction will focus on the even more abstract pairing of *yin* and *yang*. Curiously, even as philosophical interest in *yinyang* metaphysics was declining during the late imperial period, the use of *yinyang* symbolism in fiction composition and interpretation became increasingly important. It cannot be stated too strongly at the outset that even though *yin* and *yang* may be synonymous with female and male in some instances, they cannot be reduced to female or male. My hope for this book is that it will succeed in breaking down the simplistic gendered binaries with which we frequently read traditional Chinese fiction and add to our understanding of the range of meanings, even contradictory ones, that are projected onto gender.

CHAPTER ONE

The Narrative Structures of Orthodoxy

Throughout the discussions of late Ming and Qing fictional narratives in this book, I use the rather vague terms "orthodox discourse" and "orthodox rhetoric" to describe a particular mode of moralistic writing. The English term "orthodoxy" implies clearly defined and accepted textual and behavioral standards, but, as we shall see, during the late imperial period the concept of orthodoxy had more to do with claims to authority, legitimacy, and power than with the development of one universal standard. The Chinese term *zheng* 正 is typically translated in its nominative aspect as "orthodox" or "orthodoxy" and associated with the integrity of a text or person in relationship to a philosophical school. However, the word also carries a verbal aspect, meaning "to bring into order" or "to rectify," as in the central Confucian notion of rectifying names (*zhengming* 正名, usually translated "rectification of names," a concept to be discussed later).[1] At the core of a Confucian education was the belief that it was the responsibility of the sage to bring order to the world; by the late imperial period, it was believed that not only could almost everyone become a sage but, more important, that every person should strive to become sagelike in whichever ways were proper to him or her. In this sense, behavioral orthodoxy should be understood less as a fixed and clearly defined state of being and more as an active process of creating order through specific Confucian means.

The verbal force implicit in *zheng* is a crucial component of my use of the term "orthodox narrative," by which I mean those aspects of a text that allude to, even if somewhat obscurely, the mainstream Neo-Confucian belief that ritual behavior positively affects the parallel structures of the social, political, and natural orders. Orthodox narratives illustrate the rewards for

1. See also Zito, *Of Body and Brush*, p. 52.

leading a proper Confucian life or, conversely, the losses incurred by those failing to do so and actively goad the reader to aspire to the rewards of virtue. In this sense, my use of the term "orthodox" is loosely synonymous with the regulative goal of Neo-Confucian practices and must be distinguished from textual orthodoxy, a conservative and purist concept that implies the desire to define a recension of a text either as the version closest to its original state, however reconstructed, or as the most complete and best-developed expression of a particular ideology. As we shall see, orthodox discourse in traditional fiction is rarely straightforward or pure.

Chinese *xiaoshuo* texts (traditionally translated as "fiction," but actually including a much greater range of writings) are inherently noncanonical and heteroglossic;[2] despite this, they frequently promote Confucian values through a range of strategies I refer to as "orthodox rhetoric." The rhetoric and iconography used in fiction to promote Confucian behavior are closely drawn from the symbols and moral logic of syncretic Neo-Confucianism (*daoxue* 道學 or *lixue* 理學), which, it is important to note, had been deeply influenced by the tight narrative logic, symbolism, and thematic concerns of Buddhist retribution tales. With the exception of certain kinds of exemplary writings or eulogies, orthodox Confucian rhetoric is rarely pure; in order to stay fresh and compelling, it needs to keep the threat of chaos present in the readers' minds by introducing the breakdown of the social and moral order and then showing how Confucian practices resolve the crisis by restoring order. Clearly obscene and pornographic fictions, such as *Ruyi jun zhuan* 如意君傳 (The biography of Lord As You Like It) and *Jin Ping Mei*, make use of orthodox rhetoric even though they are clearly not "Orthodox." My use of the term "orthodox" (with an emphasis on the small "o") points to those aspects of fictional narratives that draw on and promote Neo-Confucian symbolism and values and that became integral to the aesthetics of *xiaoshuo* fiction as the genre developed during its golden age from the late sixteenth to the late eighteenth century. Moreover, orthodox rhetoric is frequently suggested only through isolated tropes that invoke the moral logic of Neo-Confucianism but are overshadowed by more colorful and transgressive aspects of the fiction.

The orthodox discourse used in *xiaoshuo* fiction is closely connected to late imperial Neo-Confucian ideology, a system of beliefs and practices so

2. For a discussion of the variety of texts traditionally labeled *xiaoshuo*, see S. Lu, *From Historicity to Fictionality*, pp. 39–47.

pervasive and diffuse in Ming-Qing China that it was as transparent as the air people breathed. Similar to Christianity in the contemporary U.S. context, Neo-Confucianism had many shades of meaning within the late imperial Chinese context, many with their own claims to legitimacy. Although modern scholars are justified in asking whether a real orthodoxy existed during the late imperial period, when emperors and officials alike sponsored non-Confucian beliefs and practices, the notion of the orthodox, however defined and by whom, still served to legitimate people within the political and social orders.[3] At the state level, orthodox Neo-Confucianism was defined by the system of values, practices, and philosophical interpretations of Neo-Confucian doctrine mandated and supported by the Ming and Qing governments. These teachings and practices, which were by no means uniform or consistent, were disseminated throughout the empire by means of a state-sponsored educational curriculum, aimed at both popular and elite audiences, that worked in concert with the systems of rites and laws to maintain the naturalized logic of the hierarchical and authoritarian Confucian social order.

Balanced against this institutionalized and somewhat rigid concept of Neo-Confucian orthodoxy was a living intellectual tradition that turned to the Neo-Confucian and, increasingly during the classical revival of the Qing dynasty, the Han Confucian canons in order to gain authority for its interpretive challenges to state control.[4] Despite the search for textual purity in their epistemological projects, many of these intellectuals participated in a hybrid Confucian culture. Although rejecting certain textual and metaphysical bases of Neo-Confucianism, Qing evidential scholars continued to conform to Neo-Confucian social ideals by taking part in personal, clan, and community rituals and, for many, by engaging in the conservative examination system in which they reproduced state-approved interpretations of

3. See *Orthodoxy*; and the review by Peterson in which he cautions against the desire to find a universal definition for the term "orthodoxy."

4. Wm. Theodore de Bary ("Introduction," in idem and Bloom, *Principle and Practicality*, pp. 16–17) describes this Neo-Confucian intellectual tradition as split between a more conservative philosophical orthodoxy, represented, on the one hand, by the early Ming Wu Yubi 吳與弼 (1392–1469) and the late Ming Donglin 東林 faction and, on the other, by the liberal and activist wing, which was less doctrinaire but equally committed to the preservation and promulgation of Neo-Confucianism. Representative of this latter group are Wang Yangming 王陽明 (1472–1529), Liu Zongzhou 劉宗周 (1578–1645), and Huang Zongxi 黃宗羲.

philosophical and policy issues, whatever their own intellectual beliefs.[5] However, no matter how individuals saw themselves in relation to the state or the more independent intellectual traditions, all who claimed to speak for orthodoxy shared a faith in Confucian ritual propriety and social ethics (*lijiao* 禮教) as the key to social stability.

My unorthodox definition of late imperial Neo-Confucian orthodoxy embraces this uneven and dynamic hybrid of philosophic beliefs, expedient expressions, and private and public ritual practices, all of which were associated with the Confucian tradition. Even in those instances in which the words of a person or text resist certain aspects of Neo-Confucian orthodoxy, orthodox intent can still be found in the desire to order society through reinvigorating (Neo)-Confucian values and ritual practices. The resulting definition of Neo-Confucianism may be so broad as to make the concept intrinsically meaningless; however, my definition realistically reflects the fluidly ambiguous usage of the concept of orthodoxy by various groups who either sought to legitimate themselves by claiming it or developed denigrating caricatures of it to attack what they saw as the excesses of Neo-Confucian practices. Rather than focus on defining late imperial Neo-Confucianism, I am much more interested in the discussion in this book in outlining how the notion of orthodoxy was deployed by various groups in order to legitimate themselves morally, politically, and aesthetically. No entity was more eager to identify itself with orthodoxy than the state.

Zhu Yuanzhang 朱元璋 (r. 1368–99; Ming Taizu), the founder of the Ming dynasty, was the first emperor to embrace Neo-Confucianism as state orthodoxy; moreover, he attempted to disseminate this creed directly to the masses. He did this in the form of the Grand Proclamations (*Yuzhi dagao* 御製大誥), which included codified policy on judicial and ritual matters.[6] In 1391 he honored over 190,000 commoners in the capital for their ability to re-

5. In a fascinating comparison of changes in the types of questions asked in the provincial and metropolitan levels of the examination after the rise of evidential studies, Benjamin A. Elman ("Changes," esp. p. 141) points out that the questions at the metropolitan level tended to be more conservative. Five of the leading evidential scholars of the late eighteenth century became *jinshi* in 1754 by writing essays on aspects of Cheng-Zhu doctrine they would later repudiate. Cynthia J. Brokaw ("Tai Chen," pp. 258, 275) describes Dai Zhen 戴震 (1722–80), who directed scathing attacks at Song Neo-Confucianism, as an heir to Zhu Xi's orthodox learning and interest in moral self-cultivation.

6. See Farmer, "Social Regulations," pp. 121–22; and idem, *Zhu Yuanzhang*, p. 4.

cite the 75 items of the Proclamations from memory.[7] These moral edicts, which Ming Taizu ordered be read bimonthly in each village and posted at every school, were subsequently adopted and expanded by the Qing court in its efforts to legitimate the moral authority of Manchu rule.

Although this orthodoxy was the leading currency of exchange for official recognition, legitimation, and promotion after it was institutionalized as the basis for the curriculum of the bureaucratic examination system in 1313, state-sponsored Neo-Confucian ideology was not the unchanging monolith it is often assumed to be. The Great Ritual Controversy, the power struggle over the succession of the Jiaqing emperor (r. 1522–67), which led to the death of seventeen officials in 1524, is among the best examples to show how, in Benjamin Elman's words, orthodoxy was subject to negotiation by the "overlapping but asymmetrical interests of the bureaucracy and throne."[8] When the Zhengde emperor (r. 1506–22) died heirless, his thirteen-year-old cousin was made the posthumously adopted heir of his grandfather, the Hongzhi emperor (r. 1488–1506), and enthroned as the Jiaqing emperor.[9] However, instead of recognizing the Hongzhi emperor as his imperial deceased father and his natural parents as imperial uncle and aunt as was politically expedient, the Jiaqing emperor wanted to raise his birth father's rank posthumously. In 1538, he succeeded in placing his father's spirit tablet in the Imperial Ancestral Temple, an honor reserved for ruling emperors. What had begun as a savvy decision to install a politically isolated boy as emperor, instead of a more capable adult man with a stronger claim to the throne, led to a ritual crisis.[10] Those in the faction who opposed the young emperor argued on the basis of historical precedent that it was his duty to maintain an unbroken line of succession.[11] Zhang Cong 張璁 (1475–1539) and those who defended the boy's filiality rejected the applicability of these historical examples and countered that ritual needed to be rooted in proper feelings (*renqing* 人情) in order not to be false; in so doing, Zhang Cong and the others went

7. *Cambridge History*, p. 165.

8. Elman, "Changes," p. 111.

9. Fisher, *The Chosen One*; see also the review by Chu.

10. A crucial factor that should have disqualified the Jiaqing emperor from the line of agnatic succession was that his father was born to a secondary consort rather than to an empress or a principle consort (*Cambridge History*, p. 442).

11. Fisher, *The Chosen One*, p. 56.

against orthodox Cheng-Zhu Neo-Confucian doctrine in treating feelings as a source of moral authority.[12]

Although the Great Ritual Controversy can be seen as a factional struggle between the brilliant senior grand secretary Yang Tinghe 楊廷和 (1459–1529) and those Hanlin scholars associated with him and a group of mostly junior officials who hoped to curry favor with the emperor, the arguments used by the supporters of the Jiaqing emperor borrowed from the sixteenth-century reconceptualization of human nature that questioned the orthodox Cheng-Zhu bias against the emotions as a basis for moral behavior. This political struggle, in which both sides laid claim to legitimacy, helps contextualize the sharp attacks against the rationalist bias of Neo-Confucianism discussed in the following chapter. Despite the polemical stance taken by many of the most radical critics of Neo-Confucian orthodoxy, their calls for a more flexible interpretation of ritually proper behavior was within the mainstream of Ming Neo-Confucian thought.[13]

Although scholars may quibble about the reach and uniformity of Confucian orthodoxy in the late imperial period, there is no question that Confucian ritual was a constant and dominant discourse in China among the elites up until the twentieth century. During the period of economic expansion in the Ming and Qing, the increased availability of printed materials and higher literacy levels meant an even greater absorption of orthodox values at all social levels. Guidelines for ritual behavior were also widely copied into lineage regulations, and the nominal endorsement of the rituals, if not actual practice, became an important part of elite clan identity and an indicator of literati status.[14] Even though the dominant intellectual trend of the Qing was a return to a textual basis for Confucian knowledge, the classical impetus of evidential studies was not limited to the researching and collating of more "authentic" versions of texts by stripping away the Buddhist and Daoist overlays imposed by the Song Neo-Confucians. Evidential studies also led to a revival of classical forms of ritual. A growing number of activist literati promoted and disseminated knowledge about Confucian rituals as a means to strengthen society's moral base. Local pride and prestige were bol-

12. Ibid., pp. 58, 148, 150, and *passim*.

13. For more on the growing importance of emotions to ritual practice during the late Ming and Qing, see Kutcher, *Mourning in Late Imperial China*, pp. 47–52, 92–96, 153–56.

14. See Ebrey, *Confucianism and Family Rituals*, pp. 157, 163; Chu, "Intellectual Trends"; and Brooks, "Funerary Ritual," pp. 477–80.

stered by padding gazetteers with a full complement of exemplars of virtue, including talented scholars, chaste women, and filial children.[15] Literati, and those who were trying to legitimate their social or political position, commented on and disseminated ritual texts as part of their Confucian obligation to preserve the past, as well as for the more expedient reasons of strengthening lineage identity and demonstrating their virtue to contemporaries and later generations.[16] Furthermore, during the Qing, significant numbers of Han loyalists turned to ritual practice, in what Kai-wing Chow has called "ritual purism," as a solution to internal and external attacks on the health of the Chinese state.[17] This ritual purism had the added attraction of demonstrating the moral and intellectual superiority of the Han Chinese heritage over the practices the Manchus brought with them from the steppes.

The explosion of print technology and the spread of literacy, which brought actual texts into an increasing number of communities and homes, attest to the power, attraction, and continued vigor of the great orthodox traditions, despite far-reaching social changes. Common sense and growing historical evidence indicate that although ritual texts illustrated the ideal, actual practices were often more flexible and that people, even the elites, fulfilled their ritual responsibilities with a greater or lesser degree of sincerity and enthusiasm.[18] Within this context, the performance of ritual and the voicing of orthodox rhetoric can be read as tactics to gain social legitimation and power, tactics utilized at all levels of society from the imperial court down to the poorest of widows trying to hold on to her husband's property. As the Great Ritual Controversy makes clear, however, even the emperor chafed under the demands of orthodoxy and had limited power in negotiating his ritual obligations.

15. The number of biographies of virtuous women in gazetteers swelled during the Ming and Qing (see Elvin, "Female Virtue"; and T'ien, *Male Anxiety*).

16. On the imperial level, E. F. Soulliere ("Palace Women") has drawn a connection between expanded production of imperial editions of ritual texts for women and the attempts by the Yongle emperor (r. 1403–24) to legitimate his rule after usurping the throne.

17. Chow, *The Rise of Confucian Ritualism*, pp. 33–43 and *passim*.

18. For example, scholarship on women's lives during the late imperial period reveals the extent of the disjuncture between orthodox ideals and practice in terms of family life; see Ko, *Teachers of the Inner Chambers*; Mann, "Fuxue"; and Widmer, "The Epistolary World."

ORTHODOX CONSTRUCTIONS OF SELF

If Confucian orthodoxy provided the ideological structure of society, ritual and rites were the building blocks that gave shape to the structure.[19] Ritual practices, which include the narrow prescriptions for all manner of interpersonal social forms, the rites proper, as well as broad regulatory principles for maintaining the cosmic sociopolitical order, are at the core of orthodox discourse. Commonly translated as "ritual," *li* 禮 spans a range of meanings, including religious sacrifices and social etiquette. The origins of *li* lie in the royal sacrifices made to totemic ancestors; these rites explicitly re-created the Heaven-earth-man triad that was essential to fixing and stabilizing the calendrical year and by extension played a major role in legitimating the authority of the ruling dynastic houses.[20] In its later expanded meanings, codified in the *Yili* 儀禮 (Etiquette and ritual) and *Liji* 禮記 (Book of rites), *li* never lost its connection to the numinous. In Angela Zito's words, "*Li* summarized a way of being human necessary to the cosmos: the principles and practices by which the interpenetration of the cosmic and human worlds was maintained by human intervention."[21] The metaphysical logic of the connection between the human and the cosmic, spelled out in the correlative cosmology of Han Confucianism, endowed human actions with the power and the responsibility to establish not only social harmony but also cosmic harmony. In this way, the practices defined by ritual encompass the totality of individual, social, and natural existence.

Despite Confucius' self-deprecating claims that he merely transmitted culture, he did transform ritual practice. Although many of what have been called his innovations were anticipated in texts such as the *Zuo zhuan* 左傳, which may predate him, Confucius' emphasis on morality deepened the personal and ethical dimensions of Zhou aristocratic rituals, which had been

19. As James Watson ("The Structure of Funerary Rites," p. 3) writes: "If anything is central to the creation and maintenance of a unified Chinese culture, it is the standardization of ritual."

20. Zito, "Silk and Skin," p. 105.

21. Zito, "Ritualizing *Li*," p. 322; see also idem, *Of Body and Brush*, p. 16. Studies of Confucian ritual are roughly split between those who describe it as a rational-humanist invention (this view is summarized in Mote, *Intellectual Foundations*) and those who see it more mystically as a type of performative magic (see Fingarette, *Confucius*; Eno, *The Confucian Creation*; and Zito, "Ritualizing *Li*"). Because *xiaoshuo* narratives exploit the cause-and-effect logic of ritual, the discussions of ritual in this study are limited to the latter definition.

limited to calendrical and life-cycle rites.[22] He transformed ritual into the behavioral expression of a morally perfect humanity (*ren* 仁).[23] Thereafter, the majority of Confucian thinkers followed him in believing that the raw material of human nature needed rigorous training in order to achieve its full moral potential; this process of moral self-refinement was achieved through conforming to and eventually mastering the full spectrum of rules of conduct and propriety that constitute ritual. The degree of attention paid to these daily practices intensified greatly with the spread of Neo-Confucianism during the Song dynasty and afterward.

At the heart of ritual is the Confucian imperative to rectify names (*zhengming*), to make reality conform to ritual ideal. In the best-known exposition of this principle, Confucius explained governance as, "Let the ruler be a ruler, the subject a subject, the father a father, the son a son."[24] For every role and situation, there is a proper way to act. Through studying ritual, history, the Five Classics, and, under Neo-Confucianism, the Four Books, the individual is able to learn the proper expression and response for every situation and, in so doing, train the self to embody the ideal. The Confucian self is a social being expressed through the "five relationships" (*wuchang* 五常, an expansion of the "three bonds," *san'gang* 三綱), those mutual bonds of responsibility and obligation connecting ruler and subject, parent and child, husband and wife, older and younger siblings, and friends. With the exception of friendship, these codified bonds are hierarchical and situationally contingent; everyone, even the emperor, had at least one relationship in which he or she was ritually subordinate. At the core of ritual practice is the belief that the observance of distinctions is necessary to the maintenance of domestic and social order.[25]

Traditionally, Confucianism focused on the production of self as an external process achieved through the proper performance of social roles, such as filial child, loyal statesman, or chaste widow. Historiographical and fictional biographies tend to portray their subject from the exterior as he or she exemplifies one of these prescripted typologies (*zhixing* 致性; literally "to fulfill one's nature").[26] It was not until the mid-sixteenth and seventeenth

22. *Lunyu*, VII.i.
23. Chow, *The Rise of Confucian Ritualism*, pp. 9–10.
24. *Lunyu*, XII.xi; trans. from D. C. Lau, *The Analects*, p. 114.
25. See Rowe, "Women," pp. 4–5.
26. Twitchett, "Chinese Biographical Writings," p. 110.

centuries, the period Peiyi Wu has identified as "the golden age of Chinese autobiography," that certain literati became acutely concerned about disjunctions between the interior, subjective self and the objective, ritually defined standards of the orthodox self.[27] The late Ming cult of sentiment, discussed in the following chapter, attacked excessive orthopraxy as creating a society of hypocrites devoid of both passion and compassion. In place of orthodoxy, they championed authenticity of self-expression as the foundation of true morality. Whereas the cult of sentiment championed interiority and depth of emotional experience, orthodox discourse demonized the desires and promoted the ideal of the externally defined ritual self.

In contrast to earlier theoretical conceptualizations of premodern Chinese identity, which tend to follow Confucian definitions in reifying ritual roles, recent analyses have emphasized the negotiable and fluid nature of the ritually defined self, particularly in terms of gender.[28] Angela Zito, for example, has described the relationship between male and female in spatial terms: the outer *yang* sphere (usually but not necessarily occupied by biological males) encompasses the *yin* sphere; since the boundaries between *yin* and *yang* are relative, depending on the sex, age, and status of the people involved, a woman, as mother or head of household, could occupy the dominant *yang* position over her children or servants.[29] This kind of analysis has opened up a theoretical space that makes it possible to see women, the group most likely to be subordinate within the matrix of the five Confucian roles, as empowered agents. Indeed, we can no longer assume that all women were oppressed and powerless.

However, although scholars of traditional China should no longer naïvely extend the essentialist assumption that a direct correlation exists between a person's biological identity and his or her social role or even assume that individuals conceived of themselves as having a somewhat coherent psychologically defined core identity, neither should we diminish the force of legal and ethical injunctions on individuals to conform to orthodox ideals. People of all ages and stations might maneuver and manipulate their social position to their own advantage whenever and however they could, but strict sanc-

27. P. Y. Wu, *The Confucian's Progress*, p. xii.

28. Following the work of Bell in *Ritual Theory* on ritual as a negotiation of power, Zito, Barlow (see esp. "Theorizing Woman"), and Hevia (*Cherishing Men from Afar*) have emphasized the contingent and fluid nature of ritually defined identity.

29. Zito, "Silk and Skin," esp. p. 106.

tions were in place to punish those who strayed too far from accepted norms of behavior. Furthermore, the rewards of leaving a good name behind inspired many martyrs to "fulfill their nature" through a degree of self-sacrifice that twenty-first-century Western sensibilities find difficult to comprehend. As Neo-Confucianism taught, and as reflected in orthodox discourse, human action was needed to bring order to the cosmic process, a process accomplished through the correct performance of ritual.[30]

Although it is important to acknowledge that ritual in action incorporated a certain degree of flexibility, the orthodox textual tradition stresses the need to draw absolute distinctions. The Han dynasty compendia of earlier ritual texts, the *Book of Rites*, states, "Ritual is the means by which one establishes the intimate and distant, judges what is doubtful or suspect, differentiates the similar from the different, and clarifies the right from the wrong" 夫禮者，所以定親疏，決嫌疑，別同異，明是非也.[31] A factor that led to the fiction of one uniform orthodox standard for ritual behavior is that ritual manuals reify discursive categories and treat them as unproblematic. A trenchant example of this is the discussion of the domestic boundary between inner (*nei* 內) and outer (*wai* 外).[32] Zhu Xi's 朱熹 (1130–1200) *Family Rituals* (*Jiali* 家禮), the compendium that established ritual standards for the Neo-Confucian era, follows the section on domestic regulations, the "Neize" 內則, in the *Book of Rites* in architecturally concretizing the injunction to separate the sexes into fixed inner and outer spheres: "In housing, there should be a strict demarcation between the inner and the outer parts, with a door separating them. The two parts should share neither a well nor a washroom nor a privy. The men are in charge of all the affairs on the outside; the women manage the affairs on the inside."[33] This passage obscures the processes of negotiation through which actual social boundaries were established by treating the *neiwai* distinction as a product not of language and culture but of the solidity of architectural construction. In practice, the *neiwai* separation in elite homes was complicated by the presence of the enclosed garden; the garden was an architectural gray area that

30. Ibid., p. 103.

31. *Li ji*, 1.5.

32. The boundary between inner and outer is especially important in delineating gender; see Ebrey, *The Inner Quarters*, pp. 23–25; and Ko, *Teachers of the Inner Chambers*, pp. 12–14; and Epstein, "Inscribing the Essentials."

33. Trans. from Ebrey, *Chu Hsi's Family Rituals*, p. 29; for the Chinese text, see ibid., p. 189.

was sometimes treated as an enclosed extension of the women's quarters and was sometimes open to outsiders. Significantly, this unstable division of space is not reflected in ritual texts. Yet as readers of Ming-Qing texts are aware, the ambiguity of architectural boundaries is a favorite trope in fiction and drama, which frequently exploit the garden and the courtyard as a setting for illicit romance.[34] The ritual injunctions to draw absolute distinctions further gendered the construction of the symbolic *neiwai* boundary. For example, the *Book of Rites* states that at six *sui* boys and girls are no longer allowed to share the same mat; at eight *sui* girls are restricted to the women's quarters (thereby establishing the boundary that sets off the inner from the outer); and at 10 *sui* boys are sent out to school in a process that identifies them with the outer.[35] In a process we shall see repeatedly, gender distinctions (rather than biological difference) are used to naturalize and reify discursive boundaries. Significantly, the concern in ritual texts for creating and maintaining distinctly gendered boundaries was transcribed into much of late Ming and Qing fiction and drama, even those works that display a real fascination with gender ambiguity. In novels such as *Honglou meng*, which seem to celebrate anything but the orthodox, the performance of one's proper social role is treated as so foundational to order that unless the father acts as a father, the son as son, and the wife as wife, chaos will ensue no matter how much author(s) and readers might wish things were different.

In order to understand the often obscure didactic logic of late imperial fiction, in which minor transgressions can set in motion a deadly cycle of karmic retribution, it is necessary to take account of the ways that the Song Neo-Confucian synthesis shifted the emphasis of ritual from the mastery of external forms to an internalized process of self-cultivation. Neo-Confucianism copied Buddhism in popularizing its message of universal salvation by holding out a promise of enlightenment to almost every individual who had the will to conform to moral principle. Buddhist self-cultivation is a process of freeing the self from all desires and emotional attachments, in the belief that any attachment to the illusory, phenomenal world impedes enlightenment. Although Neo-Confucianism did not go so far as to deny the

34. For the importance of boundaries, see McMahon, *Causality and Containment*, esp. pp. 25–28.

35. *Li ji*, 12.52; Legge, *Book of Rites*, 1: 478–79; Zhu Xi expands the prescriptions in the *Li ji* to include a list of age and gender appropriate works to be studied (Ebrey, *Chu Hsi's Family Rituals*, p. 32; for the Chinese text, see ibid., p. 189).

reality of the phenomenal world, it follows Buddhism in advocating detachment from it. Zhu Xi developed a clear and programmatic curriculum as the basis for the discipline of self-cultivation (*zixiu* 自修), the process by which individuals achieve their full moral potential by freeing themselves from their subjective and potentially biased reactions to the phenomenal world.

To a much greater degree than classical ritual codes, which define the self externally and emphasize proper behavior, Neo-Confucianism directs attention to the internal development of the moral will.[36] The moral will is established by training the mind to be fully objective so that it will not be aroused by external stimuli. Even the most cursory reading of Neo-Confucian texts reveals the great concern for achieving the internal states of tranquillity (*jing* 靜), seriousness (*jing* 敬), impartiality (*gong* 公), and equilibrium (*zhong* 中) as a means to overcome selfish subjectivity (*si* 私). Whereas classical Confucianism focuses on the proper expression of emotions, Neo-Confucianism emphasizes calming the mind so that it becomes like a mirror that can reflect events or stimuli without reacting to or being distorted by them; this is the goal of quiet sitting (*jingzuo* 靜坐).[37] Desires, accordingly, were seen as inimical to an enlightened state. Although Neo-Confucian discipline often seems repressive when we view from it modern individualist values, we should not ignore that its intellectual and spiritual appeal was powerful enough that it dominated Chinese and Korean intellectual traditions and was highly influential in Japan until the twentieth century. By the late imperial period in China, conformity to Neo-Confucian ritual codes was an essential component of maintaining a respectable social identity.[38]

36. Donald Munro (*Images of Human Nature*, pp. 105–96) describes the Confucian vision of people as "horizontally defined" through social relations as opposed to that of Zhu Xi, who was more intent on finding the inner self.

37. This concept is exemplified by the following quote from the Neo-Confucian primer *Reflections of Things at Hand*: "Suppose here is a clear mirror. It is its normal nature to reflect all things. It is difficult not to have it reflect them. Similarly, the human mind cannot but interact with the myriad things, and it is difficult not to have it engaged in thinking. If one wants to avoid confusion and disturbance, his mind must have a master. What can be its master? Seriousness and seriousness only. With a master, the mind will be vacuous and if it is vacuous depravity cannot enter it" (*Reflections*, pp. 143–44; *JSL*, 4.17b).

38. The expansion of Confucian practices and values beyond the aristocracy is one of the great successes of Neo-Confucianism; as Patricia Ebrey (*Confucianism and Family Rituals*, pp. 37–40) suggests, non-elite classes probably adopted Confucian ritual practices in order to legitimate their political status.

The centerpiece of Zhu Xi's cosmological system was the concept of *Li* 理, commonly translated as "principle" or "reason" (I capitalize it to distinguish it from its homonym *li*, "ritual").[39] Zhu Xi made principle into a universal standard, "a pattern for the cosmos," that structures both the natural and the moral order.[40] Although every thing and event has its own particular principle, each is just a manifestation of one universal and transcendent principle. Furthermore, although principle is inherent in all things, every blade of grass as well as every thought, human effort is needed to realize and perfect its universal potential. Counterpoised to principle is matter or ether (*qi* 氣), a dynamic energy force that gives form to principle.[41] Because of its own imperfections, *qi*, which varies in terms of purity, often obstructs the full realization of moral principle by making human nature biased and subjective.[42] The discipline of self-cultivation, based on the optimistic Confucian belief that education and ritual are spiritually and physically transformative, is designed to minimize the negative effects of the impure material nature and make of the self a fully objective and transparent vessel with which to embody moral principle. According to Zhang Zai 張載 (1020–77), one of the thinkers whose writings Zhu Xi canonized, when people "make their actions accord with ritual, their *qi* spontaneously becomes good."[43] Although Dong Zhongshu 董仲舒 (179–104 B.C.E.) had already laid the groundwork for a moral cosmology, Neo-Confucianism introduced scrutiny of the individual will as an essential process for actualizing a morally perfect cosmic order. As spelled out in the *Daxue* 大學 (Great learning), one of the central Four Books of Neo-Confucianism, making the will sincere (*chengyi* 誠意) and rectifying the mind (*zhengxin* 正心) are necessary steps toward harmonizing the entire world.

Ritual is the performative aspect of Neo-Confucian principle; it simultaneously allows individuals to achieve their full moral potential and regulates their immediate environment. As the second passage in *Jinsi lu* 近思錄 (Reflections on things at hand), the widely circulated Neo-Confucian anthology on self-cultivation compiled by Zhu Xi and Lü Zuqian 呂祖謙 (1137–81),

39. See Wing-tsit Chan, "Evolution."

40. Gardner, *Learning to Be a Sage*, p. 49.

41. Gardner's (ibid., p. 90) translation of *qi* as "psychophysical stuff" gets at its role in the formation of emotions.

42. See C. Y. Cheng, "*Li-ch'i*," p. 505.

43. Zhang Zai, *Zhang Zai ji*, p. 265; trans. from Ebrey, *Confucianism and Family Rituals*, p. 51.

puns: *Li yue li* 理曰禮, "Principle is called ritual."[44] This identification of ritual with transcendent principle departs from the classical Confucian understanding of ritual as a constructed set of practices that reached its highest stage of perfection during the Zhou dynasty and as a result gave rise to much more rigid interpretations of orthodoxy and orthopraxy under Neo-Confucianism. The uncompromising view of morality under Cheng-Zhu Neo-Confucianism is exemplified by Cheng Yi's 程頤 (1033–1107) statement that it is preferable to starve to death than to lose one's integrity.[45] This interpretation of proper behavior is much stricter than that of Mencius, who condoned expediency (*quan* 權) as a valid reason to deviate from ritual codes, particularly if it meant saving a life.[46]

The *Great Learning* seamlessly integrates the interiorized process of self-cultivation with the regulation of the social environment and spells out the process by which an individual's regulation of his subjective consciousness radiates out to the social macrocosm in ever wider circles of effect.[47]

Through the investigation of things, one can extend one's knowledge; once knowledge has been extended, the will can be made sincere; once the will has been made sincere, the mind can be rectified; once the mind has been rectified, the self can be cultivated; once the self has been cultivated, the family can be regulated; once the family has been regulated, the state can be properly ordered; once the state is properly ordered, the entire world can be kept in harmony. From the Son of Heaven to

44. *JSL*, 1.13a. For an alternative translation, see *Reflections*, p. 8. Zhang Zai (*Zhang Zai ji*, p. 326) makes the same claim even more clearly in his statement "Ritual is principle" 蓋禮者理也.

45. *JSL*, 6.6b; *Reflections*, p. 177. Orthodoxy concerns purity of ideology and belief; orthopraxy refers to purity of practice (see J. Watson, "The Structure of Chinese Funerary Rites," p. 10). As has been widely discussed, this comment by Cheng Yi was the doctrinal justification for the practice of widow suicide.

46. "Not to help a sister-in-law who is drowning is to be a brute. It is prescribed by the rites that, in giving and receiving, man and woman should not touch each other, but in stretching out a helping hand to the drowning sister-in-law one uses one's discretion (*quan*)" (trans. from D. C. Lau, *Mencius*, p. 124; *Mengzi*, 4a, no. 18). This passage justifying expediency is explicitly mentioned in several Qing novels; see the discussion of *Yesou puyan* in Chapter 5.

47. I use "he" to refer to the individual because even though women were also to adhere to strict moral codes, it was ultimately the responsibility of the Confucian male to "regulate his family." As we shall see, in fiction the ruin of a household consistently arises from a man's failure to assert moral leadership.

the common people, all must regard self-cultivation as the foundation. There is never a case where the foundation is in disorder and yet the branches are in order.[48]

By narrating the analogic connection between the individual mind and the affairs of the empire, this passage in the *Great Learning* lays bare the symbolic logic of late imperial orthodox discourse, which makes individual actions (and thoughts) directly responsible for the maintenance of the social and cosmic order.

Andrew Plaks, in his study of the four great Ming novels, which he reads as Neo-Confucian allegories, has argued that the chain of causality detailed in the *Great Learning* is a central theme of Ming literature. The *Jin Ping Mei*, the definitive Ming novel on domestic relations, illustrates how deviance from the ideal process of self-cultivation brings disaster to the individual and his household.[49] Keith McMahon, too, has demonstrated the importance of the Neo-Confucian concepts of containment and moderation as narrative tropes in seventeenth-century fiction. Neo-Confucian suspicions of desire and pride, as he has brilliantly observed, are narrated through images of gaping mouths and seeking eyes and then further projected onto the architecture of the home as cracks and openings in walls.[50] The genealogical connections between *xiaoshuo* fiction and ritual texts are made explicit in Ding Yaokang's 丁耀亢 (1599–1671) sequel to the *Jin Ping Mei*, *Xu Jin Ping Mei* 續金瓶梅, which presents itself more as a commentary to the popular morality book *Taishang ganying pian* 太上感應篇 (The Great Ruler's book of retribution) than a continuation of the novel,[51] and the eighteenth-century novel *Qilu deng* 歧路燈 (Warning light at the crossroads; preface dated 1777). The author, Li Lüyuan 李綠園 (1707–90), copied "Jiaxun zhunyan" 家訓諄言 (Earnest words of household instruction), a set of household rules written by him, into several of the manuscript copies of his novel.[52] The narrative logic of orthodox discourse follows the *Great Learning* in treating the individual as a microcosm of larger systems of order; as we shall see, this analogic relationship between the individual and the social and natural environment was an important structural feature of the novel and had a significant impact on the meanings ascribed to fictional representations of gender.

48. *Daxue*, in *Sishu jizhu*, p. 2.
49. Plaks, *The Four Masterworks*, pp. 156–67 and *passim*.
50. McMahon, *Causality and Containment*, pp. 25–28.
51. See Rolston, *Traditional Chinese Fiction*, pp. 89–90, 301–2.
52. Ibid., p. 281.

RITUAL, *YINYANG* COSMOLOGY, AND THE CONSTRUCTION OF GENDER

In contrast to contemporary Western discourses on gender that rationalize the necessity and coherence of gender differences by arguing the primacy and certainty of biological difference between male and female, the only two sexes recognized in this discourse, the emphasis in Confucian China was on demonstrating the natural and social logic of symmetrical gender roles.[53] A radical point of difference between the two ways of conceptualizing sex and gender is that in premodern China the proper performance of a social role was considered more important to social order than ensuring the congruity of biological and social identities. If necessary, for example, a woman could perform the role of a son if no appropriate males were available. As Charlotte Furth's research on naturally occurring sex changes in premodern China has shown, biological sex was conceptualized as happening along a continuum. Both legal and medical discussions of natural sex changes accepted biological fluidity as consistent with the transformations of *yin* and *yang*. These biological transformations did not threaten the natural order, itself a cultural construct based on the knowledge of constantly shifting *yinyang* permutations, so long as the person in question was properly stationed in the social order.[54] Furthermore, despite their detailed delineations of proper gender roles, orthodox texts displayed some tolerance for individuals who put aside expected gender roles, as a temporary expediency, in order to achieve higher ritual or familial ends.[55] Notably, Hua Mulan 花木蘭 is celebrated as an icon of filiality and political loyalty despite her transgression

53. Historically, the European West has been intolerant of biological fluidity and ambiguity and has created the fiction of the exclusivity of the two biologically determined sexes. Contemporary U.S. anxiety about regulating distinctions between the two sexes can be seen in the medical practice of operating on intersexed newborns to fix them firmly within one sex or the other (see Fausto-Sterling, "The Five Sexes"; for a historical perspective on Western scientific beliefs about biological sex, see Laqueur, *Making Sex*).

54. Furth, "Androgynous Males."

55. For example, Li Gongzuo's 李公佐 (fl. 810) tale of Xie Xiao'e 謝小娥, a woman who disguised herself as a male servant and worked in the household of two brothers who had murdered her husband until she was able to avenge her husband by killing the two men, was incorporated into the biographies of exemplary women in the *Xin Tang shu* 新唐書 (S. Lu, *From Historicity to Fictionality*, pp. 101–4).

of proper gender roles in disguising herself as a man in order to save her elderly father from the hardships of military service.[56]

Significantly, a slight increase in the social rather than biological foundation for identity can be detected in certain changes Zhu Xi made to ritual practice in his *Family Rituals*, the standard text on domestic rituals during the late imperial period.[57] Sections of the Han standard for ritual, the *Book of Rites*, emphasize biological as well as social identity. For example, in its prescriptions for the presentation and naming ceremony for a newborn, the *Rites* notes that the child's head is to be shaved three months after birth. The ritual includes both boys and girls, but complementarity between the sexes is produced by shaving the hair in inverse patterns (horn tufts for a boy and a circlet for a girl, or with a tuft on the left of a boy's head and the right of a girl's).[58] All children, including those born to a concubine, are ritually presented, with varying degrees of formality depending on the child's rank. In contrast, Zhu Xi went against contemporary practice in describing only the presentation of the descent-line heir, an identity that is socially, rather than biologically, determined; furthermore, Zhu Xi's description of the ritual omits any physical marking of the child's body.[59] A slight shift of emphasis in the ritual treatment of girls can also be noted in the *Family Rituals* concerning the rite of pinning. The *Book of Rites* links pinning, which marks the transition from childhood to adulthood, to the girl's physical maturation. Although it contextualizes pinning as one of the stages preparing a girl for her adult role as wife, the event is linked to the girl's age, fifteen *sui*, rather than to her betrothal status.[60] The *Family Rituals* links the rite to changes in the girl's social status and prescribes that she should be pinned when she is betrothed, but comments that a girl should be pinned at fifteen *sui* if she is not yet engaged.[61]

In contrast to the European discursive emphasis on biology and the materiality of the individual body as the essential foundation of gendered iden-

56. Joseph R. Allen ("Dressing and Undressing," p. 347) argues that by the sixth or seventh century the emphasis in the Mulan story was not on her anomalous behavior but on her reintegration into society.

57. See Ebrey, *Chu Hsi's Family Rituals*.

58. Trans. from Legge, *Book of Rites*, 1: 473; *Li ji*, "Neize," 12.54.

59. Ebrey (*Chu Hsi's Family Rituals*, p. 19) points out that expanded versions of the *Family Rituals* reflect the widespread practice of ceremonial observances for all newborns.

60. *Li ji*, "Neize," 12.54; Legge, *Book of Rites*, 1: 479.

61. Ebrey, *Chu Hsi's Family Rituals*, p. 45; for the Chinese text, see ibid., p. 192.

tity, the Chinese emphasis was on demonstrating and maintaining the symmetrical relationship between male and female, a symmetry that came to be a defining feature of both the natural and social orders. This emphasis on symmetrical patterns of order rather than the individual *sui generis* gave biology a meaning different from the one it carries in the European West. Rather than being the essential foundation of gender identity, it functioned more as an epistemological anchor for the foundational truth of gender symmetry. In this sense, Angela Zito is correct in saying that the material body was treated as a sign or vessel upon which meaning could be projected, but as the evidence from fiction will attest, she goes too far in negating the importance of sexed bodies.[62] As we shall see in the discussion of *Xingshi yinyuan zhuan* (Chapter 3), the need to keep men and women in their proper places caused a great deal of anxiety; this anxiety was frequently expressed in corporeal terms in which the leaking, transgressive body of the woman threatens the integrity of the *neiwai* boundary. Although the cultural significance of biological identity in traditional China differed from that in the West, that identity was important to the moral and natural order.

Ritual texts treat gender difference as both parallel to and metonymic of other paired status categories, such as ruler and minister or parent and child. Although filiality (*xiao* 孝) and political loyalty (*zhong* 忠) receive more direct attention in classical Confucian texts than does marital fidelity (*jie* 節), the Confucian hermeneutic tradition consistently privileges the gendered husband-wife relationship as a metaphor for other hierarchical relationships, especially in the political realm. This may be because the distinctions between male and female social roles could more easily be naturalized than the other hierarchical social roles. Orthodox discourse essentializes gender roles not by linking them to biology but by treating them as the anthropomorphic manifestation of abstract *yinyang* values. It bears emphasizing that discussions of *yinyang* values in ritual texts differ radically from the more fluid constructions of *yinyang* metaphysics in the *Yi jing* 易經 (Book of changes). In metaphysical discourse, *yin* and *yang* are posited as mutually complementary and fluidly interdependent forces: *yang* is represented by the sun, the male, brightness, fire, heat, originating activity, and the like, and *yin* by the moon,

62. Zito, "Of Silk and Skin," p. 106. Although recent discussions of the performative nature of gender in China, such as those by Zito and Barlow, owe a great deal to Judith Butler's *Gender Trouble* and *Bodies That Matter*, Fingarette's (*Confucius*, p. 11) descriptions of Confucian ritual as performative anticipated her work in the Chinese context.

Qian

Kun

the female, darkness, water, cold, passive receptivity, and so on. Generation, regeneration, the processes of change, and the full range of experiences and phenomena depend on a free and endless mixing of these two equal energies; at various points of the calendrical or life cycle, one or the other will gain in force until it is dominant, but soon thereafter it peaks and begins to recede until the other is dominant. The two can be thought of as the poles of a continuum; in the *Yi jing* the pure *yang* position is represented as the Qian 乾 hexagram; and the pure *yin* position as the Kun 坤 hexagram. Of the 64 hexagrams, only Qian and Kun do not represent a mixture of *yin* within *yang*, or *yang* within *yin*; the vast majority of phenomena are formed from a mixture of the two. The natural world is a manifestation of these fluid interactions.

Rhetorically, however, *yin* and *yang* came to be used as exclusive binomes to differentiate opposing terms. As described in Richard John Lynn's translation of the *Yi jing*, the function of the Qian hexagram is regulative:

> [Qian] manifests its fitness and constancy by making the innate tendencies of things conform to their natures. The power in Qian to provide origins is such that it can make all under Heaven fit by means of its own beautiful fitness. One does not say how it confers fitness; it is just great! How great Qian is! It is strong, dynamic, central, correct, and it is absolutely pure in its unadulteratedness and unsulliedness.[63]

The parallel description of the pure *yin* Kun hexagram reveals that its reproductive potential was considered to be unstable enough that it could result in the creation of disorder unless properly controlled:

> How great is the fundamental nature of Kun! The myriad things are provided their births by it, and in so doing it compliantly carries out Heaven's will. . . . For one who is yielding and compliant, it is fitting to practice constancy here, and the noble man who sets out to do something, if he takes the lead, will be in breach of the Dao, but if he follows and is compliant, he will find his rightful place.[64]

In contrast to the Qian hexagram, which tends toward continuation of a stable order, inherent in the very mutability of the Kun hexagram is a potential for transgressive (re)production should it fail to conform to the proper patterns established by Qian. Extreme *yin* is conceived as an inchoate and volatile space in which radical transformations occur, such as the

63. Lynn, *The Classic of Changes*, p. 130.
64. Ibid., p. 143.

changes associated with birth and death.[65] Confucian ethicists fixed the regulatory function of *yang* and the unstable fertility associated with *yin* within a hierarchical social matrix in which the *yang* position (as ruler, parent, elder, male) is dominant over the inferior *yin* position (subject, child, cadet, female). Within this dyad, the *yang* entity, equated with orthodoxy, imparts regulative order, and the *yin*, when properly controlled, supports and regenerates the meta-order. When the *yin* is not properly contained, however, it becomes a transgressive force capable of subverting the meta-order.[66] Although the two constructions of *yinyang* symbolism—the social, which arranges *yin* and *yang* into a static, hierarchical relationship; and the metaphysical, which emphasizes the fluidity of interactions—are clearly contradictory, the disjunctures between them were erased by philosophers who sought to base the Confucian social order on a discursively constructed natural order.

During the Han dynasty, competing schools of philosophers expanded *yinyang* paradigms to incorporate a host of associations worked out through cycles of four- or five-element cosmologies. Even though they might assign different symbolic values to the same concept, these philosophers were

65. The multivalent quality of *yin* is captured in the symbolism of popular life-cycle rituals in which *yin* is paradoxically associated with both life and death. As James Watson ("Of Flesh and Bones") has described in Cantonese funeral ceremonies, women play a prominent role in burial ceremonies by absorbing and controlling the polluting airs associated with death; he suggests that this passive aspect of death pollution is linked to women's fertility because the coins and cloth used in the funeral ceremony are often rewoven into the harnesses women use to carry children. Birth, although a happy event, is also seen as highly polluting. Parturition ceremonies (*zuoyuezi* 坐月子) treat the delivery of life as a highly unstable period during which great care needs to be taken with certain *yin*-associated items: the afterbirth must be disposed of properly, and the mother herself is contained within her room for a month and may not wash her hair (Ahern, "The Power and Pollution," pp. 171–73). As Watson ("Of Flesh and Bones," p. 162) explains, hair is associated with *yin*. During her confinement, the mother traditionally replenishes her *yang* energy (*buyang* 補陽) by consuming large quantities of a *yang*-rich chicken and rice-wine broth. The inherent instability of *yin* is encapsulated in the symbolism of these two transitional events: death, which is negative, is linked to fertility; and birth, a positive event, is filled with pollution. Both birth and death rituals function to contain the unstable, polluting, and even destructive potential of *yin* energy and channel it to ensure that it nurtures life.

66. The anthropologist Steven Sangren (*History and Magical Power*, p. 134) has argued that the unchanging meta-order, posited as *yang*, hierarchically encompasses the myriad manifestations of *yinyang* interactions. Zito's (*Of Body and Brush*, pp. 149–51) analyses of imperial rituals that privilege the *yang* so that it encompasses the entirety corroborate this association of *yang* with the meta-order.

united in the belief that abstract metaphysical terms could be reified in actual objects, people, or qualities.[67] The most influential of these Han cosmologists was Dong Zhongshu, who incorporated five-elements (*wuxing* 五行) correlative thinking into a *yinyang*-based moral order. In his efforts to conceptualize a coherent cosmological structure, Dong created a system of associative equivalency between otherwise discrete phenomena by equating each element of binomic concepts with an abstract *yin* or *yang* value. He then grounded this epistemological schema in a moral framework by valorizing the *yang* term as inherently good (*shan* 善) and the *yin* as evil (*e* 惡).[68] In this system, each *yang* term is analogically linked to all other *yang* terms, even though they may share no other logical connection.

The impact of this expansive rhetorical logic on the subsequent development of symbolic language in China is inestimable; it allowed abstract terms to be discursively defined by being placed in an oppositional relationship, or series of relationships, to other terms. The universality and flexibility of this rhetorical logic allowed for an extremely rich, although slippery, symbolic vocabulary in which any term could invoke multiple and frequently contradictory associative meanings. The somewhat arbitrary nature of this symbolic system was disguised by treating the signs as though they were empirically rather than discursively derived. For example, in a lengthy passage that contrasts oppositional *yinyang* qualities, Dong emphatically states: "The *yin* and *yang* of Heaven and earth are equivalent to man and woman; the male and female of humankind are *yin* and *yang*. Therefore, *yin* and *yang* can be called man and woman, and man and woman can be called *yin* and *yang*" 天地之陰陽當男女，人之男女當陰陽。陰陽亦可以謂男女，男女亦可以謂陰陽.[69] Dong Zhongshu then used this rhetorical strategy to connect ethical human behavior to the proper functioning of the Heavens:

> Heaven has its dual operation of *yin* and *yang*, and the self (*shen* 身) also has a dual nature of humanity and greed. There are cases in which Heaven restricts the operation of *yin* and *yang*, and there are cases in which the person weakens his feelings and desires. [The Way of man] and the Way of Heaven are the same. Consequently as *yin* functions, it cannot interfere with spring or summer (which correspond to *yang*), and the full moon is always overwhelmed by sunlight, so that at one moment it is

67. See Needham, *Science and Civilisation*, 2: 262–63.

68. *CQFL*, p. 52, 11.4. For the moral valorization of *yin* and *yang*, see Bao Jialin, "Yinyang xueshuo."

69. *CQFL*, p. 76, 16.6.

full and at another is not. This is the way Heaven restricts the operation of *yin*. How can [man] not reduce his desires and stop his feelings (both corresponding to *yin*) in order to respond to Heaven?[70]

As suggested in this passage and elsewhere in Dong's writings, *yin* needs to be regulated and contained, for "all that is hateful (*e*) is concentrated in *yin*, and all that is good (*shan*) is concentrated in *yang*."[71]

The abiding influence of Dong's moral cosmology on later writings on statecraft can be seen in a comment by Liu Ji 劉基 (1311–75) in which he describes the political chaos of the fourteenth century.

Although Heaven's principle is such that it has a mind to love the good and hate evil, and while it has an original bias in favor of ordered conditions, its natural substance *qi* ceaselessly oscillates between the positive and negative extremes of *yin* and *yang*. As *qi* moves toward the *yin* extreme, it loses balance, its circulation becomes blocked, it throws the seasons out of sequence and the stars out of position, it gasps and retches, and thunder, lightning, disease, flood, drought and rebellions appear on the earth. Inescapably infected with this cosmic sickness, men crazily rebel against what is normal, they become deranged and stagger about because they have contracted the diseased *qi* of Heaven and do not know what they are doing.[72]

As we shall see, this same rich lexicon of associative symbolism, which links *yin* to many variations of negative events, forms the core of the orthodox rhetoric deployed in Ming-Qing fiction.

It was through the rite of marriage that ritual texts most clearly articulated the parallels between natural *yinyang* patterns and social institutions. The *Book of Rites* describes the rite as the foundation of the social order because of the way it delineates the fundamental distinctions between man and woman and establishes the symmetrical obligations between husband and wife; from these initial structures develop the bonds of filiality and loyalty. As stated in the *Book of Rites*, "The rituals of marriage are the root of ritual."[73] The section on the rites of marriage describes how cosmic *yin* and *yang*

70. *CQFL*, p. 45, 10.1; trans. and notes from *Source Book*, p. 274. The material in parentheses was added by Chan.

71. *CQFL*, p. 52, 11.4.

72. Liu Ji, *Chengyibo wenji* in Guoxue jiben congshu series (Taibei, 1967), p. 175; cited in and trans. from Dardess, *Confucianism*, pp. 134–35.

73. *Li ji*, "Hunyi," 44.4; for a different translation, see Legge, *Book of Rites*, 2: 430. The notion that marital relations are the basis of the moral order is also explicitly stated in the Mao Preface to the *Shi jing*.

energies follow and respond to the virtuous efforts of the king and queen, the most powerful human representations of *yang* and *yin*, to regulate the inner (female) and outer (male) spheres of their home. "Therefore when the teachings of men (*nanjiao* 男教) are not cultivated, *yang* phenomena do not proceed regularly, as can be seen by the heavenly manifestation of a solar eclipse; when the obedience of women (*fu shun* 婦順) is not cultivated, *yin* phenomena do not proceed regularly, as can be seen by the heavenly manifestation of a lunar eclipse."[74] Another section of the *Book of Rites* states that "the rituals of marriage are that which clarify the distinctions between male and female" 昏姻之禮所以明男女之別也.[75]

An oft-repeated phrase in ritual texts directed specifically at women, such as Ban Zhao's 班昭 (32–92 C.E.) *Nü jie* 女誡 (Instructions for women), is "wife [as] earth and husband [as] Heaven" (*fudi futian* 婦地夫天), which further serves to naturalize the hierarchical difference between men and women. The later *Nü xiaojing* 女孝經 (Classic of filial piety for women) also draws repeated connections between cosmic *yinyang* patterns and ritual to provide a "natural" context for the social differences between male and female:[76] "The wife is earth and the husband Heaven, and one cannot discard either. Therefore the husband has a hundred responsibilities, and the wife a single resolve. It is right for the husband to remarry, but there is no textual elaboration [calling for] a woman to celebrate nuptials a second time."[77] Nowhere do these ritual anthologies refer to male and female biological differences as evidence of the distinctions between men and women. Furthermore, consistent with the vast majority of didactic texts directed at girls and women after the rise of Neo-Confucianism, although the title of *Classic of Filial Piety for Women* suggests that it might be a treatise explicitly concerned with a girl's relationship with her parents, its major focus is on the marital relations between a woman and her husband and his family; as stated in the preface, "The way of the husband and wife is the beginning of social relations" (*fufu zhi dao renlun zhi shi* 夫婦之道，人倫之始).[78]

74. *Li ji*, "Hunyi," 44.9; trans. based on Legge, *Book of Rites*, 2: 433–34. This cosmological aspect of the marriage rites is absent from Zhu Xi's *Family Rituals*.

75. *Li ji*, "Jing jie," 26.4.

76. The *Nü xiaojing* is attributed to a mid-Tang woman named Zheng 鄭, although the earliest known reference to the text does not appear until 1126 (Murray, "Didactic Art," p. 29).

77. *Nü xiaojing*, 1.6b; also see preface 1a, 7.3a, 9.4a, and 13.6b.

78. *Nü Xiaojing*, preface 1a.

The central importance of the husband-wife relationship was widely reflected during the late imperial period when there was an explosion of ritual texts directed at or about women. Lü Kun's 呂坤 (1536–1618) *Guifan tushuo* 閨範圖說 (Illustrated regulations for the women's quarters; preface dated 1590) remarks: "[The state of having] one *yin* and one *yang* is called the Way. Husband and wife are a microcosm; Heaven and earth are a macrocosm of husband and wife. Therefore the source of the myriad transformations starts in the women's quarters" 一陰一陽之謂道。夫婦一小天也。天地一大夫婦。故萬化之原始於閨門.[79] A fictional rendering of the same concept occurs in a story by Feng Menglong 馮夢龍 (1574–1646):

> When [the undifferentiated] primordial chaos split open, the way of Qian became male, and the way of Kun became female. Although creation was unbiased, still *yin* and *yang* divided and were differentiated, so that *yang* was active and *yin* quiescent; *yang* initiating, *yin* receptive; *yang* external, *yin* internal. In this way, men are master over the affairs of the four directions, and women are master over the affairs of one room.[80]

In contrast, those gendered relations that are not regulated by marriage are a significant source of anxiety in literary texts. In many examples, gendered difference immediately evokes the specter of sexual desire; it is rarely neutral.[81] As can be seen from the allegorical Mao interpretations of love songs in the *Book of Poetry*, Qu Yuan's 屈原 (ca. 340–278 B.C.E.) *Li sao* 離騷 (Encountering sorrow) in which the hero seeks an ideal and faithful sovereign, who is represented allegorically as the "beautiful one" (*meiren* 美人), and Song Yu's 宋玉 (ca. 290–223 B.C.E.) paean to imperial authority, *Gaotang fu* 高唐賦 (Rhapsody on the Gaotang Shrine), gendered relationships are sexualized and made into charged sites in which the boundaries that define power, order, loyalty, and virtue are tested, negotiated, and re-established. What more powerful way could there be to illustrate the tensions between self and duty evoked in any hierarchical relationship than to pit moral obligation against the most extreme expressions of desire? As discussed in the

79. Lü Kun, *Guifan tushuo*, 1.1b. For similar statements, see Li Zhi, "Fufu," in idem, *Fenshu*, p. 107; *Lienü yanyi*, preface 2a. Yu Zhengxie employs this analogy to criticize a man's remarriage in "Jiefu shuo," in *Guisi leigao*, 13.7a.

80. Feng Menglong, *Xingshi hengyan*, p. 226. McMahon also cites this passage in *Causality and Containment*, p. 52. For another example from fiction, see *JHY*, 1.1a.

81. See also the discussion of Xunzi's intertwined discourses on ritual and desire in A. Yu, *Rereading the Stone*, pp. 74–82.

following chapter, by the Neo-Confucian era, the problematic of desire had become so emblematic of the struggle for self-cultivation that for a character to catch sight of a member of the opposite sex, or to hear of her or his existence, inevitably sets in motion a narrative on desire, ritual, and transgression that is played out in *yinyang* symbolic terms.

The late Ming, early Qing novel *Xingshi yinyuan zhuan,* the subject of Chapter 3, is a stark expression of the Neo-Confucian distrust of sexual desire. As discussed above, maintaining the proper gender distinctions and hierarchies was a foundational aspect of the Confucian social order; the depictions of the female protagonist in *Xingshi yinyuan zhuan* are a nightmarish fantasy of all that can transpire when a man's failure to cultivate himself and regulate his home brings about the erasure of those boundaries. At the center of this orthodox allegory of the dangers of desire is the character of a shrew, who almost succeeds in the unthinkable, the destruction of her husband's lineage. Although the appearance of a shrew is not unusual in overtly didactic narratives, it is surprising the extent to which the attributes of the transgressive woman, writ large in *Xingshi,* appear in an abbreviated shorthand in more sentimental works that have been noted for their idealization of the feminine. Even though these later shrews are overshadowed by their gentler sisters and are often overlooked as incidental characters, they play an important narrative role in invoking the moral logic of orthodox discourse. As illustrated in the novel *Xingshi yinyuan zhuan,* individual performances of ritual are the means by which a stable and moral social and cosmic order is created and maintained; gender is foundational to this ethical system. To tamper with ritually prescribed gender roles is to risk destabilizing the social and cosmic order.

WEN AND THE AESTHETICS OF ORTHODOXY

Not surprisingly, the foundational importance of gender symmetry in the social and natural orders is also reflected in fiction aesthetics. Formal structuring was crucial to the reception and meaning of late imperial vernacular fiction, for the moral intent ascribed to certain novels was based on the literary qualities of the text. The structural manipulation of *yinyang* themes became a significant aspect of producing the literary (*wen*) nature of the text. Male and female are not simply naturalized manifestations of *yang* and *yin;* they also carry an explicit moral valence. For this reason, gendered depictions in fiction carry a substantial ideological and ethical weight in addition to their more straightforward narrative function.

Just as the performance of ritual brought order to the world, the cultural practices associated with *wen* were thought to be able to actualize a perfect expression of the *Dao* 道, the Way (*wen yi zai Dao* 文以載道). Within the late imperial context, *wen* is usually translated simply as "writing" or "literature." However, by the Qing dynasty, as Angela Zito has so convincingly argued, the literary activities practiced by the literati, the *wenren* 文人, came to be endowed with the same moral authority and power as the practices of ritual.[82] In her study of Qing imperial rites, Zito uses the archaic concept of a "naturally occurring text-pattern" to translate the word *wen*. Her gloss evokes the belief expressed in the *Xici zhuan* 繫辭傳 (Commentary on the attached verbalizations) on the *Yi jing* that the textual patterns (*wen*) of the hexagrams can and should reflect cosmic configurations (*wen*). "The things [that figure a hexagram, its lines and the circumstances indicated by them] are mixed together, and in consequence [the *Change*] speaks of the patterns (*wen*) [formed by those figures]" (物相雜故曰文).[83] Based on the logic of correlative cosmology, textual patterning had by extension the power to affect reality so that certain kinds of cultural production, especially music, writing, and architecture, shared with ritual a sacral power to pattern, or harmonize, various levels of existence. In the words of Wang Anshi 王安石 (1021–86), literary texts (*wen*) are the equivalent of social ethics (*lijiao*) and governing (*zhizheng* 治政).[84] Or as Zito has written, "Productions that modernity deems 'aesthetic' in fact endowed their creators with a kind of moral authority."[85]

Wen refers both to cultural production and the power of culture to civilize. These deeply held beliefs in the dual ability of *wen* to reflect cosmic truths and affect change are elegantly voiced in Liu Xie's 劉勰 (ca. 465–522) treatise on literature, *Wenxin diaolong* 文心雕龍 (The literary mind and the carving of dragons). The *Wenxin diaolong* begins with a claim for the moral efficacy of art, "The [ability] of *wen* [literary texts] to bring about virtue is great indeed" 文之爲德也大矣.[86] Human activities derive from cosmic

82. Zito, *Of Body and Brush*, pp. 70–71.
83. Trans. based on Peterson, "Making Connections," p. 81.
84. Wang Anshi, "Shangren shu," in *Wang Linchuan*, p. 489.
85. Zito, *Of Body and Brush*, p. 217.
86. Liu Xie, *Wenxin diaolong*, p. 1.

patterns: "The origins of human patterns/texts (*ren wen*) are found in the Great Ultimate" 人文之元肇自太極 (p. 2). Furthermore, cultural production and cosmic and social changes are mutually generative:

> The *Change* says: "That which stimulates the movements of all under Heaven is in the oracular judgments (*ci*), and that which enables the judgments to stimulate all under Heaven is the pattern (*wen*) of the Dao." 易曰: 鼓天下之動者存乎辭; 辭之所以能鼓天下者迺道之文也. (p. 3)

One translator of this passage comments that Liu Xie is here capitalizing on the ambiguous associations of the word *ci*, which refers both specifically to the attached commentaries of the *Yi jing* and more broadly to linguistic form, as if to claim that rhetoric has the power to engage change.[87] By translating the word *wen* in this passage as "aesthetic pattern," Stephen Owen points to the sacral power of the rhetoric and form of those literary texts, which are able to make manifest the "aesthetic pattern" of the universe.[88]

Despite the long association of *wen* with cosmic patterns, not all aesthetic patterning was viewed positively by Confucian thinkers. Confucius himself pointed out the difficulty of finding a proper balance between content and ornamentation when writing: "Substance (*zhi* 質) exceeding patterning (*wen*) results in vulgarity (*ye* 野); patterning exceeding substance results in stilted formalism (*shi* 史)" (*Analects*, VI.18). He also attacked the music of the state of Zheng as wanton and corrupting (XV.11, XVII.18). In later ideological battles for political and cultural hegemony, self-avowed Confucian camps regularly targeted the "decadent" aesthetics of their opponents as a sign of moral decline. For example, during the Confucian revival under the reign of Han Emperor Ming (r. 58–76), Confucian scholars differentiated themselves from the aristocratic elite by opting for austere and intentionally simplistic funerary monuments. In contrast to the aristocracy who favored highly ornate and opulent funerary objects, the scholar class avoided these traditional

87. Shih, *The Literary Mind*, pp. 14–15n25.

88. In Owen's (*Traditional Chinese Poetry*, p. 18) words, "A person who aspires to be *wen* will unite the semantic meanderings of the word: becoming *accomplished* through education, he may serve the government in a *civil* post, his capacity for such a position having been examined by a public test of his *writing*; he finds himself naturally drawn to *literature in which the 'aesthetic pattern'* (*wen*) *of the universe becomes manifest*" (italics in the original). Most striking in this description is the use of the word "naturally," which follows the traditional Chinese bias of viewing the appreciation of art as a reflection of a natural intelligence rather than the result of culturally formed tastes.

signs of luxury and replaced them with ornamentation that emphasized the conventional signs for filial piety, frugality, and sacrifice.[89] A better-known example of the Confucian preference for spare aesthetics over intricate ornamentation is the Confucian statesman Han Yu's 韓愈 (786–824) promotion of a more direct "ancient-prose" (*guwen* 古文) style in place of the elaborate parallel prose favored during the mid-Tang. The Song Neo-Confucians, who honored Han Yu as the equal of Mencius in defending Confucianism, followed him in rejecting ornamentation and adopting a straightforward and almost vernacular prose style to voice their Confucian message.[90] In the same letter cited above, Wang Anshi wrote that patterning (*wen*) is able to "restore the world" (*you bu yu shi* 有補於世), in contrast to ornamentation (*ci*), which, like carvings on a vessel, is superficial and not inherently useful.[91]

The late Ming was the site of another aesthetic and ideological battle between orthodox purity and expressive freedom. A small number of influential cultural figures, most important Li Zhi and the Yuan brothers of the Gong'an school, countered prevailing standards of poetry to argue that each age should produce its own literary forms. Ming poetic styles were dominated by the Archaist school, which to a greater or lesser degree drew its inspiration from Yan Yu's 嚴羽 (1180–1235) treatise on poetry, *Canglang shihua* 滄浪詩話.[92] The *Canglang shihua* identified the high Tang as the source for the "orthodox" (*zheng*) tradition of poetry and claimed that only through assimilating and mastering the orthodox tradition could one hope to become an enlightened poet. Ironically, that Yan Yu also emphasized intuition (*miao wu* 妙悟) and merged the discourses of poetic criticism and Chan enlightenment (*yi Chan shuo shi* 以禪說詩) as part of his orthodox revival shows just how malleable the term "orthodox" is in aesthetic-literary terms. For the

89. Powers, *Art and Political Expression*, p. 71.

90. For an encomium from the *Xin Tangshu* ranking Han Yu with Mencius, see *A History*, 2: 409.

91. Wang Anshi, *Wang Linchuan*, p. 489.

92. The Archaists are traditionally identified as the Former and Latter Seven Masters (*Qian Hou qizi* 前後七子). However, the political and aesthetic boundary between the Archaists and the reformers gets blurred by the fact that the innovative Wang Shizhen 王士禎 (1634–1711) was a prominent member of the Latter Seven Masters. For a discussion of how Wang Shizhen's ideas about poetry came to resemble those of the Gong'an school, see Chou, *Yuan Hung-tao*, pp. 11–14; For a more detailed discussion of Wang's theories on poetry, see Lynn, "Orthodoxy and Enlightenment," pp. 241–57.

Archaists, the practice of poetry composition, more than being a form of self-expression or exploration of aesthetic styles, was valued as a medium of self-cultivation.[93]

Unfortunately, the conservative emphasis of the Archaists on following earlier models (literally, *fugu* 復古, "returning to the past") as a form of spiritual and aesthetic discipline resulted in much of Ming and Qing poetry being woodenly formulaic and imitative. In response to this large body of uninspired poetry, the late Ming reformers called for a return to a more expressive function for poetry. Yuan Hongdao 袁宏道 (1568–1610) of the Gong'an school wrote a manifesto in which he boldly argued that an authentic (*zhen*) representation of individual experience and voice was more important to the production of poetry than was working within an orthodox tradition. As is discussed in the following chapter, this stylistic resistance to the more academic Archaists gave rise to the often decadent values of the late Ming cult of sensibility, also known as the cult of *qing*, which promoted an aesthetics based on affect, illusion, paradox, and surface patterning. In an invaluable study of the late Ming moment, Waiyee Li points out that the value of one spontaneous nocturnal dramatic performance lay precisely in its pointlessness;[94] given the morally didactic function of the dominant theory of poetry composition, it is not surprising that the reformers subscribed to a playful "art for art's sake" mentality that prized rhetorical embellishments, based on clever doublings, reversals, and the celebration of uniqueness, that were aesthetically productive but ethically ambiguous.

Although the Confucian conservatives were suspicious of excessive ornamentation, aesthetic patterning (*wen*) was frequently associated with orthodox expression, in terms of either content or style. The rhetoric of orthodoxy in traditional China was highly structured and regulated; classical prose (*wenyan* 文言), the language of philosophy, history, official documents, poetry, and the culturally more refined and therefore esteemed forms of literature, is marked by its concise descriptions and parallel syntactic and semantic structures.[95] Although it would be an exaggeration to equate formalism with orthodoxy (one school's formalism could easily be attacked as stylistic decadence by another school), there seems to have been an under-

93. Lynn, "Orthodoxy and Enlightenment," pp. 218–19.

94. W. Y. Li, *Enchantment*, p. 47.

95. For a discussion of the social uses of Classical Chinese through 1917, see Hanan, *Chinese Vernacular Story*, pp. 3–5.

lying cultural tendency to associate regular patterning with moral rigor, a bias that became a central feature of *xiaoshuo* criticism. Textual form (*wen*) functions similarly to ritual form (*li*) in taking spontaneous expressions, which may be unpredictable and messy, and shaping and organizing them into a universal, transparent, and civilizing medium. For Yan Yu, the highest achievement of lyric poetry, in which the tone and syntactic and semantic functions of each character are dictated according to patterns established within each line and strophe, was regulated verse (*lü shi* 律詩; the character *lü* also means "the law" and "to bind"); to write it is to engage in self-discipline.

It is no exaggeration to say that during the Ming and Qing dynasties, when academies were established throughout the empire to prepare young men for the rigorous bureaucratic examinations, the parallel eight-legged essay (*bagu wen* 八股文, also called *shiwen* 時文, "the prose of our time") had come to be the predominant expression of the carefully modulated voice of official orthodoxy.[96] Although it was possible for examiners and examination candidates to manipulate interpretations of the Confucian Classics to promote changes in political and ideological structures, the essays in which they did so needed to be phrased in the elegant, spare language the format demanded.[97] The very rigidity of the form and the requirement that the Classics be used as a source for argumentation functioned as a conservative straitjacket that helped keep candidates and examiners from straying too far from the boundaries of orthodox thought.[98] Tellingly, despite widespread criticism of the shortcomings of the examination system during the late imperial period, such as the seemingly arbitrary nature of success, and cynicism about the commercialization of examination preparation and the pedagogical emphasis on acquiring skill in writing eight-legged essays rather than moral or practical knowledge, as well as fears that the system was kept in

96. For a structural analysis and translation of an eight-legged essay, see C. I. Tu, "The Chinese Examination Essay."

97. To see how the content of the examination essays changed to accommodate evidential scholarship, see Elman, "Changes," pp. 135–43; and Chow, "Discourse," pp. 185–86, 198–99.

98. The low rates of success in the bureaucratic examination system no doubt dissuaded candidates from taking intellectual or stylistic risks. For the Qing dynasty, Elman ("Changes," p. 117) estimates that of the total two million candidates who participated in the examination system, 1.5 percent gained licentiate status, and only 0.01 percent made it through the highest level, the metropolitan examinations. For Ming figures, see Ho, *The Ladder of Success*, pp. 186–90.

place as a form of social control, there was also praise for the *bagu* essay as a literary creation.[99] For example, both Li Zhi, the radical critic of the bureaucratic status quo, and Yuan Hongdao praised the eight-legged essay as a Ming literary innovation.[100]

The cultural importance ascribed to literary formalism in the parallel eight-legged essay is also suggested by the fact that during the early Ming and Qing it became closely associated with a Han Chinese identity. On a popular level, because success in the examinations was the most legitimate avenue of social advancement for men, examination lore became an important aspect of the mythology of what it meant to be culturally Chinese. As a Ming innovation, the eight-legged essay seems to have been regarded as a triumphant response to the cultural inferiority of the barbarian Mongols, who had canceled the examination system for over 40 years. An early Qing attempt to de-emphasize the eight-legged essay and those sections of the examination that required rote memorization met with vehement opposition; as Benjamin Elman writes, certain literati saw these innovations as a "betrayal of Confucian orthodoxy by ignorant Manchu usurpers."[101] Seemingly, the rigid form of the eight-legged essay was regarded by some as emblematic of Han Chinese culture.

The tendency to associate formalism with orthodoxy became a central component of *xiaoshuo* criticism. Fiction commentaries regularly direct readers' attention away from unorthodox content toward aesthetic patterns that could be defined as *wen*. No more explicit and daring example of this process can be found than Jin Shengtan's defense of the *Shuihu zhuan* 水滸傳 (Brotherhood of the marsh), an unruly, anti-state novel that seems to condone rebellion. Jin ignored the political message inherent in the fictional bandits' rebellion despite the fact that he worked on his edition during the years leading up to the collapse of the Ming dynasty. In his third preface, Jin promoted the novel as not only appropriate for but also beneficial to schoolboys, because, as he argued, the structural techniques he identified in the

99. Roddy, *Literati Identity*, pp. 51–58. For discussions of the influence of eight-legged essays on the composition of novels, see Plaks, *Four Masterworks*, pp. 31, 33–34; and Rolston, *How to Read*, pp. 17–29.

100. Li Zhi, "Tongxin shuo," in *Fenshu*, p. 98; Yuan Hongdao, "Yu Youren lun shiwen" and "Chidu," in *Yuan Zhonglang*, p. 14, and "Hao Gongyan shi xu" and "Chaowen," in ibid., pp. 11–12; discussed in Chou, *Yuan Hung-tao*, pp. 42–44.

101. Elman describes the negative Chinese reaction to a 1663 attempt to reform the format of the examinations in "Changes," pp. 119–20.

novel make it a suitable primer for learning how to write eight-legged essays. Even though his legitimation of the vernacular novel as *wen* required a deliberate misreading and rewriting of the *Shuihu zhuan*, Jin Shengtan's intervention in the aesthetics of *xiaoshuo* fiction was so powerful and far-reaching that the early twentieth-century intellectual Zhou Zuoren 周作人 (1884–1969) could recall his grandfather instructing his students to study novels such as *Xiyou ju* 西遊記 (The journey to the west), *Rulin waishi* 儒林外史 (The scholars), and *Jing hua yuan* as part of their preparation for learning to write *bagu* essays.[102]

The editors, commentators, and authors of vernacular novels had to fight an uphill battle in their efforts to promote *xiaoshuo* fiction as a serious genre. Fiction had always eluded respectability; despite their best efforts to categorize and order the textual world, bibliographers were never quite sure how to codify *xiaoshuo*, a minor branch of history that deals with events outside the purview of orthodoxy by being either too trivial or too heterodox.[103] Given the dominance of historiography in the Chinese cultural context, the qualities of creating and shaping that are foregrounded in the English word "fiction" (from the Latin *fingere*, "to form," "to fashion," "to invent") served only to devalue *xiaoshuo*. The remarkable Chinese epistemological urge to classify all manner of phenomena should be seen as yet another literati activity that parallels ritual in attempting to order the world by dividing it into discrete categories. Fiction rested uneasily at the margins of canonical genres. Ban Gu 班固 (32–92) placed *xiaoshuo*, "minor talk," under the philosophers (*zi* 子) as the last of the ten schools, a category that included Confucianism, Daoism, Mohism, and Legalism. Liu Zhiji 劉知幾 (661–721) catalogued *xiaoshuo* as a type of history. Even while admitting the subjective nature of the schema, Hu Yinglin 胡應麟 (1551–1602) divided *xiaoshuo* fiction into six subgenres (*zhiguai* 志怪, records of anomalies; *chuanqi* 傳奇, tales of the extraordinary; *zalu* 雜錄, miscellaneous notes; *congtan* 叢談, collected talk; *bianding* 辨訂, inquiries; and *zhengui* 箴規, admonitions).[104] Tellingly, despite his interest in contemporary *chuanqi* drama, Hu Yinglin excluded vernacular drama and novels, the most heteroglossic of all genres, from his taxonomy. Perhaps in order to compensate for these thematic and

102. Cited in Rolston, *How to Read*, p. 21.

103. For a more detailed definition and history of attempts to categorize *xiaoshuo*, see S. Lu, *From Historicity to Fictionality*, pp. 37–52.

104. Hu Yinglin, *Shanfang bicong*, p. 374, cited in S. Lu, *From Historicity to Fictionality*, p. 50.

taxonomic shortcomings of vernacular fiction, commentators and editors introduced a formal poetics for *xiaoshuo* fiction that equated aesthetic control with moral intent.

Formalism and the Golden Age of Xiaoshuo *Fiction*

When present-day scholars of late imperial China make an analogy between the writing of texts (*xiuwen* 修文) and the physical cultivation of the body (*xiushen* 修身) through such practices as quiet sitting and ritual enactments, they refer to the editing of canonical literature—the Classics, history, philosophy, and poetry.[105] However, the value placed on the textual tradition (*wen*) during the late imperial period was such that involvement in almost any elite textual activity brought a certain cultural legitimation.[106] Those eighteenth-century endeavors that modern scholarship compartmentalizes into art, philosophy, and politics existed on a continuum alongside ritual as behaviors that partook of the sacral activities of ordering and regulating self and world.[107] During this period, aesthetic patterning achieved new levels of cultural authority.

During the Ming, the focus of interest in texts (*wen*), even histories, shifted from the text as a repository of historical truth toward the text as an example of the technical aspects of composition; this shift was instrumental to the development of the aesthetics of *xiaoshuo* fiction.[108] One of the core beliefs of the return to the ancients movement of the Ming Archaists was that mastering the rules of composition (*fa* 法) of high Tang poetry could lead to enlightenment.[109] This emphasis on technique and structure as a way of cultivating the self gave rise to a wave of commentaries on the Classics, histories, and poetry as examples of literature (*wen*).[110]

105. See Zito, *Of Body and Brush*, p. 70; Lynn, "Orthodoxy and Enlightenment," p. 219.

106. For a similar discussion of the practice of connoisseurship, see Clunas, *Superfluous Things*.

107. See. e.g., Shen Fu's (*Fusheng liu ji*, p. 25; trans. by Pratt and Chiang, *Six Records*, p. 40) admiring description of his wife Yun's efforts to restore and preserve scraps of calligraphy and printed text.

108. Space does not permit me to do justice here to the late Ming move away from viewing *xiaoshuo* as deficient historiography to valuing its stylistic features. This crucial topic is treated more thoroughly in S. Lu, *From Historicity to Fictionality*, pp. 93–150; and Rolston, *Traditional Chinese Fiction*, pp. 105–90.

109. Lynn, "Orthodoxy and Enlightenment," pp. 222, 235, 242.

110. Rolston, *How to Read*, pp. 12–13, 15–17; and idem, *Traditional Chinese Fiction*, pp. 160–63.

Commentaries to novels began to claim that in certain respects fiction was equal to the Classics and could be superior to canonical histories. Jin Shengtan, who more than any other person shaped the aesthetics of both the *xiaoshuo* and the commentary tradition, constructed a list of masterworks (*qishu* 奇書) "by and for geniuses" (*caizi shu* 才子書). He boldly placed the vernacular *Shuihu zhuan* and the drama *Xixiang ji* 西廂記 (Romance of the western chamber) on a par with the *Zhuangzi* 莊子, Qu Yuan's *Li sao*, Sima Qian's 司馬遷 (b. 145 B.C.E.) *Shi ji* 史記 (Records of the historian), as well as the poetry of Du Fu 杜甫 (712–70), one of the Tang poets most highly revered by the classical Archaist movement. Jin made even more daring claims to respectability for fiction when he purported that certain techniques in the *Shuihu* derived from the Confucian *Analects* and suggested that because fiction is not tied to fact, it is superior to history in its literary qualities.[111]

In their 1680 edition of the *Sanguo yanyi* 三國演義 (The romance of the Three Kingdoms), the father-and-son team of Mao Lun 毛綸 (1605?–1700?) and Mao Zonggang 毛宗綱 (1632–1709?), who were deeply influenced by Jin Shengtan's editing of *Shuihu zhuan* and *Xixiang ji*, went even further in suggesting that literary technique can be read as a transparent representation of cosmic order. They credited the patterning of this vast and dense historical work to the divine inspiration of the "Creator of All Things" *Zaowu zhe* 造物者.

> This is an example of the artful dispositions (*qiao* 巧) of the Creator. Though his mysteries are beyond human imagination, his artistry can be imitated by us. The Creator can indeed be said to be a master of the literary arts (善于作文矣). When the writers of our day set pen to paper they command neither such mystery nor such art (*qiao*). If this is so, we should do better to study the spontaneous patterns (*ziran zhi wen* 自然之文) of the Creator himself rather than to peruse the literary works (*wen*) dreamed up by our contemporaries.[112]

In their introductory essay (*dufa* 讀法) on how to read the *Sanguo*, the Maos state that the *Sanguo* is a worthy successor to Confucius' *Spring and Autumn Annals* and superior to the *Zuo zhuan*, *Guoyu* 國語 (Conversations of the states), and *Lieguo zhi* 列國志 (Romance of the feudal states), because it manages to organize complex historical events into one unified narrative.[113]

111. *SHZ*, p. 10 (third preface) and p. 16. Both are discussed in Rolston, *Traditional Chinese Fiction*, pp. 2, 134.

112. *SG*, "Dufa," p. 9; trans. from Roy, "How to Read," p. 166.

113. *SG*, "Dufa," p. 18; trans. from Roy, "How to Read," p. 193.

The increased importance of aesthetic patterning during the late Ming and Qing can further be seen in the many prefaces that argue that *xiaoshuo* fiction no longer needed to be based on historical fact in order to communicate universal truths.[114] As Liu Tingji 劉廷璣 (fl. 1676) wrote in his preface to the pseudo-history *Nüxian waishi* 女仙外史 (Unofficial history of the female immortal), "The words are absurd, but the meaning is true. The book is unusual, but the message is upright."[115] The aesthetic patterning of fiction allowed it to convey truth more powerfully than history.

Commentaries to *xiaoshuo* began to ask that these works of fiction be judged according to the standards of canonical writings, as historical documents that capture the moral and artistic vision of the author. Until the late Ming, due to the low repute in which vernacular fiction was held, it was published anonymously. The lack of reliable information about the provenance of most texts did not deter commentators from engaging in autobiographical readings of their favorite works. By the 1600s, the imprimatur of a known personality, as author, publisher, or commentator, increasingly added a layer of cultural and commercial value to specific texts. Li Zhi, in his commentary to the *Shuihu zhuan*, defended the politically sensitive content of the anonymous novel by drawing a parallel between it and the *Shi ji* on the basis of authorial intent; each should be read as a product of the author's righteous resentment (*SHZ*, p. 28). Jin Shengtan went Li Zhi one better and fabricated for his truncated and polished "ancient text" (*guben* 古本) version of the *Shuihu zhuan* an authorial persona, Shi Nai'an 施耐庵, who appears in no previous sources.[116] The Maos attributed their version of the *Sanguo yanyi*, a text with a long textual history, to the "Creator." In order to bolster their interpretation of *Xiyou ji* as a Daoist allegory, Wang Xiangxu 汪象旭 (fl. 1605–78) and Huang Zhouxing 黃周星 (1611–80) attributed the novel to the Yuan dynasty Daoist patriarch Qiu Changchun 邱長春 (1148–1227). They even forged a letter from one of Qiu's younger contemporaries as proof and included it along with a biography in their edition of the novel.[117] Although Zhang Zhupo 張竹坡 (1670–98) did not name the author of the *Jin*

114. See, e.g., Xie Zhaozhe, *Wuza zu*, p. 1287; Feng Menglong's preface to *Jingshi tongyan* 警世通言; and Jin Shengtan's third preface to the *Shuihu zhuan*. This point is also discussed in S. Lu, *From Historicity to Fictionality*, pp. 134–40; and Rolston, *Traditional Chinese Fiction*, pp. 131–39.

115. Trans. from Rolston, *Traditional Chinese Fiction*, p. 134.

116. Rolston discusses the creation of implied authors in ibid., pp. 114–22.

117. Ibid., p. 8.

Ping Mei, known only by his pseudonym "Xiaoxiao sheng" 笑笑生, he did claim to have special insights into the author's motivations of frustrated filiality (*kuxiao* 苦孝) and used this as a basis for his defense of the novel.[118]

These created authorial personae not only raised the value of vernacular fiction as an expressive rather than a historiographical genre but, even more important, also allowed commentators to insist that every aspect of these sprawling and often flawed texts was an intentional detail of the authorial plan. The commentators extended Confucian allegoresis, a practice of reading developed in the commentaries to the Classics, and applied it to their didactic readings of *xiaoshuo*. The commentaries to the *Spring and Autumn Annals*, in particular, treated every turn of phrase and narrative lapse as an intentional signal meant to draw attention to a specific point. The Ming and Qing creation of a controlling authorial vision for these hitherto anonymous fictional works was so successful that commentators could turn to "rents" (*pozhan* 破綻) in the surface of the text as proof of the author's skill in transcending the bare factual level of narrative.[119]

Demonstrating the structural integrity of these sprawling, heteroglossic, and frequently composite works became a primary concern of fiction criticism after Jin Shengtan.[120] In order to reveal the unified vision of the projected author or divine "creator," commentators provided aesthetic or thematic rationales for the arrangement of the text. This process simultaneously proved the existence of the author's coherent vision and allowed readers to subject fiction to the style of close moralistic readings demanded by Confucian allegoresis. Unlike the Li Zhi commentary, which praised the *Shuihu zhuan* for its style but based its defense of the novel on its vigorous political spirit, Jin Shengtan claimed canonical status for the novel by introducing it as a masterpiece of composition on a par with the *Records of the Historian*, even while admitting its problematic political content. His poetics

118. Zhang Zhupo's defense of the novel, based on his claim that the central theme of the novel is filiality, calls to mind the parallel drawn by Angela Zito (*Of Body and Brush*, p. 4) between the production of *wen* through text and through filiality, the latter being an embodied performance of ritual through the bearing and enculturating of sons.

119. See Rolston, *Traditional Chinese Fiction*, pp. 180–82. For discussions of the development of Confucian allegorical strategies, called "the historian's brush" (*shibi* 史筆), for reading and writing fiction, see also Lo, "*San-kuo*"; Plaks, *The Four Masterworks*, pp. 124, 403–4; S. Lu, *From Historicity to Fictionality*, pp. 74–92; and Ding, "Tears of *Ressentiment*," pp. 663–94.

120. For a parallel discussion of the process of canonization in *zaju* drama, see Sieber, "Corporeality and Canonicity."

of fiction, developed in his commentary to the *Shuihu zhuan*, canonized a hermeneutics of equating structural patterning with moral vision.

By Jin's time, unity of form and symmetry of structure had already been established as defining features of elite fictional production. Cheaper commercial editions of "simpler recension" (*jianben* 簡本) editions of *Shuihu zhuan* were published with irregular numbers of printing divisions (*juan* 卷) and chapters,[121] as opposed to the more luxurious "fuller recension" (*fanben* 繁本) editions, which were presumably targeted at a more elite audience and had either 100 or 120 chapters. This variation was ended by the publication of Jin Shengtan's 70-chapter truncated edition. A similar pattern emerges in the publishing history of *Xiyou ji*. Both the Shide tang 世德堂 and Zhu Dingchen 朱鼎臣 editions of the novel date from the Wanli period, but the fine Shide tang edition is divided into 20 *juan* and 100 chapters, whereas the cheaper Fujian-style Zhu Dingchen edition has 10 *juan* and 67 or 68 unnumbered sections.[122] Of the six novels recognized as canonical, *Rulin waishi* stands apart in having an irregular number of chapters. Although Jin Shengtan could not exploit structural symmetry and numerology as a way of demonstrating the structural integrity of *Shuihu zhuan*, he did point to "how marvelous" it is that the novel begins and ends with the phrase "All under Heaven is at peace" (*Tianxia taiping* 天下太平) and developed a list of fifteen rhetorical techniques to demonstrate the intentionality of the novel's design. Following him, Mao Zonggang referred to the structure of the *Sanguo*, a novel notorious for its complicated and numerous subplots, as the "Chang Mountain snake formation" (*Changshanshe zhen* 常山蛇陳), a military formation so tightly connected that the entirety responds no matter where it is attacked.[123] The sheer number of literati novels that conform to

121. Examples include the 1594 Yu Xiangdou 余象斗, *Jingben zengbu jiaozheng quanxiang Zhongyi Shuihu zhizhuan pinglin* 京本增補校正全像忠義水滸傳評林, 25 *juan*, 124 chapters; the *Xinkan jingben quanxiang chazeng Tian Hu Wang Qing Zhongyi Shuihu zhuan* 新刊京本全象插增田虎王慶忠義水滸傳, 24 *juan*, 120 chapters; the *Zhongyi Shuihu zhuan*, 115 chapters; or the *Shuihu quanzhuan*, 124 chapters.

122. Although the Chen Shibin 陳士斌 (preface dated 1696; earliest extant edition 1780) and the 1810 Liu Yiming 劉一明 editions of the *Xiyou ji* are divided into 8 and 24 *juan*, respectively, they maintain the "canonical" 100-chapter format. Andrew Plaks (*The Four Masterworks*, pp. 202–3) has argued that the inviolability of the 100-chapter length for *xiaoshuo* novels was established by 1592. For quick comparative bibliographic descriptions of these and other editions, see ibid., pp. 525–34; and Rolston, *How to Read*, pp. 404, 430, and 451–56.

123. *SHZ*, "Xiezi," p. 50, 70.1273; *SG*, 94.1145. Jin Shengtan had complained that the degree of historical detail in *Sanguo* constrains the author (*SHZ*, "Dufa," p. 16; trans. from John

the 100- or 120-chapter format (or the equally neat 20- or 40-chapter length of the shorter scholar-beauty romances) implies that the solidity and regularity of these numerical structures came to be widely preferred by editors and authors of fiction.

Given the value that both traditional Chinese and European aesthetics ascribe to structural integrity and symmetry in works of art, it is no coincidence that so much scholarship on the traditional Chinese novel, my own included, has used structuralist means to argue for the superiority of specific editions. In the Chinese tradition, structural symmetry is a sign of *wen*, an enlightened reflection of cosmic patterning. In the European West, symmetry fulfills classical aesthetic demands for rationality (often demonstrated through mathematical precision), as well as romantic notions that a masterpiece should reflect the intellectual and creative insights of the controlling mind of the genius. The more complex the pattern, the greater the genius. In *The Four Masterworks of the Ming Novel*, one of the most important studies in any language on the aesthetics of the traditional Chinese novel, Andrew Plaks organizes the chapters in reverse historical order to highlight the teleological development of the highly symmetrical and structured novel form that culminates in the intricately crafted *Jin Ping Mei*.[124]

This attention to form, influenced by both traditional Chinese concerns and imported European biases, has obscured the ways that commentators used, and continue to use, aesthetics to distract readers from problematic thematic issues.[125] Jin Shengtan, who more than any figure in the history of the traditional Chinese novel is responsible for this trend, suggested that the value of *Shuihu zhuan* lay in its appeal as a manual of style.[126] Some of his interlinear comments enable readers to distance themselves from morally questionable passages. For example, Jin's comments that punctuate and interrupt almost every sentence of the scene in which Wu Song 武松 murders

---

Wang, "How to Read," p. 132). Rolston discusses the production of narrative unity as an aesthetic ideal in *Traditional Chinese Fiction*, pp. 264–66.

124. Plaks, *The Four Masterworks*, p. 76. For a summary of the aesthetic features of the literati novel, see his "After the Fall," pp. 545–49.

125. For a fascinating history of how traditional and contemporary readers of the *Jin Ping Mei* use aesthetic issues to inoculate themselves against the novel's obscenity, see Ding, *Obscene Objects*.

126. David Rolston (*Traditional Chinese Fiction*, p. 26) makes the interesting point that Jin Shengtan also aestheticized the word "loyalty" (*zhong* 忠), which typically refers to political loyalty, to mean "something approaching self-authenticity."

his sister-in-law Pan Jinlian 潘金蓮 keep the reader's attention drawn to questions of style rather than content (*SHZ*, 25.505). Although many readers have felt that Wu Song's bloody sacrifice of Pan Jinlian can be excused as an act of revenge for his brother's death, Jin Shengtan uses many of the same techniques to distance the reader from Wu Song's vicious and pointless killing spree in the Duck and Drake Tower in which he massacres an entire household, including servants and children. Jin Shengtan distracts the reader from the carnage by keeping separate running tallies of each time the words "dagger," "light," and "moon" appear. After the troubling description of how Wu Song needs to switch blades because his first has become too dull to sever a head neatly, Jin comments:

> The nineteenth use of the word "dagger" (*yaodao* 腰刀). For half a day, one can say that the dagger is extremely busy, whereas the sword (*pudao* 朴刀) has nothing to do. This change makes people call out. [The author] is truly a real genius (*caizi*). 十九寫腰刀。半日可謂忙殺腰刀，閑殺朴刀矣。得此一變，令人叫絕。眞正才子。 (*SHZ*, 30.574)

Jin then coolly begins to count the number of times "sword" is used. In the scenes in which Li Kui 李逵 discovers that his bravado has led to his mother's death (*SHZ*, 42.801–2) or in which he ruthlessly and needlessly murders a beloved six-year-old boy in order to force Zhu Gong 朱公 to join the outlaws (*SHZ*, 50.944–45),[127] Jin's commentary continues to direct readers' attention toward stylistic features so as to privilege the literary as a more important didactic function of literature than the ethical.[128]

An even more striking example of how a commentator claims canonical status for a thematically transgressive work is Zhang Zhupo's defense of *Jin Ping Mei*. Zhang's guide to reading the novel follows Jin Shengtan's com-

127. Jin's generally positive view and sympathetic treatment of Li Kui contrasts sharply with his contempt for Song Jiang 宋江. For example, Jin coolly makes an aesthetic comparison between the description of two tiger cubs gnawing on Li Kui's mother's leg and an earlier scene but then, rather than comment on Li Kui's culpability, launches an attack on Song Jiang's lack of filiality. Curiously in the second scene, Jin does not count the number of times the word "carry" (*bao* 抱; it also means "hug") is used in the descriptions of how Zhu Gong carried the boy everywhere. Perhaps he feared that asking readers to focus on the tenderness of the relation between Zhu Gong and the child might evoke outrage.

128. Jin argued that Sima Qian's interest lay in the craft of writing (*wen*) rather than content (*SHZ*, 28.539). As we shall see, the commentator to *Yesou puyan* similarly uses discussions of stylistic issues to distract the readers' attention away from the Confucian hero's breaches of propriety.

mentary to the *Shuihu zhuan* in concentrating on structural devices (*zhangfa* 章法) and directing the reader's attention toward aesthetic issues.[129] According to Zhang, a reader who becomes aware of the structural integrity of the 100-chapter novel will be able to see through the pornography to the work's true value.

> The *Jing Ping Mei* should not be read in a desultory fashion. If you read it that way you will only read the obscene passages. Only if you take several days and read it all the way through will you perceive the connecting nerves and arteries that act like a single thread upon which the author has strung together his succession of rising and falling actions.[130]

Zhang follows this comment by revealing that his method for protecting himself against the obscene passages is "to read the book as though it were written by Sima Qian," as a compositional model. Zhang builds on Jin Shengtan's reading of the *Shuihu zhuan* to argue that a work as carefully structured as *Jin Ping Mei* must have a serious moral intent. In one of his more audacious moments, in a claim that exemplifies his penchant for conflating aesthetic control with moral control, Zhang slyly likens the author to a bodhisattva because of his ability to escape all narrative problems.[131] After calling the author a technical genius, Zhang presents him as moral genius:

> The author of the *Jin Ping Mei* is certainly a genius, but his learning is that of a Bodhisattva, not that of a Confucian sage, for his message is that everything is empty. If he had taken the further steps to nonemptiness he would have written a different book.
>
> The *Jin Ping Mei* concludes with emptiness, but if we look carefully we will see that it is not complete emptiness. This is apparent from the fact that the author brings his work to a conclusion with the transfiguration of Xiaoge 孝哥 [filial son], which signifies the fact that filiality has the power to transform all evils.[132]

Having shown the structural and philosophical genius of the conclusion (which many modern readers dismiss as highly ironic), Zhang glosses a character's name with a highly tendentious pun as evidence for his argument that the novel is morally didactic.

129. Zhang Zhupo noted the influence Jin Shengtan had on him in a statement quoted by Zhang's brother (Rolston, *How to Read*, p. 198).

130. *JPM*, "Dufa," p. 42; trans. from Roy, "How to Read," p. 232.

131. *JPM*, "Dufa," p. 42; trans. from Roy, "How to Read," p. 232.

132. *JPM*, "Dufa," pp. 44–45; trans. from Roy, "How to Read," p. 235.

> The *Jin Ping Mei* is a book that is intended to correct people's faults, as can be seen from the fact that it concludes with the example of Han Aijie 韓愛姐. The pun in her name expresses the idea of "seeking *ai* 艾 [moxa] that is three years old in order to cure an illness that has lasted seven years." [That is to say, though there may be a cure for your illness, you won't be able to find it when you need it unless you have prepared it in advance.][133]

As we shall see in Chapter 4, a similar logic of extrapolating a moral vision from structural integrity is used by the Confucian triumvirate who were published together in what has recently been titled the "Three Commentators Edition" (*Sanjia pingben* 三家評本) of the *Honglou meng*; each of the three takes great pains to show the structural and chronological coherence of Cao Xueqin's ambiguous masterpiece in order to justify their rigidly moral interpretations.

Although it is clear that participating in the production and protection of elite culture (*wen*) could evoke a sense of moral purpose, a question remains about the sincerity of those who were defending the moral status of works of fiction that were clearly less than orthodox. As will be discussed in the following chapter, the literati of the late imperial period held a broad range of attitudes toward Confucian orthodoxy. Zhang Zhupo seems sincere in his belief that his reading of the pornographic *Jin Ping Mei* could lead to an enlightened release from sexual desires; in contrast, the prolific writer, editor, and publisher Feng Menglong was not above claiming a moral seriousness for certain of his projects as a way of boosting sales (see the next chapter). Li Yu's 李漁 (1611–80) attempts to contain his transgressive stories by concluding with moralizing editorial comments create such an ironic disjunction that the reader cannot be sure if he is making fun of orthodox values, trying to reinvigorate them by applying them to preposterous situations, or subjecting these serious ideological debates to the destabilizing irony that is his stylistic trademark. Whatever the intent or beliefs of these individual authors, commentators, and editors, the thematic tension created by the conflicting orthodox desire to create patterns of order and the heterodox content of the fiction is semiotically productive. It is only fair to assume that traditional readers, like their modern counterparts, enjoyed the interpretive freedom left them by these ambiguous and heteroglossic narratives. It is

133. *JPM*, "Dufa," p. 45; trans. and notes from Roy, "How to Read," p. 236 (the material in brackets is in Roy's translation). The quotation "searching for moxa" is taken from the *Mencius*, IVA.9.

clear from the dogmatic claims of most commentaries, however, that the commentators overlooked any reservations and cynicism they might have had about state-controlled orthodox ideology and, more pointedly, the orthodox purity of the texts they promoted, in order to claim an orthodox intent for *xiaoshuo* fiction in the face of charges that it was frivolous and even dangerous. In order to accomplish this, they developed an appreciation for literature in which aesthetics displaced ethics.

Formalism and Yinyang *Symbolism in* Xiaoshuo *Fiction*

The importance of formalism to fiction commentary might explain the continued and even expanded use of *yinyang* numerology and symbolism in *xiaoshuo* fiction through the early nineteenth century. The increasingly sophisticated application of *yinyang* symbolism in Qing fiction runs counter to the marked decline of interest in *yinyang* cosmological thinking in late imperial philosophical discourse due to the rise of evidential studies.[134] Although the Ming novel *Xiyou ji* is filled with suggestive references to *yinyang*, five elements, and alchemical imagery, it fell to the commentators to flesh out the full significance of the various allegorical strands. The sprinkling of explicit references to hexagrams in the novel[135] is supplemented by the commentaries by Wang Xiangxu 汪象旭 (fl. 1605–68), Chen Shibin 陳士斌 (preface dated 1696), Zhang Shushen 張書紳 (fl. eighteenth century), and Liu Yiming 劉一明 (1734–after 1820), which apply *Yi jing* hexagrams to interpret and explain the significance of specific scenes.[136] In the first half of the nineteenth century, Zhang Xinzhi 張新之 (fl. 1828–50) continued this somewhat arcane hermeneutic practice of *Yi jing* allegoresis in his extensive commentary to the 120-chapter version of the *Honglou meng* in which he identified certain of the fictional characters as representations of hexagrams.[137]

Although it is frequently tempting to dismiss the hermeneutical zeal of these commentators as forced overinterpretation, a trend in the compositional use of *Yi jing*–based *yinyang* iconography can be observed in the fiction

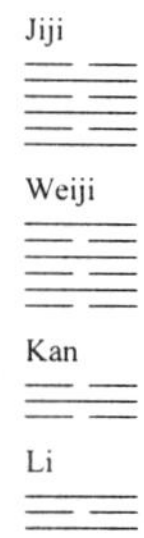

134. See Henderson, *Development and Decline*, pp. 149–60; and Elman, *From Philosophy to Philology*, pp. 13–36.

135. The hexagram terms Jiji 即濟 (fully completed) and Weiji 未濟 (not yet completed) appear in chapter 61, as do their constituent trigrams Kan 坎 and Li 離.

136. For a translation of Liu Yiming's "Dufa" to the *Xiyou ji*, see A. Yu, "How to Read."

137. For a translation of Zhang Xinzhi's "Dufa," see Plaks, "How to Read," pp. 324–40; the Chinese text can be found in the *SJPB*, "Dufa," pp. 2–7. For the connection between Zhang and earlier commentaries to the *Xiyou ji*, see Rolston, *How to Read*, p. 327*n*.

of the late Ming and Qing. Dong Yue's 董說 (1620–86) *Xiyou bu* 西遊補 (A supplement to the *Journey to the West*; written before 1650) contains some of the earliest examples of extended development of hexagram imagery to further narrative ends.[138] The sixteen-chapter novel is an interpolated dream narrative that would fall between Chapters 61 and 62 of *Xiyou ji*; the discontinuous dream adventures provide both Monkey and the readers with a sophisticated experiential version of the dangers of desire (*qing*) in its manifold aspects.[139] In Chapter 10 of *Xiyou bu*, Monkey enters the Tower of Sixty-four Hexagrams and literally walks into a visual pun based on the pure *yin* Kun hexagram. He steps through railings arranged like cracks of ice and is immediately enmeshed in a web of red threads from which he cannot escape no matter what transformation he assumes. An old man explains to the pilgrim that he is caught in the Palace of Entangling Vines (*Kun ge lei gong* 困葛藟宮). The image of the cracked ice railings is derived from the commentary on the first *yin* line of the Kun hexagram, "The frost one treads on reaches its ultimate stage as solid ice";[140] the verb *kun* "being constrained" or "bound" is an obvious homophone on the name of the hexagram. In the next chapter, Monkey enters the Palace of the Limitation Hexagram (*Jiegua gong* 節卦宮), which is also based on images suggested by the *Yi jing* commentary to the hexagram.[141] The Limitation Hexagram teaches of the necessity of self-control and the setting of limits; in this scene Monkey appropriately checks his own impulse to dash straight through the gate into the palace and instead comes up with a plan that will save him from expending all his energy.

The late Ming novel *Jingshi yinyang meng* 警世陰陽夢 (A dream of *yin* and *yang* to caution the world) makes creative use of *yinyang* imagery in its structural arrangement. The novel is divided into two parts, reflecting the *yin* and *yang* dreams of the title; most unusual is that the halves of the novel are treated as so distinct that the chapters of the two parts are numbered separately.[142] As I shall argue in later chapters, the explicit use of *Yi jing* imagery in the Qing novels *Honglou meng*, *Yesou puyan*, and *Jinghua yuan* went beyond earlier fictional texts in developing an aesthetics and semiotics based on the

138. The novel has been translated by Lin Shuen-fu and Schulz as *A Tower of Myriad Mirrors*.

139. For a discussion of the stages of desire depicted in the novel, see Andres, "Ch'an Symbolism."

140. Lynn, *Classic of Changes*, p. 145.

141. Dong Yue, *Xiyou bu*, 11.1a.

142. Described in Rolston, *Traditional Chinese Fiction*, p. 254n.

yin number six and the *yang* number nine. In *Yi jing* numerology, six and nine are the numerical values ascribed to the extreme manifestations of *yin* and *yang* when they are at the peak of their power; in interpreting hexagrams, *yin* and *yang* lines are numbered six and nine, respectively.[143] These numerological patterns inform the use of gender in these texts.

The sophisticated use of *yinyang* numerology in these Qing novels builds structural patterns important to the four great Ming novels. As has long been recognized, the *yang* formula of "nine-nines" is an important theme in *Xiyou ji*, demonstrated by the seemingly arbitrary introduction of yet another trial to bring the final total up to 81 precisely in Chapter 99 because "nine times nine" is the number needed to achieve immortality.[144] Although *yinyang* numerological structuring is not an important feature of the *Shuihu zhuan*, historically inaccurate dates in the Prologue create a symbolically suggestive set of numbers, which are exploited by Jin Shengtan. After the opening poem by the Song Neo-Confucian cosmologist Shao Yong 邵雍 (1011–77), Jin Shengtan comments that Shao was "a man of calculations" (*suanshu xiansheng* 算數先生), a diviner who based his prognostications on numerology. When the text misrepresents the Five Dynasties as "fifteen emperors who wrought chaos for fifty years," rather than the historically correct figure of twelve emperors who ruled for 53 years, Jin ignores the error and instead points out that the characters for fifteen and fifty (*shiwu* 十五, *wushi* 五十) are mirrors of each other and bring to mind the Yellow River Chart (*Hetu* 河圖), a cosmological chart based on the number five (*SHZ*, "Xiezi," p. 39). Shao Yong identified both the Yellow River Chart and the Lo River Writing (*Luoshu* 洛書), which is based on the number nine, as the main elements of the cosmological universe.[145]

Jin again treats numerological symbolism as more important than historical fact when the narrator retells how the Song emperor Renzong 仁宗 (r. 1022–63) changed his reign title nine times during his 42-year rule. The text describes how his peaceful and prosperous reign could be divided into three "peaks" (*deng* 登), each nine years long, for a total of 27 years. In actuality, the dates given for the second "peak" cover a period of twenty years, and the third "peak" spans only seven years. Although Jin had pointed to the his-

143. Wilhelm, *Change*, p. 41. Different phases of change are assigned different values, so that quiescent *yin* and *yang* are equated with eight and seven, respectively.

144. Plaks, *The Four Masterworks*, pp. 232–34.

145. Henderson, *Development and Decline*, p. 125.

torical unreliability of these figures in an interlinear comment just one sentence earlier, he mechanically repeats the line about the three "peaks" totaling 27 years and says that the meaning of these words comes from the cosmological thinkers Shao Yong and his intellectual predecessor Chen Tuan 陳摶 (906–89). Several lines later, after the date for the onset of the plague is listed as "the third day of the third month of the third year of the Jiayou reign period [1058]," a year for which there is no historical record of an epidemic, Jin Shengtan comments: "[These numbers] total nine; *yang* reaches its extreme at nine; the number has reached its full potential (*shu zhi qiong ye* 數之窮也). In the *Yi jing*, when [things] have reached their full potential, there is change; thus the processes of change have produced this *Shuihu zhuan*" (p. 41).

Jin's oblique suggestion that *yang* has exhausted itself and has thereby set in motion a period of decline would explain the earlier cryptic remark after the introduction of the hermit Chen Tuan that the two men of calculations, Chen Tuan and Shao Yong, "had already calculated that there would be 36 members [of the Shuihu band]; doubled this becomes the 72 seats" (p. 40). Jin's insertion of a direct reference to the *yin* number 36 before any of the other numbers are introduced prepares the readers to interpret the suggestive but vague numerology of the fictional text as explicit and intentional references to *Yi jing* numerological schema. Although there is no way of determining the original intent behind the insertion of the historically inaccurate dates, Jin Shengtan's glosses on these numbers articulate meanings that had only been vaguely suggested by the text. It is likely that these glosses were in part responsible for directing writers of fiction toward an explicit manipulation of numerology as part of the emerging poetics of the genre.[146]

Andrew Plaks's discussions of the poetics of the traditional novel have demonstrated that one of the benefits of the highly regular 100-chapter canonical length of the novel was that it allowed fiction writers and editors to develop complex structural patterns based on chapter numbers.[147] Mirroring chapters, those paired numbers that are inverse but symmetrical in position (for example, in a 100-chapter work, Chapter 10 mirrors Chapter 90, Chapter 25 mirrors Chapter 75), develop static structural patterns; parallel chapters, those that fall in the same position in a sequence (for example, Chapters

146. Deborah Porter's ("Setting the Tone," p. 64) observation that the actual number of years in the three "peaks" of Renzong's reign totals 36 rather than 27 would only heighten the significance of Jin Shengtan's comment that *yang* had exhausted itself.

147. Plaks, *The Four Masterworks*.

9, 19, and 29) create a rhythmic sequence of narrative progression. One of the major foci throughout my study of the aesthetics of *xiaoshuo* fiction is the evolving use of explicit *yinyang* iconography based on *yinyang* numerology as a distinct feature of orthodox rhetoric. The earliest examples of this that I have been able to find occur in the use of nines in Chapter 99 of *Xiyou ji*, discussed above, and of sixes in Chapter 33 of *Jin Ping Mei*. In his prefatory and interlinear commentary to the chapter, Zhang Zhupo three times stresses the connection between the number six and the *yin* principle (his mathematical reference here seems to have been that the two "threes" in the number 33 add up to six; *JPM*, 33.492–3, and 503). The introduction of the sexually unsavory character Wang Liu'er 王六兒, Wang Number Six, in this chapter suggests that use of *yin* thematic material was by design. As we shall see, the appearance of characters named Liu, a pun on "six," in appropriate *yin* chapters is a motif that Cao Xueqin developed in *Honglou meng*.

Although the discussions of *yinyang* symbolism and numerology in the commentaries to the *Shuihu zhuan*, *Jin Ping Mei*, and *Xiyou ji* make explicit suggestive patterns that were already being woven into fiction, they had a powerful impact on the development of the poetics of Qing fiction. Numerological puns based on the *yin* number six are an important structural principle in *Honglou meng* and the early nineteenth-century *Jinghua yuan*, and to a lesser extent, the "nine" chapters in both works provide a site for an exploration of *yang* themes. Chapter 66 of the late eighteenth-century *Yesou puyan* contains an intricately developed exploration of *yin* themes based on an *Yi jing* hexagram; the 90s chapters of the same novel contain a much rarer example of detailed *yang* iconography. Although these structural patterns are significant in that they demonstrate yet another layer of authorial control and design, they are of even more interest for the way they complicate our readings of gender in novels that have been singled out for their positive depictions of women.

As I argue in the case of *Honglou meng* in particular, Cao Xueqin's sympathy for women and girls, although undoubtedly genuine, is not as straightforward as is usually presented. For example, the contrast between the idealized depictions of women and the depictions of transgressive shrews in key *yin* chapters throws into relief the ways in which Cao manipulated gender for aesthetic and thematic purposes. By showing that the use of gender in *Honglou meng*, widely acknowledged as the most "realistic" of traditional novels and frequently cited as a source for historical studies of women and gender in eighteenth-century China, goes beyond mimetic description, I hope to deepen current understandings of the meanings ascribed to gender in late imperial Chinese fiction.[148] The close readings of specific novels in the following chapters link the structural and ideological uses of gender to the competing aesthetic and moral truths promoted by orthodox rhetoric and the cult of sentiment (*qing*).

Each of those aspects of narrative that I have identified in this chapter as representative of orthodox rhetoric—the emphasis on Confucian ritual as the foundation of the social order, the attention paid to structural patterning in *xiaoshuo* novels, and the use of *Yi jing* numerology and *yinyang* iconography—is expressed through gendered terms. As we shall see in the next chapter, which considers changing late Ming attitudes toward the Cheng-Zhu bias against desire, a new and competing matrix of gendered meanings emerged in the writings of the counterhegemonic movement known as the cult of *qing*. In contrast to orthodox discourse, which promotes as its highest value the re-establishment of a stable Confucian order, the cult of *qing* values authenticity of personal expression. Within orthodox discourse, the performance of proper gender roles is treated as foundational to social stability. In contrast, those texts that promote the "authentic" take a more playful approach to gender and seem to take a real delight in gender fluidity. Although the two discursive modes often appear simultaneously within the same text and are even interwoven, the ideological motivations for the two are contradictory. Orthodoxy is based on the ritually defined self and holds social stability to be an inherently more worthy goal than the pursuit of individual desires; authenticity celebrates the individual's expression of desires and feelings as the true foundation of identity.

148. Although space does not permit me to do justice to the thorny question of realism in traditional Chinese fiction, it is important to note that although verisimilitude was valued, realism was not a generic requirement, as is demonstrated by the freedom with which writers interwove fantastic and allegoric details into otherwise realistic narratives. Although the concept of realism still stands as one of the defining features of the classical European novel, it is now generally accepted as referring to a specific aesthetic code. In the Chinese tradition, one of the highest praises given to lively prose is that it is like a painting, which suggests the use of vivid rather than realistic detail. James J. Y. Liu discusses this absence of a theory of mimesis in *Chinese Theories of Literature*, pp. 49–73; see also Anderson, *The Limits of Realism*, pp. 1–26. The realistic details in *Honglou meng*, long recognized as among the most directly autobiographical works of Qing literature, are built upon a rich foundation of narrative conventions.

CHAPTER TWO

The Late Ming Reinterpretation of Human Nature and the Gendering of Desire

The late Ming saw the emergence of related philosophic and aesthetic movements that challenged many of the premises of orthodox discourse. The post–Wang Yangming 王陽明 (1472–1529) period in Ming China has been identified as a time of increased interest in the subjective self, an internally constructed understanding of identity that differed from the classical Confucian model based on externally observable patterns of behavior.[1] Even as the Ming literati and aspiring elite continued to follow the dicta of the *Great Learning* in training their wills and practices to conform to the ideal objective models of behavior spelled out in orthodox texts on ritual, followers of Wang Yangming's school of the mind (*xinxue* 心學) began to place increasing value on the unique potentials of the autonomous self. The central point of contention was the nature of the relationship between human nature (*xing* 性) and the emotions and desires. The polysemous word *qing* (情) became a central discursive site for these late Ming reformulations of self-identity. Within mainstream Cheng-Zhu Neo-Confucianism, although *qing* (emotions) were considered a natural expression of the mind, they were closely associated with sexual desire (*yu* 欲) and regarded as dangerously subjective and selfish and thus in need of monitoring and regulation. A counter-group of thinkers posited the emotions and even desires as an integral and positive aspect of human nature. An influential minority of thinkers and writers went so far as to champion the emotions and argue that they were foundational to the Confucian moral obligations of filiality and loyalty.

1. P. Y. Wu, *The Confucian's Progress*, pp. 116, 143, 163; Plaks, *Four Masterworks*, pp. 19–20; de Bary, "Introduction," in *Unfolding*, p. 18; and idem, "Introduction" and "Individualism and Humanitarianism," in *Self and Society*, pp. 12–14, 145–48 and *passim*.

Although this ontological dispute created a sharp schism among the various Neo-Confucian schools during the late Ming, the more holistic view of the emotions and desires had become the mainstream one by the eighteenth century. As we shall see, the most radical voices in the debate, although enjoying only a short-lived prominence in the world of philosophy, had a profound impact on the development of fiction aesthetics.

It is my contention that many of the changes in the deployment of gender in the fiction of this period can be traced to an aesthetic movement spawned by a handful of these radical intellectual figures. It is from within the context of this redefinition of the place of the emotions and desires in human nature that this chapter tries to make sense of the witty, playful, and often passionate and transgressive values of this counter-orthodox discourse I call the "aesthetics of authenticity." One of the most remarkable trends in late Ming fiction was the changing typology of gender as the traditional novel shifted away from its roots in the stern morality of orthodox discourse toward an exploration of more subjective values. In contrast to the demonization of desire in those orthodox narratives, which illustrate the necessity of Neo-Confucian self-cultivation, romances of the authentic tend to treat the expression of desire as a catalyst for personal, cultural, and even political redemption. For reasons discussed below, the feminine and a nexus of analogically associated motifs became emblematic of this representation of the "authentic." Although the changing depictions of women in fiction and drama may have influenced a change in the status of elite women, I argue that the unprecedented idealization of the feminine during the late Ming and Qing, rather than being directly reflective of social practices, was discursively derived from the late Ming philosophical and ideological debates about the nature of desire.

THE PARADOXICAL MEANINGS OF *QING*

In order to appreciate the idiosyncrasies of the Song Neo-Confucian interpretations of the word *qing*, we must first examine the full range of its classical usage; as is true of so many terms used in Chinese philosophical writings, the web of associative meanings implied by *qing* covers a broad and often contradictory spectrum, sometimes even within the usage of one person. As a means of categorizing the pre-Mencian uses of the word *qing*, A. C. Graham paired it against a number of its antonyms in order to establish a range of stable meanings. He concluded that *qing* was used to refer to facts, in contrast to reputation (*ming* 明, *wen* 聞, or *sheng* 聲), and that as a modifier it meant genuine or genuinely in contrast to false (*wei* 偽).[2] Wang Shumin has argued that in many early texts *qing* and *jing* 精, essence, were used interchangeably.[3] By the first century C.E., the "Great Preface" to the *Book of Songs* (*Mao Shi daxu* 毛詩大序) institutionalized the Confucian hermeneutic practice of reading an individual's (or a people's) emotive expressions as a microcosmic reflection of the moral-political ethos of the state: "The music of a well-governed land is peaceful and happy, its government being harmonious; the music of a disorderly land is plaintive and angry, its government being perverse; the music of a vanquished nation is sad and nostalgic, its people being distressed."[4] Emotions, particularly as expressed through lyric and music, reflect a moral essence. During the spread of Confucianism during the Han dynasty, the usage of the word *qing* changed radically. The *Shuowen jiezi* 說文解字, one of China's earliest dictionaries (compiled by Xu Shen 許慎, ca. 58–147 C.E.), adds to these earlier definitions that *qing* is "the desires contained within a person's *yin* ether" 人之陰氣有所欲.[5] This definition of the word *qing* reflects the profound influence of the great Confucian cosmologist Dong Zhongshu. In his commentary to the Confucian classic the *Spring and Autumn Annals*, Dong analogically classifies *qing* as a manifestation of embodied *yin*:[6] "The human body has within it human nature (*xing*) and the emotions (*qing*), just as Heaven has *yin* and *yang*. To speak of a person's basic stuff (*zhi* 質) and exclude emotions from this is equivalent to speaking of Heaven's *yang* while excluding its *yin*." 身之有性情也，若天之有陰陽也。言人之質而無其情，猶言天之陽而無其陰也.[7] Dong's writings anticipate the dualism of Cheng-Zhu Neo-Confucian thought in dividing human nature into the two components of selfless benevolence (*ren* 仁) associated with *yang* and covetous desire (*tan*

2. Graham, "The Background," pp. 259–60.

3. Wang Shumin, *Zhuangzi jiaoquan*, pp. 261–62.

4. For a complete translation of this passage, see J. Liu, *Chinese Theories*, p. 119.

5. Duan Yucai, *Shuowen jiezi zhu*, 10B.7. The Qing dynasty *Peiwen yunfu* dictionary includes this as its basic definition, 23B.1151.

6. Tzuey-yueh Tain ("Tung Chung-shu's System of Thought," p. 226) tentatively identifies this as one of the first such classifications, if not the first.

7. *CQFL*, 10.1/ 46/11. Translation based on *A History*, 2: 33. The *Shuowen jiezi* also contrasts a *yin qing* to a *yang* human nature.

貪) associated with *yin*.[8] This conceptualization of *qing* informed orthodox Song Neo-Confucian usage of the term: first, *qing* became identified as subjective and selfish desires in contrast to a selfless love of humanity; and second, *qing* was thought to emanate from the *yin* aspect of the self.[9]

Qing is extremely difficult to translate because of the way it was historically used to anchor a wide range of binomes in philosophical discussions. Even in the classical period, to choose one category of meaning was to silence other associations. By the late imperial era, the term had acquired even more connotations. Based on a survey of texts from the *Yi jing* to Yuan Mei's 袁枚 (1716–98) writings, Siu-kit Wong compiled thirteen definitions of *qing*; I have reduced these to four main discursive groupings.[10]

8. *CQFL*, 10.1/ 45/29. This statement is echoed in other Han writings such as the *Baihu tongyi* 白虎通義 (Comprehensive discussions in the White Tiger Hall), traditionally ascribed to Ban Gu.

9. Not everyone agreed with the categorization of *xing* as *yang* and *qing* as *yin*. For example, Wang Chong 王充 (27–ca. 100) cites Liu Xiang 劉向 (79–8 B.C.E.) approvingly to argue that since *qing* are active expressions of human nature, they should be classified as *yang*; see Yang Jialuo *Lunheng jijie*, "Benxing pian," pp. 65–66.

10. Siu-kit Wong, "*Ch'ing* in Chinese Literary Criticism," pp. 328–33. His thirteen definitions are: (1) synonymous with ambition (*zhi* 志; found in *The Great Preface*, *The Mean*, Liu Xie's *Wenxin diaolong*, and Ming critical writings); (2) universal human emotions distinct from rational thought (found in Six Dynasties critics, Tang anthologists, and Ming critics who opposed it to principle, *Li*); (3) undesirable and selfish emotions such as passion (found in *The Great Preface*, Tang writings, and Shao Yong, who opposed it to human nature); (4) emotion, chiefly erotic (found in Six Dynasties writers and Qing dynasty critics of *ci* poetry); (5) instinctive, uneducated, and universal emotions (found in Bo Juyi, Wang Fuzhi, Shen Deqian, and Yuan Mei); (6) morally refined emotions (found in *The Great Preface*, *Book of Changes*, Qian Qianyi, Wang Fuzhi, Ye Xie, and Shen Deqian); (7) reality, truth, and inner spirit, in contrast to external artificiality (found in *The Great Preface*, *Wenxin diaolong*, Bo Juyi, Wang Fuzhi, and Ye Xie); (8) imaginative truth, in contrast to mere fact (found in Lu Shiyong, Ye Xie and Yuan Mei); (9) the substance of poetry not the form (found in *The Great Preface*, *Book of Changes*, *Mencius*, Six Dynasties writers, and Xie Zhen); (10) the identity of poetry, often interchangeable with disposition, *xingqing* 性情, or *qingxing* (Six Dynasties writers, *Wenxin diaolong*, Tang writers, and Yuan Mei); (11) as elements of poetry other than the visual *jing* 景 (found in *The Mean*, Xie Zhen, Wang Fuzhi, Yuan Mei, and Qing dynasty *ci* criticism); (12) artistic sensibility, often *qingxing* (found in Yuan Yu, Wang Yuyang, and Yuan Mei); and (13) a cognate meaning of intellectual interest or even passion, as in *qingqu* 情趣 (found in Yuan Hongdao and the writers of the Gong'an school as well as Yuan Mei). As can be seen from the multiple usages, individual texts and writers exploited the polysemous nature of the word.

Physiological: the body of emotions with which the individual responds to his or her environment, as in the modern *ganqing*, 感情, "emotion," which is often reduced to the single emotion of romantic love.

Spiritual: the true and real inner spirit, always positive, contrasted to external artificiality.

Phenomenological: a morally neutral usage to describe discrete and unique phenomena in contrast to the universal and unchanging Truths (*Li* 理), as in the vernacular *shiqing* 事情, "affairs," "matters," or *qingkuang* 情況, "conditions."

Aesthetic: always positive, a true aesthetic sensibility, disposition, or intellectual interest, as in the vernacular *qingqu* 情趣, "interest," "appeal."

Qing thus paradoxically refers both to objective reality and to subjective reactions to external stimuli, as well as a transcendent merging of the two, as in the lyric dissolution of the boundary between self and other (*wuwo heyi* 物我合一).[11] These different connotations of *qing* depending on context make it particularly ambiguous; this is especially true in discussions of the emotions, in which *qing* span a continuum from subjective and selfish expressions of sexual desire to the selfless love and obligation one feels for a family member. *Qing* are simultaneously the basis for ideal social interactions and the selfish urges that threaten to destroy the social order. As we shall see, late Ming and Qing writers increasingly treated its most popular and suspect meaning, romantic love, as metonymically representative of otherwise unrelated meanings. Because of the frequent ambiguity in its usage, I leave *qing* untranslated except where there is a precise English equivalent.

SUBJECTIVE *QING* VERSUS THE OBJECTIVE IDEAL IN ORTHODOX NEO-CONFUCIANISM

Arguably, the most radical innovation that the Song Neo-Confucian thinkers introduced into mainstream Confucian thought was the division of human nature into its ideal, heavenly endowed form (*tian zhi xing* 天之性) and its material form (*qizhi zhi xing* 氣質之性).[12] Intellectually, this concept of a dual nature was a powerful one, for it drew on the traditional Mencian notion that humans are innately good in order to refute the then-dominant Buddhist be-

11. See W. Y. Li, *Enchantment*, p. 207.

12. For a discussion of how Song Neo-Confucians traced this dualism back to the human-mind, moral-mind (*renxin Daoxin* 人心道心) passage in the "Da Yu mo" 大禹謨 section of the *Shu jing* 書經 (Book of history), later shown to be an Old Text forgery, to sanction their interpretation, see Elman, "Philosophy (*I-li*) Versus Philology," pp. 176–82.

lief that human nature is bad, while still providing an explanation for the presence of evil within human behavior. The Neo-Confucians viewed the material nature as problematic because of the possibility that the matter (*qi*) from which it is formed might be turbid or corrupt (*zhuo* 濁) in contrast to the heavenly endowed nature, which is a morally perfect embodiment of principle. The process of self-cultivation laid out in Neo-Confucian teachings was designed to minimize the negative effects of the material nature on the realization of the heavenly nature. Despite the fact that Zhu Xi, the dominant figure in the synthesis of Neo-Confucian doctrine, traced a direct line of descent from Mencius to himself in his construction of an orthodox Confucian lineage (*Daotong* 道統), Buddhism had a profound influence on Neo-Confucian doctrine and practice.[13] Buddhism preached that attachment to the illusory, phenomenal world impeded enlightenment; Buddhist self-cultivation was thus a process of freeing the self from all desires and emotional attachments. Although the Neo-Confucians did not go so far as to deny the reality of the phenomenal world, they followed Buddhism in advocating detachment from it in order to gain a clearer perception of ideal principle.

Neo-Confucian attitudes toward the emotions were somewhat ambivalent. In some instances, emotions were described in neutral terms as a function of the self and an integral part of the human psyche. In the words of Cheng Hao 程顥 (1032–85), "The sage expresses joy at things which properly call for joy, and anger at things which properly call for anger. Therefore the joy and anger of the sage are not connected with his mind, but with things. Why, then, should he not respond to things?"[14] The emotions were conceptualized as having two aspects; when quiescent and in a state of undifferentiated equilibrium, *qing* refers to the capacity for an emotional response as opposed to the actual expression of those emotions. This distinction between the not yet aroused (*weifa* 未發) and already aroused (*yifa* 已發) emotions is drawn from the *Doctrine of the Mean* (*Zhong yong* 中庸), a text Zhu Xi excerpted from the *Book of Rites* and established as one of the foundational Four Books.

13. See Wing-tsit Chan, *Chu Hsi*, pp. 30, 61, 68–69, 142–3; idem, "How Buddhistic Is Wang Yang-ming?"; and idem, "Neo-Confucianism: New Ideas in Old Terminology." See also C. Y. Cheng, "Reason, Substance, and Human Desires," esp. pp. 469–73. In addition to borrowing certain Buddhist concepts such as enlightenment and quiet-sitting, the Neo-Confucians also adopted Buddhist pedagogical techniques such as the moral confession as well as the concept of the academy with its explicit set of rules.

14. Trans. from *A History*, 2: 525.

However, the emotions were understood to be situated in the material nature, and in their aroused state they became suspect as potentially subjective and biased. Shao Yong 邵雍 was the most extreme of the Song Neo-Confucians in setting *qing* and human nature in opposition to each other. For him, although the capacity for feeling was good, the aroused emotions themselves needed to be contained and regulated: "To view things from the point of view of things is human nature (*xing*); to view things from the point of view of the viewer is subjectivity (*qing*). Human nature is clear (*ming* 明) and open (*gong* 公); *qing* is dark (*an* 暗) and secret (*tou* 偷)."[15]

Neither the Cheng brothers, Cheng Hao and Cheng Yi 程頤, nor Zhu Xi discussed *qing* in much detail, since they were more concerned with the question of desire (*yu*). Cheng Yi, who was more radical than Zhu Xi in his dualism, equated the material nature with desire.[16] Zhu Xi's definition of the term *qing* was straightforward and reveals that he did not consider emotions to be innately good or bad: in two analogies, he describes human nature as what is received (*suo shou* 所受), whereas feelings are the functional aspect of human nature (情是性之用).[17] However, as shown in the Neo-Confucian compendium *Reflections on Things at Hand*, Zhu Xi was troubled by the difference between potential and aroused emotions.

> Human nature is the same as principle. Traced to its source, none of the principles in the world is not good. Before they are aroused, have pleasure, anger, sorrow and joy ever been found not to be good? As they are aroused and attain due measure and degree, they are good, no matter in what connection. When they are aroused and do not attain due degree, then they are not good.[18]

The true source of anxiety in Neo-Confucian writings is desire, which is always treated as selfish and improper and in conflict with the fully rational and impartial heavenly endowed nature. Indeed, the scholar Chung-ying Cheng has even suggested that the primacy of this opposition between universally good principle and selfish desire was a motivating factor in the Neo-Confucian formulation of the duality of principle and matter.[19] Indeed, the two form a consistent rhetorical pair. "Those who understand the higher

15. Trans. from S. K. Wong, "*Ch'ing* in Chinese Literary Criticism," p. 124.

16. Elman, "Philosophy Versus Philology," p. 178.

17. See Zhu Xi, *Zhuzi yulei*, vol. 1, j. 5, p. 82.

18. *JSL*, 1.33a–b; trans. from *Reflections*, p. 28. Also see *JSL*, 4.3a, 8a, 13a, 14a–b, and 20a; *Reflections*, pp. 125, 129, 138, 139, and 145.

19. C. Y. Cheng, "Reason, Substance, and Human Desires," p. 485.

things return to the principle of Nature, while those who understand the lower things follow human desires."[20] Because pleasure can so easily lead to desire and excess, it, too, is suspect. "Generally speaking, if one acts because of pleasure, how can he avoid being incorrect?"[21] Physiologically, emotions are problematic because of the unreliability of the unenlightened person's material nature in responding to each stimulus. Any turbid matter in a person's material nature can interfere with his or her ability to react impartially and may incite dangerous desires. "In terms of *qing*, every man is, in fact, blinded in one way or another. Hence he is unable to accord with the Dao. Generally speaking, the trouble with man is that he is selfish and mentally calculating. Being selfish, he cannot take action as a [spontaneous] response, and being mentally calculating, he cannot take intuition as his natural guide."[22] Because of its dual composition, human nature is not a reliable and objective standard of judgment; the Neo-Confucian rationalists argued that it was thus essential to establish a normative and objective standard of behavior. Ritual orthopraxy provided this standard.

Given the perception that mainstream Neo-Confucianism was repressive and somewhat anti-individualist, it is necessary to point out that, contrary to the accusations of late Ming critics, neither Zhu Xi nor the Cheng brothers advocated denying the expression of *qing*. They recognized that emotional expression is a necessary aspect of human life; however, they did subordinate emotional expression, and thus self-expression, to ritualized behavior. Their intent was not to repress or annihilate *qing* but to train the emotional responses to conform to a universal ideal. In fact, the Song Neo-Confucian masters seem to have been more tolerant of individual differences and needs than their pronouncements suggest; for example, in one selection from the *Reflections*, Cheng Hao warns against taking seriousness too far.[23] But as the teachings of the masters were transcribed and institutionalized, their oral comments became dogma in a way they likely never intended. The statement by Cheng Yi cited above that it is better to starve to death than compromise one's integrity was used to justify the practice of widow suicides; Zhu Xi, however, arranged for the remarriage of his niece.

20. *JSL*, 2.37b; trans. from *Reflections*, p. 75.

21. *JSL*, 12.5b; trans. from *Reflections*, p. 272.

22. Trans. from *A History*, 2: 524, Cheng Hao, *Mingdao wenji*, 3.1b.

23. *JSL*, 4.7a–b; *Reflections*, p. 128.

In order to understand the motivations behind the vehement reactions against Song idealism, we must consider orthodox Neo-Confucianism through the eyes of its late Ming and Qing critics. Although these later philosophers attacked the Cheng-Zhu school, it is clear that they were reacting against the contemporary practice of Neo-Confucianism. As Neo-Confucian ideology became codified, institutionalized, and increasingly removed from the intellectual and political currents that had originally fertilized it, the appeal of its strict introspective discipline inevitably faded. Sixteenth- and seventeenth-century writers often reviled Cheng Yi and the other Neo-Confucians for their inflexible stance in placing ritual above the natural expression of emotions. One well-known anecdote told how Cheng Yi objected to a friend's leaving a banquet after hearing of Sima Guang's death by citing the passage in the *Analects* that describes how Confucius did not make merry on the same day he had cried. The friend pointed out that Confucius had said nothing about crying after making merry.[24] Yuan Mei scoffed at strict followers of Neo-Confucianism whose gaze was so inverted that they were completely cut off from reality, when he wrote of a certain Lü Xi 吕希, who was so adept at quiet-sitting that when one of his palanquin bearers slipped into a river and drowned, he sat "tranquilly and did not ask" (*anran bu wen* 安然不問).[25] As we shall see, even serious Confucian thinkers who were originally devout followers of Cheng-Zhu Neo-Confucianism turned against its excesses. It was within this context of frustration with institutionalized Neo-Confucian practice and thought that some late Ming thinkers tried to revitalize the Confucian way. At the core of this project was a rethinking of the question of human nature that led to a radical re-evaluation of the function and value of *qing*.

THE LATE MING REFORMULATION OF HUMAN NATURE

The following discussion of late Ming intellectual thought is framed in terms of the trends that influenced Li Zhi 李贄 (1527–1602), a figure whose writings and reputation had a tremendous impact on late Ming fiction. Li Zhi was one of the most radical proponents of the relativist values associated with the Taizhou 泰州 school; although his positions were frequently too extreme to

24. Yao Mingda, *Cheng Yiquan nianpu*, pp. 163–64.
25. Yuan Mei, *Xiaocang shan fang chidu*, 4.216.

make him truly representative of late Ming thought, his views were not anomalous and, in fact, anticipated many representative Qing developments. Western historians of the Chinese novel have already discussed how *xiaoshuo* fiction both reflects the voices of late Ming dissent and represents a continuation of traditional historiographical hermeneutics. In order to maintain my focus on those trends in intellectual history that had the greatest impact on the changing constructions of gender in literature, I mention the elite social context only briefly and refer readers to those works.[26]

The late sixteenth and seventeenth centuries witnessed mounting literati cynicism toward the state institutionalization of Neo-Confucianism, a cynicism that achieved its sharpest expression in Li Zhi's writings. As discussed earlier, the most important manifestation of state control was the examination system (the most respected route to status and official position) and the empire-wide system of schools and academies that supported it. The requirements of the examinations necessitated that students and candidates memorize the Neo-Confucian canon and master the form of the highly structured eight-legged essay. Many literati were critical of the substitution of a curriculum based on rote memorization for morally transformative study.[27]

By the reign of the Wanli emperor (1573–1620), the liabilities of the institutional reformation of the civil bureaucracy by the founder of the Ming dynasty were fully apparent. Those close to the center of power were frustrated by the imperial paralysis and widespread bureaucratic corruption and were growing increasingly alarmed that the current system was not producing effective leadership. The weakness of the military was particularly troubling since China's borders were under constant threat of invasion. These well-justified concerns fueled a movement away from the introspective quietism of Neo-Confucian self-cultivation toward an activist interest in solid learning: statecraft, technology, and classical studies.[28] The widespread intellectual frustration can also be seen in the speed with which three-school syncretism (*sanjiao heyi* 三教合一) swept through the intellectual world during the sixteenth century and dislodged the hegemonic control Song Neo-Confucianism had held over textual interpretations and methods of

26. See Plaks, *Four Masterworks*, pp. 3–52; and Hegel, *The Novel*, pp. 1–32.

27. Wang Gen 王艮 (1483–1541) attempted to reinsert a moral aspect to examination preparation by suggesting that the examinations test knowledge of ethics as well as personal conduct (see *DMB*, p. 1384).

28. See Handlin, *Action in Late Ming Thought*.

self-cultivation. This syncretic approach was based on two premises that differed radically from those of orthodox Neo-Confucianism: that the end result of self-cultivation was more important than the means; and that the path to enlightenment might vary for each individual.[29] In this spirit, some literati began to turn to Buddhism and Daoism for answers to their spiritual questions and subsequently imported these new insights into their metaphysical and ethical discussions.[30] Both trends, the Confucian turn toward utilitarian statecraft and classical learning and syncretism, posed challenges to the quietist and idealist tendencies of institutionalized Neo-Confucianism and opened new opportunities and interest in autonomous action and individualized spiritual journeys.[31]

No person exemplified these trends better than Wang Yangming; his call for the unity of knowledge and action (*zhi xing heyi* 知行合一) sums up his contributions as governor, military leader, and philosopher.[32] Despite his popularity as statesman and general, Wang's uncertain status as a philosopher is shown by the fact that he was not included in the genealogy of Confucian sages until 1584, some fifty years after his death.[33] Wang Yangming's School of the Mind raised profound challenges to central Cheng-Zhu doctrines. Wang had voiced his concern about the excessive quietist and inward focus of orthodox self-cultivation after his famous failure to achieve enlight-

29. For a brief discussion of the development of syncretist thought, see Y. S. Yü, "The Intellectual World of Chiao Hung Revisited," pp. 32–39.

30. For a discussion of the importance of syncretist thought to Wang Yangming's intellectual development, see Tu Wei-ming, *Neo-Confucian Thought*; see also Ch'ien, *Chiao Hung*; and *Self and Society*.

31. See P. Y. Wu, *The Confucian's Progress*, p. 142 and *passim*. The late Ming is often associated with a more liberal turn toward individualism. "Individualism," however, is a problematic term to apply to traditional China because it implies a bourgeois and capitalist restructuring of feudal society. Although the late Ming redefinition of self did share some of the same impulses as European individualism, such as strengthening individual autonomy from family control and giving more credence to individual judgment rather than tradition, the two cannot be equated. The impetus behind the late Ming revision of Cheng-Zhu Neo-Confucianism was a spiritual revitalizing of the tradition in face of what was seen as its excessive rigidity rather than a rejection of tradition; even the most extreme of the "individualists," men such as Wang Gen, He Xinyin, and Li Zhi, did not reject the clan-based structuring of Chinese society. For a discussion of the problems of applying the term "individualism" to premodern China, see de Bary, "Individualism and Humanitarianism," pp. 144–48.

32. For biographies, see *DMB*, pp. 1408–16; and Tu Wei-ming, *Neo-Confucian Thought*.

33. Chu, "The Debate," p. 47.

enment after meditating by a bamboo grove for seven days.[34] After a later attempt at rigorous self-cultivation, Wang developed his concept of an innate and individually centered moral understanding (*liangzhi* 良知). According to Zhu Xi, although universal principle is embodied in each person's nature, it is an external standard that must be apprehended through investigation and study. Wang Yangming inverted Zhu Xi's dictate of extending knowledge (*gewu* 格物), a turning outward to discover objective truths, into an internalized and subjective search for moral knowledge (*zhi liangzhi* 致良知). In so doing, Wang refashioned self-cultivation into a process of turning inward to recover an innate and morally perfect knowledge rather than a discipline designed to make the self conform to an externally defined ideal.[35] In Wang Yangming's philosophy, innate moral knowledge held a centrality parallel to transcendent and objective principle in Zhu Xi's thinking.

Although Wang Yangming was responsible for introducing an individually based standard for moral knowledge into mainstream Neo-Confucianism, the real intellectual roots for the cult of *qing* should be traced to Wang Ji 王畿 (1498–1583), a disciple of Wang Yangming who rejected outright the structural duality of human nature.[36] Wang Ji was a disciple of Wang Yangming and a co-leader of the Taizhou School along with its founder Wang Gen 王艮 (1483–1541), who had established an academy at Taizhou immediately after Wang Yangming's death. Wang Ji and Qian Dehong 錢德洪 (1496–1574), another of Wang Yangming's disciples, had a disagreement over their master's teaching: Qian followed the orthodox interpretation in arguing that although the mind is good, it quickly becomes dominated by habit and loses its original clarity. From this perspective, the only way to maintain this original state of goodness is through strenuous moral cultivation (*gongfu* 工夫). Wang Ji countered that certain gifted minds could achieve sudden and spontaneous enlightenment without strenuous effort.[37] Although Qian Dehong's interpretation was likely closer

34. Tu Wei-ming, *Neo-Confucian Thought*, pp. 49–50.

35. See ibid., 165–67; and *Source Book*, pp. 655–56.

36. Wang Yangming's contemporary Luo Qinshun 羅欽順 (1465–1547) had discussed monism long before Wang Ji, but the idea did not become influential until it was taken up by the Taizhou School; see Bloom, *Knowledge Painfully Acquired*, pp. 34–36.

37. In a famous debate with Qian Dehong, Wang Ji seems to have misinterpreted Wang Yangming's "Four-Sentence Teaching" to argue that evil is external to human nature (see *MRXA*, 12.101–2; trans. in *Records*, pp. 114–17). The debate is discussed in C. Y. Cheng, "The Constancy and Meaning."

to Wang Yangming's meaning, Wang Ji's subjective standard for moral knowledge became the point of departure for the nonconformist figures associated with the Taizhou school, many of whom separated moral knowledge from textual learning.[38] Some now saw instinctive responses to stimuli, not as being flawed due to their subjective bias, but as a basis for morality.[39]

Others such as Li Zhi began to argue that the emotions are as integral to human nature as is principle. This shift toward a subjective and nontextual standard for moral knowledge had broad implications for late Ming philosophical understandings of the self and transmission of values. Descriptions of the potter Han Zhen 韓眞 (1516–85) traveling and holding huge gatherings at which he preached to over a thousand people testify to the appeal of these charismatic and unconventional teachers.[40] Yan Jun 顏鈞, a passionate but illiterate teacher who traveled widely lecturing on his theories of *qing* and unrestrained heroic activism, attracted the talented and successful scholars He Xinyin 何心隱 (1517–79) and Luo Rufang 羅汝芳 (1515–88) as disciples.[41] As is discussed below, Luo Rufang is especially important to literary history because of the influence his theories of the metaphysical power of *qing* had on the playwright Tang Xianzu 湯顯祖 (1550–1616). Huang Zongxi, the Qing historian of Ming intellectual history, attributed the subsequent rejection of Confucian teachings to Yan Jun: "All of the experiences, doctrines, and formulas reported by earlier Confucians suffice only to ob-

38. For example, when Han Zhen heard people looking for textual citations, he responded: "Why do you give up trying to understand your experience of the immediate and play with dead words instead?" (*MRXA*, 32.182; trans. from *Records*, p. 182).

39. Despite their critiques of orthodox Neo-Confucianism, many influential thinkers associated with the Taizhou School were rigorous in their own pursuit of self-cultivation and not all were as extreme as Wang Ji in their advocacy of sudden enlightenment. For example, Yuan Huang 袁黃 (1533–1606), whose father had been a friend of both Wang Ji and Wang Gen, published Confucian morality books (*shanshu* 善書) and ledgers of merit and demerit (*gongguoge* 功過格), and Luo Rufang, for whom *qing* was a central philosophical issue, stated that effort was necessary to achieve enlightenment. It is interesting to note the difference between Wang Ji's polemical style in his rejection of the necessity of rigorous self-cultivation and his actual practice. When a fire spread from his daughter-in-law's apartment and destroyed much of Wang Yangming's estate, Wang Ji blamed his own moral laxness. "I appear to be amiable and faultless enough; but in private can I really be strict with myself and commit nothing dishonorable in the eyes of the supernatural beings?" (cited from P. Y. Wu, *The Confucian's Progress*, p. 218).

40. *MRXA*, 32.319; *Records*, p. 182.

41. For biographies of He Xinyin, see *DMB*, pp. 513–15, and Dimberg, *The Sage*; Luo Rufang's biography can be found in *DMB*, pp. 975–78.

struct the Way."[42] In place of the traditional discipline of ritual, Yan Jun and He Xinyin advocated the free expression of spirit (*yiqi* 意氣). This movement away from canonical texts as the sole source of moral understanding is one factor that made it possible for defenders of *xiaoshuo* novels to argue for the didactic worth of fiction.

The sixteenth-century turning away from an external standard of truth accorded with the waning intellectual interest in the static, universal cosmological models that were the foundation of Zhu Xi's twelfth-century Neo-Confucian synthesis.[43] The late Ming and Qing saw a gradual shift from the investigation of universal truths to an emphasis on individual and unique phenomena as representative of the dynamic cosmos.[44] *Qing* and desire (*yu*) were keys to this individualistic dynamism. Despite the contempt Qing historians and thinkers held for the Taizhou school, by the eighteenth century philosophers such as Wang Fuzhi 王夫之 (1619–92) and Dai Zhen 戴震 (1722–80) had fully legitimated the Taizhou emphasis on *qing* and desire as the driving creative force of the cosmos.

LI ZHI, DESIRE, AND AUTHENTICITY

Many of the critiques of Cheng-Zhu Neo-Confucianism expressed in the writings of Wang Yangming and Wang Ji found their most radical expression in the writings of Li Zhi, a student of Wang Gen. Although his biting wit and polemical style isolated him from the mainstream of intellectual production, Li Zhi was one of the best-known literati figures of the late Ming.[45] His writings were reprinted several times during the Ming and the Qing despite their proscription after his posthumous impeachment in 1625 and during the Qianlong inquisition.[46] Despite the vilification of Li Zhi by

42. *MRXA*, 32.311; trans. based on *Records*, p. 166.

43. Henderson, *The Development and Decline*, pp. 137–47.

44. Worth noting is that although the diagrams of the Great Ultimate (*taiji* 太極) in the writings of Zhou Dunyi and Shao Yong were based on the principle of Change, their focus was on revealing the ultimate unchanging principle behind Change, not the great variety of its manifestations.

45. See *DMB*, pp. 807–18; H. L. Chan, *Li Chih*; and de Bary, "Individualism and Humanitarianism," pp. 188–225.

46. It is important to reiterate that Li Zhi and the other figures associated with the Taizhou School are anomalous within the late Ming intellectual landscape. Although many literati may have wanted to reform some aspect of Cheng-Zhu orthodoxy, Neo-Confucian rationalism continued to be the dominant intellectual school. The actual extent of the majority

the Qing historian Huang Zongxi, who blamed the fall of the Ming in part on the excesses of these "crazy Chanists," Li Zhi should not be understood as a demagogue who tried to undermine the entire Confucian ethical system.[47] He did attack Song Neo-Confucianism with particular vehemence, but this was in part motivated by his urgent plea for efficacious moral activism.[48] Perhaps it was a realization of China's military and political weakness that drove Li Zhi to value action over introspection: in one of his more outrageous comparisons, Li praised the ability of the outlaw pirate Lin Daoqian 林道乾 (fl. 1566–80), who had evaded government capture for years, and condemned those officials who could only look at each other blankly when an emergency arose.[49] In line with his pragmatic approach, Li Zhi wrote that because people's physical and intellectual capacities differed, the goal of education should not be to make all people alike.[50] Li was a relativist in many senses; for him, the good was defined not by an unchanging moral principle but by institutions and practices that were flexible enough to adapt to the times. His view that each era should have its own literary style and judgments helped fuel the rise of vernacular publishing and the anti-archaic stance of the Gong'an School.

---

of scholars' faith in the system is to some degree irrelevant since Neo-Confucianism still provided the core material for the state-sponsored examination system. The Donglin faction and other conservative groups of scholars relied on their reputation for strict adherence to orthodox ritual and study in their attempts to bring the corrupt imperial court to task. The stern ethics of Neo-Confucianism could not help but exert great appeal and power of moral suasion to many during the decadent closing years of the Ming dynasty and the founding of the Qing. For a broader intellectual context, see Crawford, "Chang Chü-cheng"; Handlin, *Action in Late Ming Thought*; Busch, "The Tung-lin shu-yuan"; Hucker, "The Tung-lin Movement"; and R. Huang, *1587*.

47. Li Zhi was so loathed by Huang Zongxi that Huang did not even give Li a biography in the *Mingru xue'an*. Gu Yanwu singled out Li Zhi as one of those responsible for the loss of public morals that led to the fall of the Ming dynasty, and Wang Fuzhi attacked him for having lost all conscience. Li Zhi was not as morally decadent as he was painted by the Qing sources, however, and was himself aware of the dangers of the excessive relativism of the Taizhou School. Despite his rhetoric, he was conventional in his values; he supported his family during the 30 years he was an official, and he also used much of his limited resources to provide proper burials for his parents and grandparents (*DMB*, p. 816). He Xinyin also emphasized regulating clan affairs (*MRXA*, 32.311; *Records*, p. 167).

48. Li Zhi, *Xu fenshu*, "Wang Wencheng," pp. 439–40; also repeated in *Xu cangshu*, pp. 275–79. Discussed in Cheang, "Li Chih as a Critic," pp. 49–51.

49. Li Zhi, *Fenshu*, "Yinji wangshi," pp. 189–90.

50. Ibid., "Lunzheng pian," p. 103.

Li Zhi is particularly important as a crossover figure between the world of intellectual history and that of fiction and drama. Although the authenticity of the many commentaries to novels and drama attributed to him is questionable to say the least, Li Zhi was closely associated with the values espoused in vernacular fiction.[51] He has been credited with commentaries to the *Sanguo zhi yanyi*, the *Xiyou ji*, and the *Shuihu zhuan*, as well as to the plays *Xixiang ji* and *Pipa ji* 琵琶記 (The lute); of these, only the preface to *Shuihu zhuan* has been established as the product of his brush. The frequency with which his name appears on editions of vernacular fiction clearly indicates that publishers, including Feng Menglong, believed that an association with Li Zhi would add commercial appeal. Li Zhi's influential friendships with the playwright Tang Xianzu and the literary theorist Yuan Hongdao also established him as a vital link between late Ming intellectual trends and the production of literary values and aesthetics.[52]

Even as Li Zhi has become a central focus of twentieth-century historiography on the late Ming, because of his emphasis on individual autonomy, some intellectual historians have argued that his importance has been exaggerated, since he had little or no direct impact on the development of seventeenth-century thought. His conceptualization of desire, however, influenced vernacular fiction profoundly, and many of the values expressed in his writings continued to shape fiction through the Qing dynasty. Moreover, although Li Zhi may not have directly influenced later thinkers, many of his critiques are echoed during the Qing. The acidity of his attacks on the status quo were perhaps anomalous, but his criticisms of institutionalized Neo-Confucian orthopraxy as spiritually bankrupt were unique neither to him nor the late Ming. It is not my intention to discuss whether or not Li Zhi's writings form a coherent philosophy (nor indeed whether he actually subscribed to his exaggerated judgments or merely used them as a stylistic tactic). Of interest here are his views on authenticity as somehow organic to the self and closely associated with desire, as opposed to his attacks on the ritually constructed self as a false self-presentation.

In opposition to the ideal of the ritually defined self, Li Zhi valued an ability to "live in the present" (*dangxia* 當下), to react spontaneously and effectively to situations without the mediation of trained responses. His ethi-

51. See Plaks, *Four Masterworks*, pp. 513–17; and Rolston, *How to Read*, pp. 356–63.

52. See Hsia, "Time and the Human Condition"; P. K. Cheng, "Reality and Imagination"; Chou, *Yüan Hung-tao*; Vallette-Hémery, *Théorie et practique*; and Hung, "Yüan Hung-tao."

cal system was based on the premise that social practice should change according to the needs of each age. Instead of defining ritual as a metaphysical or historically perfected truth, Li Zhi explained it as the practice of "what people have in common" (*ren zhi suo tong zhe* 人之所同者) in contrast to their individual tastes.[53] He argued that rituals should be based on customary practice (*su* 俗), and that what scholars defined as ritual was actually "not-ritual" (*feili* 非禮), a false construction that led to hypocritical behavior. The practices of self-cultivation made the current generation of officials useless, for "all they understand is bowing and saluting; they sit squarely all day as if they were molded of clay."[54] At worst, ritual could become a hypocritical performance based on a false external standard that would mask a person's true self, such as the case of those who affect virtue to hide their venality.[55] In a tone of disdain echoed a hundred and fifty years later by the fictional Jia Baoyu, Li Zhi associated the rote memorization of classical learning with a widespread spiritual corruption:

> Since people are false, there is nothing that is not false. In this way, if you use false speech to talk to a false person, the false person will be pleased; if you tell false matters to a false person, the false person will be pleased; if you discuss false writings with a false person, the false person will be pleased. If everything is false, everyone will be pleased.[56]

Even though Li Zhi's tone here is unduly harsh, Confucius himself had warned against the mechanical performance of ritual.[57] As was made clear in the debates surrounding the Great Ritual Controversy, discussed in Chapter 1, finding a balance between ritualized form and sincerity of feeling was a real dilemma that confronted people more conservative than Li Zhi.

In place of what he described as an artificial, externally derived moral standard, Li Zhi substituted the innate "childlike heart" (*tongxin* 童心), a concept central to his definition of the authentic (*zhen* 眞). Li's concept of the childlike mind derived from Wang Ji's teaching that evil is external to human nature. According to Li Zhi, the childlike mind has a natural and spontaneous understanding of the good and can be taken as the true source

53. Li, *Fenshu*, "Siwu shuo," pp. 120–21.

54. Ibid., "Yinji wangshi," p. 190.

55. Ibid., "Fu Jiao Ruohou," pp. 51–52.

56. Ibid., "Tongxin shuo," p. 118.

57. "*Li* performed without reverence, the forms of mourning observed without grief, how can I bear to look upon these things?" (*Lunyu*, III.26).

of authentic morality. Among Li Zhi's most extreme claims was that authenticity, which may also be translated as the "true," is subjectively determined and based on enlightened selfishness (*si* 私). In contrast to Neo-Confucianism, which teaches people to extinguish their subjective bias, Li argued that enlightened selfishness motivates people toward self-improvement.

> And how could there be a way of mindlessness? If farmers were mindless, the fields would be overgrown with weeds; if artisans were mindless, their implements would be deficient; if scholars were mindless, their studies would be useless. Without a mind, how could things be accomplished? The commentaries also say "To be mindless means being without a selfish heart." This is not true mindlessness. Selfishness *is* man's mind; people must first be selfish, and only then will their mind be revealed.[58]

Desire, which in orthodox Neo-Confucianism is antithetical to principle, here becomes the productive force that drives people to acquire wealth, to study, and even to achieve enlightenment. One of the most extreme shifts in Li Zhi's philosophy was that he rooted his concept of the good, authenticity as expressed through enlightened desires, in the material self. "Liking goods, liking sex, study, personal advancement, accumulating wealth, buying more land and property for their descendants, searching for auspicious sites with which to bless their children—all the things that order life and are productive, all these things that everyone practices, acknowledges, and speaks of as good—these are the authentic."[59] Desires were the foundation of Li Zhi's definition of authenticity; those desires shared by a community define the common good.

One of Li Zhi's favored rhetorical strategies was to take concepts reviled by orthodoxy and invest them with positive connotations; he transformed selfishness and desire, two of the most threatening components of the material nature according to Neo-Confucianism, into the basis for moral action. Oppositional rhetoric similar to that used by Li Zhi reverberates throughout much of the fiction written during the late Ming and Qing and seems to underlie the common paradoxical conceit that authentic morality is most powerfully expressed through a transgression of excessively rigid Confucian practices. Before turning to examples of fiction by several late Ming figures

58. Li Zhi, *Cangshu*, "Deye ruchen houlun," p. 544.

59. Li Zhi, *Fenshu*, "Da Deng Mingfu," p. 43; also translated in de Bary, "Individualism and Humanitarianism," p. 200. For another passage that reveals the importance of the physical to Li Zhi's definition of the self, see Li Zhi, *Fenshu*, "Da Deng Shiyang," p. 5.

who were directly influenced by Li Zhi, we will first look at how certain late Ming critiques of Cheng-Zhu orthodoxy were incorporated into mainstream Qing intellectual trends. As in fiction, ideas that had been imbued with a counterhegemonic intent during the late Ming progressively lost their transgressive edge as they were absorbed into attempts to reinvigorate Confucian practices and values.

RITUAL AND DESIRE RECONCILED IN QING THOUGHT

Historians are still debating the effects the fall of the Ming dynasty had on the generations of literati who lived through that political transition or came of age in the generation immediately following.[60] When it came time for Qing historians to evaluate the past and assign praise and blame, it was inevitable that the wild Chanists, those most extreme members of the Taizhou School such as Li Zhi, would be fiercely attacked for their excessive subjectivism. Until the last two decades of the twentieth century, most intellectual historians have followed Liang Qichao in saying that the fall of the Ming dynasty created a great watershed in traditional Chinese thought; this facile understanding of the transition from Ming to Qing explained the seeming sudden dominance of Qing evidential studies (*kaozheng xue* 考證學; also known as Han studies, *Hanxue* 漢學) as a conscious effort to break away from the empty philosophizing (*xuxue* 虛學) of the late Ming.

In actuality, just as the aesthetics of the Qing *xiaoshuo* novels were built on a Ming foundation, Qing intellectual trends followed from directions already well established during the Ming.[61] In both philosophy and fiction, ideas that had been launched as radical challenges to the hegemony of Neo-Confucianism during the sixteenth century came to represent a new status quo. Indeed, Qing classicism, as reflected in evidential studies and ritual purism, provided a platform from which to continue the critique of Neo-Confucianism.[62] Moreover, as On-cho Ng has argued, despite differences in

60. See Y. S. Yü, "Some Preliminary Observations"; and idem, "Cong Song, Ming ru lixue." For general discussions of the transition from Ming to Qing, see Adshead, "The Seventeenth-Century"; Peterson, *Bitter Gourd*; Spence and Wills, *From Ming to Ch'ing*; Struve, *Voices from the Ming*; and Chow, *The Rise of Confucian Ritualism*, esp. chap. 1.

61. See Elman, *From Philosophy to Philology*; and Ng, "*Hsing* as the Ontological Basis."

62. Chow, *The Rise of Confucian Ritualism*, p. 7.

their philosophies, mainstream thinkers such as Gao Panlong 高攀龍 (1562–1626), Liu Zongzhou 劉宗周 (1578–1645), and Lu Shiyi 陸世儀 (1611–1720), the last "an ardent Cheng-Zhu follower," were in agreement that human nature was inherently and uniformly good and that evil arose through action, not essence.[63] Clearly, there was widespread sympathy for the revisionist notion that the emotions and desires were integral to the moral nature rather than antithetical to it.

The experiences of Yan Yuan 顏元 (1635–1704), one of the best-known and most representative figures of the practical learning (*shixue* 實學) movement of the early Qing dynasty, are illustrative of the continuing frustration with Neo-Confucian orthopraxy.[64] Yan Yuan was a conservative Confucian who condemned the self-indulgent excesses of the Taizhou leaders. He made many sincere efforts at self-cultivation; when young, he erected his own shrine to the Confucian masters and worshiped there daily. As was a common practice, he also kept a detailed notebook in which he recorded his actions and thoughts; he gave himself demerits for losing his temper or letting his mind wander, both of which were considered signs of an unenlightened mind.[65] He also tried to conform to the ritual practices set out in Zhu Xi's *Family Rituals*; however, he began to rebel against them later in life when he went into mourning for his grandmother. The strict injunctions in the *Family Rituals* against eating and wearing more than the bare minimum while in mourning left him so weak that he fell ill and could no longer concentrate on his grief for his grandmother. At that point, he decided that fulfilling each punctilio of the rituals not only interfered with his proper expression of grief but also could be inimical to life itself. Implicit in this claim is his belief that a true expression of proper Confucian sentiments should allow for some degree of individual autonomy.[66] Yan later criticized the Neo-Confucian educational process for producing introverted, passive, and effete scholars who had no experience of the real world. He likened Neo-Confucian pedagogy to trying to learn how to play a musical instrument by memorizing a manual but never having any physical contact with the actual instrument.[67]

63. Ng, "*Hsing* as the Ontological Basis," pp. 83–96.

64. See *ECCP*, pp. 913–15; Tu Wei-ming, "Yen Yuan"; and Zhou Kangxie, *Yan Li xuepai*.

65. See Tu Wei-ming, "Yen Yuan" esp. pp. 517–18; and Sakai, "Confucianism," pp. 342–45. For further examples of this widespread practice, see Brokaw, *Ledgers*.

66. For more on Yan Yuan's revisions to mourning rituals, see Kutcher, *Mourning in Late Imperial China*, pp. 114–19.

67. Yan Yuan, *Yan Yuan ji*, "Cunxue bian," pp. 78–79.

The writings of the staunch Ming loyalist Wang Fuzhi reveal his attempts to bridge the gap between the orthodox Cheng-Zhu theory of the basic duality of human nature and the increasing tolerance of seventeenth-century thinkers toward the emotions and desires. Even though Wang saw himself as a follower of Song Neo-Confucianism and opposed Wang Yangming's idealism, he treated the enlightened desires as a central component of human nature. He accepted the basic Cheng-Zhu distinction between, in Wang Fuzhi's own terms, the human mind (*renxin* 人心; equivalent to Zhu Xi's material nature) and the moral mind (*Daoxin* 道心; Zhu Xi's Heavenly nature), but thought of them as unified rather than oppositional.[68] "Now with regard to *qing*, there is a clear distinction between the human (*renxin*) and moral mind (*Daoxin*). Happiness, anger, remorse, pleasure—these are the human mind. Compassion, shame, respect, right and wrong—these are the moral mind."[69] Wang argued that desire (*renyu* 人欲) is anterior to ritual expression and accused those Buddhists who tried to exterminate desire of selfishly destroying humanity.[70] "Although ritual is purely a pattern (*jiewen* 節文) of Heavenly principle, it must be lodged (*yu* 寓) in human desires in order to be seen. Although [desires] may abide in stillness, when aroused they use changing and mixing to display their function. Then, therefore, there cannot be Heaven apart from people, nor principle apart from desire."[71] As one scholar put it, "As principles were 'lodged in' the desires, if one tried to 'subdue one's self by eliminating the desires one would be left with no vehicle for principles.'"[72] Despite his condemnation of Li Zhi and the other Taizhou figures, Wang Fuzhi shared with them the view that the desires are necessary for the realization of morality. Wang even emphasized the desires as the first link in the chain of strenuous self-cultivation.

The Classic [*Great Learning*] says: "Those who desire to cultivate their persons must first rectify their minds." It says you must first desire it, and then you will have it. . . . Thus, unless you take the desires to regulate, to rectify, and to make sincere as the

68. For a study of Wang's philosophy, see McMorran, "Wang Fu-chih."

69. Wang Fuzhi, *Shangshu yinyi*, p. 26; citation and trans. from Elman, "Philosophy Versus Philology," p. 206.

70. Wang Fuzhi, *Chuanshan yishu*, "Du Sishu daquan shuo," 8.11a.

71. Ibid., 8.10b; trans. modified from C. Y. Cheng, "Reason, Substance and Human Desires," p. 488.

72. McMorran, "Wang Fu-chih," p. 445.

basis for study, your investigations will not be investigations, and your knowledge will not be knowledge.[73]

Wang allowed that certain desires could be problematic, but he sought to limit his definition to those aspects of them that are positive and life-affirming. As he put it, "Bloodthirstiness is outside [the scope of] human desires" 嗜殺人，自在人欲之外.[74]

Wang's primary philosophical inspiration came from Zhang Zai and his materialist interest in *qi* as the basic stuff of the universe. Wang turned away from the primacy given to principle in Cheng-Zhu thought and focused his attention on the Way (*Dao*), a term he used to replace *Li*. Wang wrote that in place of a transcendent principle that pre-exists and predetermines reality, each age and each vessel (*qi* 器) must develop forms to meet its own needs.[75] Each vessel, because of the variability of its material form (*qi* 氣), is of necessity unique. The Way depends on vessels in order to be made manifest.

Under Heaven, there are only vessels. The Way is the Way of vessels. . . . Before there were bows and arrows, there was no Way of archery. Before there were chariots and horses, there was no Way of driving. Before there were sacrificial oxen and wine, presents of jade and silk, bells, chimes, flutes, and strings, there was no Way of music or ritual. Thus, before there was a son, there was no Way of the father; before there was a younger brother, there was no Way of an older brother. There are many potential Ways that do not exist [in material form]. Therefore without the vessel, there cannot be a Way.[76]

Again, despite the profound political and philosophical differences between Wang Fuzhi and Li Zhi, one cannot help but be struck by the parallels between Wang's materialist relativism and Li's defense of new forms of literature for changing times. In a significant departure from orthodox Neo-Confucian metaphysics, Wang also stripped away the long-standing moral overlay on *yin* and *yang* in favor of a purely materialist understanding of their function. "When *yang* mixes with *yin*, there is humanity and rites; thus, although rites are pure *yang*, they are embodied in *yin*."[77] The contrast between

73. Wang Fuzhi, *Chuanshan yishu*, "Du Sishu daquan shuo," 4.19a–b.

74. Ibid., 8.4a.

75. Wang Fuzhi, *Chuanshan yishu*, "Du Tongjian lun," 42b; trans. from *Source Book*, pp. 701–2.

76. Wang Fuzhi, *Chuanshan yishu*, "Zhou Yi waizhuan," 5.25a; trans. modified from *Source Book*, p. 695.

77. Wang Fuzhi, *Chuanshan yishu*, "Du Sishu daquan shuo," 8.10b.

Wang's *yinyang* materialism and the Neo-Confucian moral valuation of the terms can be seen in the following quote from his mentor Zhang Zai: "If *yang* that is clear dominates, one's moral nature will function. If *yin* that is turbid dominates, one's material desires (*wuyu* 物欲) will have their way."[78] Because Wang Fuzhi's writings were not published until 1842, due to his virulently anti-Manchu sentiments, he cannot be said to have had any direct influence on mid-Qing intellectual history. What is important to note in his writings is that despite the vast ideological chasm that separated him from Li Zhi, both men questioned the universal and transcendent authority of Neo-Confucian principle, and both identified desire as a positive and even moral aspect of human nature. Both, moreover, affirmed the integrity of the individual as a unique expression of larger processes. Although Wang Fuzhi never let go of the notion that people need to pursue and conform to strict moral standards, he demonstrates the extent to which certain ideas that had been highly controversial during the sixteenth century had moved into the mainstream of Qing thought.

One cannot fully appreciate the extent of the change of attitude toward the desires during the two centuries that separate Wang Yangming and the high Qing without turning to the writings of the influential philosopher Dai Zhen, a scholar widely respected during his own lifetime. He penned what was, because of his stature, one of the most damning responses to the excesses of institutionalized Neo-Confucianism:

> Alas, that people today have not thought about this! The Way of the sage allows all under Heaven to achieve their emotions (*qing*) and fulfill their desires (*yu*) while all under Heaven is well governed. Later Confucians (*hou Ru* 後儒) do not know that [achieving] emotion to the most minute degree without regret is called principle (*Li*). What they called "principle" is equivalent to what a rapacious minor official calls "law." [Just as] rapacious minor officials use laws to kill people, these Confucians use principle to kill people. What has gradually permeated the law and is discussed as principle is death! Nothing can remedy [this situation].[79]

78. *JSL*, 2.36b, *Reflections*, p. 74. Zhu Xi's comment on the passage is a classic statement of the negative value placed on *yin*: "As has been said, 'The nature is of course good, but it cannot be said that evil is not nature.' Both come from Heaven. *Yang* is good and strong, while *yin* is evil and weak. With *yang*, a thing becomes bright and clear. With *yin* it becomes dark and turbid."

79. Dai Zhen, "Yumo shu," in Hu Shi, *Dai Dongyuan*, p. 58; also see Elman, "Philosophy Versus Philology," pp. 216–17.

Dai blamed Cheng-Zhu Neo-Confucianism for instituting a dangerous repression of emotions and desires. In order to find a textual basis to decenter principle as the foundational moral concept, Dai turned to the earliest definitions of *Li* as patterns innate to objects (*wenli* 文理) and as the individual qualities that differentiate things (*fenli* 分理).[80] He defined principle as an aspect of emotional expression: "When an individual is among people, it is called *qing*. Principle is the state when *qing* is neither excessive nor insufficient."[81] Significantly, Dai substituted the word *qing* for the Confucian term *ren*, "humanity," to describe the force that connects the individual to the universal community. He also argued that physical desires and emotions are natural and positive components of human nature, for the desires root individuals in the creative activities of the universe and people interact with their environment through emotional reactions.

> The desire for sounds, colors, smells, and tastes helps to enrich one's life. The feelings of joy, anger, sorrow, and pleasure respond to and bring one into contact with [external] things. The knowledge of beauty and ugliness, or right and wrong, when developed to the utmost, enables one to penetrate Heaven, earth, and the divine spirits. . . . Only when the desires and feelings are supplemented by knowledge do these desires gain fulfillment and these feelings gain expression. All activities in the world should consist of nothing more than ensuring this fulfillment of desires and expression of feelings.[82]

Dai defined the emotions (*qingxu* 情緒) as those things that enable people to interact with the world around them, and desires (*yuwang* 欲望) as an internal life force, essential to the continuation of a physical existence. "The Way of procreation and nurturing lies in the desires" 生養之道存乎欲者也.[83] In his discussion of human nature, Dai Zhen argued that the Song rationalists had mistakenly confused selfishness with desire; much like Wang Fuzhi, he refined the discussion of desires by distinguishing between good desires and the obscured (*bi* 蔽) and selfish (*si*) desires.[84] Since the truest desires are to "love life and hate death," Dai also attacked the Neo-Confucians

80. Dai Zhen, "Mengzi ziyi shuzheng," in Hu Shi, *Dai Dongyuan*, appendix, pp. 40–41.

81. Ibid., sect. 1, p. 43.

82. Ibid., sect. 3, p. 105; trans. from *A History*, p. 660.

83. Dai Zhen, "Yuanshan," in Hu Shi, *Dai Dongyuan*, appendix, sect. 1, p. 7.

84. Dai Zhen, "Mengzi ziyi shuzheng," in Hu Shi, *Dai Dongyuan*, appendix, sect. 1, p. 55. He states this even more clearly in a letter to his friend Duan Yucai (reprinted in Yu Yingshi, *Lun Dai Zhen*, pp. 291–93).

for going contrary to human nature in placing greater value on cultivating the self according to a narrowly defined orthopraxy than on life itself.[85] Dai, of course, was not suggesting individual standards of moral knowledge, for he stressed that people need to guard against the dangerous potential of "obscured" emotions to cloud individual judgment.

Dai advocated the rigorous study of specific institutions, laws, and rituals mentioned in the Classics as a form of intellectual discipline; for him, moral enlightenment was a direct consequence of knowledge rather than a result of introspective self-cultivation.[86] The process of self-cultivation Dai Zhen proposed was no less arduous than that found in Cheng-Zhu orthodoxy; the main difference lies in Dai Zhen's intellectualism and his understanding that each person might fashion an individual methodology in this moral process. Despite the influence of Dai Zhen's evidential scholarship, his attempts to refashion philological research into a tool for moral learning had "little representative value."[87] What is of interest to us is the respectability his voice lends the polemical critiques of Cheng-Zhu orthodoxy made by Li Zhi and others of the Taizhou school.

Vast differences in belief about the need for effort and for an external standard in the process of moral self-cultivation separate these mainstream Qing philosophers from the most radical followers of Wang Yangming. What unites them is their use of the emotions and desires as a discursive site from which to critique Cheng-Zhu Neo-Confucianism. Several other areas of concern loosely connect the writings of Yan Yuan, Wang Fuzhi, and Dai Zhen to Li Zhi and the other figures who had a direct influence on the production of literature. They shared an uneasiness that the emphasis on the introspective and quietist practices of self-cultivation had diverted the attention of scholars from a more activist and pragmatic engagement in society and pursuit of knowledge and experience; they also shared a loss of faith in the concept of Neo-Confucian principle as a universal and transcendent moral standard and object of knowledge. Most important for this study, each also rejected Neo-Confucian dualism in favor of a more materialist, organically integrated, and individualistic definition of self. These thinkers re-

85. "In terms of human life, there is nothing more sick than someone not fulfilling his or her own life" 人之生也，莫病無以遂其生 (Dai Zhen, "Mengzi ziyi shuzheng," in Hu Shi, *Dai Dongyuan*, appendix, sect. 1, p. 53).

86. Brokaw, "Tai Chen," pp. 266, 278.

87. Ibid., p. 260.

conceptualized *qing* and desire as positive forces that, with proper restraint and guidance, drive people to live moral and fulfilling lives. And with the exception of Yan Yuan, they treated the expression of *qing* as a basis for morality. In fact, there was a growing recognition that individuals needed some autonomy in the performance of ritual and that to follow the ritual prescriptions too closely, without allowing space for emotional engagement, could undermine the integrity of the act.[88]

We must not forget, however, that this gradual shift, between the mid-sixteenth and the late eighteenth century, toward a more positive conception of *qing* occurred within an intellectual and moral environment that was still dominated by Cheng-Zhu Neo-Confucianism. All educated people were expected to be conversant with, if not fully steeped in, orthodox writings; even the illiterate memorized ritual codes. Canonical Neo-Confucian texts continued to serve as the basis for the official examinations until the examination system was abandoned at the end of the Qing dynasty; and despite the grumbling about the system, its conservative shape and content were proud symbols of the cultural achievements of Han culture under Manchu rule. Clan practices continued to draw on Zhu Xi's *Family Rituals*, despite the evidential scholarship that undermined that text's canonical authority. Clearly, during these two centuries multiple constructions of *qing* circulated simultaneously, and depending on the context within which a person was communicating, he might, and likely did, invoke a number of contradictory usages of the term. As we shall see, these conflicting discursive uses of the various terms for desire, implying either self-destruction or liberating passion, are widely reflected in the vernacular fiction of this period, frequently within the same text.

Although too little is as yet known to judge what impact the more liberal attitudes toward *qing* and self-expression had on actual domestic practices for any other than the most exceptional cases,[89] the late Ming and Qing reevaluation of human nature had a profound impact on the production of literature. Fueled by the cult of *qing*, fiction moved away from its didactic roots in orthodox discourse toward a more lyric and self-reflexive aestheticism. Fictional poets and lovers began to supersede the traditional biographical models of self-sacrificing chastity or political and filial virtue as part of the creation of a new cultural ideal. Fictionalized representations of sexual desire

88. Kutcher (*Mourning in Late Imperial China*) also makes this argument.

89. See Ko, *Teachers of the Inner Chambers*; and Mann, *Precious Records*.

no longer needed to be disguised as political or moral allegory,[90] for passion in all its forms had become a complement to, and even basis for, moral principle.[91] In many instances the expression of *qing* came to be the marker of an authentic moral performance.

FROM PHILOSOPHY TO FICTION: THE AESTHETICS OF *QING*

Strong currents of influence connect the textual worlds of philosophical theory and literary practice during the late Ming. The philosophical attempts to reclaim *qing* as a vital and essentially moral quality provided an ethical defense for the publication of fictional texts that from other perspectives could be seen as morally suspect. Whereas fictional narratives with an orthodox intent, such as *Jin Ping Mei* and *Xingshi yinyuan zhuan*, treat sexual yearnings as inherently threatening, the fiction and drama influenced by the cult of *qing* depict sexual desire as a positive instinct that can lead toward moral regeneration.

In order to redefine *qing* as redemptive, however, writers of fiction practiced a sleight of hand whereby they reinscribed the liberating power of *qing* within a stable Confucian frame. In these dramas and novels, the protagonists' most deeply felt desires, which initially challenge hegemonic moral codes, are eventually made to express the highest Confucian values of filiality, loyalty, and chastity; true *qing* resolves any tensions between authentic self-expression and orthopraxy. In many instances, an uneasy ideological balance results from narrative attempts to celebrate individual expression, particularly in the area of sensual enjoyment, while claiming for it the moral purity historically reserved for orthodox self-restraint. Those texts inspired by the philosophic redefinition of *qing* gave rise to a new aesthetics. The remainder of this chapter briefly surveys several key Ming texts in order to map out the emerging aesthetics of *qing* as it was appropriated and championed by the writers and publishers of fiction and drama.

90. This form of Confucian political allegoresis is discussed in P. Yu, *The Reading of Imagery*, pp. 50–53, 67, 124–27; and Robertson, "Voicing the Feminine."

91. W. Y. Li, *Enchantment*, pp. 60–62.

Qing, *Cultural Redemption, and the Ideological Appropriation of the Feminine*

By the late imperial period, the rewards for participating in the examination system were widely perceived as incommensurate with the sacrifices demanded. Even if a man were talented and lucky enough to win a degree, the breakdown of the official bureaucracy stymied his chances for meaningful service to the state. Born of these frustrations was a nostalgic yearning for a simpler, less regulated, and less commodified basis for self-identity to take the place of the official route. Because of the nominally apolitical status accorded women in the premodern period, they were easily transformed into icons of cultural purity. Indeed, during the late Ming, the feminine began to be idealized as an authentic subject position untainted by the frustrations, sacrifices, and moral compromises demanded by participating in the bureaucratic system.[92] In fiction, particularly in the scholar-beauty genre, sentimental characterizations of beautiful and talented young women became the norm. The increasing social mobility of the late Ming caused many literati to become concerned with the problem of distinguishing authenticity from mimicry and pretense; many of these anxieties about literati status and identity were resolved in fiction by having women enact roles traditionally reserved for their male counterparts. One gets the sense reading through Ming-Qing vernacular fiction that women, by their apolitical status, could redeem the moral authority of orthodox values and the imperial bureaucracy, both of which had become debased through their conflation with men's career ambitions.

Moreover, the novelty of a woman's engagement in culture lent otherwise clichéd concepts a freshness they might not otherwise enjoy. The image of beautiful young women as politically pure and virtuous was not a Ming invention; it had long been enshrined in the Confucian hermeneutic practice of reading a woman's desire for her lover as allegorical of a worthy scholar's desire for political recognition. Yet the use of the trope exploded during the late Ming and Qing, and even courtesans and prostitutes were held up as emblems of integrity, whereas scholars, in contrast, were depicted as in-

92. For a discussion of how the Wanli official Lü Kun identified with women during times of moral uncertainty, see Handlin, "Lü Kun's New Audience," pp. 30–31.

creasingly weak or corrupt.[93] The idealization of women's subject position became so accepted that even the socially conservative scholar Zhang Xuecheng 章學誠 (1738–1801), a moralist who criticized Yuan Mei for taking on female students, seems to have felt that the life of a cloistered woman could provide the best site for nurturing the disinterested ideals of classical learning.[94]

The growing idealization of the feminine during the late imperial period cannot be separated from two paradoxically intertwined value systems: the counterhegemonic cult of *qing* and the Neo-Confucian cult of female chastity. By making the ultimate sacrifice to prove their virtue, which for women was synonymous with chaste loyalty to a husband, virtuous women became emblematic of orthodoxy. As one scholar has argued, virtuous women began to displace male scholars as local symbols of orthodox achievement.[95] In fiction and drama, the lines between courtesans and maidens from elite families were being blurred, creating hybrid characterizations that functioned as potent symbols of purity. The narrative insistence on demonstrating the sexual attractiveness and potential for passion of female protagonists even while proving their chastity sometimes leads to improbable twists of plot.[96] In the drama *Mudan ting*, which I discuss in detail below, Tang Xianzu improves the moral integrity of the Tang dynasty tale "The Biography of Yingying" ("Yingying zhuan" 鶯鶯傳) by having the heroine give herself to her lover in a dream; this narrative stratagem allows her to maintain the chastity of her physical body. In fact, as is supported by the fact that Feng Menglong's 24-chapter *Qingshi* 情史 (Anthology of *Qing*) begins with a chapter entitled "*Qing* and Chastity" ("Qing zhen lei" 情貞類), the sensualism associated with the literary cult of *qing* frequently supported, rather than challenged, the widespread social concern for female chastity.

In addition to the transformation of female characters into fit guardians of the classical heritage due to their ability to transcend ambition, the voices of women began to be privileged as producers of authentic and even elite culture. This of course goes against the ubiquitous Ming adage that "lack of

93. For a discussion of changing depictions of courtesans during the late Ming, see K. Y. S. Chang, *The Late-Ming Poet*, pp. 9–18; and W. Y. Li, "The Late Ming Courtesan."

94. See Mann, "*Fuxue* by Zhang Xuecheng," p. 42.

95. See T'ien, *Male Anxiety*.

96. For example, the seventeenth-century scholar-beauty romance *Haoqiu zhuan* 好逑傳 (The fortunate union) concludes triumphantly with proof of the heroine's chastity in the climactic finale.

talent is virtuous in a woman." Unlike a highly trained scholar whose literary expressions would likely be mediated through an artificial style acquired through years of mimicking classical models, women and the unlettered were vaunted as having a more natural and powerful form of expression because of their more direct access to emotions. Even for those literati who preferred the more refined aesthetics of the allusive and ornate classical language, women's voices were accorded a special affective power and purity denied their male counterparts. As Ellen Widmer has commented, the almost legendary literary status achieved by the young courtesan Xiaoqing 小青 (d. 1612), despite the slim corpus of writings that survived her, is emblematic of the special interest paid to female writers and artists after the early seventeenth century.[97]

By the eighteenth century, it had become normative to construct the apolitical feminine as a source of authentic expression in contrast to the decadence of the official center. The two most prominent examples of this are *Honglou meng*, in which Baoyu's girl cousins are demonstrably more talented and refined than he, despite his renunciation of orthodox learning, and the lengthy celebration of Qing literati culture conducted by the hundred successful female examination candidates in *Jinghua yuan*. Even the eighteenth-century novel *Yesou puyan*, which counters the aesthetics of the scholar-beauty genre in that its values are distinctly masculinist and orthodox, describes the Confucian hero noticing

> a young girl of four or five, clapping her hands and singing a tuneless melody. Because she was so young and because it was in Miao dialect, he couldn't make out a word. Her pure child's voice sounded like the piping of Heaven; as she shook her head in time to the music, her demeanor was wildly captivating. Suchen felt that she was better than any of the famous opera singers, more graceful to watch and more pleasing to listen to. 見一個小女孩子，約有四五歲光景，兩手拍著，唱那没腔的歌兒；本是小孩子，又是苗語，吉伶古魯的一字也聽不出；既純是童音，居然天籟；兼以顛頭播腦，姿趣橫生。覺比著名優演唱，更是嬝嬝可觀，渢渢可聽.。 (*YSPY*, 87.12a–b)

97. Widmer, "Xiaoqing's Literary Legacy." As recent scholarship suggests, however, there remained a great deal of ambivalence about protecting a talented woman's reputation for virtue while allowing others to see or hear her words. One practical solution to this conundrum was apparently to wait until the demise of the woman in question so that her literary fame would not tarnish her reputation for modesty.

That the girl is an illiterate Miao barbarian, in addition to being female, heightens the allure of her unselfconscious and "natural" charm, as well as strengthens the purity of her expression; this young performer, who is marginalized by sex, age, ethnicity, and education, is presented as a transparent vehicle for art itself.

Concomitant with the idealization of the feminine as the potentially pure embodiment of *qing* was the increasing importance of women as the emotional and intellectual counterparts to men. The concept of companionate marriages developed from the ideal of the soulmate (*zhiji* 知己), a relationship that refers to those rare friendships in which genuine intellectual and spiritual communion occurs. These relationships connote a willingness to defy social custom and place affective bonds above career or the more conventional orthodox loyalties to family and state. Likely for these reasons, the platonic *zhiji* bond is a staple of the biographies of the eccentric Seven Masters of the Bamboo Grove celebrated in the Six Dynasties *Shishuo xinyu* 世說新語 (A new account of tales of the world) and the knight-errant tradition. Although many examples of romantic *zhiji* relationships predate the Ming, such as those between the Han dynasty Sima Xiangru 司馬相如 and Zhuo Wenjun 卓文君 or Scholar Zhang and Yingying in "The Biography of Yingying," these early scholar-beauty love affairs typically carried a taint of sexual impropriety.

During the late Ming, however, the notion of companionate marriage lost its subversive edge and became a dominant expression of the selfless *zhiji* ideal. The rise in popularity of literary companionate marriages was a parallel to the late Ming philosophical preference for friendship over family bonds based on obligation rather than an authentic expression of feelings.[98] Despite the profound influence of courtesan culture on the literati ideal of companionate marriage, the textual re-creations of scholar-beauty marriages downplay the sexual component of these relationships in order to foreground the more respectable passions of political loyalty and sexual fidelity.[99] Even *Mudan ting*, one of the more boldly erotic manifestos of *qing*, denies and delays

98. Li Zhi and He Xinyin both praised friendship as being the most authentic of all bonds; see de Bary, "Individualism and Humanitarianism," p. 185.

99. Kang-i Sun Chang (*The Late-Ming Poet*, pp. 3–18) shows how the popular romanticization of scholar-beauty couples was influenced by relationships between highly literate courtesans and leading late Ming literati, such as those between Liu Shi 柳是 and Chen Zilong 陳子龍 (1608–47), and Li Xiangjun 李香君 and Hou Fangyu 侯方域 (1618–55) in which *qing* and loyalism were intertwined.

the reality of the lovers' corporeal relationship until they have been properly married. The irony of making the courtesan type "the metaphorical equivalent of the *qing* idea"[100] fits well with the historical associations of *zhiji* as unconventional and marginal while building on the polemical rhetoric of late Ming philosophy, which promoted the socially abject as morally superior.

Despite the somewhat subversive genealogy of companionate marriages, the trope became aestheticized in scholar-beauty romances to such a degree that the lovers become intellectually, spiritually, and sometimes physically interchangeable. Male scholars take on many of the positive qualities attributed to beautiful women, and the women appear as purer and more accomplished reflections of the male self, even to the extent of temporarily displacing the male from his public role. Although on the surface these idealizations of women and the feminine appear to empower women insofar as women are given opportunities to succeed in public roles, these idealized couples are, as has been recently argued, ultimately a narcissistic reflection of the male protagonist in which the man appropriates his lover's positive attributes.[101] In this sense, the talented female beauty (or her feminized homosexual counterpart), similar to any beloved object of connoisseurship, is made into a site on which the male protagonist's (as well as authors' and readers') potential for *qing* is projected and displayed, either through shared passions or through the gaze that focalizes the male subject's ability to appreciate an object's unique and unorthodox qualities.[102]

Mudan ting *and the Iconography of* Qing

For understanding the rich associative symbolism of the literary treatment of *qing* during the late Ming, no text is better than Tang Xianzu's influential drama, *Mudan ting*, written in 1588. The play is famed for its lush poetry, the dreamed atemporality of the love scenes in which the boundaries between fantasy and reality are blurred, and its triumphant vindication of youthful passion over sterile orthodox rationalism. *Mudan ting* borrows heavily from the *Xixiang ji*, but the influence of the sixteenth-century cult of *qing* can be

100. Ibid., p. 12.

101. This point is made in discussions of *Honglou meng* by M. Huang, *Literati and Self-Re/Presentation*, pp. 81–97; Yee, "Self, Sexuality, and Writing," esp. p. 388; and Saussy, "Reading and Folly," p. 31.

102. Ellen Widmer ("Xiaoqing's Literary Legacy," p. 128) draws similar conclusions about male writers' interest in Xiaoqing as a "vehicle" for their own self-promotion.

seen in a shift in the thematic conflict. The drama is no longer centered on the scholar's choice between passion and career, as in the earliest versions of the *Xixiang ji*, but on the heroine's choice between passion and life. The orthodox definition of self, represented by an official career and a socially approved marriage, is subordinated to the expression of self through love. *Mudan ting* is dominated by the exquisitely rendered Du Liniang 杜麗娘, an ethereally beautiful adolescent girl and the daughter of strict Confucian parents. As has frequently been pointed out, her lover, the ambitious but unsuccessful scholar Liu Mengmei 柳夢梅, is in comparison exceptionally unremarkable and bland.[103] Although it is Liu Mengmei's dream in the second scene that takes us into the world of sensual fantasy and nominally focalizes the romance through his perspective, it is through the character of Du Liniang that life is breathed into this dramatization of desire. In fact, she immediately eclipses him as the narrative focus.

Structurally and thematically, the play contrasts the young lovers' world of *qing* with the rigid orthodoxy of Du Liniang's parents. Liniang embodies the aesthetics of *qing*: she is young, delicately beautiful, passionate, and sensitively intelligent. Her essence transcends form: she is equally compelling to Mengmei and readers alike as corporeal being, painted image, and disembodied phantasm. Her sensibilities are organically attuned to the dynamic processes of nature, and, like those of a plant, her beauty and strength are ephemeral. Furthermore, her identity is formed not so much through ritualized Confucian roles as through her ability to respond to the world subjectively. Her artistic expressions are motivated by a self-reflexive desire to give voice to her emotional state rather than a Confucian desire to shape or pattern the world. When Liniang first discovers the secret garden behind her parents' official residence, spring is in its full glory: birds are mating, and all the flowers except the peony, which is associated with sexual maturity, are in bloom. Her response to this "expanse of green" (*yi pian qing* 一片青), a transparent pun on "an expanse of *qing*," is immediate and unmediated (*MDT*, 10.43); her own *qing* aroused, she lies down and enters a dream of sexual passion with Liu Mengmei. Much to Mengmei's delight, Liniang's ability to love is absolute; she falls for him spontaneously and, initially, without consideration for ritual propriety. Her body, unlike her spirit, is the one

103. One noteworthy feature that would distinguish him as a lover worthy of Liniang may be his surname Liu, perhaps an intentional pun on the *yin* number six; it is his only attribute that might explain his special affinity for *qing*.

weak link in her identification with *qing* as a positive force since it allows for the possibility of moral transgression. Before her flawed corporeal state is redeemed by Liu Mengmei, who authors her rebirth, she allows herself to indulge in excessive passion (*MDT*, 34.169).[104] Until the two lovers are properly married, however, Liniang's passion is enacted only in disembodied states. As she explains it, "A ghost may beguile through *qing*; living people must substantiate themselves through ritual" 鬼可虛情，人須實禮 (*MDT*, 36.175).

In contrast to Liniang's refined sensitivity to her environment, her father Prefect Du and his crony Tutor Chen, a parody of the Confucian pedant, seem to have no emotional or subjective connection to the world around them. Ritual and duty determine Prefect Du's engagement with life. When spring arrives, he responds as a Confucian: he hires a bombastic scholar to tutor his lovely young daughter in the Classics and then presides over the communal spring plowing rites. Prefect Du's subordination of his private emotional responses to public duty is painfully illustrated at the time of Liniang's death when he accepts a letter of official promotion to serve as pacification commissioner, thereby denying himself and his wife the opportunity to mourn the loss of their only child. His limited ability to respond emotionally to circumstances is revealed even more forcefully in the concluding reunion scene when he clings to his narrow rationalist perspective and refuses to allow himself to hope that either his wife or daughter might be alive, even though they are standing in front of him.

A more humorous treatment of the ideological differences between *qing* and orthodoxy is brought out in the interactions between Tutor Chen and Liniang and her lively maid Chunxiang 春香, Spring Fragrance, in scene 7. As the world outside and inside the classroom window bursts with spring vitality, Tutor Chen comments, without interest, on the presence of flowers and insects, traditional symbols of sexual passion, and remains oblivious to Liniang's radiant beauty. During their lessons, he follows the conventions of Confucian allegoresis and imposes a moral reading on the simple love poem with which the *Poetry Classic* begins; in response, the earthy Chunxiang tries to subvert the lesson by turning Tutor Chen's Confucian readings into sex-

104. The patch from Tutor Chen's trousers, added to the wine potion used to bring Liniang back to life, is a parody of a common motif about the resurrection of amorous female ghosts through the reception of their lover's blood and semen. In terms of *yinyang* theory, the motif suggests the power of *yang* to redeem excessive *qing*.

ual puns. She eroticizes the practice of writing by bringing out cosmetic brushes, dyes, and fancy letter paper in place of the proper writing implements that make up the four treasures of a scholar. Chunxiang's attempts to teach the parrot to call for tea playfully highlight the emptiness of this exercise in classical learning in which the mistress learns to parrot the words of the commentaries (*MDT*, 7.25).

Despite the sharp contrasts between the worlds of Du Liniang and that of her parents, the oppositional values ascribed to Neo-Confucianism and *qing* in *Mudan ting* are more important on the structural and aesthetic levels than the ideological. The conclusion to the play, in which the marriage of Mengmei, now the leading candidate in the imperial examination, and Liniang finally receives imperial and parental sanction, strongly suggests that Neo-Confucian principle should be supplemented rather than replaced by the dynamic, regenerative power of *qing*.[105] Although the two philosophical visions are presented as antithetical in the first half of the play, Tang brilliantly uses the comic structure of the finale to bring them into harmony by showing the power of *qing* to reinvigorate orthodoxy and make it more responsive to individual circumstances. The artifice of containing the lovers' illicit sexual relationship within a dream permits Tang Xianzu to achieve the impossible: Liniang keeps her chastity while giving herself in passion; she thereby transforms her transgressive and daring show of authentic passion into a triumphant expression of her moral nature. Her spontaneous love is both passionate and moral. Tang's preface to the play spells out the transcendent metaphysical power of *qing*:

> The origins of *qing* are unknown, but it runs deep. The living can die of it; the dead can be reborn with it. If it cannot cause the living to die or the dead to be resurrected, it is not supreme *qing*. . . . Human affairs cannot be fully experienced within human life. I am not one who has full understanding, and I cannot consistently use principle (*Li*) to comprehend all things. How can it be known that where principle (*Li*) cannot be is where *qing* must be. (*MDT*, p. 1)

Here *qing* cannot be translated simply as "love," for although *qing* is expressed in its most narrow form as romantic love in the play, its import is more akin to the dynamic life force that generates Liniang's miraculous resurrection. Tang Xianzu's use of *qing* in *Mudan ting* was deeply influenced by

105. For a similar statement made by the scholar Chen Jiru (1558–1639) in a 1623 preface to *Mudan ting*, see W. Y. Li, *Enchantment*, pp. 60–61.

the late Ming re-evaluation of concepts of desire; he was an admirer of Li Zhi and a student of Luo Rufang, the unconventional *jinshi* who was a disciple of the illiterate Yan Jun.[106] In Luo Rufang's synthesis, *qing* is identified as the energy that drives cosmic vitality; for him, the ultimate universal good is not the ordered regularity of principle, as it is in Neo-Confucian metaphysics, but the constant generation of life (*shengsheng* 生生) in all its varied manifestations. *Qing*, in its more mundane and intimate forms of love and passion, is the axis through which humans participate in this dynamic and intrinsically moral cosmic process of regeneration.[107] The love affair between Liu Mengmei and Du Liniang metonymically encompasses this expanded metaphysical definition of *qing*; Tang Xianzu, however, exploited *qing* in the more restricted sense of romantic love, as a way to structure the play around the conflict between Du Liniang and her parents.

Mudan ting enshrined gardens as an essential component of the late imperial iconography of *qing*. The garden in *Mudan ting*, on which the Grand Prospect Garden (*Daguan yuan* 大觀園) of *Honglou meng* is based, endowed the literary garden with a new structural and ideological meaning. The garden in *Mudan ting* is a literal *mise-en-scène* of *qing*, an architectonic rendering of the protagonists' affective selves that encodes everything within its walls with the rhetorical valence of *qing*. Within this aesthetic construction, the garden takes on a symbiotic relationship with its occupants. Although readers of *Mudan ting* first see the garden through Liu Mengmei's oneiric gaze, the space comes to life through the combined sensibilities of the refined Du Liniang and the earthy Chunxiang. As is frequently seen in dramas, Tang Xianzu uses the character of Chunxiang to split Liniang's character in half: the transgressively sexual, performed by the maid, which Liniang eventually disavows; and the transcendently sensual. The girls discover the enchanting garden when Chunxiang goes outside to urinate (*MDT*, 7.27). As I have discussed elsewhere, in traditional Chinese fiction the image of a woman urinating is a trope that frequently initiates or stands in for some sort of sexual transgression.[108] In this instance, Chunxiang's trip into the garden to empty

106. See C. T. Hsia, "Time and the Human Condition," esp. pp. 249–51; Xu Shuofang, *Lun Tang Xianzu*, esp. pp. 1–4, 21–23; and P. K. Cheng, "Reality and Imagination."

107. *MRXA*, 34.2a; *Records*, pp. 187–88.

108. See Epstein, "Inscribing the Essentials." Another detail in this scene that hints at transgression is the entry of Liniang into the garden either late in the second or early in the third month; this raised the possibility of the double-three date (the association between the third day of the third month and women's transgression is discussed in the following chap-

her bladder motivates Liniang's entrance into the garden. Whereas Chunxiang enjoys the garden's beauty, Liniang is literally enraptured when she sets foot there and is immediately swept into a "spring dream," a euphemism for a sexual dream. The older characters also find in the garden a reflection of their own attitudes toward *qing*. Although Prefect Du obliquely refers to a garden when inviting Tutor Chen to join him in a scholarly drink, he seems never to have entered the garden of Liniang's dreams. As for Chen, he claims never to have strolled through a spring garden. And in striking contrast to the vibrant and compelling atmosphere Liniang finds in the garden, her mother describes it as a deserted, decaying, and threatening wilderness filled with malevolent spirits (*MDT*, 11.50).

Before the late Ming, the Chinese literary garden was more likely to invoke a rhetoric of ethics than one of desire. As Andrew Plaks has written, literary gardens existed along a continuum, anchored on one end by gardens as a place of almost numinous encyclopedic fullness, as celebrated in the *fu* poetry that catalogues the richness of imperial domains, and on the other by the garden as site of retreat from the injustices and corruption of bureaucratic service, exemplified by Tao Yuanming's Peach Blossom Spring.[109] Both ideals connote a rhetoric of virtue; the lushness of the former is both reward for and proof of a ruler's ability to assemble and govern "all under heaven"; the latter is a more intimate reflection of the integrity of the hermit who deliberately chooses straitened purity over corrupting ambition. Even though the aesthetics of the literati garden were by no means naturalistic, gardens were appreciated as a microcosm or summation of the metaphysical forces of nature because of the way they foreground the dynamic processes of complementary *yinyang* bipolarity and five-elements periodicity.[110] Literati gardens were frequently encoded within a moral frame that linked the proper progression of the seasons, or an eternal spring, to virtuous behavior or that constructed specific seasonal markers, such as autumn chrysanthemums or the four friends of winter (those four species of tree that flourish in the harshest cold), as emblems of an indomitable moral spirit. Whether situated within primarily Daoist or Confucian sensibilities, these literary

---

ter). Scene 9, entitled "Sweeping the Garden" 肅苑 ("Suyuan"), alludes to the Qingming holiday, traditionally a time to sweep family tombs; by the late imperial period, the symbolism of the double-three date and Qingming had merged.

109. Plaks, *Archetype and Allegory*, p. 150.

110. Ibid., pp. 43–53.

gardens were idealized spaces in which privileged individuals could demonstrate their personal and political integrity.

Even those erotic encounters that took place in gardens were incorporated into a moral framework based on allusions to the encounter with the goddess on Mount Wu.[111] As in the *Chuci* tradition, the sexual act, in which the goddess willingly gives herself to her lover, is proof of the man's virtue. However, since Liu Mengmei is practically incidental to the lovemaking in *Mudan ting*, their sexual union in the garden asks to be read as a reflection of Liniang's passion rather than of Mengmei's virtue. He can be said to stand in for all romantic young scholars; the only quality that sets him apart from other young men is Liniang's willingness to give herself to him.

In addition to invoking timeless ethical and metaphysical truths, the literati garden was also a setting in which scholars could showcase their cultural achievements. The owner's taste would be shown through the artful arrangement of rocks, plants, structures, vistas, paintings, and curios in ways that transformed them from the level of mere objects or acquisitions into a statement of aesthetic values. As important as the objects themselves was the scholar's ability to turn the garden into a living oasis of culture by gathering a community of like-minded cognoscenti who engaged in displays of poetic and artistic talent and knowledge that evoked deep resonances with the cultural tradition. This cultural aspect of the literati garden was a favorite theme of Ming and Qing textual representations of gardens. The cultural knowledge and aesthetic judgment that made it possible to transform what might be dismissed as a crass display of wealth into an exquisite display of refined taste distinguished a true literatus from the parvenu, an issue of great concern during the socioeconomic expansion of the late Ming and Qing.[112] Although a merchant-turned-gentry, such as Ximen Qing of *Jin Ping Mei*, might be able to purchase the best of Chinese material culture, he would fail to legitimate his access to culture unless he could envelop his purchases in a patina of cultural refinement.

According to the Confucian view, talent (*cai* 才), the ability to reproduce established patterns (*wen*) that were anchored in cultural tradition and moral purpose, reflected a person's moral worth. Under the influence of the late Ming cult of *qing*, connoisseurship, the sympathetic ability to appreciate

111. Ibid., p. 151.

112. For a discussion of the importance of taste and connoisseurship as strategies to legitimate social status during the late Ming, see Clunas, *Superfluous Things*.

cultural worth, became just as important a marker of literati identity as cultural production itself (a subject examined in more detail below). More so than in *Mudan ting*, the idyllic gardens in *Honglou meng*, *Jinghua yuan*, and Shen Fu's 沈復 (1763–after 1809) *Fusheng liu ji* 浮生六記 (Six records of a floating life) are settings for poetry competitions and exhibitions of literati knowledge. Each illustrates the importance of the garden as a venue, protected from any taint of political ambition, in which to demonstrate one's cultural sensibilities and accomplishments.

Although the display of talent in the garden of *Mudan ting* is comparatively sparse, with the exception of Du Liniang's self-portrait, it does provide Liu Mengmei a setting in which he can express his appreciation of and enthusiasm for the previously undiscovered beauty and passion of Du Liniang. Unlike other romances, in which the love affair between scholar and beauty inspires an exchange of verse or music, Du Liniang and Liu Mengmei do not compose poetry for each other. However, from the readers' and audience's perspective, the characters' lack of literary production is more than offset by the elegant and richly intertextual lines Tang Xianzu composed for them to sing. Du Liniang's painting, in which she captures the essence of her beauty, is a perfect icon of *qing*; through this self-reflexive image, Liniang transcends her flawed corporeal state and becomes an immortal representation of unobtainable beauty and desire.[113] The qualities of absence, loss, illness, and ephemerality associated with beauty all enhance the affective power of *qing*.[114]

Although the garden in *Mudan ting* is both an idealized "natural" retreat from repressive social demands and an apolitical site for lyric self-expression, its primary function is to give Liniang a stage to voice her emotions fully.[115] Like the affective correlative of European romanticism, the garden serves as

113. In a parodic reversal of the usual narrative in which a painted image of a goddess appears to a scholar as a flesh and blood woman, Liu Mengmei mistakes Liniang's portrait for the image of the goddess Guanyin or Chang'e (scene 26).

114. Loss, absence, and sickness as motifs associated with *qing* are discussed in Plaks, *Archetype and Allegory*, pp. 62–63, 75; W. Y. Li, *Enchantment*, pp. 171–75; and Zeitlin, "Shared Dreams."

115. In the terminology of Yu-kung Kao ("Lyric Vision," pp. 227–30) and Wai-yee Li (*Enchantment*, esp. pp. 222–25), the garden is a spatialized representation of the central protagonist's "lyric consciousness," which they describe as a state of heightened emotional self-awareness wherein time is suspended and the individual strains to overcome the boundaries between self and other in order to encompass the totality of existence.

a symbolic extension of her affective state. For example, the passage of the seasons, illustrated through the flourishing and decay of vegetation in the garden, parallels Liniang's merged emotional and physical states: her passions blossom in the spring; she begins to yearn for her unfulfilled passion as the flower petals drop in the summer; desolate, she wastes away and dies just as autumn turns to winter; Liu Mengmei revives her, and the two are finally reunited in the spring. The following autumn, the lovers separate again when Mengmei leaves to pursue his career. Significantly, given the affective importance of the seasonal details throughout *Mudan ting*, the comic resolution, which reinscribes the lovers' transgressive passions within an orthodox framework, is strangely atemporal. Even though the scenes directly preceding the conclusion are filled with images of late autumnal gloom, the final scene, in which the emperor personally incorporates their unconventional love affair into the imperial order, literally glows with the radiance of imperial splendor as "sun and moon radiate Heaven's virtue" 日月光天德 (*MDT*, 55.260). The triumph of orthodoxy is shown by its power to stabilize the unpredictable mutability of both time and passion into an utopic state of eternal spring.

Much of the iconography of *qing* employed in Tang Xianzu's *Mudan ting* is carried to an even more rarified aesthetic level in Wu Ren's 吳人 *Three Wives' Commentary to "Peony Pavilion"* (*Wu Wushan sanfu heping Mudanting huanhun ji*, 吳吳山三婦和評牡丹亭還魂記), published in 1694, in which the voices and actions of his three stunningly beautiful wives merge into one text.[116] In his preface to the commentary, Wu follows *Mudan ting* in blurring the lines between text and life by explaining how the first of his three wives, Chen Tong 陳同, to whom he was betrothed, was obsessed with *Mudan ting* and wrote a commentary to it, of which only the first volume survived. Her untimely death was seemingly caused by her excessive passion for the play.[117] Although Chen Tong passed away before they could actually marry, Wu managed to obtain this one remnant of her writings and was so moved by it that, like Liu Mengmei on discovering Liniang's portrait, he began to mourn his loss. In turn, Wu Ren's second wife was so taken with Chen Tong's commentary that she added her own annotations to the second volume of

116. See Zeitlin, "Shared Dreams," pp. 132–36; and Ko, *Teachers of the Inner Chambers*, pp. 69–71.

117. For the ability of the play to trigger a fatal response in susceptible readers, especially women, see Zeitlin, "Shared Dreams," pp. 130–31.

the play in a style identical to that of her dead counterpart. Wu Ren was so enchanted with the product that he circulated a transcription of the joint commentary under his own name in order to protect the identities of the two women. Unfortunately, his second wife also died in the bloom of her youth, but her literary reputation was secured by Wu's third wife, who selflessly volunteered to sell her own jewelry in order to see that the precious commentary was republished and properly attributed to the two women. This final edition includes annotations by this third of Wu Ren's talented wives.

As Judith Zeitlin has pointed out, the circumstances surrounding the lives and deaths of Wu Ren's three wives bear a striking resemblance to the life and death of Xiaoqing, a beautiful and young concubine who herself seems to have been modeled on Du Liniang. Xiaoqing became a *cause célèbre* after her untimely death, which resulted from her emotional fragility. The circumstances of Xiaoqing's death actualize the passions of *Mudan ting*. She was driven to death in part by the jealous attacks of her husband's primary wife and in part by her own enervated state after reading *Mudan ting*.[118] A double martyr to the two emotional complexes of empathy and virtuous resentment, Xiaoqing follows Liniang in her devotion to passion. Only after her death did this unknown concubine assume a culturally significant existence, for her death, like Liniang's, was proof of the depth and selfless purity of her emotions. The historicity of Xiaoqing, 小青, whose name is a rebus for *qing* 情, has been debated from the seventeenth century to the present; however, as Ellen Widmer argues, much of her appeal derives precisely from the way her characterization straddles the conventions of fiction and historiography.[119] One of the signature features of late Ming narratives of *qing* is the way they challenge the ontological boundaries between reality and fantasy, history and fiction.[120] The blending of history and art in the production of Xiaoqing and the *Three Wives' Commentary* made of the tragic lives of these women a text better than fiction.

Wu Ren, in particular, employed so many of the conceits associated with *qing* in the joint biography of his three wives that it is tempting to read his project as a sequel that surpasses *Mudan ting* by pulling the fictionalized passions of the drama even further into the realm of reality by having actual women re-enact many of its most important tropes. Whereas Du Liniang's

118. Ibid., p. 129.

119. Widmer, "Xiaoqing's Literary Legacy," p. 131.

120. Also discussed in W. Y. Li, *Enchantment*, pp. 47–50.

claims to moral purity are undercut by her dreamed sexual relationship with Liu Mengmei, the shared passion of the three wives is desexualized, made completely selfless, and projected into the realm of artistic production. Each of Wu Ren's wives becomes the intellectual and emotional soulmate to her predecessor(s), and the affective power of their bonds is magnified with each tragic loss. The three wives are more talented along conventional literary lines than is Liniang; but like her, they sacrifice themselves for an ideal of love, leaving behind only a textual memory. As with Liniang, these talented women are carefully protected from any taint of ambition or vanity; Wu Ren, too, protects himself from the charge that he might be exploiting their talents by attributing the motivation for publishing their writings entirely to the third wife's desire to honor her older sisters. Wu Ren, like Liu Mengmei, is both patron and voyeur of the consuming passions engendered by these women's artistic sensibilities, even as true *qing* remains the exclusive domain of women. Moreover, the wives outdo Liniang in combining physical frailty with unusual talent, a stereotyped attribute of *qing*; whereas the poignancy of *Mudan ting* is necessarily limited by the comic ending of the drama, Wu Ren's first two wives are irrevocably lost and exist only through the sympathetic memories of their admirers.

Although ephemerality and lack are important features of the aesthetics of *qing* that informed the tragically young deaths of many talented beauties in Ming and Qing romances, it is important to note that the transitory nature of *qing* is balanced by its ability to transcend the limits of both death and reality. A favorite theme of Ming-Qing fantasies of *qing* is the painting or image of the beauty that comes to life.[121] Although it is passion that causes Du Liniang to waste away and die, it is also passion that allows her to flourish in her various transformations as daughter, painted image, ghost, and wife. The most remarkable transubstantiation of all occurs in the serial projection of Liniang onto Wu Ren's three wives. Although Chen Tong died before Wu Ren had a chance to see her, her exact likeness appears in Wu's dreams for three consecutive nights. And parallel to the process in which Liniang's self-portrait becomes a substitution for her corporeal self,

121. In the case of *Honglou meng*, Baoyu refuses to differentiate between paintings or stories about beautiful women and the women themselves. See, e.g., the scenes in which Baoyu thinks that a painting has come to life (*HLM*, 19.187) and believes an old lady's story about a beautiful statue come to life. In his words, "Although this kind of person [a beautiful girl] may have died, she is not dead" 這樣人是雖死不死的 (39.416–18).

traces of Chen Tong's passionate spirit can be seen on her one surviving manuscript, which seems to glisten almost as if her tears and calligraphy were still fresh.[122] As suggested by the multiplication of the singular Liniang into three wives, *qing* is so powerful a fantasy that it does not lose intensity as it is exponentially reproduced; in fact, each additional loss only serves to magnify the pathos. Although there is no evidence that Cao Xueqin knew the *Three Wives' Commentary*, the autobiographical frame, the vast list of characters who embody one or more aspects of *qing*, and the multilayered blurring of boundaries between illusion and reality in *Honglou meng* demonstrate that he had mastered these compositional techniques. These successful narratives of *qing* create highly aestheticized illusions that clothe lyric desire in flesh and blood so alluring that readers want to make it true.

Many of the iconographic markers associated with *qing* in *Mudan ting* reproduce the traditional *yin* symbolism so prominent in the writings of Dong Zhongshu. That the imagery of *qing* is based on the feminine, the sensuous, the private, the mutable and unstable, the sick or dead, the phantom and illusory, in contrast to the solid, orthodox stability of *yang*, may have lent these often fantastic narratives a sense of credibility, if only because of the familiarity of the *yinyang* symbolic logic. Even though the rhetoric of *qing* stands certain Neo-Confucian values on their head, especially the call to subordinate individual desires to a rigid moral code, its symbolic logic builds on the paradigms of orthodox narrative that had long codified desire as a *yin* and female trait linked to the transgression of boundaries. This deep cultural association between *qing* and *yin* had a profound impact on the meanings projected onto the feminine in the aesthetics of *qing*.

Gender, Wit, Performativity, and the Construction of Lyric Identity

One paradoxical aspect of the concept of *qing* during the late imperial period was that it was simultaneously associated with a philosophical school that promoted authenticity of self-expression and an aesthetic movement that prized wit, illusion, and enchantment. As Wai-yee Li has so masterfully articulated, writers' and readers' commitment to and fascination with the aesthetic surface of texts parallel the intensity of emotional engagement so fundamental to the cult of *qing*.[123] Fictional texts such as *Mudan ting*, Dong

122. Zeitlin, "Shared Dreams," p. 134.
123. W. Y. Li, *Enchantment*, pp. 160–62.

Yue's seventeenth-century *Xiyou bu*, and most especially *Honglou meng*, each a detailed exploration of the theme of *qing*, delight in developing intricately structured narrative patterns. In contrast to orthodox writings, which proposed a singular and universal truth, the fiction and drama of the late Ming embraced paradox and wit in ways that challenged the claims of Confucian discourse to a monopoly on virtue.[124] The compositional priority given to surface aesthetics in narratives of *qing*, especially through the techniques of doubling, inversion, and paradox, over the development of clear didactic plots creates dazzlingly patterned texts that undermine the epistemological and ontological boundaries between fiction and history, orthodoxy and heterodoxy. I defer a full treatment of this topic until the discussion of *Honglou meng* (see Chapter 4); for now, I focus on the dissolution of gender boundaries in narratives of *qing*.

As writers of fiction and drama moved further away from the historiographical roots of *xiaoshuo* in favor of exploring and exploiting the craft of fictionality, they began to incorporate images of actors, masks, and plays-within-plays into their elaborately structured narratives. It is no coincidence that references to theatricality and performance abound in narratives of *qing*, for the cult of *qing* emerged during that period of the late Ming when literati were increasingly interested and involved in the writing, publication, and production of drama and fiction. The influence of drama had significant implications for the depiction of gender in fiction because of the highly constructed system of gender used in staged performances. Since actors specialized in certain role types, regardless of the sex, gender, or age of the character, stage identities were not rooted in the actor's physical characteristics but were conveyed through performative conventions. As in Elizabethan drama, playwrights playfully manipulated the disjunctures between actor and character. Hu Yinglin 胡應麟 (1551–1602) described *chuanqi* drama as a "literature of play" based on paradox and inversion of the familiar.[125]

Gender switching, one of the most striking features of late imperial fiction and drama to an early twenty-first-century eye and the central issue I explore

124. In Keith McMahon's (*Causality and Containment*, p. 3) words, "The xiaoshuo tells us that the orthodox way is never as interesting as what strays from that way, that the story is interesting precisely because it shows how to stray. Once that is said, it is necessary to emphasize that the xiaoshuo is not purely heterodox, nor is orthodoxy necessarily so narrow."

125. Cited in W. Y. Li, *Enchantment*, pp. 87–88*n*. See also her reference to Tuo Shi, who admires the playwright Xu Wei's "reversal of name and reality" (*diandao mingshi* 顛倒名實).

throughout this book, became a common form of inversion.[126] In the didactic *Xingshi yinyuan zhuan*, the shrew Sujie's appropriation of power is depicted as fundamentally transgressive because of the way it threatens the stability of the social order. In contrast, the gender-bending in pro-*qing* fictions is more a witty flourish that adds new twists to conventional plots than a commentary on power. As I shall argue of the mid-Qing novels *Honglou meng*, *Yesou puyan*, *Jinghua yuan*, and *Ernü yingxiong zhuan*, reversals of gender roles, although never entirely losing their counterhegemonic edge, gradually became incorporated into fiction as an uncontroversial aesthetic inflection. Xu Wei's 徐渭 (1522–94) well-known *zaju* 雜劇 drama *Nü zhuangyuan* 女狀元 (The female first-place candidate), about a woman who disguises herself as a man and takes first place in the imperial examination, is an example of a play that adds a simple twist to a conventional topic. Wang Jide's 王驥德 (d. 1623) *zaju* drama *Nan wanghou* 男王后 (The male queen) exemplifies the tendency to manipulate gender as an aesthetic device in these Ming comedies of error.[127] A young soldier, Chen Zigao 陳子高, is played by a *dan* 旦 role. The actors who specialized in *dan* roles typically played young female leads and came to define the elite ideal of femininity. Captured by enemy soldiers, the beautiful Zigao is told to dress as a woman. The enemy king becomes smitten with him and makes Zigao his queen. The king's sister also falls in love with the new queen, but after discovering that Zigao is a man, she forces him, still disguised as a woman, to marry her in secret. The king eventually sanctions their marriage in order to preserve his own access to Zigao, and Zigao resumes his identity as a man. By the end of the drama, although Zigao's gender is stabilized as male, his sexual identity, as lover to both brother and sister, continues to be fluid. Moreover, the incongruity of a feminine *dan* role playing a male character remains. The self-reflexive layering of gender inversions and shifting pairs of lovers completely destabilizes any link between the sex of the actor and the fluid gendering of Zigao. In *The Male Queen*, Wang Jide treats gender as a performative aspect of Zigao's character that, like a mask, can be donned or removed to enrich the aesthetic texture.[128]

126. Discussed in McMahon, "The Classic 'Scholar-Beauty' Romance"; K. I. S. Chang, *The Late-Ming Poet*, p. 15; and M. Huang, *Literati and Self-Re/Presentation*, pp. 82–83.

127. For a discussion of the doubled identities and homoerotics of the play, see Volpp, "The Male Queen," pp. 63–65.

128. Although Wang Jide's monograph on dramatic writing, *Qulü* 曲律, deals more with questions of prosody than structure (and thus does not comment on structural or thematic inversions), in it he does draw associative links between various complementary paired terms

More so than any fiction writer, Li Yu, among the most inventive and witty storytellers and dramatists of the seventeenth century, delighted in using gender and sexual inversions as a way to create multiple plot twists in his cleverly structured works.[129] His female characters regularly outsmart their male counterparts, and some plots contain characters who change sex or engage in homosexual and lesbian liaisons, while the narrator slyly argues for the moral and social propriety and even superiority of these inverted practices.[130] The playfulness of Li Yu's treatment of gender in his narrative fiction may in part have been due to the close connection between his narratives and his dramas; his stories are filled with references to the structure and conventions of drama, and Li Yu is unique in simultaneously publishing his work in short-story and dramatic form.[131] Several links connect Li Yu to the traditional novel. Although there is no proof that Zhang Zhupo knew Li Yu's writings (Li Yu was an acquaintance of Zhang's father, however), Li's name appears on the title page of some of the Zhang Zhupo commentary editions of *Jin Ping Mei*.[132] Li Yu was also connected to the grandfather and great-grandfather of Cao Xueqin, and his name is mentioned in the Red Inkstone commentary.[133] That Cao Xueqin originally conceived *Honglou meng* as a *chuanqi* drama rather than a *xiaoshuo* fiction might in part explain his use of multiple layers of gender inversion. The ideological implications of the playful and highly constructed aesthetics of gender in late Ming *zaju* and

---

that are alternated as part of the aesthetic design, such as *yin* and *yang* tones, or oral (*kai* 開) and nasal (*bi* 閉) pronunciations, which he metaphorically links to gender. For example, he writes: "A character (*zi* 字) that has open and nasal pronunciations is like *yang* encompassing *yin*, male encompassing female" (*Qulü*, p. 98). Each section of the monograph illustrates how Wang conceptualized prosodic features in terms of maximizing aesthetic complementarity. By frequently inserting examples of "male" and "female" pairs as concrete expressions of *yin-yang* complementarity, Wang Jide rendered the aesthetic more "natural" and compelling.

129. See Hanan, *The Invention of Li Yu*, esp. pp. 76–110; and Volpp, "The Discourse on Male Marriage."

130. See, e.g., "A Female Chen Ping Saves Her Life with Seven Schemes" 女陳平計生七出; "A Male Mencius' Mother Educates His Son and Moves House Three Times" 男孟母教合三遷; "A Daughter Is Transformed into a Son Through the Bodhisattva's Ingenuity" 變女爲兒菩薩巧 (all in *Wusheng xi* [Silent operas]); "The House of Gathered Refinements" 萃雅樓 in *Shi'er lou* (The twelve towers); and for lesbianism, the drama *The Fragrant Companion*, 憐香伴.

131. For four stories Li Yu transposed as dramas, see Hanan, *The Invention of Li Yu*, pp. 17–18, 138–42.

132. Rolston, *Traditional Chinese Fiction*, pp. 43, 59.

133. Ibid., p. 59.

chuanqi drama are radically different from the gender inversions in those *xiaoshuo* narratives that are genealogically and hermeneutically closer to the more orthodox genres of history and ritual.

The interchangeably beautiful and talented protagonists in scholar-beauty romances (*caizi jiaren xiaoshuo* 才子佳人小說) seem to have been particularly influenced by the aesthetics of drama. As we shall see in subsequent chapters, the inverted and fluid gender roles of drama became normative in Qing sentimental fiction, even in those works that seem to promote a conservative Confucian agenda. However, the feminization of gender roles within the aesthetics of *qing* is less an attempt to challenge normative gender roles than the naturalization of the feminine as the most appropriate site in which to represent *qing*. Indeed, the cultural markers of femininity became such an important attribute of *qing* that the trademark feminine beauty (*mei* 美) of the idealized male scholars in these romances should be seen as a corporeal manifestation of *qing*. The power of *qing* to feminize underlay the emotional and physical transformation of the male ideal in seventeenth- and eighteenth-century fiction from virile leader to gentle, introspective aesthete who is as beautiful as the women he hopes to marry and who searches for personal and emotional fulfillment through romance and poetry rather than through a public career as scholar or statesman.[134] This gradual process of feminization culminated in the stereotyped pairs of lovers in scholar-beauty romances who are interchangeable in looks and talent.[135]

Even though much of the gender fluidity in late Ming and Qing narratives can be explained as an aesthetic choice, the resulting inversions in which the socially debased—women, and more pointedly, courtesans—were

134. Keith McMahon (*Causality and Containment*, pp. 52–59) has pointed out the seventeenth-century replacement of the virile and gruff *haohan* 好漢 protagonist by the effeminate *fengliu* 風流 type: unlike his coarse predecessors, this light-skinned, delicate, and beautiful man is sensitive and open to subtleties and opportunities.

135. See Hessney, "Beautiful, Talented and Brave," p. 5. McMahon discusses the symmetry of the beauties and scholars in "The Classic 'Scholar-Beauty' Romance," p. 234. *Yesou puyan* contains one pair of lovers whose oddly speckled bodies are physically identical (83.2a). The vocabulary for beauty is so closely associated with the feminine that there does not seem to have been a separate vocabulary to discuss male beauty, as can be seen in the humorous presentation of male beauty in Chapter 30 of *Rulin waishi*. For texts that attempt to distinguish male from female beauty, see Li Yu's story "Nan Mengmu," trans. by Hanan in *Silent Operas* as "A Male Mencius' Mother Raises His Son Properly by Moving House Three Times," pp. 97–135. Also see Chen Sen's late Qing homoerotic novel, *Pinhua baojian* 品花寶鑒, esp. chap. 1, pp. 11–12.

suddenly endowed with higher claims to truth and purity frequently enjoyed a certain ideological power to challenge and disrupt accepted ethical structures. This polemical use of gender can be seen most particularly in the writings of the Gong'an 公安 School, also known as the School of Native Sensibility (*xingling pai* 性靈派) of the three Yuan brothers, Hongdao 袁宏道 (1568–1610), Zongdao 袁宗道 (1560–1600), the most important of the three, and Zhongdao 袁中道 (1570–1624). Perhaps more than any other late Ming belletrists, the Yuan brothers exploited the counterhegemonic values associated with *qing*. In many of their essays, they follow Li Zhi's polemical style in promoting the socially abject as the morally superior. The three were friends and admirers of Li Zhi, and their writings form an important bridge between the textual worlds of philosophy and belles lettres.[136] Gender was just one of an associative matrix of terms they used to undermine and destabilize traditional values; in the same way as the playful gender inversions in drama, their references to women and the feminine are abstractions in which the feminine stands for whatever orthodoxy is not, rather than referring to some essential female quality.

Although the Gong'an school was active for only a short time, from 1595 until Zongdao's death in 1600, it was very influential among the circles of late Ming writers and publishers who experimented in the production of new types of prose, including brief essays (*xiaopin wen* 小品文), vernacular *xiaoshuo* novels, and story collections.[137] The brothers met Li Zhi in 1593 and discovered many common interests; they subsequently introduced many of Li's ideas into the literary forum. What was spontaneity of experience (*dangxia*) for Li Zhi became spontaneity of poetic expression for them. Yuan Zongdao, in an essay entitled "On Prose" ("Lunwen" 論文), which André Lévy has described as a "manifesto" for the Gong'an School, argued against slavish imitation of famous literary models in favor of a more spontaneous

136. Biographies for all three can be found in *DMB* under Yuan Hongdao, pp. 1635–38. Also see Chou Chih-p'ing (Zhou Zhiping), *Gong'an pai*, translated as *Yüan Hung-tao*; Lynn, "Tradition and the Individual"; see Chaves, *Pilgrim of the Clouds*, for translations of poems and essays by all three brothers. Hung, "Yüan Hung-tao"; A. Lévy, "Un document"; and Vallette-Hémery, *Théorie et practique*, includes a study and translations of several important essays and prefaces. Chinese references are to Yuan Hongdao, *Yuan Zhonglang quanji*.

137. For a discussion of the Yuan brothers' involvement in the circulation of early manuscripts of *Jin Ping Mei*, see Plaks, *Four Masterworks*, p. 67; A. Lévy "About the Date"; and Hanan, "The Text," p. 39.

self-expression.[138] He saw formal and stylistic rigor as potentially impinging on the expression of genuine sentiments. Yuan Hongdao followed Li Zhi and Xu Wei, the author of *The Female First-Place Candidate*, in making spontaneity, authenticity, and sensualism the slogans of the Gong'an movement. He was also a great admirer of and advocate for Xu Wei's theory that emotion is the essence of literature and that poetry is the refined expression of emotion.[139] Yuan Zhongdao in particular valued straightforward language, by which he meant a more colloquial idiom with less emphasis on allusion and form. Emotionally direct expression was more authentic and therefore more powerful as a way of affecting readers than was mimicry of past forms.[140] The following quote from Hongdao suggests an organic basis for authentic writing.

> If the emotions are authentic (*qing zhen*), the language will be straightforward. Therefore men who are troubled or women filled with yearning sometimes surpass scholars. . . . Although sickness cannot serve as literature, the emotions associated with sickness are enough to be used as literature. It is not that the emotions associated with sickness are all literature, but that the literature of sickness has no false ornamentation. This is why all people value sickness.[141]

Rhetorically, the passage echoes Li Zhi's style in the way it reverses normative values in order to arrive at the contentious claim that illness is good. Furthermore, similar to *Mudan ting*, it bases authenticity on the ability to feel emotions and associates a deficiency or weakness (here associated with illness and the frailty of the female sex) with a heightened intensity of emotion.[142]

138. For a translation of Zongdao's "Lunwen," see A. Lévy, "Un document," p. 255. For the Chinese, see Yuan Hongdao, "Xu Xiaoxiu shi," in *Yuan Zhonglang quanji*, "Wenchao," p. 6. This passage is remarkably similar to Li Zhi's discussion of the relativism of historical judgment in his "Zongmu houlun," in *Cangshu*, p. 61 (trans. in de Bary, "Individualism and Humanitarianism," p. 201). This admiration for stylistic authenticity can also be found close to a century earlier in the writings of Li Mengyang 李夢陽 (1472–1529), who also searched for the authentic in songs and poetry (see Lévy, "Un document," p. 253).

139. Chou, *Yüan Hung-tao*, pp. 17–21.

140. Yuan Hongdao, "Xu Xiaoxiu shi," in *Yuan Zhonglang quanji*, p. 5.

141. Yuan Hongdao, "Tao Xiaoruo Zhenzhongyi yin," in *Yuan Zhonglang quanji*, "Wenchao," p. 14. Zhongdao also described his brother's illness as having enhanced his sensibilities in "Xu Xiaoxiu shi," ibid., p. 6.

142. See Furth, "Blood, Body and Gender," pp. 50–51, for a medical treatise that cites female emotionality as one of the reasons women are more vulnerable to serious diseases.

Self-expression through an authentic literary style was not enough; self-expression was best extended into performances of taste and style. The individualistic philosophy of the Gong'an School fits into what James Cahill has described as a wave of eccentricity during the late Ming in which the unconventional became a sign of authenticity.[143] Although iconoclastic and eccentric behavior had historically been an accepted and expected aspect of *qing*, the trope seems to have reached new heights of self-reflexive performativity during the late Ming.[144] As important as demonstrating one's own unique qualities was the ability to appreciate the eccentric behavior of others. Yuan Hongdao's admiring essay on the old drunkard who eats nothing but scorpions, centipedes, and larvae clearly expresses his appreciation of "authentic" behavior.[145]

This appreciation for the authentic was frequently demonstrated through a passionate appreciation for and desire to collect physical objects; the more unique, transgressive, and obsessive the passion the better.[146] Women were a popular object of fascination; as shown so clearly by Wu Ren's collection of three unusual wives, a man could easily transform his passion for a woman into a statement of his taste and social values, sometimes with serious implications.[147] In Hongdao's refined words, women are just one aspect of connoisseurship.[148] "Pleasure (*qu* 趣) is like the color of a mountain, the flavor of

143. J. Cahill, *Fantastics and Eccentrics.*

144. For earlier associations between *qing* and individualism, see Yingshi Yu, "Individualism and the Neo-Taoist Movement," esp. pp. 137–40. See also the description of Zhang Dai's 張岱 (1597–1679) pointedly pointless late night performance of *Dream Memories of Dao'an*, in W. Y. Li, *Enchantment*, pp. 47–48.

145. Yuan Hongdao, "Cuisou zhuan," in *Yuan Zhonglang quanji*, "Wenchao," pp. 2–3 (trans. in Chaves, *Pilgrim of the Clouds*, pp. 110–12).

146. Chou, *Yüan Hung-tao*, pp. 99–100.

147. Several influential late Ming and Qing aesthetes took women on as students. The highly individualistic painter Chen Hongshou 陳洪綬 (1598–1652) painted a scholar with two female students (see J. Cahill, *Fantastics and Eccentrics*, pp. 36–37); Li Zhi and Yuan Mei were attacked for their open relationships with women as students and friends. In literature this eccentric behavior is mimicked by Jia Baoyu; Du Shaoqing of *Rulin waishi*, who appears in public walking hand-in-hand with his wife; and the first-person narrator of Shen Fu's *Fusheng liuji*, who introduces the topic of his wife as the first and most important of a series of objects he appreciates.

148. For the connoisseurship of women, see Carlitz, "Desire, Danger, and the Body," pp. 122–24.

water, the radiance of flowers, the bearing of a woman."[149] The same sensual enactment of taste can be observed in Jia Baoyu's obsession with girls (and for that matter, in the conversations of latter-day enthusiasts of the novel, who continue to argue for their favorite among the girl cousins). The aesthetic of the obsession (*pi* 癖) did not disappear with the collapse of the Ming; the figure of the impassioned collector runs as a motif through the writings of both Li Yu and Pu Songling 蒲松齡 (1640–1715).[150] A splendid parody of the pursuit of an eccentric hobby as a way to express the core of one's spiritual worth appears in *Yesou puyan* in the anecdote about a man so attuned to his kennel of dogs that he learns to distinguish them by the taste of their feces (*YSPY*, 72.8a–b). It seems that the more obsessive the interest, no matter how transgressive (and perhaps the more transgressive the better), the more expressive it is of an authentic, untrammeled self. As we shall see in the discussions of *Yesou puyan* and *Ernü yingxiong zhuan*, the whole nexus of performative qualities associated with *qing* became regularly equated with moral authenticity and, ironically, became used as shorthand to imply integrity of character even in those texts that reject many of the premises of the cult of *qing*.[151]

Popular Culture and the Commercial Appeal of Qing

Thus far I have discussed the discursive roots of the cult of *qing* and their relation to the aesthetics of gender; more materialist studies have shown, however, that the affluent, highly literate, and increasingly commercial urban culture of the late Ming Jiangnan region also played a crucial role in reshaping social values and aesthetic tastes. The merchant backgrounds of Wang Gen and Li Zhi, two of the most radical Taizhou intellectuals, underscores the importance of the changing economic and social conditions to the spread of the late Ming philosophical interest in materialism, pragmatism, individualism, and direct expression of emotions.[152] With the weakening of the central authority during the last century of the Ming, a culture of self-

149. Yuan Hongdao, "Xu Chen Zhengfu huixin ji," in *Yuan Zhonglang quanji*, "Wenchao," p. 5.

150. See Zeitlin, *Historian of the Strange*, pp. 61–74.

151. For more on the performative aspects of authenticity, see W. Y. Li, "The Late Ming Courtesan," pp. 53–60.

152. For an economic argument for the late Ming changes in social values, see Lu Kan, "Shi lun Mingdai"; see also Yu Yingshi, *Shi yu Zhongguo wenhua*, pp. 524–40.

indulgence and decadence flourished in the wealthy cities of the Jiangnan region.[153] Even though the majority of the upwardly mobile continued traditional patterns of legitimating economic privilege through the cultivation of orthopraxy and classical learning, this growing market for leisure reading materials hastened the breakdown of a clear distinction between orthodox and popular texts.

The impact of the rapid spread of print culture in the Jiangnan region on emerging late Ming moral and aesthetic values is only just beginning to be evaluated.[154] The cities of Jiangnan and Fujian, where most of the commercial publishing houses were located, were far from the more conservative and regulated center of political control in Beijing. Although little is yet known about the regional or historical specifics of reader reception or consumption in premodern China, it seems likely that the sophisticated audiences of the urban centers of Jiangnan, whose taste for popular entertainment had been shaped in large part by the witty dramas produced during this period, demanded a higher degree of titillation, in terms of sensualism, novelty, and perhaps even irony, than did audiences in other parts of the empire. The growth of commercial publishing as well as developments in modes of production had a significant impact on the blurring of boundaries between once distinct genres. An example of this is the way the late Ming *Lüchuang nüshi* 綠窗女士 (Women scholars of the green windows) casually intersperses *The Four Books for Women*, a staple of women's moral education, with piquant tales from the lives of courtesans.[155] As Katherine Carlitz has written, the fact that the same printing houses were simultaneously publishing exemplars of virtuous women and tales of romance literally changed the face of virtue. Female virtue, as was true of so many other facets of women's lives, became an aestheticized object of connoisseurship that enhanced the commercial value of romances by giving them a veneer of respectability; in a parallel process, didactic anthologies absorbed materials that once would have been considered too risqué for inclusion.[156] A collection of stories that emerged from this hybrid publishing culture was Feng Menglong's *Qingshi lei lüe* 情史類略 (An anatomy of *qing*).[157]

153. Ho, "The Salt Merchants of Yang-chou," pp. 155–56.

154. See Hegel, *Reading Illustrated Fiction*, esp. pp. 13–17.

155. Discussed in Carlitz, "Desire, Danger, and the Body," p. 122.

156. Carlitz, "The Social Uses of Female Virtue."

157. *Qingshi* was most likely published during the 1640s or 1650s, several decades after it was compiled. The confusion in dating exists because there is no extant Ming edition, and neither of the two prefaces is dated; the latest date appearing in the anthology itself is 1617.

The prefaces and commentary to this extensive anthology package the collection as an exposition on *qing* and promote the philosophical claim that *qing* can lead to moral renewal, even though many of the anecdotes themselves are more voyeuristic than exemplary.

Feng Menglong was extremely active and commercially savvy as a writer, commentator, and publisher in Suzhou. Unlike Tang Xianzu and the Yuan brothers, who wrote for an elite circle of literati readers, Feng consciously strove to appeal to a broad audience.[158] Moreover, Feng, like Li Zhi and the Yuan brothers, was in the vanguard of the movement to promote the vernacular as a more authentic and affective form of writing; he associated the vernacular with the expressive power of *qing*. Despite the philosophical and moral defenses of his writings inserted in the prefaces to his collections, Feng Menglong's publishing efforts seem on occasion to have been driven as much by a desire for profit and pleasure as by artistic or ideological concerns.[159] These attempts to appeal to an audience whose tastes were shaped by the more flexible standards of popular culture rather than the stricter discursive standards of canonical writings allowed Feng's work to reflect hybrid urban values. Whereas in other works the truly *qing*-crazed are stereotypically unmoved by, and even disdainful of, references to anything as utilitarian as money, Feng assimilated commercial culture into the cult of *qing*. In the first preface to *Qingshi*, he uses cash as a metaphor for *qing*:

The myriad things are like unstrung coins,	萬物如散錢
Qing is the cord that binds them together.	一情爲線索
When the scattered coins are at last bound together	散錢就索穿
Those at the ends of the world become one family.[160]	天涯成眷屬

Qing, elsewhere treated as an ethereal and transcendent force, has become the stuff of mercantile relations.

Hanan (*The Chinese Vernacular Story*, p. 95) dates the compilation of the anthology itself to before 1631. Hua-yuan Li Mowry ("Ch'ing-shih," p. 452) dates the compilation to no earlier than 1626. Selections from *Qingshi* are translated in Mowry, *Chinese Love Stories*. For a discussion of Feng Menglong's use of the concept *qing*, see Hsu, "Celebrating the Emotional Self."

158. See Hanan, *The Chinese Vernacular Story*, pp. 77–78.

159. Other critics have referred to this ideological compromise as Feng's split personality; see ibid., pp. 80–81. Carlitz ("Desire, Danger, and the Body," p. 122) calls him a "literary chameleon" for his simultaneous involvement in producing expurgated versions of *Mudan ting* and more ribald compilations. Feng's interest in promoting sales of *Shuihu zhuan* may also have spurred him to attribute commentaries to Li Zhi (Plaks, *Four Masterworks*, p. 516).

160. Feng Menglong, *Qingshi*, Preface, pp. 8–9.

Feng's loose arrangement of extant materials into a compendium of *qing* suggests that the polysemous concept was enough of a curiosity and commodity to justify the publication of such a lengthy anthology. Although many of the entries do not directly reflect the late Ming aesthetic of *qing*, the prefaces and majority of the comments boldly state their claims for the philosophical centrality and orthodoxy of *qing*. For example, the second preface begins with the assertion, "All Six Classics use *qing* to teach [the Way]." The collection mimics canonical form in its arrangement into linked biographies: *Qingshi* contains over 850 biographies and anecdotes in classical Chinese, organized thematically into twenty-four chapters.[161] Significantly, the first section is entitled "*Qing* and Chastity" ("Qingzhen" 情貞), as if to dispel any fears that this anthology might confuse *qing* with wanton sexuality. Less edifying materials are saved for later chapters entitled "The *Qing*-Passionate" ("Qing'ai" 情愛), "The *Qing*-Crazed" ("Qingchi" 情痴), "Degenerates of *Qing*" ("Qinghui" 情穢), and "*Qing* Succubae" ("Qingyao" 情妖). Needless to say, the examples of romance illustrated in the tales are not as socially or morally redemptive as the two prefaces would suggest. In the style of historiography, judgments follow many of the entries, and longer comments conclude each chapter. These concluding remarks are signed "Master of *Qing*," 情主人 or "Historian of *Qing*," 情史氏; although many of the signed comments are consistent with the prefaces in treating *qing* as a uniformly positive concept, others carefully distinguish between *qing* and those passions that can lead to self-delusion. "The Historian of *Qing* says: *Qing* generates love (*ai* 愛), and in return love generates *qing*. Just as *qing* and love generate each other without end, there must be incidents of death and destruction. Those without mishap are fortunate" (6.506).

Whatever the motives for the compilation and publication of the anthology, the prefaces to *Qingshi* represent an audacious defense of an idealized *qing* that is frequently at conflict with the content of the collection. For example, the author of the first preface, Zhanzhan waishi, 詹詹外史, one of Feng's pseudonyms, exploits the positive connotations of *qing* in his introduction of himself as someone selflessly "*qing*-crazed":

> It has always been one of my ambitions to compile a history of *qing*, and ever since I was a young man, I have been known to be *qing*-crazed (*qingchi* 情痴). In dealing with my friends and my equals, I always pour out my heart, sharing with them in

161. For a list of these 24 chapters, see Mowry, "*Ch'ing-shih*," pp. 40–42.

both good times and bad. Whenever I hear about a person who is in unusual straits or is suffering a great wrong, even though I may not know him, I always seek to help; if I do not have the power to help, I sigh for days and toss and turn sleeplessly at night. When I see a person of *qing,* I desire to bow before him. (Preface, pp. 1–2)

This daring advocacy of *qing* in the preface is tempered throughout the collection by an overwhelmingly conservative vision of the dangers of *qing.* For example, despite the proud self-introduction of Zhanzhan waishi in the preface, each of the twenty biographies in the chapter entitled "The *Qing*-Crazed" elucidates the Confucian teaching that indulgence in *qing* leads to self-destruction. The post-chapter comment begins, "All of men's troubles and worries are generated from having *qing*" (7.542). In other places, the language of the preface and comments makes use of the polemical rhetoric associated with the late Ming critique of institutionalized Neo-Confucianism: "The Historian of *Qing* says: Ever since ancient times, when acts of loyalty, filial piety, chastity, and heroism are performed out of principle (*DaoLi*), they are necessarily forced (*mianqiang* 勉強). However, when performed out of utmost *qing* (*zhiqing* 至情), they are necessarily thoroughly authentic (*zhenqie* 眞切)" (1.82).

Despite the passionate tone of the commentary, the anthology reproduces the traditional Confucian values of filiality and chastity and reinforces a suspicion that *qing* is not always positive. The prefaces clearly state the anthology's didactic purpose: "I have also desired to select the most beautiful acts of *qing,* both ancient and contemporary, and write up a brief narrative for each, to let people know that *qing* can endure and thereby transform those without *qing* into people of *qing* and selfish (*si* 私) *qing* into impartial (*gong* 公) *qing*" (Preface, p. 4).

I quote at length from the first preface to show the extent to which Feng Menglong substitutes *qing* for the now-discredited principle as the central moral truth, remaking *qing* as an objective standard.

Had Heaven and earth had no *qing,*	天地若無情
They would not have produced the myriad things.	不生一切物
Had the myriad things had no *qing,*	一切物無情
They would not engage in the cycles of generation.	不能環相生
Life gives birth to life without being extinguished,	生生而不滅
Because *qing* itself is not extinguished.	繇情不滅故

The four great elements all are but illusion,	四大皆幻設
Only *qing* is neither empty nor false.	惟情不虛假
With *qing* the distant are close,	有情疏者親
Without *qing* the intimate become distant.	無情親者疏
Between those with *qing* and those without *qing*,	無情與有情
The difference is immeasurable.	相去不可量
I desire to establish a school of *qing*	我欲立情教
To teach all who have been born,	教誨諸衆生
So that a son will face his father with *qing*,	子有情於父
And a subject will face his lord with *qing*. (Preface, pp. 7–8)	臣有情於君

In addition to ensuring the continuation of life, *qing* has become the foundation of both principle and ritual, rather than their antithesis.

In anticipation of my discussion of the hybrid romances *Yesou puyan* and *Ernü yingxiong zhuan*, which blend the conventions of scholar-beauty and knight-errant narratives, the sections of *Qingshi* in which *qing* is shown to motivate heroic deeds are of particular interest. The section entitled "Knights of *Qing*" ("Qingxia" 情俠) transforms the usual chivalric ethics of morally superior heroes from a code of personal honor (*yi* 義) to one based on *qing*.[162] This interest in knights-errant may in part reflect the influence of the lives and teachings of Wang Yangming and those leading Taizhou figures, such as Wang Gen, Yan Jun, and He Xinyin, who preached a more activist ethics.[163] The heroic figures celebrated in *Qingshi* display two qualities associated with late Ming redefinitions of *qing*: an instinctive ability to respond to those in need and the understanding that authentic morality must come from an individual standard that frequently needs to break with established rules of propriety in order to reinstate a proper order. That almost half the biographies in the "Qingxia" section feature female knights-errant is a reflection of the strong cultural association linking *qing* with the feminine and the unconventional. As we shall see in the discussions of *Yesou puyan*, *Jinghua yuan*, and *Ernü yingxiong zhuan*, eighteenth- and nineteenth-

162. Discussed in ibid., p. 108, and W. Y. Li, *Enchantment*, pp. 90–91.

163. For example, Li Zhi's master Wang Gen, a commoner from a farming background who held no degrees but went on to found the Taizhou School, organized the local wealthy to distribute grain during a famine in 1523; see *DMB*, p. 1383. See Hanan, *The Chinese Vernacular Story*, pp. 78–79, for a discussion of Feng's popularization of the biography of Wang Yangming.

century authors mixed the conventions of knight-errant and scholar-romance novels to create new models of authentic morality.

The *qing* referred to in *Qingshi* is so powerful that it inspires people to sacrifice themselves for others (*juan* 4 and 5) and stimulates animals and plants to selfless acts of loyalty and compassion (*juan* 23). The ability of *qing* to transcend boundaries between nature and culture is further emphasized in the final section, "Traces of *Qing*" ("Qingji" 情蹟), in which the various forms of lyric poetry are likened to the expressive songs and cries of birds and insects. Although neither the prefaces nor the contents of *Qingshi* break new ground in developing the philosophy or aesthetics of *qing*, the collection testifies to the broad appeal of *qing*, in all its shifting meanings and manifestations. The appeal of the collection seems to have derived in part from the paradoxical ability of *qing* to destroy and redeem, to transgress and revitalize. The careful apologetics of *qing* in the prefaces and commentary to *Qingshi* reveal that Feng Menglong and the others involved in the compilation and publication of the anthology were fully cognizant of *qing*'s subversive and creative potential and that this dynamic paradox imbued the discourse of *qing* with a marketable fascination.

The lines in the ideological and aesthetic battles between the proponents of *qing* and the adherents of Neo-Confucian orthodoxy seem to have been drawn most sharply during the late sixteenth and early seventeenth centuries. This period was marked by a rapid growth of material wealth and the expansion of printed texts, conditions that weakened the social and ideological cohesiveness of the early Ming. These diffuse challenges to the hegemony of traditional routes to respectability created a greater tolerance for the relatively individualist, anti-establishment, and sensual values associated with the cult of *qing*. The lengthy reign of the Wanli emperor (r. 1573–1619) was so marked by decadence and corruption that imperial rule ground to a halt; this no doubt added further impetus to the interest in developing standards for individual moral and social worth independent of state-controlled institutions. However, as shown by the conservative Confucian critique of the status quo adopted by the Donglin faction and the growing interest in the pragmatics of statecraft and activist engagement, as well as the intellectual movement away from Cheng-Zhu Neo-Confucian philosophy in favor of classicism and evidential studies, the cult of *qing* was just one among many reformist attempts to reinvigorate late Ming elite values. Although interest in statecraft and evidential studies continued into the Qing dynasty, the collective soul-searching brought on by the shock of the humiliating defeat of the Ming dynasty to the culturally inferior Manchus spelled an end to the philosophical interest in *qing*, an intellectual movement that came to be blamed for contributing to late Ming self-indulgent decadence. Many late Ming intellectuals questioned the moral integrity and intellectual validity of the basic premises of Neo-Confucianism and began imagining possibilities of a more humanist and activist social order that decentered Neo-Confucian principle. The philosophical defense of emotions, even those acknowledged as selfish, as a positive and fundamental part of human nature led to an impassioned heralding of the unorthodox, the private, the individual, and the eccentric.

The great flourishing of prose fiction during the late Ming drew inspiration from this multifaceted critique of orthodox Neo-Confucianism, and the new fictional protagonists achieved success less through the traditional economic or bureaucratic routes to power than through unconventional but authentic acts of self-expression as lovers, aesthetes, and heroes. A new class of hybrid fiction blended the conventions of individualist and activist knight-errant fiction with the lyric expressions of scholar-beauty romances.[164] The protagonists of these works are depicted as having an authentic morality; their rebellious actions and emotions represent a corrective to the spiritually empty gestures of stereotyped scholars and bureaucrats who try to profit from an increasingly ineffective and corrupt status quo.

Despite the vilification of the proponents of *qing*, their legacy lived on into the Qing dynasty. Certain of their challenges to idealist Cheng-Zhu metaphysics were incorporated into the mainstream of Qing materialist philosophy. More important to this study was the direct importation of the rhetoric of *qing* into all genres of fiction; as we shall see, a broad nexus of terms associated with the cult of *qing* became standard iconographic elements of fiction. Many of the sentimental narratives written during the Qing dynasty imagined a reinvigorated moral order and sense of self based on the subjective and dynamic qualities of *qing*. The feminine enjoyed a privileged position within this aesthetic of resistance and reform; fictional characters, male and female, freely adopted feminine personae as part of their nonconformist performances of authenticity. In *Honglou meng*, *Jinghua yuan*, and

164. Among these hybrid novels, I count *Haoqiu zhuan*, *Rulin waishi*, *Jinghua yuan*, *Yesou puyan*, and *Ernü yingxiong zhuan*.

Ernü yingxiong zhuan, it is the female characters who offer the promise of cultural and political redemption. Rather than being a straightforward celebration of women's lives and talent, the cult of *qing* signaled a literati appropriation of the feminine and the female subject position. *Qing*, or a character's capacity for *qing*, is expressed through physical, emotional, and intellectual attributes that include beauty, artistic talent, purity of intent, emotional empathy, and passion, as well as physical frailty. Within this context, the feminine became an essential attribute of *qing*. However, even though their plots rely on the regenerative potential of *qing*, each of the novels discussed in the following chapters concludes with a return to the normative Confucian social order and the re-establishment of traditional patriarchal social structures.

CHAPTER THREE

Xingshi yinyuan zhuan: Orthodoxy and the Making of the Shrew

> If there is a master in the center (*zhu yu zhong* 主於中), external depravity (*waixie* 外邪) cannot enter. —Zhu Xi

> Men and woman have an order of superiority and inferiority; husbands and wives have a principle of leading and following. These are constant principles. If people follow their feelings, give free reign to desires, and act because of pleasure, men will be driven by their desires and lose their strength of character, and women will covet pleasure and forget their place of following. Consequently, there will be misfortune, and none will benefit. —Cheng Yi

These two epigraphs from the Neo-Confucian handbook *Reflections on Things at Hand* make clear the logic of the Neo-Confucian discourse that improper desires open the door to disaster. Within orthodox narratives, the ultimate responsibility for the maintenance of domestic order lies with the male members of the household; women are treated less as subjects of their own moral cultivation than as reflections of the moral failures or virtues of their fathers or husbands. This view is confirmed in the writings of several seventeenth-century writers who explained antagonism between a husband and his wife as a result of the man's moral deficiency. Lü Kun, for example, wrote that men ruined their wives by indulging them.[1]

EPIGRAPHS: Zhu Xi: *JSL* 4.17b. Cheng YI: *JSL*, 126a–b; trans. based on *Reflections*, p. 272.

1. Lü Kun, *Guifan tushuo*, 1.13b–14b. Yenna Wu ("Marriage Destinies," pp. 118–20) notes other late Ming explanations for the problem: Feng Menglong blamed shrewish women on male weakness, Xie Zhaozhe 謝肇淛 (fl. 1592–1607) attributed jealousy to karmic retribu-

The figure of the shrew, because of her power to threaten normative Confucian social structures on a number of levels, became emblematic of the breakdown of the sociopolitical order within orthodox discourse. Chinese shrews are most often beautiful young women who use their sexual attractiveness to dominate men; their beautiful exterior hides a power-hungry, cruel, jealous, and degenerate nature. Some, however, with their big feet, coarse features, and slovenly dress, are as ugly and unregulated as their natures. These young wives or concubines, at the center of the home or imperial court, are perfectly situated to invert, and even shatter, the proper functioning of familial and state relations. The Chinese terms for shrew, *yinfu* 淫婦, *hanfu* 悍婦, and *pofu* 潑婦, highlight shades of difference unremarked in the English usage. Central to the characterization of the *yinfu* is her insatiable sexual desire; the *hanfu* is a vicious and ferocious harpy. Least well defined are the particular attributes of the *pofu*; as Keith McMahon has described her, she is a woman who "spills" or "splashes," whose behavior, like the various liquids she scatters, is unconstrained, transgressive, and frequently polluting.[2] These categories are not exclusive; depictions of shrews frequently combine characteristics from each type or build on implied associations.

The late Ming, early Qing novel *Xingshi yinyuan zhuan* 醒世姻緣傳 (Marriage bonds to awaken the world) is remarkable for the ways it brings its anxieties about self-cultivation and social stability directly to the surface of the text through the persona of the shrew. The plot and structure of *Xingshi*, a didactic story of karmic retribution, are fairly conventional in terms of its usage of orthodox rhetoric, although it goes further than almost any other text in its development of the character of the shrew. The twenty-chapter prologue shows how a dissolute and weak-willed young man named Chao Yuan 晁源 sets in motion a karmic cycle by killing a fox-spirit (*huli jing* 狐狸精).[3] Chao Yuan's name can be glossed as the "source."[4] He in turn is murdered in chapter 19 by the husband of a woman with whom he is having an adulterous affair. Chao Yuan is reborn as Di Xichen 狄希陳, and the

tion, and Shen Defu 沈德符 (1578–1642) suggested that men had ceded power to their wives so that the women would not speak against them.

2. See McMahon, *Misers*, p. 55; for a lengthy exploration of the jealous nature of the shrew, see Y. Wu, *The Chinese Virago*.

3. For translations and summaries of the first twenty chapters of *Xingshi*, see C. C. Wang, "Marriage as Retribution."

4. Plaks, "After the Fall," p. 566.

fox-spirit returns as his wife Xue Sujie 薛素姐. Throughout their marriage, Sujie torments Xichen: she beats and burns him, ties him up for days, and eventually drives his parents to death. Xichen tries to escape his fate by marrying Jijie 寄姐, a woman who had always been friendly to him; but because Jijie is the reincarnation of his own wife, whom Chao Yuan had earlier driven to suicide, she, too, turns against him. In the final chapters of the novel, Xichen finally chants the *Diamond Sutra* and brings the cycle of retribution to completion: Sujie dies, and Xichen and Jijie live into ripe and contented old age, surrounded by their children.

Despite numerous attempts to identify "The Scholar of Western Zhou" Xi Zhou sheng 西周生, the pseudonymous author of *Xingshi*, little is known about the authorship or the date of the novel. Based on similar uses of Shandong dialect in Pu Songling's vernacular writings, the fact that several key sections of the narrative are set in the counties of Shandong in which Pu lived, and that there are thematic similarities to the story "Jiang cheng" 江城 in *Liaozhai zhiyi* 聊齋誌異 (Strange tales from Make-Do Studio), Hu Shi tentatively ascribed the novel to Pu Songling.[5] However, the Pu Songling attribution is largely circumstantial, and it has come under question. Wang Shouyi dates the first edition to the Chongzhen period (1628–44) based on the avoidance of Ming taboo characters and reflections of institutional changes.[6] Recently, based on linguistic, biographical, and thematic evidence, Zhang Qingji has argued that *Xingshi* was written by Ding Yaokang, the author of the *Xu Jin Ping Mei*.[7] The question of authorship will likely remain unsolved until an early edition with clear biblio-

5. Hu Shi, "*Xingshi yinyuan zhuan*" *kaozheng* 醒世姻緣傳考證. The claim of Pu Songling's authorship is, of course, dependent on the dating of the first edition of the novel. Based on internal evidence, Sun Kaidi and Hu Shi proposed that the first edition was printed during the Kangxi period (1662–1723); Hu Shi argued that the flood scene was based on a flood that took place in Shandong in 1703 and caused mass starvation and cannibalism. The theory of Pu's authorship had already gained currency by the 1880s; the famous publisher Bao Tingbo 鮑廷博 (1728–1814) supposedly attributed *Xingshi yinyuan zhuan* to Pu Songling (see Deng Zhicheng, *Gudong suoji*, j. 7, p. 235). Liu Ts'un-yan ("Introduction," pp. 6–11) follows Hu Shi and Sun Kaidi in attributing the novel to Pu Songling.

6. Wang Shouyi, "*Xingshi yinyuan zhuan* de chengshu niandai." For a thorough review of the authorship debate see Y. Wu, "Marriage Destinies," chap. 1; and Chen Bingzao, "Pu Songling ye shi Xi Zhou sheng ma?"; and briefly, Plaks, "After the Fall," pp. 554–56.

7. Zhang Qingji, "*Xingshi yinyuan zhuan*" *xinkao*; Xu Xialing ("*Xingshi yinyuan zhuan*"), while admitting Ding may have been involved in the publication, suggests that the author was Jia Fuxi 賈凫西.

graphic information surfaces. The earliest mention of the book is found in the 1728 catalogue of Chinese books imported into Japan, the *Hakusae shomuku* 舶載書目.[8]

All attempts to date *Xingshi* place it well after the circulation of the *Jin Ping Mei cihua* in the early seventeenth century and most likely after the 1695 publication of the Zhang Zhupo commentary to the 100-chapter *Jin Ping Mei* since there are both stylistic and thematic indications that the author of *Xingshi* was familiar with *Jin Ping Mei*. Andrew Plaks has noted that despite *Xingshi*'s meandering structure, the 100-chapter novel roughly breaks into 10-chapter segments, which, like *Jin Ping Mei*, climax in the chapters ending with nine.[9] Although not as tightly structured as *Jin Ping Mei*, *Xingshi* does mimic that novel's use of mirroring chapters, so that, for example, Chao Yuan's killing of the fox-spirit with an arrow in Chapter 1 is framed by Sujie's attempt to shoot Xichen with an arrow in Chapter 100 (Sujie, of course, being the reincarnation of the fox-spirit).[10] We enter into the main fictional world of *Jin Ping Mei* with the opening of Ximen Qing's garden in Chapter 20; Chao Yuan's death in Chapter 20 neatly divides the prologue from the main narrative in *Xingshi*. Other stylistic similarities mentioned by Plaks are the use of irony, the frequent repetitions of certain themes or topoi, figural recurrence, and the use of prosy verse summaries to introduce a chapter rather than the conventional inclusion of vaguely related poems.[11] Thematically, *Xingshi* also mimics *Jin Ping Mei* in using the character of a shrew to illustrate the male protagonist's self-destructive inability to order his home or control his excessive desires. *Xingshi*, however, surpasses *Jin Ping Mei* in the depiction of conjugal violence and a wife's relentless and sadistic cruelty toward her husband; Pan Jinlian 潘金蓮 is at least capable of acts of kindness and concern. And although *Xingshi* focuses more narrowly on the specific

8. Oba, *Hakusai shomoku*, 30/31.28b–29a.

9. Plaks, "After the Fall," p. 557.

10. There is some indication that the author of *Xingshi* may have borrowed some chapter headings from *Jin Ping Mei*. The second line of the chapter title in chapter 79 of *Xingshi* reads "Jijie raises a ruckus at the grape arbor" 寄姐大鬧萄架; the second half of the couplet in chapter 27 of *Jin Ping Mei* reads "Pan Jinlian raises a drunken ruckus at the grape arbor" 潘金蓮醉鬧葡萄架. The swing scene in chapter 97 of *Xingshi* hints at the same sexual improprieties as the famous scene in chapter 25 of *Jin Ping Mei*. Furthermore, Plaks ("After the Fall," p. 566) has suggested that the death of the sexually depraved Wang Weilu 汪爲露 in chapter 39 is modeled after Ximen Qing's death in chapter 79.

11. Plaks, "After the Fall," pp. 558–62.

events within the Di household, it, too, depicts the male protagonist as a microcosm of the larger political environment.

Although *Xingshi* is less skillfully crafted than the accepted masterworks of *xiaoshuo* fiction, it is methodologically important to establish the structural, stylistic, and thematic similarities between it and *Jin Ping Mei* in order to legitimate readings of *Xingshi* as somehow engaged with the same late Ming literati debates about the nature and issues of personal responsibility as *Jin Ping Mei.*[12] Like *Jin Ping Mei, Xingshi* is one of the many novels from the late Ming and Qing that can be read as a fictional exegesis on the process of self-cultivation. Ximen Qing 西門慶 of *Jin Ping Mei* provides a deadly example of what can happen if a man does not try to contain his desires through self-cultivation. At another extreme, the scholar-turned-monk in the seventeenth-century *Rou putuan* 肉蒲團 (Prayermat of flesh) resorts to self-castration as a shortcut to mastering his corporeal desires. Di Xichen of *Xingshi* falls between these two models; although Xichen is almost destroyed by Sujie, he manages to triumph over her when he finally achieves enlightenment. Furthermore, as in *Jin Ping Mei,* images of women and sexuality are central to the symbolic vocabulary of self-mastery in this syncretic Neo-Confucian parable.

Xingshi features one of the fiercest shrews in all of Chinese literature; from the moment of their marriage, Xue Sujie is locked in a literal life-and-death struggle with Di Xichen. The battle between the two is not resolved until the hundredth and final chapter of the novel when Xichen finally learns to control his desire by chanting the *Diamond Sutra.* Unlike *Jin Ping Mei,* in which the struggle for power in Ximen Qing's household is interwoven with the search for sexual pleasure, Sujie's battles with Xichen are never confused with a desire for sexual gratification. Although the narration of their conflict is sexualized, sex is clearly a metaphor for other issues. As the narrator states explicitly, Sujie and the chain of karmic events in the novel that threaten to destroy Xichen are a manifestation of the male protagonist's troubled psyche: "The ghosts and strange things that Chao Yuan [Di Xichen's prior incarnation] saw were born from his own guilty conscience (*kuixin* 虧心). All along it was not that real ghosts were disturbing

12. For a Neo-Confucian interpretation of *Jin Ping Mei,* see Plaks, *Four Masterworks,* esp. pp. 156–80; in contrast, David Roy ("Introduction," in *The Plum in the Golden Vase,* esp. pp. xxiv–xxxii) links the novel to the philosopher Xunzi's pessimistic view of human nature.

him" (*XS*, 17.177). Sujie, with all her ferocious energy, is a creation of Xichen's unrestrained desires.

The shrew, the epitome of uncontrollable destructive energy, is central to the theme of self-cultivation narrated in *Xingshi*. Sujie's body, which is repeatedly stripped and displayed, reveals the inescapable corporeality of human existence through the ways that her physical nature resists the socializing discipline of ritual. In one episode, Sujie shamelessly refuses to veil herself when visiting a temple and is beaten and completely stripped, even of her foot bindings, by a group of local youths (73.790). Not long after, she is even further deprived of any veneer of propriety. On the occasion of her birthday, Sujie dresses a pet monkey in Xichen's clothing and begins to beat it (76.825). After Sujie begins to beat it, the monkey attacks her and rips the flesh on her face, blinding her in one eye and tearing out a nostril, suggestively leaving two gaping holes along the bright red lips which split her face, earlobe to earlobe. After disfiguring Sujie, the monkey continues its frenzied attack that extends the sexualized subtext. Mistaking Mrs. Long (龍氏), Sujie's mother, for her, "[The monkey] jumped off the roof onto Mrs. Long's shoulders, struck her face and pulled her hair, and bored down between her legs, tearing her leggings to shreds" (76.825). In an intensification of the sexualized attack by the youths who had stripped Sujie in the temple, the monkey seems to be attempting to unmask Sujie of any guise of humanity. A suggestive parallel to this attack can be found in a macabre anecdote in Yuan Mei's anthology on the weird entitled *Zi bu yu* 子不語 (What the Master [Confucius] would not discuss). In this story a strange creature, half-ape and half-human, kidnaps and murders a woman, leaving large scars on her lips and ripping open her vagina (*yinchu kuilie* 陰處潰裂).[13] In the Yuan Mei anecdote, the wounds on the woman's face are explicitly linked to her sexual organs, a connection that is only hinted at in *Xingshi*. One character later refers to Sujie's "stinking (*bi* 屄) face" (87.939), using a term for vagina that Sujie had earlier invoked to curse her mother-in-law (64.693).

Although the indomitable Sujie "loses face" after this scene, her power and presence are anything but diminished. She continues to circulate in the world of the novel as a cipher of transgression. Despite Xichen's requests that the women keep themselves hidden from the people in the neighboring yamen, Sujie insists on swinging above the level of the wall, which incites the

13. Yuan Mei, "Da maoren juenü" 大毛人攫女, in *Zi bu yu*, p. 123; discussed in Epstein, "Inscribing the Essentials."

neighbor to send over a series of poems, the last two of which mock her disfigurement (chap. 97). In contrast to the body of a virtuous woman, which is invisible to those outside the family, Sujie's body, like a gaping wound that resists suppression, is repeatedly exposed and thrust into the public gaze. In this sense, the transfiguration of Sujie parallels the grotesque description of the foreign monk who sells Ximen Qing aphrodisiacs in chapters 49 and 50 of *Jin Ping Mei*;[14] Sujie has become the embodiment of female sexuality.

INVERSIONS OF ORTHODOXY: *XINGSHI* AND FAILED SELF-CULTIVATION

Xingshi illustrates what happens to human relations when those who should be in control abdicate their responsibilities. Chao Yuan's inability (or unwillingness) to contain his sexual desires in the prologue sets in motion an elaborate parable detailing the dangers of loss of self-mastery. Although Di Xichen's transgressions are not as overtly sexual as those of Chao Yuan, transgressive sexual desire runs as a motif through the novel. As we shall see, the conflict between Xichen and Sujie is sexualized in a number of indirect ways. An example of this is the figural association between Xichen and monkeys, already hinted at in the scene in which Sujie abuses a monkey she has dressed in his clothing.[15] Monkeys were a frequent motif in seventeenth-century fiction and used to symbolize the restless energy, often sexual, of the unenlightened mind, as in the proverbial expression "Monkey of the mind, horse of the will" (*xinyuan yima* 心猿意馬).[16] The mind-monkey refers to

14. The monk is the color of purple liver, is wearing a flesh-red robe, has a beard bristling out from under his chin, a shining pate, and a jade column of mucous running from his nose. When Ximen Qing first approaches him, the monk's head is sunken down to his shoulders; but once aroused, the monk straightens himself up and opens his one sunken eye. The Chongzhen commentary notes that the motion is "not far off from a penis" (*yangwu* 陽物) (*Xinke xiuxiang piping Jin Ping Mei*, p. 635).

15. In addition to the scene where Sujie dresses her pet monkey in Xichen's clothing, Xichen's behavior is described as monkey-like in 37.397 and 50.547. His first illicit affair is with a woman named Sun 孫 (a pun for "monkey" made famous in the monkey Sun Wukong's 孫悟空 name in *Xiyou ji*). In a direct allusion to Sun Wukong, an actress lays an egg that hatches into a monkey (27.286).

16. For a discussion of the legend of the sexual white ape that kidnaps women for its harem, see Dudbridge, *The "Hsi-yu chi,"* pp. 114–28; see also Plaks, *Four Masterworks*, p. 236. Keith McMahon (*Causality and Containment*, pp. 138–40) describes the story "On a Journey to

that part of the ego that must be fixed or stabilized (*ding* 定) during the process of self-cultivation. Xichen's inability to control his own restless nature is reflected in a later scene in which the "apelike" energy of Sujie and the other women of the household wreaks havoc with domestic propriety. A new upright district magistrate, Li Weizheng 李爲政, whose name can be glossed as "ritual makes government," has moved into the yamen next door. Since the women are sensitive enough to issues of "face" that they are afraid Magistrate Li might overhear their vicious fighting, they try to restore a semblance of order. However, the temporary peace does not last long.

How could this group of apelike furies stand this kind of stifling boredom? They cornered Di Xichen and told him [to build a swing]. He got several cedar-wood poles outside, found some thick rope to which he attached a colorful board, and fastened it all together into a tall swing. Sujie was first, Jijie followed; all the mistresses, maids, and nannies spent the entire day monkeying around on that swing, me up you down, you up me down, in an endless cycle of swinging and playing. (97.1050)

The restless "monkeying around" of the women on the swing echoes the sexual undertones of the swinging scene in *Jin Ping Mei* where Pan Jinlian, her double Song Huilian 宋蕙蓮, and the other women of the household vie to outdo each other in the presence of their son-in-law Chen Jingji 陳敬濟 (*JPM*, 25.377).[17] Although there are no overt sexual motivations behind the women's swinging, the sexual undertones to the topos are confirmed by the poems their neighbor, Judge Wu (吳), composes after catching sight of Sujie.[18] In a pattern that is illustrated on a number of levels, although the narrative focus in *Xingshi* is more on grotesque violence than sexual excess, the diffuse employment of motifs traditionally linked to sexual themes keeps the problematic of desire central to the meaning of the novel.

Although the larger political implications of the failure to regulate the self are not as well developed in *Xingshi* as *Jin Ping Mei*, both show institutions at the state and the family levels disintegrating into chaos in the absence of proper leadership. Woven into the prologue of *Xingshi* are details of the

---

Annam a Jade Horse Is Exchanged for Orangutan Velvet" as a satire of containment in which a boy, who is as "hard to contain as a monkey in a cage," riots after he sees a pretty woman.

17. Zhang Zhupo (*JPM*, 25.375) criticizes this scene as "without order, without sequence, without propriety, without morality."

18. It is also suggestive that Judge Wu's two concubines are described as climbing all over him in bed like monkeys (91.986).

Tumu 土木 incident, one of the worst military disasters of the Ming dynasty, in which the Zhengtong emperor 正通 (r. 1436–50) was captured and held for ransom by a much smaller force of Mongol troops.[19] The campaign, whose primary advocate was the eunuch Wang Zhen 王振, the most powerful member of the inner court, unnecessarily took the emperor out of Beijing and temporarily left the country without a ruler.[20] Thematic resonances from this historical incident appear in the lives of both Chao Yuan and Di Xichen, who are similarly plagued by an inability to lead others or engage in self-control. The political implications of Xichen's lack of domestic leadership come to a head in the closing chapters of the novel when Xichen is cashiered from a minor yamen post on the charge that he is unable to regulate his home (*buneng qijia* 不能齊家, 99.1076).[21] Leading up to his dismissal are a number of incidents, including the swing scene, in which Sujie's imperious "dragon nature" (*longxing* 龍性, 96.1047) makes a mockery of Xichen's authority.[22] After receiving a violent beating from Sujie outside the yamen walls, Xichen tries to explain to his neighbor Judge Wu exactly who runs his home: "'The period my concubine was acting as king was when my wife had still not arrived. The one who got me good yesterday was my wife; it wasn't that concubine who used to act as king'" (97.1050). Shortly after this conversation, Sujie pours burning embers down Xichen's back and burns him so badly that he is unable to show up at the court (97.1055). It is this collapse of domestic peace that causes his dismissal.

An anecdote in the same chapter, which tells of the two tribal chiefs who launch attacks on each other when their children's marriage alliance turns sour, further emphasizes the political significance of the failure to maintain harmonious conjugal relations. The tribal feud erupts into a state emergency when three thousand imperial troops are sent in to quell the "insurgency." In a clear illustration of the analogic relationship between the microcosm and

19. See *DMB*, 416–20; and Mote, "The T'u-mu Incident," pp. 243–272; also discussed in Plaks, "After the Fall," pp. 573–74.

20. Wang Zhen appears in *Xingshi* in chaps. 5, 7, 8, 12, and 15.

21. Other examples of familial strife affecting the public sphere include Jijie cutting up the gifts Xichen had planned to present to his superiors at Chengdu (87.937); Sujie publicly charging Xichen with plotting a rebellion (89.960); and Sujie keeping Xichen from his official duties when she whips him bloody (95.1034). For similar examples in *Jin Ping Mei*, see Plaks, *Four Masterworks*, pp. 158–67.

22. At one point Xichen ironically claims that without Sujie he would be without a ruler (*zhu'er* 主兒, 74.803).

macrocosm spelled out in the *Great Learning*, the maintenance of order within the family is necessary to public stability.

Balanced against Xichen's increasing passivity and impotence at home is the growing dominance of his wives, which turns the household into an inversion of the Confucian ideal. As discussed in Chapter 1, many late Ming and Qing Confucian thinkers referred to the husband-wife relationship as the concrete embodiment of a hierarchical *yinyang* duality. Since women are a manifestation of *yin*, they should naturally be subordinate to their husbands. Sujie, by her refusal to fulfill any of her marital responsibilities, becomes a grotesque antithesis of the ideal wife and daughter-in-law. Of the three ways to be unfilial, failure to provide an heir is the most egregious.[23] Not only is Sujie barren, as is typical of shrews, she also tries to destroy the children of the other women in the household. When the maid Tiaogeng 調羹 is elevated to be the concubine of Xichen's father, Sujie accuses both father and son of engaging in an incestuous relationship with her.[24] Sujie throws doubt on the paternity of any child Tiaogeng might bear by claiming that there is no way of telling if it is old Mr. Di's, Xichen's, or even the servant Di Zhou's 狄周 (56.609).[25] In order to prevent the birth of any new rivals to clan property, Sujie then tries to castrate her father-in-law (56.609). When Tiaogeng does bear a son, Sujie's behavior is similar to that of Pan Jinlian after Guan'ge 官哥 is born. She sets off firecrackers by Tiaogeng's window, "beats dogs and grabs chickens" (*dagou naji* 打狗拿雞) in the courtyard to "scare the child to death," and picks fights with Tiaogeng by accusing the child of illegitimacy (76.819). Even as late as the end of the novel, Sujie is scheming of a way to drown the concubine Jijie's son (99.1078).[26]

Sujie's greatest transgression, however, is her lack of filial concern toward either her own or Xichen's parents. Her willful refusal to obey their wishes eventually drives all four parents to their deaths. Her mother and father-in-law are so enraged by her repeated visits to temples that both suffer strokes (56.604), and her mother-in-law dies of rage when she is unable to stop Sujie from torturing Xichen with a pair of pliers (59.643). Not only is Sujie di-

23. *Mengzi*, IVA.26.

24. Tiaogeng's strange name, "ladle," reflects her role as a cook; it may also highlight the contrast between her fertility, in that she can contain something, and Sujie's infertility.

25. Pan Jinlian also questions Guan'ge's paternity (*JPM*, 41.615 and 617, and 48.707).

26. Murdering a rival's child is a shrewish quality perfected by Pan Jinlian, who trains her cat to maul Guan'ge (*JPM*, 59.877); Wang Xifeng 王熙鳳 uses a second shrew, Qiutong 秋桐, to cause her rival You Erjie 尤二姐 to miscarry a male fetus (*HLM*, 69.775).

rectly responsible for her parents' deaths, she prevents Xichen from fulfilling his most important ceremonial duties as eldest son. She "imprisons" him for the duration of his mother's funeral ceremony and releases him only after the initial mourning period has been concluded (60.652). Later, in a perversion of the Mulian story, the Buddhist paragon of filial piety, Sujie prevents Xichen from reciting prayers to lessen his mother's suffering in Hell, even though he has had a vision of her torments (69.750).

Equally egregious is Sujie's violation of the *neiwai* boundary. Her frequent excursions out of the sequestered women's quarters evoke almost as much disgust and horror from the narrator and interdiegetic spectators as her all-out physical attacks on Xichen's person. Iconographically, the most significant of Sujie's outings is the self-contained narrative of her pilgrimage to Taishan in chapters 68 and 69.[27] In terms of *yinyang* numerology, the placement of this episode in the sixties decade of chapters suggests a deliberate attempt to manipulate *yin* themes parallel to the bitter cold in chapters 67 to 69 of *Jin Ping Mei*, which forms the backdrop to Li Ping'er's 李瓶兒 death.[28] One indication that the author of *Xingshi* may have consciously manipulated *yin* iconography here is the presence of a Mrs. Liu Shangren 劉尚仁 as Sujie's companion. Mrs. Liu, unlike other women with the name Liu, who are typically sexually corrupt, is the sole female voice of virtue in this section as her name "Upholding Humanity" suggests. It is she who reminds Sujie that "A husband is Heaven; a foolish man fears his wife, and a virtuous wife honors her husband" (69.744). Chapter 68 begins with a poem warning against allowing the "six classes of women" (*liupo* 六婆) into one's home, and the opening verse in Chapter 69 comments negatively on the mixing of men and women in public (*nannü hunza* 男女混雜).[29] The description of the crowd of women preparing to set out on the pilgrimage to Taishan is an offensive scene of pollution: women are running back and forth "like a pack of dogs," cursing, defecating, menstruating, nursing babies, and yelling orders back and forth (68.742).[30] As will be discussed below, the unruly, leaking female

27. On the extreme irony used in this episode, see Dudbridge, "A Pilgrimage," pp. 234–43.

28. More sophisticated examples of *yin* imagery in the sixties chapters will be examined in the analyses of *Honglou meng*, *Jinghua yuan*, and *Yesou puyan*.

29. For similar comments, see *XS*, 1.10 and 3.22.

30. Dudbridge comments, "The author shares with us all his refined male disgust at the public sight of so much private female business that should be decently concealed at home" ("A Pilgrimage," p. 245). For more on the disruptive nature of women's pilgrimages as seen from the Neo-Confucian male's perspective, see Pomeranz, "Power, Gender."

bodies in this scene are naturalized and foregrounded as emblems of social transgression.

The pilgrimage is simultaneously a moment of triumphant exposure for Sujie and a humiliating loss of face for Xichen. Although Sujie should be in mourning for her mother, she proudly wears all her finery and rides atop a mule with her face exposed. She treats Xichen as a servant, even though he is wearing his licentiate's cap, and forces him to lead her mule. In contrast to Sujie, who makes a great show of exhibiting herself to the throngs of people, Xichen tries to hide his face in his sleeve so that a friend on the side of the road will not recognize him. It is at Haoli, the final stop for the souls of the dead before they enter the underworld at Taishan,[31] that Sujie not only prevents a distraught Xichen from praying for his mother but loudly insults her memory.

The third time Sujie visits a temple is on the birthday of Xiwangmu 西王母, Mother-Queen of the West, on the third day of the third month, a date widely exploited in fiction for its *yinyang* significance. This chapter weaves together three transgressive elements: Sujie's refusal to attend the rituals marking the anniversary of the death of her mother-in law, Mrs. Di; the introduction of Big Sister Cheng 程大姐, a prostitute who quickly befriends Sujie; and Sujie's visit to the Temple of the Jade Emperor.[32] It is significant that the celebration Sujie attends is the birthday of Xiwangmu, for in China this date was a traditional festival day associated with women, and in Japan it continues to be celebrated as the girls' holiday.[33] According to the "Yueling" 月令 (Monthly ordinances) section of the *Book of Rites*, the third day of the third month marks that point of the lunar calendar at which cosmic *yin* energy is at the peak of its strength; this is a critical juncture in the calendrical cycle, for if *yin* fails to cede to *yang* on this date, the cosmic order is thrown into disarray.[34] In Ming-Qing fiction, the date is often associated

31. Dudbridge, "A Pilgrimage," p. 246.

32. The temple name, Yuhuang 玉皇, suggests a pun on *yu* 慾, desire. Wang Guowei ("*Honglou meng* pinglun," p. 250) suggests a similar pun may resonate in the jade of Baoyu's name in *Honglou meng*.

33. See S. Cahill, "Performers and Female Taoist Adepts."

34. Another possible explanation for the association of this date with women was its conflation with the Cold Food Festival (*hanshi* 寒食) and the later Qingming 清明 (tomb-sweeping) holiday. Originally, Qingming was determined by the solar calendar and thus had no fixed date in the commonly used lunar calendar. However, the Yuan dynasty *Sanguo zhi pinghua* records Qingming as being fixed on the third day of the third month (p. 1). Qingming

with periods of political upheaval or excessive female power. Both *Nüxian waishi* and *Jinghua yuan*, two novels in which women usurp male power, begin with a celebration of Xiwangmu's birthday.[35] Chapter 72 begins with the narrator explaining that the interment of Sujie's mother-in-law falls on the double-three holiday. Instead of attending the burial ceremony, Sujie decides to accompany Big Sister Cheng, one of the most sexually depraved women in the novel, to the Temple of the Jade Emperor. The narrative juxtaposes the description of the burial preparations and the long anecdotal introduction of Cheng Dajie. It is during this expedition that a group of thugs recognizes Cheng Dajie as a prostitute and begins to taunt and flirt with both her and Sujie; the young men finally beat and strip them both completely naked (73.790). Although the narrative does not condone the actions of the hooligans, their violence, like that of the monkey who "unmasks" Sujie, provides the necessary orthodox response of punishing and exposing Sujie's lack of ritual propriety.[36]

In addition to breaking down the ritual distinctions between *nei* and *wai*, the shrew also inverts gender roles and challenges the proper hierarchical domestic order. This narrative pattern, in which the male protagonist loses

---

replaced the Lustration Festival (*xi* 禊), also known as the Festival of Purgation (*fuchu* 祓除), which had been celebrated on the third day of the third month. Although the roots and significance of the latter festival are unclear, it was associated with a number of *yin* events, including spring fertility, sexual rites, purification, and the care of the dead (see Bodde, *Festivals in Classical China*, pp. 273–88). Bodde (ibid., pp. 299–301) also describes the Han dynasty "Fire Renewal Festival," which predated the Cold Food Festival and Qingming. The practice of using *yang*-firemakers to renew the fire also indicates a concern for ensuring the dominance of *yang* forces at this critical calendrical moment. For associations of the double-three date with shamanic rites of purification, see Yen, "*Shang-ssu* Festival," esp. pp. 56–61.

35. See the discussions of *Honglou meng* and *Jinghua yuan* for more on the double-three date. As mentioned above, the first precise date mentioned in the *Shuihu zhuan* is the third day of the third month of the third year of the Jiayou reign period (*SHZ*, p. 41). More than evoking a sense of chaos, the double-three date has its strongest connections to illicit sexuality. For example, the notorious swing scene in chapter 25 of *Jin Ping Mei* also takes place on this date. Du Fu's 杜甫 "Liren xing" 麗人行 (Ballad of lovely women), a poem that exposes the excesses of Yang Guifei 楊貴妃 and her cousin, the Chief Minister Yang Guozhong 楊國忠, also begins by mentioning the double-three date. Dong Yue's allegory on the dangers of desire, the *Xiyou bu*, is also set early in the third month (see 1.7a and 2.6a), as is the celebrated dream meeting between the two lovers in *Mudan ting* (*MDT*, 12.44 and 14.63).

36. For a discussion of punitive motifs directed at women who expose themselves in orthodox narratives, see Epstein, "Inscribing the Essentials."

his "will to rule" and is displaced by women or other *yin* actants who destroy the normative order, is repeated in each of the novels discussed in this study. In *Xingshi*, these inversions range from the playful to the destructive. A lighthearted example is the scene where Sujie punishes Xichen and a friend, who have drunk themselves into a stupor, by making up their faces with red and black ink stolen from Xichen's studio and rebraiding their hair in a style worn by young girls (58.632). The theme becomes more serious when Xichen is dethroned and "ruled" by his two dominating wives. An elite wife of the Ming and Qing dynasties was to follow her husband as lord; she was dually contained by her bound feet and the restrictions against leaving the women's apartments of the home. Sujie ties up Xichen and imprisons him in her rooms, while she roams over vast geographical expanses seeking to wreak vengeance on him. A proper woman should be sparing in speech; Sujie curses and yells in public and leaves the boisterous Xichen uncharacteristically silent.[37] Although physically stronger than his wives, Xichen is impotent to protect himself against their abusive treatment. Their usurpation of his privileged position of power within the home leaves him passive and "wife-fearing" (*junei* 懼内).

Inserted in the midst of these perverse images of the collapse of the Confucian social order at the macro- and microcosmic levels is the biography of Chao Yuan's mother, an idealized Confucian matriarch who is the antithesis of Sujie. Sujie refuses to be cloistered and does everything she can to destroy Xichen's family, from attempting to castrate her father-in-law to causing her mother-in-law's death to bleeding the Chao family dry of its savings to interfering in the official business of her husband's yamen. In contrast, Madame Chao is a model of Neo-Confucian containment and household management. Sobered by Chao Yuan's death at the hands of his lover's husband, Madame Chao uses her family's ill-gotten wealth to relieve the suffering of the poor in times of famine and flood. After failing to reform her own son, she raises her husband's concubine's son as her own and makes of the new household a model of ideal Confucian hierarchical order in which the younger generation subordinates itself to the older and wife follows

37. Sujie and the other shrews yell and scream throughout the novel. Although Xichen originally calls for help when being beaten (48.525 and 59.642), he loses the ability to speak (60.652–55, 63.683, and 64.693). His speechlessness peaks when Sujie's arrival in Chengdu makes him faint dead away.

husband. There is not a hint of jealousy or rancor in her treatment of the concubine; her only concern is for the safety of Chao Liang 晁梁, her husband's posthumous heir. In return, this son remains absolutely loyal to her and shows no attachment to his birth mother. Chao Liang sleeps at the foot of Madame Chao's bed and at first refuses to leave her side even to sleep with his wife (49.531–32). Chao Liang's preference for sleeping near his mother rather than his wife seems to be a cliché for demonstrating a son's filial devotion; the motif is repeated in *Yesou puyan*. Theirs is depicted as an ideal mother-son relationship in other ways as well; Chao Liang is prepared to cut the flesh from his thigh to prepare a stew for Madame Chao when she is ill (36.394). Although the government tried to end this cannibalistic practice, the use of one's own flesh was popularly regarded as one of the greatest filial acts a son or daughter could perform for his or her parents since the broth was considered to have miraculous healing powers.[38] Significantly, in a perversion of one of the traditional acts of filiality popularized in the *Twenty-four Exemplars of Filial Piety* (*Ershisi xiao* 二十四孝), Sujie makes Xichen sleep outside the bed curtains to draw the mosquitoes away from her (75.806–7).[39] Unlike Sujie, Chao Liang's modest wife is an exemplary daughter-in-law; she is so respectful of the *neiwai* boundary that we never learn her name. She acquiesces to her mother-in-law and husband in all things and gives birth to a plump son within a year of marriage.[40] As for the virtuous Madame Chao, in an episode inserted into the middle of a lengthy narration of Sujie's excesses, she is rewarded at 104 *sui* with deification as a goddess of Mount Yi (90.979). Even though it is too late to save her son Chao Yuan from his miserable fate, Madame Chao's belated adoption of proper Confucian household regulation saves her family from complete ruin. Her enlightenment in Chapter 90 foreshadows that of Di Xichen when he learns to master his own life by stabilizing his restless "monkey of the mind" with the recitation of the *Diamond Sutra*. In so doing, he brings an end to Sujie's transgressions.

38. Discussed in T'ien, *Male Anxiety*, pp. 152–61. This filial practice also appears in *Yesou puyan*.

39. This motif also appears in *Jin Ping Mei* when Pan Jinlian, wearing nothing, chases mosquitoes inside the bed netting while Ximen Qing, her "Dada," sleeps (18.277).

40. Also in contrast to Sujie, this idealized daughter-in-law is so quiet and passive that her presence is rarely mentioned.

FOX-SPIRITS AND THE WOUNDS OF SELF-CULTIVATION

Even though the treatment of sexual desire is somewhat muted in *Xingshi*, it is nonetheless the theme that drives the logic of this orthodox narrative. As I shall argue in this section, the denaturalized construct of the shrew was used as a surface onto which literati projected their anxieties about the need to contain and master sexual desire. The problematization of desire and sexuality figure prominently in the portrayal of Sujie, whose very name indicates her fundamentally sexual nature. As related in the novel, Sujie was named after a female spirit dressed in white silk (*suyi* 素衣) who had appeared in her mother's dreams shortly before she gave birth to Sujie (25.269). Although the thematic use of the color white associated with Sujie links her to the white fox-spirit killed by Chao Yuan, the name likely alludes to Sunü 素女, the Plain Maiden, a central figure in Daoist esoteric sexual teachings.[41] Sunü's conversations with the Yellow Emperor were republished during the Ming dynasty in a manual entitled *Sunü miaolun* 素女妙論 (Marvelous teachings of the Plain Maiden).[42] Even though Sujie's name may not be a direct allusion to Sunü, Sunü was such a well-known figure within the Daoist tradition that the resonance highlights Sujie's sexualized function in the novel.

Underlying Sujie and Xichen's antagonistic relationship is the common cliché of battle as a metaphor for sexual intercourse. Battle imagery is widely used in the large body of erotic fiction that circulated during the late Ming and early Qing, of which *Jin Ping Mei* and *Rou putuan* are only the best-known examples today.[43] It derives from the Daoist sexual practices that promise longevity, or at least better health, through certain sexual techniques. The goal of intercourse is not enjoyment per se but the obtaining of the essential *yin* or *yang* energy from one's partner(s). The partner is sometimes described as the "enemy," and the sex act itself as a battle fought in

41. See Monschein, *Der Zauber der Fuchsfee*, p. 302.

42. For a discussion of the importance of Sunü in the Daoist canon, see Gulik, *Sexual Life*, pp. 74, 270–77.

43. For these and other examples, see McMahon, *Causality and Containment*, pp. 78–81; and Gulik, *Sexual Life*, pp. 156, 304, 313–16, and *passim*.

rounds, with each side using various weapons in the hope of victory.[44] The Daoist medical belief that excessive loss of sperm (*jing* 精), a man's *yang* essence, is debilitating to a man's well-being is undoubtedly one of the sources of the fictional stereotype of women as sexual aggressors, an image that continued to appear in the sentimentalized fiction of the mid- and late Qing (see the discussions of *Honglou meng, Yesou puyan,* and *Jinghua yuan* in the following chapters). Although military metaphors to describe sexual relations are often used playfully, they take a deadly turn when attributed to shrews such as Pan Jinlian, Xue Sujie, and Wang Xifeng.

The destructive aspect of Sujie's sexuality is brought out most clearly in her identity as a fox-spirit.[45] Fox-spirits had long been associated with the dangers of sexual desire. In early texts, fox-spirits transform themselves into both men and women, but by the Song dynasty they had become increasingly associated with beautiful, and often lascivious, young women.[46] A matrix of *yin*-associated qualities, including beauty, sexual desire, unregulated nature (in contrast to regulated society), death, the supernatural, and mutability, are deployed in the characterization of these feminized spirits. The most likely model for the development of Sujie as fox-spirit is Pan Jinlian of *Jin Ping Mei*. In that novel, the fox-spirit theme is evoked through Jinlian's deadly association with cats and dogs, the urbanized manifestations of their wilder cousins, foxes, tigers, and lions. Zhang Zhupo comments on the importance of Lion Street (Shizi jie 獅子街) as the place where Ximen Qing

44. See Gulik, *Sexual Life*, pp. 157–59, 278–79, and *passim*. The *Xiyou ji* contains the following description of a monster's attempts to obtain Tripitika's semen, naturalized as struggle between an aggressive *yin* and a regulated *yang* (trans. A. Yü, *Journey to the West*, 55.73.):

> The fiend wished only to seek a mate;
> The monk refused to leak his primal sperm.
> Yin and yang at odds now clashed together,
> Each flaunting its might in this bitter strife.
> Quiet yin, to nourish being, quickened in lust;
> Tranquil yang purged desires to guard its health.

45. See J. Lévy, "Le renard"; Mathieu, "Aux origines de la femme-renarde"; and Monschein, *Der Zauber der Fuchsfee*.

46. The early fourteenth-century *Wu Wang fa Zhou pinghua* 武王伐紂平話 (King Wu's campaign against Zhou) casts the historical beauty Daji 妲己 as a fox-spirit. Especially noteworthy in light of Sujie's "change of heart," described below, is that the fox-spirit possesses Daji (a detail that is repeated in the *Fengshen yanyi* 封神演義 and the *Lieguo zhi*). King Zhou's self-indulgence and moral decline are blamed on the fox-spirit's supernatural interference rather than on his own weakness.

carries on many of his affairs: Hua Zixu 花子虛 and Pan Jinlian are gruesomely murdered there, and Ximen Qing is almost killed there.[47] Dogs and cats frequently appear as a seemingly neutral detail in the background of Jinlian's sexual assignations. The first chapter of the *Jin Ping Mei cihua* juxtaposes Wu Song's heroic slaying of the tiger with his uneasy encounters with his sister-in-law Pan Jinlian. Most striking is the way Jinlian trains her cat, Snow Lion 雪獅, to maul her rival Li Ping'er's son (*JPM* 59.877).[48] It is this subtext of violence in Sujie's depiction as fox-spirit that comes closest to the spirit of the vicious *hanfu* shrew.

In *Xingshi*, the theme of the fox-spirit is introduced in the first chapter when Chao Yuan leads the members of his household on a winter hunt after a big snowfall. The scene invokes associations of imperial hunts: a long descriptive poem, reminiscent of a Han dynasty *fu* rhapsody, describes the party's luxurious costumes. Chao Yuan's decision to bring a concubine along as part of the hunting party explicitly motivates the appearance of the fox-spirit. "[The fox-spirit] then saw that young master Chao was a lascivious and depraved man, [for] he was leading a singing-girl on a hunt without distinguishing man from woman. If this wasn't the opportunity to try her luck, what would be?" (1.10). The fox appears in human form; as soon as Chao Yuan catches sight of the beautiful woman standing to the side of the hunting party, his desire is aroused, and he dreams of obtaining her as a concubine to create "a lifetime of romance" (*fengliu yishi* 風流一世). His dogs, however, are able to see through her disguise and immediately give chase. The spirit transforms herself back into her original form as a white fox in order to escape, and Chao Yuan ruthlessly kills her with an arrow.[49] (As mentioned above, the white prefigures the vision of the white-clad woman

47. *JPM*, "Dufa," p. 35; trans. Roy, "How to Read," pp. 220–21.

48. Cat and animal imagery appears in *Jin Ping Mei* in 7.127, 12.180 and 196, 13.205, 39.583 and 590, 57.843 and 845, 60.894, 62.926, 68.1042, 75.1182, and 86.1373 and 1376. See also Plaks, *Four Masterworks*, pp. 99–101. For a discussion of the association between cats, dogs, and killing in *Jin Ping Mei*, see Ding, *Obscene Objects*. Worth noting is that when Sujie tries to frighten Tiaogeng's child to death, she sets off firecrackers and "beats dogs and grabs chickens" 打狗拿雞 outside the baby's window (*XS*, 76.819). The violently sexual associations of dogs and cats may explain the odd scene in *Honglou meng* in which the mad Wang Xifeng runs about the garden with a knife stabbing in a frenzy described as "see a chicken kill a chicken, see a dog kill a dog, see a person kill a person" 見雞殺雞，見狗殺狗，見人就要殺人 (*HLM*, 25.258).

49. In Buddhist iconography, arrows are sometimes used to represent desire; once an arrow strikes us, we can think of nothing other than pulling it out.

from whom Sujie takes her name.) From that evening on, Chao Yuan is racked with fevers and nightmares, ailments typically ascribed to lovesickness. A doctor is called, but after he checks Chao Yuan's pulse and notices a copy of the Ming pornographic novel *Ruyi jun zhuan* by the young man's pillow, he concludes that the fevers are a result of an internal wound (*neishang* 內傷, 2.18). Chao Yuan then ignores his grandfather's exhortations to chant the *Diamond Sutra* as the only means to cure himself, and over the space of the next 98 chapters his "internal wound" gradually transforms itself into an external projection of his unenlightened condition. Only when Xichen chants the *Diamond Sutra* for earnest, after Sujie attempts to shoot him with an arrow in Chapter 100, does Sujie collapse and the cycle of karmic retribution come to a close. In an echo of Zhu Xi's words cited as an epigraph in this chapter, Di Xichen's self-mastery finally eradicates this external depravity.

Sujie's underlying identity as a violent fox-spirit is foregrounded throughout the novel. The night before her wedding, Sujie dreams that her own "good" heart has been ripped out and replaced with another (44.480–481).[50] From this time on, Sujie, who had been a perfectly unremarkable young woman, becomes increasingly vicious and bestial in appetite and behavior. A servant from the Xue family confides to Xichen that before she married, Sujie had had a small appetite and a low tolerance for alcohol, but on her first visit home after the wedding she devoured six or seven boiled eggs and two bowls of wine (45.492). That same night, when she thinks that Xichen has already fallen asleep, she again eats a huge meal of chicken.[51] Sujie's bestial appetite is again mentioned during the period of mourning for her mother-in-law; Xichen catches sight of her, and she is "like a starved tiger, clutching it [the chicken] to her chest, with mouth biting and teeth tearing in one swoop" (60.652). Later Sujie is again depicted as a savage animal when she attacks Xichen and bites his arm so viciously that he bleeds heavily from the wound (73.791).[52]

Castration imagery is an important component of the fox-spirit theme in *Xingshi*. Castration refers to the physical loss of the penis as well as the loss of the symbolic phallus, that is, those privileges that historically legitimated

50. For literary antecedents to this image, see note 47.

51. Sujie's insatiable appetite for chicken is also mentioned in 44.484, 48.520, and 61.663. Xia Jingui 夏金桂, the shrewish wife of Xue Pan 薛蟠, also likes to chew on chicken bones (*HLM*, 80.918).

52. Unruly women are described as wolves or dogs in *XS*, 76.824, 89.970, and 91.985.

male authority. We have already seen how Xichen is feminized by being cloistered, bound, and silenced, while Sujie assumes the public and dominant identity traditionally reserved for men. The struggle for power between the two of them, however, gets played out in pointedly sexual terms. Xichen is several times referred to as a chicken (*jiba* 雞巴, 59.634 and 639, 89.967), a common pun for the slang term *jiba* 㞞髱, "penis" (as used in 56.609).[53] After Sujie and Xichen's wedding night, the family servants find an unusual amount of blood on the bedding (45.495–96). The opening poem in chapter 97, which describes Xichen's gaping wound leaking blood and pus onto the bed, recalls the copious amounts of blood on the wedding sheets, although in this latter instance the wound is caused by the hot coals Sujie pours down Xichen's back (97.1054–55). The opening poem to chapter 59, an episode in which Sujie launches one of her most vicious attacks on Xichen, puns, "Harboring a voracious tiger and fierce snake, [Sujie] maliciously slaughters a chicken" (*geji* 割雞). This same verb *ge* is used in the descriptions of the decapitation of Chao Yuan and his lover in chapter 19 and Sujie's attempts to castrate her father-in-law in chapter 58.[54]

The events in chapter 66 are also suggestive of castration. After spying on Xichen, Sujie discovers that he is at a party with a courtesan and sends for him to return home immediately. His irresponsible friend, Zhang Mao 張茂, holds him back, hoping to get Xichen into even more trouble. In his frantic haste to get away, Xichen cuts (*ge*) at his own arm with a scythe and inflicts a deep wound (66.713). Although it might seem inappropriate to read this as an act of symbolic self-castration, the events that follow justify this sort of psychological interpretation. Before Xichen is able to escape, Sujie arrives and angrily attacks Zhang Mao. She grasps him tightly by the waist of his pants, "as if she were holding a chicken," and begins to hit him

53. This slang expression is also used in *Jin Ping Mei*.

54. In a more lighthearted vein, the fight between Xichen's wives for control over him often centers on his sex organ. (Sexual possessiveness as a defining quality of the shrew is discussed in Y. Wu, "Marriage Destinies," pp. 133–40.) For examples of jealous possessiveness in *Xingshi*, see 1.6, 59.642, 62.674, 66.713–15, 79.858, and 87.944. During their first fight, Sujie offers Jijie "generous" terms: Sujie agrees to call her "sister" and share her clothing with her, but she will allow Jijie only two or three nights a month with Xichen (95.1027). In an earlier scene, Jijie had marked Xichen's penis with ink every morning so that she can tell if he has been unfaithful (79.858).

(66.715). Zhang Mao only manages to escape when his wife rips his pants off, "exposing his limp three-inch penis."[55]

Other studies of fox-spirits have linked the red of their fur to the red of blood and fires, both common metonyms of desire.[56] These deadly associations are foregrounded in the scene in which Chao Yuan is murdered. Chapter 19 begins by introducing a new character, Xiaoya'er 小雅兒, who, together with his wife, has rented a home on the Chao estate after his own had been destroyed in a fall flood. (I return to the flood image below.) As soon as he catches sight of Xiaoya'er's beautiful wife, Chao Yuan is smitten and arranges a tryst with her on a night when Xiaoya'er is out. Chao Yuan brings along one of his female servants, and the three lock themselves in the house to enjoy an evening of pleasure together. After the servant has "gone wild for a bit" (*kuangle yihui* 狂了一會), she discovers that her menstrual period has started and withdraws to her own room. Unfortunately for the two remaining lovers, Xiaoya'er unexpectedly returns that night. The first thing he notices after climbing through the window is the servant fast asleep like a "dead dog" and naked except for the cloth between her legs. He then enters the bedroom to find his wife and Chao Yuan in bed, also naked and fast asleep. At first worried that he might kill them without justification, he takes a lamp and has a closer look only to discover that his wife is holding Chao Yuan's "thing" (*na jian wushi* 那件物事) in her hands. Without a further thought, he takes out the knife from his waist and cuts off (*ge*) their heads. The chapter ends with his departure.

The following chapter begins the next morning with the servant worrying that someone else might see her menstrual blood on the floor. She hurriedly pulls on a pair of pants, leaving her upper body exposed, and goes to get ashes to spread on her blood. To her horror, the blood appears to have spread all over the floor. Another servant comes in: "When he entered, he saw the two bodies of a man and a woman, stark naked. One 'head' (*tou* 頭) still lay on the bed, but the two human heads (*rentou*) had gone who knows where, while at the head (*tou*) of the bed had flowed a big pool of blood" (20.209). The insistent repetition of the word "head" in the above passage makes clear that the symbolic connection between decapitation and castra-

55. Pan Jinlian bullies Ximen Qing by pulling open his pants and exposing his limp penis when he returns from one of his early assignations with Li Ping'er in chapter 13.

56. See Mathieu, "La femme-renarde," p. 94.

tion is not specific to the Western imaginary. Although the link between the blood in this episode, which associates sexual transgression with violent death, and the fox-spirit motif is quite indirect, the figural repetition of excessive blood found here, as well as on Xichen and Sujie's marriage bed and on the frequent wounds Sujie inflicts on Xichen, draws tighter the symbolic connection.

A particularly disturbing incorporation of violently sexual fox-spirit imagery appears in an otherwise unmotivated anecdote in Chapter 92. A man who needs more money for gambling disguises himself in a fox skin to steal from his mother while she sleeps in bed. He fails to dislodge her money belt the first night, and on his second attempt he again dons the fox skin, and "again used his tail to brush her face, and then nuzzled her lips with his cold mouth; pressing down on her body, he stuck his hand down beneath the bedding and pawed all over until he found the money belt encircling his mother's waist" (92.1002). After calling to her son to come save her from the thief, the mother grabs the scissors she keeps by her bedside and stabs and kills the intruder. Fresh blood flows all over the bed. This odd episode weaves together many of the motifs associated with fox-spirits used elsewhere in the novel, including a muted expression of illicit sexuality, violent death, and copious amounts of red blood. In this example, the son's unfilial desire to steal from his mother is oddly sexualized. Given the analogy made earlier in the novel between Chao Yuan's head and penis, the placement of the mother's scissors in the son's neck suggests a symbolic castration to parallel his "pawing" around her waist.

Underlying the characterization of Sujie as fox-spirit is the fact that she is barely human; she is the reincarnated product of Chao Yuan's originating sin of desire. After the monkey defaces her in Chapter 87, Sujie's true identity is revealed, and she enters the realm of the symbolic as a raw and monstrous emblem of irrepressible sexuality. At this point in the novel, it does not matter that Sujie is no longer desirable; just as in certain Buddhist parables that depict death as the logical conclusion to narratives of desire, sex, when taken to an extreme, is no longer desirable. It is dangerous, repugnant, and overpowering. Sujie embodies these dangerous and destructive aspects of sexuality as she engages Xichen in a violent power struggle that is ultimately about control and not desirability.

THE SHREW AND *YINYANG* SYMBOLISM

One of the most powerful expressions of Confucian orthodoxy is found in the deployment of *yinyang* symbolism. A number of stereotypical motifs in *Xingshi* analogically linked to *yinyang* symbolism echo and amplify the loss of normative order that is the central theme of orthodox narratives. The presence of the sexually dissolute *yinfu* directly evokes *yinyang* symbolism. A common epithet in traditional fiction for women, "watery-natured" (*shuixing* 水性), meaning "fickle" or "dissolute," draws on the analogical connection between women, who are identified with the *yin* principle, and water, a *yin* element.[57] A semantic association between the *yin* principle and the *yin* meaning "excess," as in the terms *yinshui* 淫水, "flood," or *yinxing* 淫性, "dissolute," most often in a sexual sense, was fully consolidated by the time of Dong Zhongshu. The "Wuxingzhi" 五行志 (Records of the five elements) section of the *Hanshu* 漢書 (Han history) explicitly connects floods to women of the inner court who used their sexuality to empower themselves.[58] It is this analogic association between female transgression and flooding that seems to motivate the cataclysmic flood that follows the karmic rebirths of Chao Yuan and the fox-spirit.

The flood takes place in the utopic town named Mingshuizhen 明水鎮, "Bright Waters," where Xichen and Sujie first meet. The name Mingshuizhen resonates with the name of Qinghe 清河, "Clear River," in the prefecture of Dongping, the setting of Ximen Qing and Pan Jinlian's first meeting in the *Jin Ping Mei*. As noted by David Roy, the original name of the town in the *Shuihu zhuan* version of the story was Yanggu 陽穀 but was changed probably to allude to the following passage by Xunzi: "The ruler is the source of order. The officials maintain the regulations; the ruler nurtures the source. If the water of the source is clear, the lower reaches of the stream will be clear. If the water of the source is muddy, the lower reaches of the source

57. On the term *shuixing*, see McMahon, *Causality and Containment*, pp. 65–66.

58. For example, in their anticipatory commentary to a passage from the *Spring and Autumn Annals*, Dong Zhongshu and Liu Xiang blame a flood (*dashui* 大水) in the 24th reign year of the Duke Zhuang 莊 of Lu 魯 (670 B.C.E.) on the "excessively wanton and unladylike" (*yinluan bufu* 淫亂不婦) behavior of the Duke's wife Ai Jiang 哀姜, although at that time she had not yet become involved in the murderous intrigues to have her lover succeed her husband (*Hanshu*, 27A.1344).

will be muddy."[59] A further allusion to moral decay worked into the *Jin Ping Mei* by its redactors is the fallacious placement of the district of Qinghe in the prefecture of Dongping.[60] Dongping recalls a *fu* rhapsody written by the well-known poet Ruan Ji 阮籍 (210–63), who served there as a governor. The *fu* lists the excesses and debauchery that take place at Dongping and, in David Roy's words, describe it "as a sink of unparalleled iniquity."[61] The moral collapse of Mingshui in *Xingshi* can be read as an elaboration of Ruan Ji's rhapsody. The initial description of Mingshui serves as an intentional narrative break immediately following the chaotic and unsavory events of Chao Yuan's murder. Chapter 23 begins with a long, unhurried, almost lyric description of the local geography, which features a "sacred mountain" (*xianshan* 仙山) on which Mingshui is built; the names of mountains and streams in the region are listed in loving detail. The seasons pass in perfect harmony, and men and women alike are described as conforming to Confucian ideals of behavior.[62]

> Those who are estimated to be capable of study are prepared for the civil service examination; those who cannot learn either work at agriculture or learn some manual skill. There are no vagrants or loafers, nor are there any people who are completely illiterate. Even those who sell vegetables can show off a couple of classical phrases. Even if you wanted one, there had not yet been even one person who stole a chicken or nabbed a dog, nor had the jail ever held any criminal sentenced to death. As for the women, from whichever small household you choose, there has never been any who has exposed her face outside or walked around the streets or markets. Even though fearing one's wife is a common occurrence both now and in antiquity, in Xiujiang county [the location of Mingshui] for one, husbands are husbands, and wives wives. Those types of situations where *yin* and *yang* are inverted, or hard and soft are imbalanced, or where the hen announces the dawn, are extremely rare. (23.248)

Like *fu* rhapsodies, which by listing places and objects create the order they describe, the enumerative descriptions in Chapter 24 transform Mingshui

59. *Xunzi yinde*, j. 12, p. 44, 1.15; trans. from Roy, "Introduction," *The Plum in the Golden Vase*, p. xxxvi.

60. See Roy, *The Plum in the Golden Vase*, pp. 435.

61. Ibid., p. 435. For a translation of the poem, see Holzman, *Poetry and Politics*, pp. 40–42.

62. The only date mentioned in this section is the ninth day of the ninth month, the propitious double *yang* festival (23.340; on which more later). It is on this date later in the novel that a bolt of lightning, an appropriate *yang* emblem, kills the morally offensive You Cong 尤聰 (54.789).

into a symbol of cosmic order.[63] The waters, from which the town takes its name, are a physical gauge of the moral level of the town; the Confucian purity of Mingshui, a stable community in which everyone knows and accepts his or her place without harboring any selfish ambitions, is mirrored in the purity and the regularity of the water.

However, it is in the town of Mingshui that Chao Yuan is reincarnated as Di Xichen, an event that skews the town's ideal *yinyang* harmony in such a way that both social and cosmic order go out of kilter. On the day the Di and Xue families first meet, the skies become overcast (*jianjian yin lai* 漸漸陰來) and "*yin* and *yang* were somehow out of balance" (*zhe yiri yinyang que shi bu zhun* 這一日陰陽卻是不準); this leads to an unusually heavy period of rain (25.266). Concurrent with the cosmic *yinyang* imbalance that besets Mingshui, a number of greedy and rapacious characters who try to profit from other people's suffering begin to plague the town's social environment (chaps. 26–28). Shocking examples of almost every type of sordid and debauched behavior are described, including the death of parents caused by their unfilial sons, incest and other acts of sexual depravity, treachery, and cannibalism. The harmony that originally defined the community of Mingshui is replaced by patterns of selfish and violent abuse.

This section of the novel is filled with both explicit and implicit references to the loss of proper *yinyang* order. A dangerous imbalance of *yin* and *yang* (*hunluan yinyang* 混亂陰陽, 27.292) erases the boundary between the living (*yangshi* 陽世) and the dead (*yinshi* 陰世); this allows ghosts and gods to appear and kill a number of the worst offenders.[64] A succession of weird anomalies is reported: of the miserly Yan Liexing's 嚴列星 three sons, two are born without anuses, and the third is riddled with holes and dies dripping of blood (2.294);[65] and an actress lays an egg that hatches into a monkey (27.285). As expressed so clearly in the passage by Liu Ji cited in Chapter 1, unusual weather patterns indicate a cosmic imbalance. In a gradually worsening cycle, the transition of seasons in Mingshui becomes unreliable (27.285), and severe droughts bring about ravaging famines and disease. The

63. For a discussion of how the expansive descriptions in *fu* poetry evoke a sense of plenitude and completeness, see Plaks, *Archetype and Allegory*, pp. 163–64.

64. Gods and ghosts also appear in 3.21–22, 6.56, 14.154–55, 17.176–77, 27.292–94, 28.297–99, and 28.304–5.

65. As Keith McMahon (*Misers*, pp. 5–6, 86–89) has written, images of diarrhea or constipation are frequently associated with misers who are so tight they "value their feces as though it were gold" (*xi fen ru jin* 惜糞如金).

townspeople's excessive debauchery (*yinyi* 淫泆) finally culminates in a massive flood (*yinshui* 淫水) that wipes out most of the town (chap. 28). Just as a minor flood in chapter 19 of *Xingshi* preceded Chao Yuan's deadly affair with Xiaoya'er's wife, this catastrophic deluge, explicitly linked to the town's moral decay, provides the narrative backdrop for Xichen's relationship with Sujie. It is instructive to contrast Sujie's introduction into the text at this juncture with the last act of the beatified Madame Chao: before ascending to Heaven, Madame Chao distributes food and medicine after a sudden flood caused by heavy *yin* rains (chap. 90). Unlike Madame Chao, who re-establishes a proper *yinyang* balance, Sujie is born of *yin* excess.

Floods were a common motif in Ming-Qing fiction used to signify the loss of orthodox order, as illustrated through a number of *yin* signs such as political chaos, sexual transgression, and female subversion of male control.[66] Flooding had always been a potent signal of the collapse of order in China;[67] Peter Perdue writes of the Qing that the legitimation of the state was tied to the success of water conservancy.[68] During the late imperial period, flood imagery in fiction capitalized on the real increase in floods due to the over-development of flood plains while simultaneously exploiting an ethically charged *yinyang* symbolic vocabulary in ways that other natural disasters could not.[69] The connotations of flooding, including notions of excess, flu-

66. In addition to the examples found in *Honglou meng*, *Yesou puyan*, *Jinghua yuan*, and *Ernü yingxiong zhuan* to be discussed below, see also the Women's Country episode in the *Xiyou ji* story cycle and Feng Menglong's "Bai Niangzi yongzhen Leifeng ta" 白娘子永鎮雷峰塔, in *Jingshi tongyan* 警世通言. The trope of flooding as a sign of political disorder has continued into the modern period in Liu E's 劉鶚 (1857–1909) *Lao Can youji* 老殘遊記 (The travels of Lao Can) and Zhang Xianliang's 張賢亮 (b. 1936) *Nanren de yiban shi nüren* 男人的一半是女人 (Half of man is woman).

67. As political scientists from Guanzi to Karl Wittfogel and Pierre-Etienne Will have argued, water control was a crucial issue in traditional China; see Rickett, *Guanzi*, "Overseeing Government" pp. 102, 107; Wittfogel, *Oriental Despotism*; and Will, "Un cycle hydraulique." Although the exact involvement of the government bureaucracy in hydraulics projects is still under debate, the government clearly saw water control as one of its primary responsibilities. Failure to contain or avert floods was a potent symbol of moral failure. This continues to be true today; according to some reports, the PRC government tried to repress news of the extent of the damage caused by the flooding of Lake Taihu in the summer of 1991 (*Human Rights Tribune* [1992], pp. 6–8).

68. Perdue, *Exhausting the Earth*, p. 170.

69. Since the majority of literati were from flood-prone regions in the south, it was perhaps inevitable that floods would be used more than devastating frosts, epidemics, earthquakes, or droughts as examples of natural disasters. Significantly for my argument, Ping-ti

idity, erasure of boundaries, and loss of control, were particularly inimical to the Confucian goal of creating a stable, harmonious order. As we shall see in *Yesou puyan* and *Jinghua yuan*, flood imagery also gained power from its ability to evoke the paradigmatic figure of the Sage-King Yu 禹, whose great virtue enabled him to regulate the floodwaters.[70] Resisting floods was a common metaphor for moral integrity; as can be seen in the following quote from Wang Fuzhi, for example, describing the members of the Donglin Academy as men who "held fast to their virtue and resolutely took their stand and were not drowned (*jinyin* 浸淫) in the [tide] of Buddhism and Daoism."[71] The devastating flood in *Xingshi* marks the onset of *yin* excess, which quickly overwhelms the weak Di Xichen.

A facet of Sujie's behavior that draws on the semantic connection between the transgressive potential of *yin* and water is her willful refusal to contain her excreta. Sujie, in a motif associated with other shrews, repeatedly dumps her chamber pot over the heads of her enemies (58.631 and 97.1055). Although the etymology of the term *pofu* is uncertain, the word *po* literally means "to spatter"; this epithet for shrews seems to point specifically to this stereotypical shrewish act. The master storyteller Li Yu featured the motif in a story about a childless and weak-willed husband who enlists the help of a famous local shrew-tamer to force his wife to allow him to bring home two concubines. His jealous wife locks him out, and the husband leads the village men in two all-out attacks on his home, where the woman has barricaded herself. During the second attack, the wife locks herself upstairs with all the maids. The wife then uses her sweetest voice to call the men forward to negotiate; when they come close to hear what she has to say, she dumps buckets of nightsoil on their faces.[72] One of the odder details of Wang Xifeng's entrapment of Jia Rui in

---

Ho (*Studies in the Population of China*, pp. 233–36) has estimated that the death toll from droughts was actually higher than that from floods.

70. See Maspero, "Legendes"; and Gu Jiegang, *Gushi lunwenji*, 2: 143–52.

71. Wang Fuzhi, *Chuanshan yishu*, "Saoshou wen" 搔首問, 64.1b–2a. McMorran ("Wang Fu-chih," p. 428) points put that Huang Zongxi used the same metaphor to describe the stand of the Donglin partisans.

72. Li Yu, "Duqi shou youfu zhi gua, nuofu huan busi zhi hun" 妒妻守有夫之寡，懦夫還不死之魂 (A jealous wife becomes a widow while her husband is still alive, the soul of a living cowardly husband returns), in *Liancheng bi* 連城壁, in *Li Yu quanji*, 8: 345–46. The story begins with another violent *yin* motif when the "Vinegar Queen," Cu Dawang 醋大王, forces her husband to drink a glass of cold water to prove his fidelity. When the husband, who has been lying to protect the life of a maid, drinks it, he contracts a *yin*-ailment (*yinzheng* 陰症) and dies within three days (ibid., p. 318).

chapter 12 of *Honglou meng* is the bucket of nightsoil that is dumped on his head before he is allowed to escape.

As I have argued elsewhere, the power ascribed to women's bodily effluvia in Ming-Qing fiction naturalizes the shrew's inherently transgressive identity.[73] Women's bodily wastes imply menstrual blood, which was believed to have great power to contaminate.[74] Evidence of how powerful women's effluvia were thought to be can be found in the following description of the use of women's effluvia by defenders trying to break the power of an attack by rebels during the Wang Lun 王倫 uprising of 1774. The city defenders had prostitutes position themselves on the city walls; the women loosened their hair (hair being a *yin* substance), and urinated and bled over the wall. "So as to increase the potent *yin* force . . . , chickens and black dogs were killed and their blood was poured over the side, simulating the polluting menstrual blood of women, and dogs' excrement and urine were thrown at the enemy."[75] That the associations between women, menstrual blood, and disaster were very present in the mind of the author of *Xingshi* is evident in the odd narrative foregrounding of the maid's menstrual blood in the events that lead to Chao Yuan's murder. The taboo and transgressive connotations of women's effluvia also explain the sense of outrage in the narrator's description of the women's pilgrimage to Taishan in chapter 68. The menstrual rags, urine, and leaking breast milk in the scene are reminiscent of the *pofu*'s socially disruptive unwillingness to respect the Confucian injunction for women to sequester themselves. The pollution of women's bodily functions gives full weight to the horror of Sujie "imprisoning" Xichen by her nightsoil bucket in chapters 60 and 63.

A further aspect of Sujie's characterization which points to her symbolic value as a *yin* cipher is in her family name Xue. The pun between the name Xue and the *yin* .ubstance snow (*xue* 雪) is developed most fully by Cao Xueqin in his depiction of the plump, white, and distinctly cool Xue Baochai 薛寶釵 in *Honglou meng*.[76] Xue, along with the surnames Wang 王, a pun on *wang* 亡, "to perish," or in the causative, "to kill," and Liu 劉 or 柳, which, as discussed above, exploit the pun on the archetypal *yin* number six, are common names assigned to those go-betweens who are only too happy

73. Epstein, "Inscribing the Essentials."

74. See Ahern, "The Power and Pollution"; and Seaman, "Sexual Politics."

75. Naquin, *Shantung Rebellion*, p. 101.

76. Discussed in Plaks, *Archetype and Allegory*, pp. 63–64.

to corrupt the morals of decent women in return for handsome cash payments. The most famous examples of this type of bawd are Old Woman Xue, who serves as go-between between Ximen Qing and Meng Yulou's 孟玉樓 family, and Old Woman Wang, who arranges Ximen Qing's seduction of Pan Jinlian.[77] Not incidentally, the boy Yunge 鄆哥 happens to be carrying a basket of snow pears (*xueli* 雪梨) when he discovers Ximen Qing having an affair with Pan Jinlian at the end of chapter 4, and Jinlian names her beloved and murderous cat Snowy Lion 雪獅. This same *yin* encoding resonates in the name of Xue Sujie.

Although I shall have to wait until the discussions of *Honglou meng* and *Jinghua yuan* to argue more conclusively that the iconography and structural patterns associated with the depiction of shrews is inextricably imbedded in *yinyang* symbolism, it is important to note the degree to which *Xingshi* makes use of an explicit *yinyang* vocabulary. The seeds of this cosmic truth are planted early in the novel in the name of one of the friends who visits Chao Yuan when he is tormented by lovesickness. The friend's name is Yin Pingyang 尹平陽, a transparent pun for "*yin* subdues *yang*" (2.17). The entire novel illustrates the chaos that ensues when *yin* overpowers *yang* and threatens the integrity of the individual, domestic, and natural worlds. In line with the late imperial emphasis on marriage as the foundation for the social order, the narration of the loss of proper *yinyang* regulation is focalized through Xichen's domestic relations with Sujie. The symbolic importance of marriage as a microcosm of larger *yinyang* processes is stated at Xichen and Sujie's wedding (44.481–82) and reiterated as the novel draws to a close. As one character observes: "'In the course of events, when *yang* wanes and *yin* waxes, and the gentleman fears the mean person and the living fear ghosts, how can a husband not fear his wife?'" (91.991). Only in the final pages of the novel, after Xichen has taken a medicine that stabilizes his mind (*dingle xin* 定了心), does he gain an understanding into the need to regulate the women's quarters and "tame and harmonize the order of *yin* and *yang*" 馴協陰陽之則 (100.1088).

A number of iconographic elements associated with shrews are deployed in the characterization of Xue Sujie. Sujie, the reincarnation of a fox-spirit, circulates through the novel as the reminder of Chao Yuan's uncontrolled and illicit desire. As fox-spirit, scattering *pofu*, sexualized *yinfu*, and verbally and

77. The go-between in the "The Pearl Sewn Shirt" is also surnamed Xue.

physically abusive *hanfu*, Sujie is an amalgam of Buddhist, Daoist, and Neo-Confucian discourses on the dangers for a man of losing self-control. Sujie is gendered as female, but she is never quite fully human; instead, she is a monstrous personification of *yin* threats to *yang*-identified orthodoxy. Although Sujie is one of the most extreme characterizations of the shrew, reflections of the dangers of *yin* excess she embodies surface in sentimental novels considered to be much more sympathetic to women. Even though these texts incorporate the positive views of women and the feminine so central to the cult of *qing*, they invoke the orthodox message of the shrew through the use of specific and frequently isolated motifs, such as transgressive sexuality, the displacement of those who should be master, the dumping of nightsoil, the specter of a fox-spirit or ghost, the mention of a flood, the presence of a cat or dog. The conjunction of all these motifs in the characterization of Sujie enables us to fill in the narrative ellipsis when we meet her more fragmented sisters in other texts.

The narrative lesson taught so clearly by *Xingshi* is that without Chao Yuan's initial loss of self-mastery, Sujie would never have come into being. Even though she is nothing more than a karmic projection of the male protagonist's desire, Sujie quickly displaces him as the focus of narrative interest. This narrative model, in which the narrative elaboration of the state of transgression overwhelms the didactic point, is common to much of Ming-Qing fiction. Sujie's domination of Di Xichen is an obvious inversion of the Confucian "natural" law in which a superior *yang* must regulate *yin*. Throughout *Xingshi*, the feminine and analogically related *yin* concepts are powerfully disruptive; in a point I return to in the discussions of *Honglou meng*, *Yesou puyan*, and *Jinghua yuan*, the loss of normative Confucian order is frequently gendered as female. In these later Qing works, even though certain aspects of the feminine are idealized, the central male protagonists continue to be as weak, passive, and marginal as Di Xichen. More important to our interpretations of these lengthy texts, the *yinyang* motifs employed as narrative elements in *Xingshi* are woven into the structure of these novels in ways that unify episodes that might otherwise seem arbitrary and out of place. As I shall argue, the orthodox structural frame employed in those largely sentimental novels frequently clashes with the central idealization of the feminine. As we shall see in the analyses of *Honglou meng* and *Jinghua yuan*, the two novels most frequently interpreted as sympathetic to women, these contradictory constructions of the feminine are employed simultaneously.

CHAPTER FOUR

Reflections of Desire in Honglou meng

No discussion of the contradictory late imperial yearnings for authentic self-expression and the stabilizing influence of orthodoxy can be complete without turning to the great eighteenth-century masterpiece *Honglou meng* 紅樓夢 (Dream of the red chamber, also known as *Shitou ji* 石頭記, Story of the stone).[1] The characters and events celebrated in the novel represent the ultimate exploration of the shifting meanings of *qing*. Although there has never been any question of the novel's literary value, since the time of its publication its admirers and detractors have debated whether the world depicted in *Honglou meng* represents the purity of the creative spirit or licentiousness. Enthusiasts have recopied and reprinted the novel and published dozens of commentaries and numerous sequels and fictional responses. The Qing government repeatedly tried to ban the work, even as late as 1844 and 1868. Premodern commentators made equally passionate claims for the novel as either a work of great sentiment or an alluring and somewhat slippery text that illustrates profound Neo-Confucian truths. Much recent scholarship continues to idealize the depiction of life in Grand Prospect Garden (Daguan yuan 大觀園).

Yü Yingshih's pathbreaking analysis of the two worlds in the novel describes the novel as a moral allegory based on the tensions between the pure utopia of the garden and the polluting forces outside its walls.[2] Louise Ed-

1. For convenience, I refer to the novel by the title by which it was known to Qing readers, although I predominantly work with the 80-chapter *Shitou ji* manuscript. Despite detailed comparative analyses of style and diction, there is still no consensus as to how closely Gao E's 高鶚 120-chapter edition, entitled *Honglou meng*, incorporates or reflects Cao Xueqin's original text or vision. The pages cited in the text and notes refer to the *Honglou meng bashihui jiaoben* (*HLM*), although I also refer to the *"Honglou meng" sanjia pingben* (*SJPB*). Unless otherwise noted, all translations are my own.

2. Yu Yingshi, *"Honglou meng" de liangge shijie*.

wards and Angelina C. Yee have applied this dualistic approach to *Honglou meng* to a discussion of gender in the novel to argue that women embody the positive values of the garden world in contrast to the degenerate world of Baoyu's male cousins.[3] Yee, in particular, has linked Cao Xueqin's use of gender to structural patterning in the novel. In her discussion of counterpoise, Yee has shown how gender is central to Cao's laying out of themes and values in a kaleidoscopic arrangement of characters and events that appear as opposites, doubles, and mutual complements. As she notes, the real aesthetic complexity of the novel's use of bipolarity is brought out in the way pairs and groups of characters, most important the emotional and delicate protagonist Jia Baoyu 賈寶玉 and his ruthless cousin Wang Xifeng 王熙鳳, form dynamic complementary axes.[4] For Yee, Xifeng stands "at the crossroads of the masculine and feminine worlds," where she "underpins, shapes and qualifies [Baoyu's] world of poetry" (648).

My own analysis of *Honglou meng* builds on these dualistic approaches; however, rather than locate the dualism of the novel in the architectural structure of the fictional world or in the deployment of gender, I see Cao Xueqin's use of both as part of his exploration of the multiple meanings associated with desire in the late imperial cultural imaginary. Although gender certainly has symbolic and structuralist uses in *Honglou meng*, Cao simultaneously destabilized and subverted the social and physical boundaries that separate masculine from feminine, even while he utilized them as categories of meaning. As I shall argue in exploring these themes, Cao made use of multiple constructions of gender, which cannot be reduced to an easy dualism. To reduce the use of the masculine and the feminine to ciphers, respectively, for "the world of ineptitude, corruption, and concupiscence" and "that of beauty, wit, and talent"[5] is to ignore how gender is deployed in the novel's exploration of Buddhist and Confucian themes. Rather than being counterpoised against one set of decadent values, the garden community is just one of a number of competing social and ideological systems, including Confucian ritual, participation in government, and Buddhist detachment. Deca-

3. See Edwards, "Gender Imperatives" and "Women in *Honglou meng*"; and Yee, "Counterpoise."

4. See especially chaps. 13–15, where the two are repeatedly juxtaposed through the events of Qinshi's 秦氏 death and funeral, and chap. 25, where both are victims of a curse and go mad simultaneously. For a detailed discussion of the complex complementarity that links them, see Yee, "Counterpoise," pp. 638–50.

5. Yee, "Counterpoise," p. 621.

dent caricatures of each of these value systems appear outside the garden, from Jia Zhen's 賈珍 incestuous relationship with his daughter-in-law[6] to Jia Zheng's 賈政 ineffectual Confucian rigidity (ironically, Jia Zheng's name means "government") to Jia Jing's 賈敬 irresponsible attempts at Daoist self-cultivation to Xifeng's brazen economic exploitation of the Jia family name. Despite the obvious contrasts, events in the garden frequently echo the more serious breaches of decorum that take place outside. Idealized life-sustaining representations of these virtues are also found in the garden, however. The relationship between the quiet young widow Li Wan 李紈, whose name, "Plain Silk," evokes the spinning that is the proper calling of a Confucianized woman, and her industrious son, Jia Lan 賈蘭, exemplifies filial devotion. The decisions of Xichun 惜春 and Daiyu's maid Zijuan 紫鵑 (Nightingale in Hawkes's translation) to take vows (as well as Baoyu's, if one accepts the ending of the 120-chapter version) model Buddhist detachment. The fiscal economies of Tanchun 探春 represent one of the few efforts to slow the family's penchant for depleting its resources. Although the discussions below touch on all these themes, my focus is on those that foreground gender as part of their construction of meaning.

THE FEMINIZATION OF BAOYU'S WORLD

Perhaps nowhere in the corpus of Ming-Qing fiction is the connection between *qing* and the feminine as closely intertwined as it is in *Honglou meng*. In fact, the novel has long been appreciated as a text that gives women a special place. So striking are the positive depictions of the feminine in *Honglou meng* that many readers from the May Fourth period to the present have argued that it contains an incipient feminist vision. As I argue below, however, the highly sentimentalized femininity celebrated in *Honglou meng* builds on the late Ming appropriation of the feminine as an expression of the "authentic," and its positive treatment of the feminine should hence be read as an attribute of *qing* rather than as a direct statement about the status of women. Those characters, male and female, who personify the values associated with *qing* are feminized by it. Baoyu, in his embodiment of an idealized lyric sub-

6. Zhang Xinzhi (*SJPB*, 2.32) pointedly glosses Jia Zhen's name 珍 as *zheng* 烝, a term used in the *Zuo zhuan* to refer to incestuous sexual relations between a male of lower rank and a woman of higher rank.

jectivity, surpasses historical literati who borrowed only the voice of the cloistered woman in their lyric poetry; Baoyu would become a girl.[7] What stands out for most readers as the vision of femininity in the novel is Baoyu's highly sentimentalized idealization of girls as purer and more authentic in their emotions and intelligence than men. However, the much vaunted sympathy for women in *Honglou meng* is based on a conceptualization of the feminine that is as available to men as it is to women. Moreover, the novel incorporates multiple visions of women and femininity. In this discussion, I reserve the term "feminine" to refer to those idealized qualities Baoyu associates with girls.

Within the context of scholar-beauty romances in which a feminine beauty (*mei*) was an ideal attribute of young scholars, it is not at all unusual that Baoyu is as beautiful as a girl.[8] Baoyu's femininity is more than skin-deep, however. As was customary on a child's first birthday, a wide range of objects is placed before the infant Baoyu. The objects the child chooses are supposed to foretell his future orientation. By picking out rouge and women's jewelry, Baoyu identifies himself with the feminine (*HLM*, 2.19).[9] Both he and his double, Zhen Baoyu 甄寶玉, value girls more than men; although they were not the first to reverse the normative gender hierarchy and idealize young women in Chinese culture, the Baoyus may be the most adamant spokespersons for the view that proclaims the inferiority of men.[10] As they put it, girls are formed of the spiritual essence of the myriad things (*wanwu zhi ling* 萬物之靈), whereas men are made of the leftover dregs.[11] Jia

7. For a discussion of a literati assumption of a female voice, see Robertson, "Voicing the Feminine," pp. 69–72.

8. More unusual is that Baoyu is frequently mistaken for a girl (*HLM*, 30.320, 50.543), a confusion that extends to Baoyu's living quarters (41.442, 51.556). Grandmother Jia mistakes Shi Xiangyun for Baoyu (31.329).

9. The remarkable scene in which Baoyu rips off his jade, the symbol of his identity, after meeting his beautiful cousin Lin Daiyu further suggests his desire to destroy his masculine privileged identity in order to be more like his girl cousins (*HLM*, 3.33). For Baoyu's jade as a phallic sign, see Yee, "Self, Sexuality, and Writing," pp. 393–94.

10. Goyama Kiwamu ("*Honglou meng* de nü xing") traces the phrase "The fine and numinous breath of Heaven and Earth converges not in man but in woman" 天地秀靈之氣不鍾於男而鍾於婦女 back to the Song dynasty figure Xie Ximeng 謝希孟 (*jinshi* 1184). Through various examples culled from narrative fiction and drama, he shows how this phrase and others expressing the same sentiment became increasingly common during the late Ming and Qing.

11. This statement is echoed in *HLM*, 2.20, 20.204, and 111.314.

Baoyu believes that "girls are made of water, and boys are made of mud," and Zhen Baoyu insists that their very presence makes him feel more alert: "I must have two girls with me when I study so that I can understand the characters and my mind will be clear. Otherwise my mind will be confused" (*HLM*, 2.20). The concept of "girls" has numinous powers. All Zhen Baoyu has to do is yell out the word "girl," and he becomes oblivious to the pain of his father's beating. His girl "madness" (*chitai* 痴態) is so excessive he instructs his pages: "The word 'girl' is very precious and pure; it is even more sacred than the expressions for Buddha or the [Daoist] Primal Celestial Excellency. It is important that you don't foul this word with your coarse, stinking mouths. But whenever you do need to use it, you must first rinse your mouths out with clean water and fragrant tea" (*HLM*, 2.20–21).

Despite Baoyu's passionate defense of girls, it is not a reliable category of meaning for him. Toward the end of the 80-chapter version of the novel, Jia Baoyu passionately distinguishes between unmarried girls and married women: "How is it that as soon as these people [girls] marry a fellow, they are infected by his male air (*qi* 氣) and get all ruined. They're even worse than men!" (*HLM*, 77.873). In actuality, neither age nor marital status is a reliable predictor of Baoyu's admiration for or closeness to women, as demonstrated by his intimacy with Qin Keqing 秦可卿, who is married to his cousin Jia Rong 賈蓉, and Wang Xifeng, who is married to his cousin Jia Lian 賈璉. Youth is no prerequisite for inclusion in the category, as can be seen by the aged Grandmother Jia's 賈母 close association with the idealized world of the girls. As Shi Xiangyun 史湘雲 warns:

> "If I were you, I would go only to Grandmother Jia's and the garden. All we have to do in these two places is play and joke, eat and drink. At Lady Wang's, if she is in the room just talk to her, there is no problem spending more time there. But if Lady Wang is not in the room, don't go in. The people there have evil in their hearts, and all want to harm us." (*HLM*, 49.525)

Grandmother Jia, of course, is the primary patron and defender of the social microcosm of the garden. All those who curry favor with her follow her in indulging Baoyu's desires. Despite the close cultural connection between the capacity for emotional sensibility and poetic production, Baoyu does not make artistic ability one of the conditions for admiring a girl. He is as infatuated with the simple country girl he meets on one of the Jia tenant farms in chapter 15 as with any of the other refined beauties he meets. Paradoxically, given Baoyu's expressions of admiration for the purity and emotional refinement he claims is concentrated in girls, he is surprisingly tolerant of several women associated with the family, including the figurally linked Xifeng, the You 尤 sisters, and Xue Pan's 薛蟠 shrewish wife, Xia Jingui 夏金桂, who, in increasing degrees, exhibit all the most destructive qualities of *yin* depravity. As we shall see, Baoyu is as attentive to the You sisters as he is to any pretty girl in the garden, despite the You sisters' unsavory reputation (*HLM*, 66.737). Only in the case of the vicious Xia Jingui does Baoyu question his assumption that physical beauty is evidence of spiritual purity (*HLM*, 80.918). Clearly, although *qing* is closely associated with the feminine in *Honglou meng*, there is no immediate correlation between the female sex and the ideal lyric.

Nor are all positive qualities associated with femininity reserved for biological girls; a chain of young men, identifiable by their femininely delicate good looks and depth of feelings, form an alternative web of sensibility that balances the world inside the garden. This group of beautiful men who blur the boundaries between male and female include the two Baoyus, Qin Zhong 秦鍾, the Prince of Beijing, the numerous pretty male cousins who appear in the schoolroom scene in chapter 9, and the actors Jiang Yuhan 蔣玉函 and Liu Xianglian 柳湘蓮. Baoyu's sexually ambiguous relationships with Qin Zhong and Jiang Yuhan further suggest that a biological male can enter Baoyu's affective world as easily as a woman.[12] The thread that connects various aspects of Baoyu's world is not his love of girls but his affinity for *qing*; those characters, male and female, who personify the values associated with *qing* are feminized by it.

PROSPECT GARDEN AND THE STAGING OF *QING*

The iconography of *qing* deployed by Tang Xianzu in his creation of the garden in *Mudan ting* provided much of the basis for Cao Xueqin's depiction of Grand Prospect Garden. Parallel to Du Liniang's dreamed relationship to the garden in her father's yamen, Baoyu's dream in chapter 5 comes to fruition with the construction of his family's garden. The first time he tours the garden with his father, various sites transport Baoyu back into the seductive

12. For Baoyu's bisexuality, see Edwards, "Gender Imperatives"; Bai Xianyong, "Jia Baoyu de suyuan"; and P. L. Chan, "Myth and Psyche," p. 169. On Baoyu's homosexual behavior, see Han Huiqiang, "*Honglou meng* zhong de xing guannian."

world of his dream.[13] Although the garden was built to welcome the imperial concubine, its official opening on the Lantern Festival, similar to Baoyu's dream, constructs it as an ephemeral mirage of unworldly splendor, and once Baoyu and his cousins move into the garden, it becomes his domain. The design, shape, and placement of the structures in the garden architectonically represent Baoyu's affective bonds with his cousins.[14] Rather than being defined by hierarchical status, relations in the garden are determined by emotional bonds and poetic talent. It is a space in which Baoyu is able to express his "authentic" nature. When Baoyu withdraws into the enclosed world of the garden, he constructs an identity based on spontaneous and unrestrained emotive responses rather than prescribed protocol.

The microcosmic world of the garden is an intricately staged setting in which orthodox social structures are progressively deconstructed. By escaping into the garden, Baoyu avoids externally imposed roles and responsibilities and creates an identity that is a projection of his "authentic" and unconstrained self. Baoyu exemplifies the conventions of literati "authenticity" by not allowing his unique eccentricities to be restrained by orthodox expectations. With the exception of the obligatory visits to his grandmother and parents, Baoyu manages to reduce all his relationships to friendship, the least formal and most authentic relationship as defined by certain late Ming philosophers.[15] Interactions between the cousins in the garden are spontaneous and unrestrained and evolve from emotional responses, not ritualized patterns. With the exception of the decorous and restrained Xue Baochai 薛寶釵, who is often castigated by commentators for her cold reserve,[16] the cousins and even the maids set aside conventional manners and terms of address and speak their minds at will. Unrestrained by traditional notions of propriety, the girls do not check their emotions either, and Baoyu's interactions with his cousins and the maids alternate rapidly between moments of excessive intimacy and peevish distancing.

13. For a discussion of Grand Prospect Garden as a re-creation of the Land of Illusion, see Yu Yingshi, *"Honglou meng" de liangge shijie*, pp. 43–45.

14. Ibid., 54–56.

15. He Xinyin and Li Zhi are best known for their emphasis on nonhierarchical relationships; see de Bary, "Individualism and Humanitarianism," pp. 180–81, 185–87, 197–98.

16. See, e.g., Hong Qiufan's (fl. 1885) *Du "Honglou meng" suibi*; his commentary at the end of chapter 5 compares Baochai to a "petty person" (*xiaoren*) and says that Daiyu would not be willing to mix with "petty people."

This emotional freedom contrasts with the world outside the garden, which is organized according to the conventions of ritual. Those who live in the public world, such as Jia Zheng, his retainers, and Yuanchun 元春 the imperial concubine, must subordinate their personal feelings in order to maintain the larger social order. Interactions in the public world are hierarchical and based on status and convention rather than on affection. At the formal reception for her, the imperial concubine is unable to express her grief at being separated from her family; it is only in the private, informal reception within the women's quarters that she dare express her true feelings. As shown by Jia Zheng's stiffness at family gatherings, his is a world unaccustomed to spontaneity. His scholarly retainers also hesitate to express their own opinions in front of Jia Zheng for fear of offending him. The public world, it seems, has no room for individual spontaneity or self-expression, the values most highly esteemed by Baoyu.

Unlike orthodox society, which is shaped by the hierarchical principles of the five cardinal relationships, life in Grand Prospect Garden seems to reflect a natural, organic order based on five-elements iconography. Fittingly, with the exception of the Confucian-identified Li Wan, the inhabitants of the garden have the names of flowers, birds, or stones. The landscaping of the garden reflects each character's intrinsic, "natural" identity. Each of the cousins lives isolated in a cottage nested in a bower of vegetation. Lin Daiyu's 林黛玉 modest residence, Xiaoxiang cottage 瀟湘館, is surrounded by a forest of bamboo. The bamboo puns on her family name Lin (forest) and her associations with spring; it also recalls the poetic image of the tear-speckled bamboo associated with the Xiaoxiang region and its obvious reference to her tearful demeanor. Xue Baochai's residence, Hengwu court 蘅蕪院, is more formal and substantial and contains a large rock garden, which is appropriate to her identification as a metal, winter character.

The organic nature of the garden is also manifested in the seasonal patterns that drive the rhythms of daily life according to the time of year and birthdays. These gatherings provide a naturalistic motivation for the production of poetry and riddles on a wide range of conventional themes. More original is the way that the characterizations of three of the cousins are rooted in seasonal imagery.[17] Lin Daiyu, a flower spirit, is linked to spring: she suffers physically when she sees late spring petals fall to the ground, and her exquisite poetry is filled with anguished references to the ephemeral na-

17. Discussed in Plaks, *Archetype and Allegory*, pp. 66–69.

ture of life. The hot temper of the powerful Wang Xifeng, the phoenix, flares during the summer heat of chapters 29 and 30, but she is strangely vulnerable the following fall when she discovers her husband in their bed with the wife of one of the family servants (chap. 44). The fall/winter identity of Xue Baochai, established by the snow and gold of her name (*chai* is a hairclasp made of precious metals), is reflected in her frequently cold demeanor, remarkably white skin, and cool scent. The ebb and flow of their fortunes closely follow seasonal rhythms.[18] Yet, as implied by Baoyu's discussion of artifice, the representation of nature in the garden is highly aestheticized rather than naturalistic (*tianran* 天然, *HLM*, 17–18.167).[19]

It is with the creation of the poetry club, immediately following Jia Zheng's departure to serve as commissioner of education in another province, that the aesthetic values associated with *qing* become foregrounded. From this point on, the cousins engage in poetry competitions, landscape painting, and musical composition. Lin Daiyu, the character who most fully personifies the values associated with *qing*, is also shown to be artistically the most talented and expressive.[20] In a trope that will be repeated and expanded in *Jinghua yuan*, the reproduction of literati culture by beautiful and genteel women endows their poetry and painting with a freshness and appeal they cannot achieve when produced by males.

The cousins themselves are a major feature of the aestheticized landscape: in one of the most famous scenes in the novel, all the women of the household tour the garden "to speed the flowers" at the end of spring, while Lin Daiyu mourns the passing of spring by collecting the fallen petals and burying them (chap. 27). They versify on chrysanthemums and eat crabs in autumn (chaps. 37 and 38); they appear wearing dazzling feathered capes in the brilliant winter snowscape (chap. 49); and in an echo of the *Mudan ting*, Shi Xiangyun falls asleep in the peony garden and wakes up covered in crimson peony petals early in the third month (62.687).

Cao Xueqin directs the readers' attention toward these conventional painterly motifs when he has Grandmother Jia insist that Xichun should in-

18. Ibid., pp. 61–70.

19. When Baoyu's father praises the naturalistic quality of Li Wan's rustic cottage in Grand Prospect Garden, Baoyu dismisses it as even more artificial than the other fanciful buildings because its artifice is disguised as mimicking nature (*HLM*, 17–18.167).

20. Daiyu, for example, first teaches Baoyu musical theory about the *qin*, the Chinese lute, and then plays it in chapters 86 and 87.

corporate the winter scene into her painting of the garden (50.545). This connection between *qing* and culture (*wen*) is the most legitimate aspect of *qing*, for a talented artist is able to transform the raw and frequently transgressive passions of *qing* into culturally acceptable forms of artistic production.[21] The admiration and sympathy of many readers for Qingwen 晴雯 (Skybright in Hawkes's translation) seems to be linked to her passionate outbursts, the most celebrated of which is her ripping of the fans (31.328). One Qing commentator eulogized her by glossing her name as *qingwen* 情文, "passion and literary writing."[22] Historically, the patina of respectability associated with cultural production was one of the most important defenses mounted for potentially risqué narratives about *qing*.[23] This refinement of raw *qing* into an impassioned sensibility is synonymous with what Yu-kung Kao and Wai-yee Li refer to as the "lyric consciousness."[24] There is no doubt that the unusually high quality of verse in the novel along with its celebration of lyric aesthetics have prevented readers from dwelling on the excesses of Baoyu's "lust of the mind" (*yiyin* 意淫); we would all like to believe, along with Baoyu, that a text this beautiful must be pure.

The performative aspect of the theme of nature in *Honglou meng* is brought out with the introduction of the troop of actresses into Grand Prospect Garden. "Like weary birds escaping from their cages, they played around in the garden every day" (58.640). Their aimless energy is spent picking over their clothing and food and squabbling and fighting among themselves. The lovelorn actress who, as Baoyu looks on, scratches characters in the dirt makes a contemptuous comparison between herself, cooped up in the garden, and the trained sparrow that performs acrobatic feats with a flag inside its cage (36.380–81). Parallels between masters and actresses are repeatedly drawn.[25]

Although Wang Xifeng is the only one of the masters to have the name of a bird, Baoyu and Daiyu have the strongest connection to the theme of

21. For a summation of this view, see the section "*Qing cai*" 情采 in Liu Xie, *Wenxin diaolong*, pp. 537–42.

22. "Er zhi Daoren" 二知道人, "*Honglou meng* shuo meng," 紅樓夢說夢, in *HLMJ*, p. 83.

23. Zhou Ruchang ("*Honglou meng* yu qing wenhua") has recently defended the meaning of *qing* in *Honglou meng* as an expression of *wen*.

24. Y. K. Kao, "Lyric Vision"; W. Y. Li, *Enchantment*, pp. 22–24 and *passim*.

25. The final poem of the song suite performed by the Fairy Disenchantment, "The Birds into the Woods Have Flown," predicts the desolation of the garden after all the girls have left (*HLM*, 5.56); trans. from Hawkes and Minford, *Story of the Stone*, 1: 144.

birds. The only servant who accompanies Daiyu to the Jia household is Xueyan 雪雁, Snowgoose; once Daiyu arrives, Grandmother Jia presents her with another maid, Yingge 鸚哥, Parrot. One of Daiyu's first impressions of the interior of the Rongguo estate is of the caged birds lining the entrance to the hall where Grandmother Jia greets her; Baoyu, too, keeps birds around his residence (*HLM*, 3.25, 36.377). Like the actresses, Baoyu and Daiyu constantly squabble between themselves.[26] Baoyu's maid Qingwen, a shadow of Daiyu, is consistently linked with bird imagery. Like Daiyu, her moods are unpredictable, and she is vain and cocky even when speaking to Lady Wang. She exemplifies the quick, violent, careless energy associated with birds as seen in the passage in which she stabs madly at the hand of one of the junior maids with a needle. "What do you want this claw for? It can't hold a needle, it can't pull thread, it's only good for stealing food to eat. Your eyes don't see [what needs to be done], your claws are light [to move], they only bring disgrace. Much better stab them raw" (52. 568). Baoyu and Baoqin strut and preen to everyone's delight in their ostentatious display of avian brilliance when wearing the shimmering red and green mallard and peacock down robes given to them by Grandmother Jia (49.525, 52.566).[27] Significantly, Qingwen's fatal illness sets in the night she stays up to repair Baoyu's peacock robe, a task only she is skilled enough to perform (52.570–71). That the bird imagery is tied into the theme of illusion is brought out when Grannie Liu (Liu Laolao 劉姥姥) mistakes a parrot for a sparrow: "Who would know that not only are city people grander, even their sparrows are grander. When a sparrow comes to your place, it becomes so talented it can speak" (41.436). The lines between performance and reality blur, however, when Daiyu's caged parrot repeats its mistress's most heartbreaking lines of poetry:

> "Let the others laugh flower-burial to see:
> Another year who will be burying me?" (35.362)[28]

Another aspect of artifice that is foregrounded by the performances of the girl actresses is the somewhat arbitrary distribution of gender identities within the aristocratic Jia family. Just as the social world of the garden reaches its apogee, Baoyu decrees that Fangguan 芳官, one of the actresses

26. Xiren describes them as "two sparrows fighting" 兩個雀兒打架 (*HLM*, 32.339).

27. For more examples of birds as emblematic of the girls "caged" up within the garden, see *HLM*, 30.320–21, 32.339, 35.363, 52.568, and 58.640.

28. Trans. from Hawkes and Minford, *Story of the Stone*, 2: 174.

who specializes in male roles, should be called by a male name and permanently dressed in boy's clothing. The cousins Xiangyun, Li Wan, and Tanchun quickly follow suit and rename the actresses who are in their service (63.705–6). During this same scene, Baoyu receives a note from his intimate friend the nun Miaoyu 妙玉, who points to the ambiguity of her own identity as "neither monk nor lay, neither male nor female" (僧不僧，俗不俗，男不男，女不女, 63.704). Clearly, within the aestheticized world of the garden, just as the cousins assume the roles of poets, painters, fishermen, and farmers, they play at gender, too. Baoyu's femininity, Lin Daiyu's hyperfemininity, Shi Xiangyun and Wang Xifeng's variations of masculinity,[29] and most especially the mutability of the gendered performances of the actresses, indicate that Cao's depictions of gender exploit a performative and aesthetic impulse that is not founded on a biological basis.[30]

Cao's original concept of *Honglou meng* as a *chuanqi* drama rather than *xiaoshuo* fiction may in part explain the fluidity and symmetry of its gender inversions. Baoyu, along with many of the other delicate young men in the novel, seems to be modeled after the effeminate male *xiaosheng* 小生 role of *chuanqi* drama, who was conventionally paired with a *dan* female lead. It is no coincidence that two of the young men to whom Baoyu is instinctively drawn, Jiang Yuhan (Bijou in Hawkes's translation), who specializes in *dan* roles, and Liu Xianglian, an amateur who performs arias from romantic plays with *sheng* and *dan* roles, are both actors. Moreover, the provenance of Shi Xiangyun's stylish tomboyishness (31.328, 49.528) is likely found among the actresses, many of whom excel at playing the more boisterous male roles. That all of these performances of gender in *Honglou meng* are shifted toward the feminine is indicative of the way that these identities are derived from nexus of aesthetic values associated with the cult of *qing*.

More than being a performative aspect of *qing*, the gender fluidity in *Honglou meng* becomes part of the aesthetic surface of the novel. Gender complementarity as an aesthetic device is comparable to the use of heat and cold, which, as Zhang Zhupo pointed out in his influential commentary to the *Jin*

29. Wang Xifeng, who is as delicately beautiful as any of the women in the novel, was raised as a boy, is sometimes described as masculine, shares her name with a man (*HLM*, 54.588), has a great aptitude for numbers and little or none for literary pursuits, and displays a remarkable competency in manipulating the broad networks of power and relationships that typically exclude women.

30. See also Yee, "Self, Sexuality, and Writing," p. 395.

Ping Mei, is one of the central aesthetic features of that novel. The complementary interplay of heat and cold forms the basis of the bipolar categories used in *Honglou meng* criticism of movement-stillness, elegance-baseness, joy-sorrow, union-separation, harmony-conflict, and prosperity-decline.[31] As is true of the depictions of gender, the most artistically compelling examples of the use of the heat and cold motif are found in those scenes which depict cold-within-heat or heat-within-cold.[32] The failure of traditional commentators to identify gender complementarity as one of the specific manifestations of *yin-yang* conceptual categories that structure *xiaoshuo* fiction should not prevent modern readers from recognizing its structural and thematic importance. On a purely aesthetic level, gender complementarity expands the range of resonances that make up the novel's aesthetic surface. Gender in *Honglou meng*, as in Wang Jide's drama *The Male Queen*, derives its meaning not from being biologically rooted in the individual but from being situationally produced through a progression of complementary pairings. Baoyu, a sentimentalized rendering of feminine-within-male, is paired against a seemingly endless variety of possible complements, from the coarse masculine-within-female of Wang Xifeng to the gentler masculine-within-female of Shi Xiangyun to the utterly feminine Lin Daiyu, not to mention the feminine dyad composed of Qin Keqing (her name in Baoyu's dream is Jianmei 兼美, "Two-in-One," referring to the pairing of Daiyu and Baochai) and her equally charming brother Qin Zhong, who, like Baoyu, alternates between being paired with other feminized men and women (including the nominally sexless nun Zhineng 智能). Rather than being an exclusive male-female dichotomy, gender in *Honglou meng* occurs along a continuum with a seemingly infinite possibility of positions and variations; yet, for the ideological and aesthetic reasons suggested above, the entire continuum is shifted toward and favors the feminine. A contrast to the process of feminization in Grand Prospect Garden can be found in the garden of the Confucian *Yesou puyan*, in which the character roles are shifted toward the masculine (see the following chapter).

31. Discussed in Plaks, *Archetype and Allegory*, pp. 55–56.

32. On the importance of heat and cold to Zhang Zhupo's poetics of *Jin Ping Mei*, see Plaks, "Terminology," p. 120; and Roy, "How to Read the *Chin P'ing Mei*," pp. 204–5, 216–17, 239, 240; for a discussion of scenes where Cao Xueqin mimicked the use of hot and cold in *Jin Ping Mei*, see Scott, "Azure from Indigo," pp. 96–101. Consider also the use of heat and cold in the characterizations of the cool Xue Baochai and heated passion of Lin Daiyu. On the thematic and structural influence of *Jin Ping Mei* on *Honglou meng*, see Xu Shuofang, "*Honglou meng* he *Jin Ping Mei*"; and Wang Rumei, "Zhang pingben," pp. 83–85.

DESIRE AND THE DISSOLUTION OF RITUAL IDENTITIES

The meaning of *qing* in *Honglou meng* cannot be considered separately from Baoyu's deep connection to Qin Keqing and her brother Qin Zhong. Several traditional commentators noted the obvious pun in their names to *qing*, and one glossed Qin Zhong's name as the "seed of *qing*" (*qingzhong* 情種).[33] The visceral intensity of Qin Keqing's connection to Baoyu and Wang Xifeng is brought out in the scene in which she appears in their dreams at the moment of her death. Baoyu awakes from his dream spitting blood. The first time they meet, Baoyu is symbolically married to Keqing; he is ushered into her bedroom, which is decorated with erotic objects, and placed in her bed.[34] It is in her bedroom, calling out her childhood name, that Baoyu is sexually initiated and introduced into the World of Illusion, where he discovers the intertwined values of *qing*, sentiment, and lust (*yin* 淫).

Keqing is not important to Baoyu alone; on a narratological level, her death surpasses all other ritual moments in the novel, including the imperial concubine's visit home, Baoyu's marriage, and the deaths of the elders Jia Jing and the matriarch Jia, in motivating the most complete listing of all the male members of the Jia family (13.128). The placement of a full genealogy at the moment of Keqing's death is striking because such a formal presentation of names typically occurs only at moments of great ritual significance. In addition to underscoring the perverse degree of honor the Jia family pays her, it suggests Keqing's importance as a central cipher that connects the interlocking narratives of Xifeng's ambition, Baoyu's *qing*, Jia Zhen's sexual licentiousness, and Jia Zheng's Confucian ritualism. As is hinted by her illustration in the registers of love Baoyu examines in chapter 5 and by the Red

33. See the Red Inkstone comment in *ZYZ*, p. 207; and the Huhua zhuren 護花主人 chapter-end comment to chapter 9 in *SJPB*, p. 152.

34. That Wang Xifeng's husband, Jia Lian (a cousin of Baoyu), and Baoyu share the title Er Ye 二爺, Second Master, suggests a similar symbolic union between Baoyu and Xifeng. Disturbing parallels between Baoyu and Lian are foregrounded in chapter 21, in which Baoyu's petulant tiff with his cousins and maids precedes a more rancorous quarrel in Jia Lian's quarters concerning his sexual access to Xifeng's maid Ping'er 平兒; in chapter 44 in which Lian's paramour, Bao Er's wife 鮑二家的, hangs herself on the birthday of Lady Wang's maid Jinchuan 金釧, who had drowned herself in disgrace after Baoyu had flirted with her in his mother's presence; and in chapter 66 where Baoyu joins Jia Lian in persuading Liu Xianglian to marry You Sanjie 尤三姐.

Inkstone commentator's discomfort with earlier versions of the chapter, Keqing's untimely death stems from her incestuous relationship with her father-in-law, Jia Zhen.[35] The crucial role of Qin Keqing as the person who simultaneously introduces Baoyu to the World of Illusion and the registers of *qing*, as well as to sexual experience, demonstrates the dual nature of the *qing* explored in *Honglou meng*, as both redemptive aesthetic bond and self-destructive sexual desire. That Qin Keqing's beautiful younger brother Qin Zhong, "the seed of *qing*," through whom Baoyu continues his connection to Keqing, also dies from desire in chapter 16 further undermines any clear distinction between the purity of *qing* and transgressive desires, the protests of Baoyu and many readers to the contrary.[36]

The novel explores two major means of guarding against the dangerous allure of desire—Buddhism and Confucianism. Although these philosophies often appear only in caricature, as in the depictions of the strange monks on Greensickness Peak and the literati Jia Yucun 賈雨村 and Zhen Shiyin 甄士隱, these philosophic strands resurface regularly through the entirety of the 120-chapter novel. Anthony Yu has recently discussed the symbolic and overlapping functions of jades, mirrors, and dreams in relationship to the Buddhist theme of enlightenment explored in the novel.[37] Baoyu's jade (*yu* 玉), which Wang Guowei glossed as a pun on yu 欲 "desire," is at the center of this allegory of enlightenment.[38] Paradoxically, in line with Buddhist teachings that enlightenment can be approached through immersion in illusion, Baoyu's jade represents both desire itself and the knowledge that will bring enlightenment. Baoyu's violent wish to smash his jade when he meets Daiyu, whose name can be glossed as a pun on *daiyu* 帶欲 "carrying desire," is thus interpretable as an attempt to rid himself of this

35. As will be discussed below, Red Inkstone had a special relationship with Cao Xueqin and was familiar with early drafts of the novel. Red Inkstone's comments suggest that an earlier manuscript depicted Qinshi committing suicide in shame (*ZYZ*, pp. 240 and 253). It is unclear whether Baoyu, a proclaimed passionate lover of purity, is aware of this blot on Keqing's reputation; he seems not to understand the slang phrase *pahui* 爬灰 (crawl in the ashes) in reference to Keqing's relationship with Jia Zhen when used by the family retainer Big Jiao (*HLM*, 7.80), but could very well have asked someone else what it means after Xifeng's refusal to answer.

36. The Huhua zhuren commentator tellingly blames Qin Zhong for initiating Baoyu's interest in male homosexuality (*nanse* 男色, literally, "male beauty"; *SJPB*, 9.152).

37. A. Yu, *Rereading the Stone*, pp. 137–71.

38. Wang Guowei, "*Honglou meng* pinglun," p. 250.

mirror of enlightenment.[39] Yu masterfully reviews the deployment of these symbols in the 120-chapter novel to argue that Baoyu's trajectory from one extreme of willful immersion in desire to enlightenment conforms to the structure of classic Buddhist enlightenment tales. I will return to these crucial symbols of Buddhist enlightenment in my discussion of the Precious Mirror chapters.

Less frequently discussed is the treatment of Confucian themes in *Honglou meng*. Early in the novel, the unscrupulous parvenu Jia Yucun connects the theme of jade to Confucius' self-referential comment about his willingness to serve in government when he says that if he had a jade, he would be willing to sell it to the right purchaser (1.9).[40] Baoyu's double, Zhen Baoyu, again refers to a jade in the Confucian *Analects* when he talks of his desire to "carve" and "grind" himself as part of his educational regimen (115.355).[41] Although the jade as an object of Confucian self-cultivation is a less well developed metaphor in the novel than that of the jade as desire, the two associations are linked in the Neo-Confucian anxieties over loss of self-mastery. As we saw in *Xingshi yinyuan zhuan*, the male protagonist's inability to master his desires led to the reversal of proper hierarchies in his household and to the household's eventual collapse. The Jia family is similarly beset with the absence of a male figure who is willing to "regulate the household" (even Jia Zheng does not pay attention to household finances until chapter 106, when it is too late). It is suggestive that Jia Zheng's beloved but deceased oldest son was named Jia Zhu 賈珠, a possible pun on *zhu* 主, master.[42] Zhu's widow, Li Wan, and his young son, Jia Lan, are the only characters in the Jia household who uphold Confucian ideals. Although loss and ephemerality are aesthetics associated with the cult of *qing*, the loss of this central young master is too ominous not to be read as a sign of collapse in a family in which, according to Leng Zixing 冷子興, the voice of cold awakening, "each generation of males compares less and less favorably with the previous generation" (2.18). Given this air of decline, it is tempting to read the surnames of the families with whom the Jias intermarry, Shi and Wang, as puns on *shi* 失 "loss" and *wang* 亡 "death." Zhu, the master, has been lost.

39. A. Yu, *Rereading the Stone*, p. 117.

40. *Lunyu*, IX.13; cited from A. Yu, *Rereading the Stone*, pp. 159–60.

41. *Lunyu*, I.15; cited from A. Yu, *Rereading the Stone*, pp. 160–61.

42. A similar pun may function in the Ming story "The Pearl Sewn Shirt," in which pearls and masters are repeatedly and disastrously misplaced.

Although histories of the late imperial period stress that the intellectual preoccupation with self-cultivation had been displaced by more scholastic concerns by the eighteenth century, it is erroneous to assume that the literati no longer felt compelled to fulfill the moral responsibility to be engaged in government of home and state. This yearning for meaningful involvement is powerfully expressed in other Qing novels such as *Yesou puyan*, *Rulin waishi*, and *Jinghua yuan*. Dai Zhen, who was roughly contemporaneous with Cao Xueqin, was among those eighteenth-century Confucian thinkers who stressed the importance of personal agency in the construction of a moral universe. His moral system is based on the distinction between the natural (*ziran* 自然) and the morally necessary (*biran* 必然); the morally necessary refers to the necessity of human action to perfect the workings of nature, as in the famous example from the *Mencius* of reaching out to prevent a child from falling into a well.[43] Although the theme of Confucian activist engagement is muted in *Honglou meng*, the Fairy Disenchantment voices it early in the novel when she warns Baoyu, "Be mindful of the teachings of Confucius and Mencius; entrust yourself to the Way of government to benefit the people (*jingji zhi Dao* 經濟之道, 5.57)." Baoyu's failure to heed her Confucian message underscores the failure of all the men in the Jia clan to accept their responsibilities. Jia She 賈赦, like the younger males of Jia Lian's generation, is too busy indulging his interests in sex and material pleasures to pay attention to household management; Jia Jing is too near Daoist enlightenment to bother with worldly affairs; and Jia Zheng, who is genuinely concerned about the clan's future, is too engaged in his textual world to be of any practical use.[44]

As in *Jin Ping Mei* and *Xingshi yinyuan zhuan*, the moral decline of the Jia household is expressed in gendered *yinyang* terms. In contrast to the increasing male turpitude of the Jia men is the widely acknowledged superiority of the women. As the dispassionate Leng Zixing says of Baoyu, "Look at this type of boy—it's certain that he'll never maintain the family traditions or listen to the advice of teachers or friends. It's a pity, though, that the girls of the family are [of a quality] rarely seen" (2.21). Even the maid Xiren 襲人

43. See Dai Zhen, "Mengzi," in Hu Shi, *Dai Dongyuan*, pp. 21, 387–88; see also *A History*, 2: 661–62.

44. Jia Zheng suffers a collapse of will before his mother (*HLM*, 33.348), and in chapter 99, he fails as an official, not because of corruption but because of his idealistic incompetence.

is praised as being "ten times" better than Baoyu (36.376).[45] The weakening of the male line and flourishing of the female in the Jia family is given a metaphysical basis in Jia Yucun's theory that the entire age is beset by a cosmological imbalance in primal stuff-matter (*qi*).[46] Jia Yucun recasts the more usual discussion of *yinyang* forces into a moral discussion of *zhengqi* 正氣, "correct or orthodox matter," and *xieqi* 邪氣, "perverse or heterodox matter." Yucun explains that those born with an excess of orthodox matter are greatly benevolent (*ren*), whereas those with a preponderance of heterodox matter are greatly perverse (*xie*, often translated "evil"; *HLM*, 2.19). Although explicit *yinyang* terminology is not invoked here, the two types of *qi* conform to Neo-Confucian descriptions of the differences between the bright, buoyant qualities of pure *qi*, equated with *yang*, and the dark, damp heaviness of turbid *qi* associated with *yin*.

Yucun provides a further metaphysical explanation for Baoyu's eccentricities when he concludes by saying that those with an extra dose of the perverse are predestined to stand out; those born into wealthy aristocratic families will be *qing*-crazy or sentimental (*qingchi qingzhong* 情痴情種; *HLM*, 2.21). Baoyu is clearly an example of someone born with an unfavorable mixture of correct and perverse airs. Although the heavier *yinqi* takes a relatively benign, aestheticized form as *qing* in Baoyu, it assumes its more usual expression in the behavior of various shrews whose destructive behavior runs as a subcurrent throughout the novel and even impinges on the supposedly pure world of the garden. In an echo of the narrative structure of *Xingshi yinyuan zhuan*, in which the collapse of the larger environment is motivated by the moral failures of the male protagonist, Baoyu's rejection of his role as heir and master results in the entropic collapse of Grand Prospect Garden in a rapid accumulation of *yin* signs of sexual transgression, sickness, death, and ghostly appearances, until the garden is reduced to a threatening wilderness.[47] Read in hindsight, even though the ascendancy of women in the Jia

45. Xue Baochai is universally acknowledged to be "ten times" better than her barely literate and dissolute brother Xue Pan (4.42).

46. Shi Xiangyun and her maid have a similar discussion about the complementary nature of *yin* and *yang*. Xiangyun explains to the maid that "everything in Heaven and Earth is created from a mixture of *yin* and *yang*: the orthodox, the heterodox, all that is strange and weird, the myriad transformations are all the [result of] the flowing together or the opposition of *yin* and *yang*" (31.331).

47. Although most of the *yin* signs of decay occur after chapter 80, the process is set in motion in chapter 71; see chapters 71, 73–75, 88, 93–95, 97, 98, 101–2, 105, 108–12, 114.

household is idealized in the assembly of talented and beautiful women, the air of *yin* dominance from the very beginning of the novel foretells the eventual collapse of the Jia household. We will return to the question of a *yinyang* meta-structure in the discussion of the Precious Mirror chapters.

Nowhere is the conflict between the values celebrated by the cult of *qing* and Confucianism brought out more forcefully than in the relaxation by the garden community of the hierarchical social order. Although initially appealing, particularly in contrast to Jia Zheng's stilted interactions, this relaxation of ritual protocol eventually results in a loss of identity. The proper use of names is an important component of the ritually defined identity because it immediately evokes the Confucian injunction to impose a moral order on society through the rectification of names; furthermore, difference and distinction (*fenbie* 分別), rather than affective bonds (*qing*), are the basis of hierarchical ritual identities. As discussed above, language is prescriptive within Confucian thought; the work of the sage is to make social reality comply with the ideals laid out in language. In *Honglou meng*, the power to name is most closely associated with Baoyu and Daiyu, the two characters who most fully embody the values associated with *qing*. Baoyu names most of the sites in the garden, and Daiyu helps him write the descriptive poems. Baoyu, as the main conjurer of illusion, also renames certain of the girls as they enter his world. Much to his father's intense distaste, he renames his maid Hua Zhenzhu 花珍珠, "Pearl Flower," Hua Xiren 花襲人, "Floral Aroma," foreshadowing the alluring nature of the garden.[48] Baoyu's first impulse on meeting Lin Daiyu is to give her the nickname Pinpin 顰顰, "Frowner" (3.32). His power to rename and remake reality according to his aesthetic vision reaches its apogee when he willfully decrees that the actress Fangguan should be called by a male name and permanently dress in boy's clothing. From this point on, artifice and whimsy, dominant facets of the aesthetics of *qing*, displace the Confucian imperative to establish a stable truth.[49]

The garden community enters a new phase in chapter 37 with the founding of the poetry club.[50] At the first meeting of the club, Daiyu sug-

48. Red Inkstone (*ZYZ*, p. 88) comments, "A strange name, a novel name. It must have an origin."

49. Wai-yee Li (*Enchantment*, esp. 47–50) has identified a fascination with artifice and illusion as a central aesthetic of *qing*.

50. Ironically, the motivation for the club comes from Tanchun, who generally distinguishes herself from the other cousins in her no-nonsense and somewhat orthodox style of management and is not known for her poetic aspirations. Moreover, the plain and industrious

gests that the cousins should take *noms de plume* in order to avoid the awkwardness of referring to each other by kinship terms. Chinese kinship terms encode within them differentiations of status marked by age and gender; to do away with this formal nomenclature is to erase the hierarchical social markers that within a Chinese context are synonymous with social order. The literary names the cousins take are innocuous enough as an imitation of the honored literati practice of assuming a pen name, but the founding of the poetry club seems to initiate an entropic process whereby the crucial social boundaries that distinguish generations, sex, and social class are erased. This process culminates in chapter 49 when the population of the garden explodes. With the arrival of all the new cousins, there is such a crowd that all the usual formalities are dropped, and with this all sense of order is lost.

> In terms of ages, except for Li Wan, who was the eldest, the twelve were all fifteen, sixteen, or seventeen; if it was not that these three were born in the same year, then it was these five having the same age, or these two having been born on the same day of the same month, or those two having been born at the same minute of the same part of the day, so that in terms of their horoscopes the only differences were the minute, time of day, or month. Even they themselves could not distinguish their ages, so that they indiscriminately called each other "older sister," "younger sister," "older brother," or "younger brother." (49.524–25)

The placement of this disintegration of ritually defined identity in chapter 49 is particularly significant given the structural parallels between *Honglou meng* and the 100-chapter *Jin Ping Mei*, for it is precisely in chapter 49 of the latter novel that Ximen Qing's fortunes begin to decline, with the entrance of the foreign monk who provides him with the aphrodisiac that is his undoing.[51]

---

widow Li Wan, who seems to be a stereotype of the belief that moral virtue and poetic talent are contradictory, quickly assumes responsibility for organizing the club, and Xifeng is soon after drawn in as one of the major financial supporters. Appropriately, Tanchun states that her inspiration for the club comes from the ancients who turned to nature and poetry as a retreat from the pressures of official life (37.383).

51. The increasingly insistent references to sickness, loss, and death after chapter 50, arguably the intended midway point in the novel, suggest that Cao Xueqin was following the structural model of *Jin Ping Mei*. A series of losses marks the transition into the decade following chapter 50: Qingwen's fatal illness sets in in chapter 51, serious shortfalls in clan income are reported in chapter 53, the New Year's celebration in chapter 54 is disturbingly hollow, and Wang Xifeng miscarries a male fetus in chapter 55.

The confusion becomes even more pronounced in chapters 62 and 63 when the garden bursts into a riot of activity to celebrate all the spring birthdays. Individual identities begin to collapse when Tanchun reels off a long list of characters who share the same birthday (62.680). During Baoyu's birthday party in chapter 63, social and architectural boundaries simultaneously dissolve. Early in the chapter, one of the older serving women chastises Baoyu for his disrespect toward his mother and grandmother in addressing their maids by their personal names (63.695). Baoyu likewise ignores other crucial barriers when he has the garden gates opened in order to invite his girl cousins to join the private party long after they are supposed to have retired for the night. That night, at Baoyu's insistence, he, his maids, and the actresses arrange themselves intimately on his kang in informal clothes and, with the cousins, begin to play drinking games little different from those played by courtesans when entertaining their patrons. Individual identities continue to implode: further coincidences regarding the ages and names of maids and cousins are revealed during the party, and it is at this juncture that Baoyu decrees that the actress Fangguan, who is so physically similar to him that they could be twins, should permanently take on a male identity. It is also at this point that the nun Miaoyu sends the note that points to the ambiguity of her identity as "neither monk nor lay, neither male nor female." This season of partying comes to an abrupt and ominous end when the death of the family patriarch Jia Jing is announced.

Despite the general laxness toward names and titles on the part of the garden inhabitants, they are nonetheless quite attuned to the significance of naming. For example, Baoyu treats Jia Yun 賈芸, a distant relative and opportunist, with derision when Yun refers to him as "father" (37.384). The charges of impropriety brought against the maid Qingwen when she fails to refer to Baoyu by his title come early enough to warn Baoyu of the dangers of ignoring ritual forms (52.569). Tanchun sticks to a rigid definition of propriety and provokes a terrible row with her birthmother, a concubine, when she indignantly refuses to recognize the woman's brother as her uncle (55.601). Baochai reacts with disgust when Xia Jingui orders that Xiangling 香菱 change her name to Qiuling 秋菱 (80.913). And finally, one of the reasons the Jia family loses imperial favor is the revelation that the unscrupulous Jia Yucun, with whom the novel begins and who has been enjoying Jia Zheng's patronage in his rapid rise to power, has been smuggling arms under his real name, Jia Hua 賈化 (104.245).

A parallel can be drawn between the collapse of the social order because of a failure to observe ritual distinctions and the collapse of meaning within Cao Xueqin's use of complementary bipolarity. Although complementarity was a standard aesthetic feature of late imperial fiction, *Honglou meng* stands apart from other works of fiction in the extent to which the paired terms are mutually interwoven; each term becomes so implicated in its opposite that each loses its distinct meaning. Rather than stress how the aesthetic of bipolarity sharpens the distinctions between the poles of meaning (as Plaks has done),[52] I find it useful to look at the ways that Cao Xueqin's aesthetics destabilize epistemological and ontological categories by collapsing the stable boundaries that separate linked terms. Perhaps the clearest example of this is the deliberate confusion of *zhen* (true) and *jia* (false) summed up in the couplet "Truth becomes fiction when the fiction's true, Real becomes not-real where the unreal's real" 假作眞時眞亦假，無爲有處有還無 (1.7).[53] Echoes of this paradox can be heard in the pairing of the two characters Zhen Shiyin and Jia Yucun in chapter 1, and Zhen Baoyu and Jia Baoyu. By establishing Zhen Baoyu and Jia Baoyu, the true and the false, as mirror images of the other, Cao subverts the claim of either to a higher truth.[54] Similar repetitions of signs and density of aesthetic patterning throughout the novel further contribute to the ambiguity of meaning. The repetition of the character *yu*, "jade," in the names of Jia Baoyu, Zhen Baoyu, Lin Daiyu, Lin Hongyu 林紅玉, Miaoyu, and the actress Yuguan 玉官, as well as the use of the phoneme in the name of Jia Yucun, creates a sprawling web of suggestive but vague connections.[55] These ambiguous repetitions erase the possibility of drawing absolute distinctions between characters or categories of meaning. In place of a clear moral frame, Cao has substituted an aesthetically productive but ethically meaningless chain of verbal relationships.

This confusion of boundaries between ontologically defined levels of reality is one of the rhetorical features of narratives of *qing*. Lighthearted examples of this aesthetic are shown in the scenes in which Baoyu willfully re-

52. Plaks, *Archetype and Allegory*, pp. 48–49.

53. Trans. from Hawkes and Minford, *Story of the Stone*, 1: 55.

54. The ambiguity between the two Baoyus is maintained throughout the 80-chapter *Shitou ji* manuscript; Zhen Baoyu's moralizing lecture on the virtues of studying in chapter 93 contradicts the careful vacillation between the two characters in the original manuscript.

55. Similar webs of connection can be drawn for the character Bao in the names Baoyu, Baochai, and Baoqin, as well as the phonemes Qin and Qing in the names of Qin Keqing, Qin Zhong, Baoqin, and Grannie Liu's granddaughter Qing'er 青兒.

fuses to distinguish between fiction and reality. When he visits his cousin Zhen's apartment thinking a girl in a painting there might be lonely, he discovers his own servant in *flagrante delicto* with a maid (chapter 19). Later, he sends the same servant to discover the whereabouts of a shrine to a young woman the countrywoman Grannie Liu had invented in one of her many yarns (39.417–18). More serious, however, is Baoyu's unwillingness to distinguish between dream and reality when, like Du Liniang, he refuses to put the dream of chapter 5 behind him. Instead of waking up, he enters ever deeper into the world of the dream by actualizing the sexual lessons taught him by the Fairy Disenchantment when he initiates sexual relations with his maid Xiren.[56] Baoyu does not wake up from this self-deluding sensual dream until chapter 116. As in *Mudan ting*, where the "reality" of the dream vision is proved by the fact that it is shared by Liu Mengmei, Du Liniang, and Xiangchun, this initial dream is shared by both Zhen Baoyu and Jia Baoyu, but with very different results.[57] The lines between reality and dream, self and other, continue to be blurred when Baoyu dreams of his double Zhen Baoyu and wakes up looking for himself in the large mirror in his apartment (chapter 56), and again when Baoyu and Daiyu experience the same dream of Baoyu cutting open his chest and discovering he has no heart (chapters 82 and 83).[58]

Wai-yee Li has recently proposed that the axial terms *qing* and *buqing*, which she variously translates as "feeling" and "not feeling" or "enchantment" and "disenchantment," are to be read not as opposites but as one semantic unit. She interprets the judgment on Baoyu, "*qing buqing*," as "feeling not-feeling, feeling even for the sentient or nonfeeling" in such a way that "the boundary between self and other is effaced."[59] The merging of epistemological opposites in the phrase *qing buqing* is a potent example of the aesthetic tendency of *qing* to dissolve boundaries between discrete terms. Parallel to the combining of *qing* and *buqing* into one semantic unit, Cao's usage of *qing* and *yin* also muddies the distinction between these two terms, which are normally treated as opposites. As the Fairy Disenchantment states in chapter 5, it is precisely Baoyu's lust of the mind that makes him so sympathetic

56. See A. Yu, *Rereading the Stone*, p. 144.

57. Zhen Baoyu's dream is mentioned by the servant Bao Yong 包勇 (93.131).

58. On a more playful note, the poetry-crazed Xiangling writes her best poem in her sleep in chapter 48.

59. Li, *Enchantment*, pp. 205, 207, 226.

to women; his empathy for and admiration of women, it seems, paradoxically arise from lust. And indeed, much of the novel calls into question the supposed distinction between *yin* and *qing*. However, although the fusion of two oppositional terms is very much in keeping with the aesthetics of *qing* (as is the blending of male and female, or dream and reality), it is anathema to ritual discourse. The kaleidoscopic figural density, so central to the aesthetics of the text, seems to parallel the incestuous sexual involution that comes from the collapse of generational and kinship relationships in the Jia family.[60] Paradoxically, *qing*, treated as the basis for the authentic self, eventually leads to a collapse of identity unless it is contained and regulated by ritual practices.

YINYANG NUMEROLOGY AND THE PRECIOUS MIRROR CHAPTERS

Concurrent with the rhetoric and iconography of authenticity associated with *qing* that configure most readers' experience of *Honglou meng* runs a strain of orthodox discourse. As in *Xingshi yinyuan zhuan*, this orthodox rhetoric constructs sexual desire (*yu*) as dangerous and presents punishment, frequently death, as a logical consequence of sexual excess. In *Honglou meng*, the chapters associated with the "Precious Mirror of Love" (*fengyue baojian* 風月寶鑒) materials form an orthodox narrative strand that punctuates and balances the alluring and enchanting presentation of *qing* in the novel. "The Precious Mirror of Love" is one of the alternative titles given the novel in the prologue and refers to the double-sided mirror given to Jia Rui 賈瑞 by a mysterious monk in chapter 12. Many details in the Jia Rui episode, such as the violence, cold weather, and inversion of gender roles, link it genealogically to a stereotypical shrew narrative. When Jia Rui makes an advance on Xifeng, she lures him to his death. On both nights he sneaks to her apartment, the weather is bitterly cold. Xifeng and her victim switch positions so that she symbolically "cloisters" Jia Rui within the locked gates of the Rong household; Jia Rui jumps "like a hungry tiger" (*ehu yiban* 餓虎一般; 12.121) on a hooded figure he assumes to be Xifeng. When he is locked outside in the cold, a bucket of nightsoil is dumped on him. Like Chao Yuan

60. See Plaks, "The Problem of Incest." Yee ("Self, Sexuality, and Writing," p. 401) interprets this expansive chain of interconnected but hollow identities as reflective of the emptiness and futility of language.

in *Xingshi yinyuan zhuan*, Jia Rui is tormented by his desire and falls deathly ill. When the monk gives him the mirror to help him cure himself of love-sickness, Jia Rui brings about his own death by ignoring the monk's warning to look only at the image of a skull reflected in one side of the mirror. Jia Rui turns the mirror over and discovers the beautiful Xifeng beckoning him. He then follows her into the dream world of the mirror and exhausts himself in a sexual frenzy. The family members who examine his corpse discover a large pool of cold, wet semen (12.124).

One of the unresolved questions in the textual history of *Honglou meng* is the nature of the relationship between the Precious Mirror chapters and the final 80-chapter version of Cao Xueqin's *Shitou ji*. The style of characterization in these chapters is strikingly different from that Cao used in the garden world; one scholar has described these chapters as melodramatic in contrast to the lyric quality of much of the rest of the novel.[61] Clearly, the Precious Mirror chapters stand out from the rest of the novel, and most scholars concur that these chapters are vestiges of an older version of the text and do not accord with Cao's final artistic vision. I will argue, however, that their inclusion is integral to the full meaning of the novel. Parallel to Jia Rui's double-sided mirror, which simultaneously reflects two contradictory images of desire, the full meaning of the novel is contingent on its weaving together of multiple and opposing constructions of desire.

All the chapters the eminent "redologist" Yu Pingbo has identified as belonging to the Precious Mirror narrative—the Jia Rui, Qin Keqing, Qin Zhong, and You sisters episodes (chapters 9 through 16 and the second half of chapter 63 through chapter 69)—contain harsh depictions of the dangers of lust more typical of conventional orthodox narratives than of the nuanced aesthetics of the rest of the novel.[62] Theories about the provenance of these chapters range from the widely held view that they are remnants of an earlier draft of the novel written by Cao Xueqin himself to a dual-authorship theory which proposes that they were drawn from a pre-existing text written by someone else.[63] A comment ascribed to Red Inkstone, Zhiyan Zhai 脂硯

61. Wai-yee Li (*Enchantment*, p. 233n) categorizes the Precious Mirror chapters as melodramatic and "closer to 'popular' vernacular narrative in its inspiration, naiveté and energy."

62. Yu Pingbo, "Yingyin *Zhiyan Zhai*."

63. Wu Shih-ch'ang (Wu Shichang) discusses the dual-authorship theory and his own belief that the five titles listed in the first chapter of the novel represent its different stages of composition in his "Cao Xueqin yu *Honglou meng* de chuangzuo" 曹學芹與紅樓夢的創作

齋, an intimate of Cao Xueqin who was closely associated with the composition of the novel, suggests that these materials formed a separate book: "*A Mirror for the Romantic* was the name of a book that Cao Xueqin once had. It had a preface by his brother Tangcun 棠村. Now that Tangcun is dead, I am reminded of the old when I look at the new. That is why I have continued to use it."[64] This identification of *A Precious Mirror for the Romantic* as a separate text is repeated in comments by the bannerman Yurui 裕瑞, who, although not born until after Cao Xueqin's death, was related to him by marriage and claims to have seen early manuscripts of the novel.[65] Recently, Dai Bufan has argued that Baoyu's sometimes contradictory behavior stems from the competing visions of two authors.[66] Likening the Precious Mirror chapters to sediment left over from an earlier version of the novel or a separate text has allowed scholars to diminish the importance of these materials in order to promote the view that Cao strove to write a seamlessly integrated idyll about life in Grand Prospect Garden. Although this might enhance the impression that *Honglou meng* conforms to the aesthetics of the classic European novel, which historically has been understood as reflecting the coherent vision of an author, it robs *Honglou meng* of some of its polyvalent richness.

Conceptualizing the Precious Mirror narrative materials as part of a vision, or even text, that predates and stands apart from the composition of the 80-chapter *Shitou ji*, forces us to confront the question of why Cao Xueqin did not excise or rework these materials in later revisions of the novel. After all, he did rewrite certain details of the novel, most famously the events surrounding Qin Keqing's death. Red Inkstone underscored the thematic importance of the Precious Mirror episode in his comment "This is where the author states his purpose; since he wants to write about the seeds of *qing*, he attempts to write profoundly here" 這是作書者之立意，要寫情種故于此試一深寫之 (*ZYZ*, p. 237). However, as has frequently been charged, some of the most glaring lapses in the unity of the text appear in the stylistic and chronological inconsistencies found in the You sisters epi-

---

and "Lun *Shitou ji* de jiugao wenti" 論石頭記的舊稿問題 in idem, *"Honglou meng" tanyuan waibian*. For a review of these textual issues in English, see Hawkes, "The Translator."

64. See Red Inkstone's comments to the 1754 Jiaxu edition in *ZYZ*, 12; trans. from Hawkes, "The Translator," p. 10.

65. Pertinent passages of Yurui's *Zaochuang xianbi* 棗窗閒筆 can be found in *HLMJ*, pp. 112–13; for a translation, see Hawkes, "The Translator," pp. 10–11.

66. Dai Bufan, "Jiekai *Honglou meng* zuozhe zhi mi" 揭開紅樓夢作者之謎, in idem, *"Honglou meng" zhuzuo*.

sode.[67] The compositional integrity of this same episode must also be questioned, for, as Yu Pingbo has pointed out, chapters 64 and 67 of the You Erjie 尤二姐 episode are missing from the 1759 Jimao and 1760 Gengchen editions.[68] Although the Precious Mirror materials do stand apart and may even, to borrow Yu Pingbo's words, form a separate narrative sequence, I argue below that they are much more coherently integrated into the novel than is generally recognized and that they play an important structural role. In fact, I propose that their structural placement may have taken priority over the subsequent fine-stitching of the seams between episodes.

Structuring the Precious Mirror chapters is a numerological framework based on the *yin* number six. As explained earlier, the use of *yinyang* numerology is a significant expression of didactic orthodox rhetoric; although the use of *yin* numerology is much less prominent in *Honglou meng* than in either *Jinghua yuan* or *Yesou puyan*, chapters associated with the *yin* number six nevertheless form a figural chain in which the Precious Mirror chapters, especially the You sisters episode in chapters 63 to 69, provide critical links. The minor characters whose surnames pun on the number six, *liu*, suddenly become the narrative focal point in chapters 6, 60–62, and 66, and this makes it tempting to read these chapters as an intentional sequence.[69] Indeed, the details of the incestuous web of relationships depicted in chapters 65 and 66 form a nightmarish variation of the theme of desire introduced in chapters 5 and 6.[70]

Baoyu's dream of enchantment in chapter 5 introduces the thematic and structural motifs used in the Precious Mirror episodes. Much to the disapproval of the older family servants, Baoyu is ushered into the bedroom of his cousin's wife Qin Keqing. Not only is her name an obvious pun on *qing*, her bedroom is filled with erotic curios that are so aesthetically refined they blur the distinction between sex and sensuality, realism and fantasy. Among the

67. See Hawkes, "The Translator"; Yee, "Counterpoise," pp. 624–25.

68. Yu Pingbo, *"Honglou meng" yanjiu*, p. 194.

69. Grannie Liu enters and takes over the narrative thread in chapter 6, Cook Liu 柳 dominates chapters 60 to 62, and the actor Liu 柳 Xianglian is central to chapter 66. The traditional commentator Zhang Xinzhi 張新之 (fl. 1828–50; about whom, more below) makes much of these puns on the number six and *yinyang* symbolism; see his introductory *dufa* essay, *SJPB*, p. 6; translated in Plaks, "How to Read," pp. 335–36.

70. That Baoyu's enchantment with desire is not resolved until a repetition of his dream, in an example of chiasmus, in chapters 115 and 116 suggests the careful structuring of the last 40 chapters.

objects decorating her room is a mirror that had belonged to Empress Wu Zetian, as well as the quince that An Lushan had thrown at Yang Guifei's bosom, and the headrest used by Yingying when she welcomed her scholar-lover in the *Xixiang ji*. As Baoyu drifts into sleep, an apparition of Qin Keqing leads him into a landscape filled with greens and reds, the archetypal colors of passion (*se* 色), and it is here that he meets the Fairy Disenchantment and is symbolically married to Keqing's double, "Two-in-One," Jianmei. The Fairy Disenchantment warns Baoyu about the interrelated nature of lust and *qing* and tells him: "To enjoy sensual pleasures is lust; to know *qing* is even more lustful" *haose ji yin, zhiqing geng yin* 好色即淫，知情更淫 (5.57). Baoyu's dream voyage to the land of *qing* in chapter 5 culminates in chapter 6 when he awakes to find cold, sticky semen on his thigh, proof of his dream experiences. In chapter 12, Jia Rui's entrance into the microcosm of desire reflected in the mysterious mirror also concludes with him ejaculating. Although most readers point to the contrasts between the two dreams in chapters 5 and 12, one could also argue that the large disorienting mirror that stands at the entrance to Baoyu's residence in Grand Prospect Garden builds on the associations of the *baojian*, the precious mirror of chapter 12. This mirror shares the character "precious" *bao* of Baoyu's name and is presented to Jia Rui by the same monks who are the caretakers of Baoyu's precious jade; both facts suggest the thematic parallels between the two images.[71]

Chapter 65 provides a perversion of Baoyu's dream of enchantment in the liminal world of the You sisters' home: it narrates the unsavory details of the openly tangled and incestuous relationships between the You sisters and Jia Lian and his cousin Jia Zhen as well as Zhen's son Rong in the household set up just outside the Jia family compound. Direct parallels to chapter 5 include the marriage of the other "Second Master," Jia Lian, to You Erjie and the reappearance of the Fairy Disenchantment at the end of the episode.[72] In these chapters, the lack of propriety and discretion on the part of the masters is so flagrant that even the normally tolerant servants are disgusted.

Chapter 66, however, marks a turning point in the narrative with the redemption of the fallen You Sanjie and her betrothed, the actor Liu Xianglian. The agent of their enlightenment is the pair of matched "mandarin

71. For an alternative reading, see W. Y. Li, *Enchantment*, pp. 225–28, 235–37.

72. That Jia Lian's trusted servant throughout this episode is named Bao Er also seems more than coincidence.

duck and drake" swords that Liu Xianglian had presented as an engagement token (mandarin ducks and drakes are a reference to marital bliss). The swords are ironically described as cold and gleaming pools of autumn waters, adjectives that are typically ascribed to mirrors but that also echo the descriptions of the cold pools of semen concluding Baoyu and Jia Rui's dream sequences (6.59, 12.124).[73] In contrast to Baoyu, who enters an even deeper level of sensual illusion in chapter 6, You Sanjie, who, for most of her life had been a caricature of decadence, is awakened by these symbolic mirrors and uses one to cut her throat as a sign of her renunciation of her past life. Liu Xianglian follows suit and slashes off his hair to mark his decision to become a monk. The unlikely joint enlightenment of You Sanjie and Liu Xianglian in chapter 66 underscores the depth of Baoyu's failure to comprehend Fairy Disenchantment's lesson in chapter 6. The figural parallels between Baoyu and Liu Xianglian further suggest a connection between the two scenes. Baoyu and Xianglian, who enjoy a suggestively intimate friendship and are both strikingly beautiful young men, share the title "Second Master" with Jia Lian. Baoyu's admission of "having fooled around with [You Sanjie] at [the Ning household] for a month" 我在那裏和他混了一個月 incriminates him in the transgressive sexual behaviors detailed in these chapters (66.741). The final image of You Sanjie's ghost, holding the swords in one hand and a register of names in the other on her way to the Land of Enchantment to guard over other *qing*-deluded ghosts, is the final ripple of Baoyu's original dream (66.743).

The figural repetition and numerological patterning that link chapters 5 and 6 with chapters 65 and 66 might also explain the placement of the Precious Mirror narrative in chapter 12, midway between Baoyu's dream visit to the Land of Illusion and his sexual initiation in chapters 5 and 6 and the architectural realization of his dream in the construction of Grand Prospect Garden in chapters 17 and 18. Exactly six chapters from both sequences, the Precious Mirror episode is perfectly positioned to caution readers, and Baoyu himself, against getting caught in the illusory beauty of the sumptuous garden world. Jia Rui's failure to demystify desire underscores Baoyu's inability to recognize that his jade, too, is presented to him as a tool of en-

73. The description of the swords as similar to "two traces of autumn waters" (*lianghen qiushui* 兩痕秋水) also suggests the "Qiushui" (Autumn waters) chapter from the *Zhuangzi*, which Baoyu reads before his own enlightenment (118.390).

lightenment.[74] That the mirror in chapter 12 was made by the same Fairy Disenchantment who introduced Baoyu to the pleasures of love in chapter 5 makes the parallelism between the experiences of Baoyu and Jia Rui, not to mention You Sanjie, more compelling.

Chapters 33 and 36 complete the sequence of *yin* chapters. Although 33 is not a compound of six, Zhang Zhupo had identified chapter 33 of *Jin Ping Mei* as a key *yin* site, perhaps because 33 is half of 66 and numerologically three plus three equals six. Provocatively, the events of chapter 33 anticipate chapter 66 in providing Baoyu a lesson on the dangers of failing to control his desires. In chapter 33, the household watches in horror as Jia Zheng beats Baoyu bloody to punish him for his involvement in the suicide of his mother's maid Jinchuan and for publicly lying about his relationship with the *dan* actor Jiang Yuhan. Although Zhang Xinzhi 張新之 (fl. 1828–50), who, as we shall see, is typically interested in numerological patterns, does not comment on the significance of chapter 33, he does note that the father's lack of compassion, the son's lack of filiality, the older brother's lack of goodwill, and the younger brother's lack of fraternal respect in this chapter are emblematic of a "failure to instruct" (*shijiao* 失教), a damning charge he also makes in chapter 9 (*SJPB*, 33.526).

Despite the grim warning delivered in chapter 33, chapter 36, identified as a key *yin* chapter by the traditional commentator Zhang Xinzhi, takes Baoyu several steps deeper into the Land of Illusion.[75] Early in chapter 36, Baoyu's mother, Lady Wang, announces her decision to raise the maid Xiren, with whom Baoyu had initiated sexual relations in chapter 6, to the informal status of chamberwife. That afternoon, Baoyu falls into a deep sleep and dreams again; although this time the readers are not permitted to follow Baoyu into his dream vision, we overhear him arguing with several monks that his destiny is a marriage of jade and wood, not jade and gold, an indication he has re-entered the mythic world of either the prologue or the Land of Enchantment (36.378). While he sleeps, a succession of girls who are either symbolically or physically paired with him appear in his bedroom: first Xiren, then Baochai, who takes her place at the head of Baoyu's bed, and finally Daiyu and Shi Xiangyun, who peer in from the window. Al-

74. Recall the warning inscriptions on the surface of the jade (8.84–85).

75. Zhang Xinzhi (*SJPB*, 36.574) wrote: "This chapter is appropriately the thirty-sixth, a heavenly number; being six times six, the ultimate *yin* number, it is an important juncture in the novel."

though the commentator Zhang Xinzhi's insistent gloss on the rhinoceros horn whisk by the side of Baoyu's bed as a phallus (*yangwu* 陽物; *SJPB*, 26.567) seems hysterically overstated (such whisks are conventionally associated with enlightenment), Baochai's presence next to Baoyu's sleeping, undressed body is highly disquieting, particularly because this re-enactment of his visit to the Land of Illusion follows so quickly on Baoyu's complicity in Jinchuan's suicide (chapter 32) and Xiren's plea that Baoyu be removed from the garden lest some scandal arise (chapter 34).[76] Life in the garden world truly comes into its own immediately after this with the ironic departure of Jia Zheng to serve as commissioner of education and the subsequent organization of the poetry club in chapter 37. As Yu Pingbo has observed, the narrative stitching between chapters 35 and 36 is uncharacteristically weak, as is the transition after the You sisters' biography. The much-noted gaps after chapters 36 and 69 strongly suggest that Cao worked from a structural template that gave priority to placing these thematically linked scenes in key *yin* chapters over streamlining the narrative flow.[77]

Although chapters 30 and 31 are not part of the sequence of Precious Mirror materials, a number of topoi familiar from *Xingshi*, including a small flood, further suggest that the structural design manipulates *yinyang* themes. The heat in chapters 29 and 30 is oppressive; it is the height of summer and all the garden inhabitants seek ways to avoid the heat. (Chapter 29 in *Jinghua yuan* is similarly filled with *yang* topoi.) The Duanyang 端陽 holiday, more commonly called the Dragon Boat Festival, occurs in chapter 30. Although a lunar holiday, falling on the fifth day of the fifth lunar month, Duanyang had long absorbed the cosmological significance of the summer solstice. The summer solstice marks a critical moment in the calendar where *yin* and *yang* struggle for dominance. The "Yueling" (Monthly ordinances) section of the *Book of Rites* describes the symbolic importance of containing *yin* energy during this period.

76. Zhang Xinzhi's (*SJPB*, 36.566–67) comments stress the sexual pollution of details in the chapter: from this moment on, the girls cannot be "clean and pure," Lady Wang's secret decision to raise Xiren to chamberwife is crafty (*yinxing* 陰行), and Baochai's entrance into Baoyu's bedroom while he is fast asleep is the "ultimate *yin*" (*yinji* 陰極).

77. Yu Pingbo, "*Honglou meng*" *yanjiu*, p. 2. Wu Shih-ch'ang (*On the Red Chamber Dream*, 159, 198) notes the gaps between chapters 35 and 36 and between 70 and 71. Hawkes discusses the awkward grafting of the Jia Rui and the You sisters materials in "The Translator," p. 12.

In this month the longest day arrives. The *yin* and *yang* contend with one another. There is a parting of ways between death and life. The superior man [the ruler] fasts and restrains himself, and remains in retirement at home, avoiding violent activity. He puts a halt to music and visual attractions, makes no approach [to women], reduces his diet, avoids piquant condiments, restrains his desires, and tranquilizes his spirits. The various officials remain quiescent and inflict no punishments. In these ways the consolidation of the quiet *yin* is assured.[78]

Baoyu's activities in chapter 30 are in blatant disregard of this orthodox warning.

The main event in chapter 30 is Baoyu's flirtation with his mother's maid Jinchuan while she is fanning Lady Wang in the oppressive heat. His actions might seem innocent enough if they did not lead directly to Jinchuan's dismissal and suicide and if they did not so clearly foreshadow the lecherous Jia She's much-maligned attempt to get his mother's maid, Jin Yuanyang 金鴛鴦, for himself (chapter 46). (The parallelism between those two scenes is further brought out in the two maids' shared metal affinity.) In the second half of the chapter, Baoyu escapes his mother's explosive anger by running away into the safety of the garden. In the garden, Baoyu stands behind a trellis to spy on one of the actresses who is scratching her lover's name into the dirt. The narrator comments that "since it was the period of *fuzhong* [the height of summer], clouds and clear skies were not predictable, and a wisp of cloud could bring rain; suddenly a gust of cool wind blew by, followed by a downpour of rain" 伏中陰晴不定，片雲可致雨，忽一陣涼風過了，刷刷的落下一陣雨來 (30.320).[79] Zhang Xinzhi commented, "This refers to the accretion of *yin*" 乃云陰其凝矣 (*SJPB*, 30.480). Since the actress is oblivious to the sudden outburst of rain, Baoyu calls out to warn her.

When the girl heard someone's voice, she jumped with fright; but when she raised her head to look, she just saw a person beyond the flowers telling her not to write for it was raining heavily. For one, Baoyu's face was quite refined; second, the vegetation was quite thick, and the leaves and branches revealed only part of his face. The girl thought he was a maid, and since it did not occur to her that it might be

78. Trans. from Bodde, *Festivals*, p. 292. Bodde cites Legge's comment that during the solstice "decay begins to set in, while growth and vigor seek to maintain their hold."

79. As Zhang Xinzhi (*SJPB*, 30.482–83) noted, it is extremely unlikely that the *fuzhong* period and Duanyang should overlap; however, he continues, since *fuzhong* is ruled by the metal element, it initiates the ascension of Baochai's power.

Baoyu, she laughed and said: "Sister, thank you for reminding me. But, sister, what do you have to protect you from the rain?" (30.320)

Baoyu's feminine appearance, the shade of the vegetation, and the confusion concerning his identity complement the heavy rain as *yin* details. The *yin* motifs continue when Baoyu runs to his residence to escape the rain and is again mistaken for a maid. Inside the locked courtyard of Yihong yuan 怡紅院, the maids and several actresses have taken advantage of the heavy rain to block off the stream and flood the yard. They then release some ducks and other waterfowl "to fool around" on the new pond.[80] Instead of rushing to open the gate when their master knocks, the maids delay, thinking it is only another servant. When Xiren, who is soon to be made Baoyu's unofficial chamberwife, finally opens the gate, Baoyu punishes her with a swift and painful kick to the ribs. Although Baoyu's aimless roaming in search of amusement is treated in a lighthearted way in this chapter, his inability to contain himself, "to remain in retirement at home" in the words of the "Yueling," culminates in the death of a maid and the beating that leaves Baoyu bloody but unreformed. Given the implications of flooding in *Xingshi* and the other novels discussed in this book, the miniature flood that the girls have created in the symbolic heart of the garden reinforces a sense of emerging chaos just at that calendrical moment when the *yang* principle is beginning to yield to *yin*.[81] The lecture by the boyish Shi Xiangyun on the complexities of *yin* and *yang*, on the day of the Duanyang holiday itself, may be another playful attempt to foreground *yinyang* patterning.

One of the distinctive features of the Precious Mirror chapters is the extent to which shrews displace the more typical sentimental and nuanced portrayals of women for which *Honglou meng* is renowned. Whereas elsewhere in the novel the characterization of Wang Xifeng is softened through her affinity with Baoyu and her occasional kindnesses to others, in the Precious Mirror chapters her depiction is flattened to conform to the stereotype

80. Red Inkstone (*ZYZ*, p. 200) was the first to comment on the significance of this stream of water, which threads through the entire garden before pooling in front of Yihong yuan and flowing out of the garden: "Of all the facets of the garden, the most important is water; it is marvelous that it is described so explicitly." See also Yu Yingshi, *"Honglou meng" de liangge shijie*, p. 42.

81. In a further repetition of the topos, a more threatening flood occurs later in the novel at the end of the third month; this flood forces Jia Zheng to delay his return home (70.785). Significantly for the development of *yin* themes, Baoyu's dementia is mentioned early in that same chapter as occurring around the second or third day of the third month.

of the vicious and jealous *yinfu* and *hanfu* stereotypes. As described above, her entrapment of Jia Rui is filled with conventional motifs associated with shrews. The connection between transgressive sexual desire, shrews, and death is brought out even more starkly in the You sisters episode. So magnified is the *yin* trope in these chapters that four shrews compete for dominance: You Erjie, once the lover of Jia Zhen and now the unofficial wife of Jia Lian; her sister You Sanjie, whose actions, until she has decided to marry Liu Xianglian, are unbounded by any sense of shame or propriety; Lian's new concubine, Qiutong 秋桐 ("Autumn" in Hawkes's translation), who is overtly vicious toward her rival Erjie; and Wang Xifeng, who wants nothing more than to destroy both Erjie and Qiutong. Xifeng's cunning ruthlessness reaches new heights in these chapters when she uses Qiutong to kill Erjie while she pretends great solicitude toward Jia Lian's new wife. As mentioned above, sexual depravity peaks in these *yin* chapters, and in comparison to the indirect allusions made elsewhere in the novel the explicit sexual depictions are shocking.

A less well developed use of *yang* numerology based on the number nine also seems to be at work in the 80-chapter *Shitou ji* manuscript. The *yang* images invoked in these chapters are connected to male activities and explorations of external spaces (*wai*) as opposed to the female-identified interior (*nei*) of the household. Chapter 9 is uncharacteristically set outside the usual domestic scene in the Jia family schoolroom and depicts chaos in the male world of education. Although it may only be a coincidence that Baoyu's trip outside the family compound to visit his maid Xiren at home occurs in chapter 19, the family outing to a temple in chapter 29 seems intentional. The transition from spring to summer was already marked in chapter 27 (9 × 3). (As we shall see, *Jinghua yuan* also uses chapter 27 to explore *yang* themes.) By chapter 29 the summer heat has become oppressive, and it is at this juncture that the power of the fiery Xifeng begins to dominate the narrative. The members of the household again empty out of the Jia compound in chapter 59 for the funeral of the consort dowager.

Whatever one thinks of the authorship of the final 40 chapters of the 120-chapter novel, an argument can be made in defense of the quality of these materials based on their use of *yinyang* numerology and symbolism. For examples, in chapter 81 (9 × 9), Baoyu is re-enrolled in the family school; chapter 90 alludes to the return of Daiyu's strength as "*yin* reaching its peak and generating *yang*" (*yinji yangsheng* 陰極陽生; 90.100); and in chapter 99, the events are suddenly focalized through Jia Zheng, who is serving away from home as a grain intendant. In chapter 119, Jia Lan and Baoyu leave the family compound to participate in the official examinations. The fact that chapters 115 and 116 return us to the events of chapters 5 and 6 in order to rewrite Baoyu's failure to grasp the import of his initial dream leads me to believe that this numerological structuring in the last 40 chapters is intentional. Although the oppressive *yin* symbolism in chapters 101 and 102 (the cold evening, Xifeng's sighting of a black dog and Qin Keqing's ghost, the sudden illnesses, and the encroaching sense of decay and even entropy in the garden) is more than a touch overwritten, the evidence clearly suggests a manipulation of *yinyang* patterning at some stage in the editing of the novel. We shall see a similar *yinyang* structuring in the novels *Yesou puyan* and *Jinghua yuan*. Although the last 40 chapters of *Honglou meng* continue the *yinyang* numerological structures established in the *Shitou ji* manuscript, they do not continue to exploit the ambiguous slippage between the various meanings of *qing*. Instead, they settle on a more conservative interpretation of desire as destructive and promote the routes of Confucian engagement (through Zhen Baoyu and Jia Lan) and Buddhist detachment (through Xichun and Jia Baoyu).

RESPONDING TO DISCURSIVE AMBIGUITY: THE COMMENTARIES OF RED INKSTONE AND ZHANG XINZHI

The rich interplay between the two discourses of orthodoxy and authenticity is crystallized in both the compositional history of *Honglou meng* and the large corpus of commentaries and fictional works that attempt to bring closure to some of the issues raised within the novel. Inscribed in *Honglou meng* are two main conflicting views of desire: the orthodox view of desire (and ambitious greed) as self-destructive, and the sympathetic view of *qing* as a self-expressive and aesthetic lyric urge that leads to authenticity. Balancing these two constructions of desire are the Confucian and Buddhist responses of restraint and detachment. Few readers of the novel have been comfortable with the often playful ambiguity of meaning created by the novel. One of the pleasures of reading *Honglou meng*, however, is the richness of the critical context, the layers of commentaries that make up the immediate hermeneutical context. These commentaries include the writings of moral conservatives and nostalgic aesthetes; both groups have found in the novel a powerful representation of their own desires for orthodox stability or authentic self-expression.

The Red Inkstone commentators take pride of place among the commentators to *Honglou meng*. The first important readers and critics of *Shitou ji*, the Red Inkstone commentators had some advisory role in Cao Xueqin's process of writing and revising; indeed, Cao Xueqin may have penned some of the comments attributed to Red Inkstone.[82] (For convenience' sake, I refer to the persona of Red Inkstone in the singular, even though it is likely the comments attributed to "him" are a compilation of voices.) These comments identify strongly with the novel's lyric vision. Although the comments occasionally point to allegorical or moral readings and frequently draw attention to the compositional superiority of *Shitou ji*, they most often echo the emotions evoked in the novel and are filled with heightened affective expressions referring to the tears, sighs, nostalgia, admiration, and indignation Red Inkstone shares with both the author and the fictional characters.[83] Throughout he engages with the fiction and creates for himself a literary mask as a person of *qing*, the equal of the author or any of the fictional characters.

Red Inkstone's enthusiasm for affect overshadows his persona as literary critic, as can be seen from the following example. In comments to the first chapter, Red Inkstone uncharacteristically provides glosses for the obvious puns in the names of the characters Zhen Shiyin (眞事陰, "true events are herein hidden") and Jia Hua (假話, "false speech," a character who circulates throughout the novel exclusively under his stylename Yucun 雨村); Calabash Temple, Hulu miao 葫蘆廟, where the "true" character Zhen Shiyin meets the Daoist and Buddhist monks from the mythological prologue, is glossed as *hutu*, 糊塗, the Daoist state of enlightened undifferentiation, whereas the "false" Jia Yucun's place of origin, Huzhou, is glossed as *huzou* 胡謅 (farce).[84] However, despite his negative reactions to the depictions of Jia Yucun's un-

82. Although the Red Inkstone commentary is a compilation of several people's reactions to the novel and evolved along with the expanding versions of the *Shitou ji* manuscripts, Red Inkstone's comments predominate. For detailed studies on the commentary and discussions of Red Inkstone's possible identity, see Rolston, *Traditional Chinese Fiction*, pp. 331–35; Chen Qinghao's prefatory material in *ZYZ*, pp. 1–84; Wu Shih-ch'ang, *On the Red Chamber Dream*; and J. C. Y. Wang, "The Chih-yen-chai Commentary."

83. For a review of Red Inkstone's discussion of compositional techniques, see J. C. Y. Wang, "The Chih-yen-chai Commentary," pp. 208–17.

84. *ZYZ*, pp. 15, 23, 24.

scrupulous careerism throughout the novel, Red Inkstone cannot restrain from vicariously empathizing with Yucun's sudden infatuation with Zhen Shiyin's maid Jiaoxing 嬌杏 (Lucky in Hawkes's translation).[85] In this example, as elsewhere, the commentary mimics the novel in foregrounding aesthetics (here the aesthetics of sentimentalism) over consistency of moral code.

Red Inkstone so thoroughly immerses himself in the conventions of *qing* that he intentionally blurs the emotions evoked by fictional events with his grief at Cao Xueqin's early passing; he also writes as if he, too, were caught up in the web of fictional dreams.[86] His appreciation of the novel builds on several of the literary conceits associated with the late Ming celebration of *qing* in which illusion is confused with fact, text becomes more real than reality, and dreams are more true than waking. Thus, even though the biographical and textual information that comes from Red Inkstone's position as an intimate of Cao Xueqin is invaluable, we should recognize the degree to which "his" literary persona is derived from the semiotics of *qing* and perhaps rethink the privileged hermeneutical position that the commentary enjoys.

In contrast to Red Inkstone, whose literary mask is symbiotically intertwined with the novel's fascination with *qing*, dream, and illusion, Zhang Xinzhi and the other two commentators whose writings have recently been compiled as the "Three Commentators' Edition" 三家評本 (*Sanjia pingben*) went to great lengths to stabilize the 120-chapter novel within a Confucian field; as we shall see, their orthodox interpretations are frequently based on structuralist evidence.[87] Zhang took an explicitly Neo-Confucian hermeneutical stance and drew frequent, and disapproving, comparisons between the fictional world depicted in *Honglou meng* and the *Daxue* and the *Zhong yong*.[88] Although Wang Xilian 王希廉 (fl. 1832) did not explicitly refer to

85. *ZYZ*, p. 25.

86. See, e.g., *ZYZ*, pp. 12, 633.

87. The *Sanjia pingben* was originally published as the *Zengping buxiang quantu Jin Yu yuan* 增評補像全圖金玉緣 (Shanghai: Tongwen shuju, 1884) and includes prefatory material, interlinear comments, and post-chapter comments by Taiping xianren 太平閑人 (Zhang Xinzhi, preface dated 1850); Damei shanmin 大某山民 (Yao Xie 姚燮, 1805–64); and Huhua zhuren 護花主人 (Wang Xilian 王希廉, preface dated 1832). A reprint of this edition is now available in a 1988 two-volume set published by the Shanghai guji chubanshe.

88. For extended biographical notes on Zhang Xinzhi and a translation of his introductory essay, "How to read *Honglou meng*" 紅樓夢讀法, see Rolston, *How to Read*, pp. 316–40. The last three items of the *dufa*, which are not included in the *SJPB* edition, can be found in *HLMJ*, pp. 153–59.

Confucian texts in the way Zhang does, he, too, provided moralistic glosses on characters and specific events and gave extremely detailed structural analyses by identifying longer episodes and breaking them down into thematically discrete units. Wang also provided an extremely nuanced commentary on the type of intratextual correspondences Andrew Plaks has called "figural density."[89] For his part, Yao Xie 姚燮 (1805–64), the third commentator, focused almost exclusively on chronology; his comments treat the novel as if it were a history by situating the events in each chapter in an exact year and seasonal moment, a challenging task given the notoriously vague, and often contradictory, references to the passage of time.[90] For example, in his summary comments to chapter 12, Yao Xie fitted the disjointed chronology of the Precious Mirror materials into the surrounding narrative without acknowledging that the narrative is playing fast and loose with the temporal frame.

> Earlier in chapter 3 when Daiyu enters the Rong household, she brings us into the first year of the central narrative (*zhengzhuan* 正傳) in an *jiyou* 己酉 year; the tumult in the schoolroom in chapter 9 brings us into the second year, a *gengxu* 庚戌 year; the second year concludes at the end of this chapter [12]. From the funeral arrangements for Qin Zhong in the spring of the third year, a *xinhai* 辛亥 year, we go to chapter 18 and the imperial concubine's visit in the spring of the fourth year, a *renzi* 壬子 year. In order to keep clear the passage of time, the reader must not read hurriedly. (*SJPB*, 12.190)

The insistence of these three commentators on the intentionality of the structure and their frequent working out of how a specific chapter fits into several different narrative configurations exemplify the Confucian urge described above to equate literary formalism, *wen*, with moral order. The three used the traditional tools of allegoresis, developed in the *Zuo zhuan* commentary to the *Spring and Autumn Annals*, to point out meaningful omissions, repetitions, double entendres, and juxtapositions in their search for any slippages between the surface layer of the text and the eternal moral principles they saw encoded within it. The concerns of Confucian historiography impelled the three to focus on inconsistencies in chronology, the use of names, and the logic of associative structural patterns to produce moral meanings from the complex aesthetic surface of the text. The following passage from

89. Plaks, *Four Masterworks*, pp. 95–96.

90. Yao Xie determinedly provides exact dates for the chronologically confusing You Erjie narrative in chapters 64 to 69.

Zhang Xinzhi shows how a commentator could use formalism to construct an orthodox reading of a passage. In this comment, Zhang presented the schoolroom brawl in chapter 9 as structurally parallel to the mythological prologue and introductory sections that precede it and as thematically integral to what follows.

> The two previous structural sections total eight chapters and portray Baochai and Daiyu; they are called "Story of the Stone" and "Dream of the Red Chamber" and are intended to set forth their names [and characters]. The [following] four chapters are an important section that aims to narrate "The Precious Mirror for the Romantic" and bring life to the phrase "condemnation for failure to instruct" from the *Zuo zhuan*.[91] Therefore [this section] begins with Baoyu entering school and concludes with Jia Rui looking into the mirror. (*SJPB*, 9.151)

In this passage, we can see how Zhang used a structuralist argument to justify his imposition of a moral interpretation on what many readers have enjoyed as lighthearted slapstick.[92] In a parallel to ritual practice, the moral integrity of literature is equated with formal integrity. One result of the three commentators' efforts to situate the novel within a stable, orthodox field of meaning is that their Confucian readings ignore and obscure any sense of the ambiguities and excesses of meaning created by the complex and fluid aesthetic patterning of the text. Parallels can be drawn between these overdetermined formalist readings and the continued popularity of interpreting *Honglou meng* as autobiographical or as a historical *roman à clef*. Both hermeneutic approaches grow out of the tradition of Confucian allegoresis and its tendency to contain potentially subversive ambiguities within a proper and stable moral frame.[93]

91. Zhang had earlier referred to this phrase from the *Zuo zhuan* in his *dufa* essay. The allusion is discussed in Plaks, "How To Read," p. 326.

92. The Red Inkstone commentary also takes an uncharacteristically moral and stern approach to chapter 9; this may in part be because the only extant comments to this chapter come exclusively from the Wangfu edition of the 120-chapter *Honglou meng*, which supplements the Red Inkstone comments. For more information on the Wangfu edition, which was not recovered until 1961, see Chen Qinghao's introductory essay to the collated Red Inkstone comments (*ZYZ*, pp. 13–17).

93. Historically, readings of *Honglou meng* have been dominated by attempts to find correspondences between the lives of Jia Baoyu and actual people, be they Cao Xueqin or the first emperor of the Qing dynasty, or to decode the Ming-restorationist allegory hidden in the novel. Red Inkstone was the first to point to a historical basis for some of the characters and events in the novel; Yuan Mei, another early enthusiast, went so far as to identify the site of Grand Prospect Garden; Zhou Ruchang's *"Honglou meng" xinzheng* is the most thorough at-

Because of his interest in the *yinyang* structural patterns in the novel, Zhang Xinzhi's commentary is of particular importance to this study. Although his commentary can be criticized as the mechanical formulations of a Confucian pedant, it articulates more clearly than any other traditional commentary the *yinyang* numerological patterns that structure *Honglou meng* and other Qing novels. Throughout his commentary, but most succinctly in his prefatory essay, Zhang argued that *Honglou meng* should be read as an elaboration of concepts found in the Confucian classics, especially the *Yi jing*, the *Daxue*, the *Zhong yong*, and the *Zuo zhuan*.[94] Modern readers may not find his attempts to identify certain characters with particular *Yi jing* hexagrams either persuasive or illuminating, but, as argued above, a structural consideration of *yinyang* numerology may take us several steps closer to solving the puzzle behind the inclusion and the placement of the Precious Mirror chapters. Furthermore, prefaces written by other people and included in the *Miaofu xuan* 妙伏軒 (Zhang Xinzhi's studio name) commentary edition that suggest that *yinyang* symbolism is important to interpreting the novel indicate that Zhang's interpretation was not anomalous.[95]

One of the most unusual aspects of Zhang Xinzhi's commentary is the importance he attached to the minor character Grannie Liu, the earthy distant relative of the Jia family who first appears in chapter 6. Her value to his commentary, as the following makes clear, stems from the fact that he anchors his *yinyang* interpretation on her presence:

---

tempt to reconstruct a biography of the author, about whom little is known, based on evidence drawn from the novel. Most recently, Martin W. Huang has read the novel as a psychological autobiography in his *Literati and Self-Re/Presentation*. The *Honglou meng suoyin* 紅樓夢索引 (published in 1916) is a detailed interpretation of the novel as a retelling of the Shunzhi emperor's tragic romance with his concubine Dong Xiaowan 董小宛. (See Yu Yingshi, "Cao Xueqin de Hanzu rentonggan bulun," for a discussion of anti-Manchu sentiments in the novel.)

94. See *dufa* items no. 2, 3, 7, 17, and 26; *SJPB*, pp. 2–7, translated in Plaks, "How to Read," pp. 323–38. In response to the maid Cuilü's 翠縷 comment that everything since the creation of the earth is composed of *yin* and *yang*, Zhang eagerly writes "Yes, yes, yes" (*shi, shi, shi* 是，是，是) and goes on to say, "The hidden meaning of the book is derived entirely from the principles of the *Yi jing*" (書中隱義，無非易理; *SJPB*, 31.496–97).

95. See especially the preface by Zilang shanren 紫琅山人, the Recluse of the Purple Pendant, which begins, "The idea of the waxing and waning of *yin* and *yang* is discussed in terms of man and woman, in order that people might understand it more easily" (陰陽消長之義，皆以男女言，示人以易知也; *HLMJ*, p. 37).

When I first read the *Story of the Stone* and came to the [first] part depicting Liu Laolao, I took it to be an interlude of comic relief, like the appearance of a clown figure in a dramatic work, designed to keep the book as a whole from becoming too somber. Afterward, I went on to consider whether or not the author had indeed designed this to be comic relief, for then he should have been expected to insert comic scenes at periodic intervals. But, in fact, in the entire 120-chapter text I have only noted six visits [by Liu Laolao] to the Rongguo fu compound, with three toward the end of the book to balance out the three earlier visits, still people only talk of "three visits." . . . Moreover, the third visit takes place during a chaotic period of mourning observance, in which there is no point using comic relief, so I began to have my doubts about this. When I later read carefully through the song entitled "The Survivor," I saw that the rescue of Qiaojie 巧姐 [Xifeng's daughter] is in reward for Wang Xifeng's kindness to her in her poverty, and this seemed to me to be the answer. But at that point in the novel, it is only the sixth chapter, and a lot of the principal characters have not yet been introduced; also, immediately after the scene of Baoyu's first taste of "clouds and rain," precisely where one would expect an extended treatment of *qing*, the narrative comes to a conspicuous halt and she [Liu Laolao] is singled out for special attention. Pointing up her importance, special attention is given to tracing her roots and to laying out her genealogical connections over a number of generations. Considering all this greatly increased my doubts. . . . Yet it was not until three years later that I finally hit upon it: it was the way of the *Yi jing*, the whole book was nothing more or less than the *Yi jing*! In fact, the commentary of the *Story of the Stone* by the "Man of Leisure of the Great Peace" [Zhang's style] really began from this point.[96]

Although Zhang did not spell out the pun on the number six in the old woman's name, a fact that might be so evident he believed it does not bear comment, Zhang's main proof of the importance of the *Yi jing* to the interpretation the novel is based on the repetitions of the number six associated with Grannie Liu's entries into the narrative: the six of her name, her first appearance in chapter 6, and what he counts as a total of six symmetrically spaced visits. So important is Grannie Liu to Zhang's cosmological reading that he makes of her a wide-reaching (and somewhat far-fetched) symbol of the individual pitted against predetermined fate; it is in this light that he invokes her repeatedly in his interlinear comments as an abbreviated reference

96. *SJPB*, p. 6; trans. from Plaks, "How to Read," pp. 335–36, with the exception of the word *qing*, which I have chosen not to translate. "The Survivor" is from the song cycle Baoyu hears in chapter 5 and refers to Qiaojie's rescue.

to the inevitability of the principle of Change depicted in the *Yi jing*.[97] Despite the fact that Zhang consistently posits *yin* as a negative quality, his treatment of Grannie Liu is entirely positive. This is no doubt because she is his irrefutable proof that the events depicted in *Honglou meng* are based on the processes of Change, and as such she is neutral evidence of these cosmic forces. Zhang also makes much of the sudden importance of Cook Liu in chapters 60 and 61, the exact midpoint of the 120-chapter version of the text and in his mind the turning point in Lin Daiyu's fortunes.[98]

One of the least persuasive aspects of Zhang Xinzhi's commentary is his practice of assigning specific hexagrams to certain characters or events. As he explained in the preface, Grannie Liu, because of her numerical value of six, the *yin* number, is the Kun hexagram, which is composed entirely of *yin* lines. Baoyu is the embodiment of the Qian, the pure *yang* hexagram. As *yin* gradually accumulates in the fictional world, the sequence of hexagrams progresses from the Qian to the Dun 遯, the Pi 否, the Guan 觀, and finally the Bo 剝, which marks the collapse of the Jia household from within. The cycle ultimately culminates in the appearance of the pure *yin* Kun hexagram. Based on Yuanchun's birthday on New Year's Day and some interpretive sleights of hand whereby Zhang reverses the value of the lines, he makes Yuanchun the embodiment of the Pi hexagram; the next younger sister Yingchun 迎春 is the Guan hexagram; Tanchun the Bo hexagram; while the youngest, Xichun 惜春, joins Grannie Liu in embodying the Kun hexagram.[99] Zhang's comments point out to readers how the narrative cycle develops according to this ineluctable accumulation of *yin* energy. The hexagrams he assigns to the four "Springs," Yuanchun, Yingchun, Tanchun, and Xichun, mark the progression from the pure *yang* state associated with Baoyu in the beginning of the novel to the gradual accumulation of *yin* energy. Zhang spelled out this process in the preface:

Dun

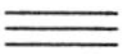

Pi

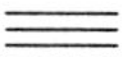

Guan

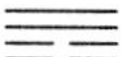

Bo

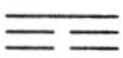

97. See, e.g., *SJPB*, p. 4; Plaks, "How to Read," p. 332; see also interlinear comments such as "Furthermore, after chapter 40, [the maid] Yuanyang is a stand-in for Grannie Liu; these people are used to enact the Way of the *Yi [jing]*" 又鴛鴦在四十回以後爲劉姥姥之替身，借演易道之人 (*SJPB*, 31.496), and "The hidden meaning of the book is derived entirely from the principles of the *Yi jing*. In the character of Grannie Liu it is portrayed indirectly; in the character of Shi Xiangyun it is portrayed overtly" 書中隱義，無非易理，在劉姥姥用暗演，在史湘雲用明演 (*SJPB*, 31.497; see also 120.1972).

98. See esp. *SJPB*, 61.992.

99. *SJPB*, p. 7; Plaks, "How to Read," pp. 336–37.

Gou

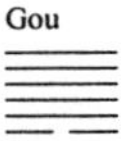

But *yin* does not suddenly become *yin*; it must begin from a single *yin* line. When a single *yin* line appears at the initial position at the bottom of the hexagram, it forms the new hexagram Gou 姤. If we take Baoyu to be the embodiment of pure *yang*, the "first taste of clouds and rain" represents the entry of a *yin* line into the first position, thus forming the hexagram Gou. That explains why this scene is immediately followed by the scene of "Liu Laolao's first entry into the Rongguo fu." After the *yin* line has moved into place, the process continues in orderly sequence, bringing us to the hexagram Bo.[100]

In this *yin*-based logic, the first of the three major narrative sections that Zhang identified spans chapters 6 to 36 and is dominated by Grannie Liu, the *yin* sign.[101] His comments to chapters 6 and 36 indicate that he demarcated this section to show the progression from the entry of the first *yin* line, signaled by Grannie Liu's appearance and Baoyu's first sexual experience, in chapter 6, to what he describes as the sexual excess of chapter 36, the "ultimate *yin* number." However, according to Zhang, despite the preponderance of *yin* energy throughout the novel, *Honglou meng* ends on a note of hope with Grannie Liu's rescue of Qiaojie, who, because she was born on the seventh day of the seventh month, is given the numerical value seven, making her a "young *yang*."[102] Qiaojie's rescue and return in chapter 119 is just one of the signs of the appearance of the Fu 復 hexagram, literally "to return."[103] In *Yesou puyan*, as we shall see, this hexagram also marks the end of *yin* dominance and the return of *yang* ascendancy.

Fu

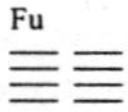

Consistent with his use of hexagrams is Zhang's simplistic application of numerology to read numbers as cosmological signs. Two of his most brilliant, but far-fetched, numerological readings occur in chapter 119, when Zhang extrapolates the Fu hexagram from the announcement that Baoyu has placed seventh in the provincial examination; Zhang's basis for the connection is the attached commentary to the Fu hexagram, which reads "On the seventh day comes return." In response to the news that Baoyu's nephew Jia Lan has placed 130th, Zhang commented:

100. *SJPB*, p. 6; trans. from Plaks, "How to Read," pp. 336–37.

101. The logic determining the shape of the second and third units is less clear: the second segment spans chapters 40 to 69; the third chapters 71 to 113; see *SJPB*, p. 5; Plaks, "How to Read," pp. 333–34.

102. *SJPB*, p. 6; Plaks, "How to Read," p. 336.

103. *SJPB*, 119.1952, 1953, 1955, and 1956. Zhang (ibid., p. 1956) specifically identifies Jia Lan, the Jia family's hope for renewed bureaucratic success, as an embodiment of the Fu hexagram.

One hundred and 10 are complete numbers, 1 and 3 are *yang* numbers; as for Lan being a "filial and incorrupt" provincial graduate,[104] [the novel] must therefore bring up the examination list to demonstrate the true meaning of the numbers; it must be a male servant who ushers in the news to show that it is *yang*. In the case of [Baoyu's] seventh place, it is merely a young maid who announces the news and it is an empty announcement, nothing more than empty talk, since both "maid" and "young" are *yin*. 百十成數，一三陽數；此蘭之爲眞孝廉也，故比提報單，見其眞也；必用家人接進，見其陽也。若第七名只是小丫頭傳進之，空言而已，丫頭爲陰，小爲陰。 (*SJPB*, 119.1958)

Zhang's mechanical projection of a limited number of hexagrams onto characters and events may explain his reluctance to question the authenticity of the last 40 chapters. Although Zhang did raise this hotly debated textual issue in the preface, he quickly dismissed it by pointing to the structural integrity of the 120-chapter text and dramatically claiming that even if his father were to command him, he would be "unable to add half a chapter."[105] For Zhang, the scandals ushered in by Cook Liu in chapters 60 and 61 represent the re-entry of old *yin* into the narrative, and his comments assert the cosmological significance of the names of Cook Liu and her granddaughter "Number Five," Wu'er 五兒, exactly halfway through the 120-chapter novel. The actual divinations of hexagrams in chapters 101 and 102 strengthen the argument in favor of his hermeneutical strategy, and as a result, the scope of Zhang's *Yi jing* exegesis expands dramatically in the final 20 chapters, which are heavily larded with references to specific hexagrams.[106] Indeed, as suggested by the frequent use of supernatural imagery to demonstrate the collapse of the garden world in the last 40 chapters of the novel, including ghosts, an exorcism, unseasonable weather, sudden and inexplicable sickness, loss, and death, it seems that Zhang's comments legitimately reflect a more clichéd *yinyang* symbolic vocabulary than that used in the first 80 chapters.

Underlying Zhang's Confucian interpretation of the novel is the premise that *yang* engenders orthodoxy and order and that *yin* functions as a source

104. Here, the commentary substitutes the term *xiaolian* 孝廉, "filial and incorrupt," for the official title of *juren* 舉人, "provincial graduate," used in the text of the novel. The commentary claims that the narrative concludes with this mention of filiality and integrity to combat the themes of licentiousness (*yin*) and greed (*tan* 貪; *SJPB*, 119.1958).

105. *SJPB*, p. 5; Plaks, "How to Read," pp. 334–35.

106. For Zhang's responses to the divinations, see *SJPB*, 101.1673–74 and 102.1681. See his comments on chapters 119 and 120, in particular, for his final, all-out attempt to persuade readers of the logic of his cosmological hermeneutics.

of heterodoxy and destruction. Frequently repeated in his comments is the statement: "Thus in the philosophy of the *Yi jing*, the principle of *yang* is regarded as superior and the principle of *yin* as inferior; hence the sage suppresses *yin* and elevates *yang*."[107] His moral stance is stated most explicitly in the following: "To rectify is to do good; the good is *yang*. To oppose the good is to do evil; evil is *yin*. The theory of *yin* and *yang* resides in this; it is what is called 'coming to rest in the highest good.'" 正即爲善，善即是陽；反善爲惡，惡即是陰，陰陽之論，至此而住，所謂“在止於至善” (*SJPB*, 31.497). Significantly, Zhang's moral framework for *yinyang* values creates a disjuncture between his metaphysical understanding of the inevitability of the processes of change and his *yang*-based ethical system. As we shall see later, the formal *yinyang* structuring of *Jinghua yuan* also invokes a moral value system that is at odds with that novel's idealization of the feminine.

As useful as Zhang Xinzhi's commentary is in identifying certain structural principles, his need to delineate clear *yinyang* patterns severely limits the range of his commentary. For example, although one might hope for a nuanced interpretation of Baoyu's effeminate qualities based on Zhang's understanding of the fluid interactions of *yin* and *yang* energies, he constructed Baoyu as a pure and positive *yang* sign.[108] Predictably, Baoyu's *yang* identity shields him from Zhang's criticism, and the moral decay that Zhang eagerly pointed out is attributed to others, not Baoyu. In chapter 33, where one might expect some admission that Baoyu has gone too far and might have something to learn from his father's beating, Zhang remains silent about Baoyu's faults and lays the blame squarely on Jia Zheng's failure to regulate his family (*SJPB*, 33.526).

The manner in which Zhang's equation of *yin* and *yang* with moral values skews his interpretation of the novel is expressed most transparently in his discussions of Lin Daiyu and Xue Baochai. Based on his reading of the two girls as anthropomorphic representations of the five elements, the tirelessly Confucian Zhang was an unceasing advocate for Daiyu as the proper mate to Baoyu, but he seems to loathe Baochai, whom he blamed for Daiyu's

107. *SJPB*, p. 4; trans. from Plaks, "How to Read," p. 331; see also *SJPB*, 2.22, 99.1643–44, and 104.1717.

108. The one comment I have found regarding Baoyu's effeminacy follows a remark by You Sanjie on Baoyu's girlishness. Zhang blandly remarks, "[You] Sanjie has a male air, Baoyu has a female air; this is just how one *yin* and one *yang* form the Way" 三姐有男子氣，寶玉有女兒氣，正一陰一陽之爲道 (*SJPB*, 66.1089).

tragic death. He consequently constructed Daiyu as a *yang* sign and established a complementary balance between her and Xue Baochai, whom he identified as *yin*.[109] Despite his warning to readers against being too much like either Daiyu or Baochai, he found Baochai so insidious as an emblem of *yin* power that he interjected the following comment into the maid Baochan's 寶蟾 account of how the shrew Xia Jingui came to poison herself instead of her intended victim. "[Bao]Chai killed Dai[yu]; when one method did not work she used another, her methods were innumerable, and all are in the novel." 釵殺黛，一法不行更有一法，其法多多，具在書中 (*SJPB*, 103.1699).[110] Even though the reserved Baochai exhorts Baoyu and Daiyu to be more restrained and pay more attention to Confucian texts, qualities that should endear her to the conservative Zhang Xinzhi, Zhang was one-sided in his praise of the *yang*-identified Daiyu and her shadows.[111] In one of the more extreme examples, Zhang glossed the incident in which the maid Qingwen, the quick-tempered shadow of Daiyu, thoughtlessly tears fans for her own pleasure as a veiled reference to goodness and filiality. "Her fan (*shan*) is the good (*shan*). To tear fans (*sishan*) is to think of the good (*sishan*)" 扇，善也。撕扇，思善也. Even more implausibly, he equates her laughter (*xiao* 笑) with filiality (*xiao* 孝; *SJPB*, 51.500).[112] Clearly, Zhang's hermeneutic need to shore up his rigid cosmological interpretations led him to make judgments that contradict what one would expect to hear from a stern Confucian.[113]

109. Zhang aligns the two girls with *yinyang* values when he claims that Xue Baochai's surname should be read as "snow" and therefore *yin*, whereas wood, Lin Daiyu's surname, "being engendered by the sea, and the sea being in the south-east" is a *yang* element (*SJPB*, p. 4; Plaks, "How to Read," p. 332).

110. Negative comments linking Baochai to the "poisonous heat" (*redu* 熱毒) of summer solstice also appear in chapters 30 and 31; worth noting in this instance is that excess *yin* is blamed for a negative *yang* imbalance. This same logic is used in *Yesou puyan*.

111. Anthony Yu (*Rereading the Stone*, pp. 173–78) describes Baochai as the voice of Confucian orthodoxy.

112. Zhang Xinzhi's optimistic interpretation seems particularly forced if one reads Qingwen's tearing of the fans against Pan Jinlian's actions (*JPM*, 8.138).

113. Zhang's positive view of Daiyu and Baoyu stemmed, in part, from the fact that he never equated them with *qing*. His silence on the topic of *qing* and the sensualism in the novel is remarkable, particularly since there was no lack of detractors who decried the power of the novel to weaken morals and seduce readers. Despite his critical debt to *Jin Ping Mei* and his warnings against the desires for wealth and sexual pleasure, Zhang Xinzhi did not attack the seductive dangers of the sensual and aesthetic pleasures associated with *qing*; nor, for that matter, did he comment on the creative or emotional expressions in the novel.

Zhang Xinzhi's commentary demonstrates how orthodox allegoresis uses formalist arguments to stabilize the meaning of a complex and heteroglossic fictional text. Despite the interpretive shortcomings of Zhang's commentary, it provides valuable insights into early nineteenth-century interest in *yinyang* numerology as a structural device in fiction. Although we need not be convinced by Zhang's claims that the author(s) of the 120-chapter *Honglou meng* composed the novel with a sequence of hexagrams in mind, or that the novel is an exegesis on Neo-Confucian principle, his comments provide a context for interpreting the *yinyang* symbolism found in other late eighteenth- and early nineteenth-century novels.

The complex aesthetic codes used in *Honglou meng* exemplify the centrality of what I describe as the competing discursive constructions of desire to the interpretation of late imperial fiction. The positive, liberatory promise of Grand Prospect Garden is conveyed to readers through an elaborate semiotic code that incorporates many of the meanings associated with *qing* discussed in the previous chapter. Twentieth-century readers and critics have been drawn to the novel's anti-authoritarian depiction of *qing* because it fits so well with both the individualist ideology of the liberal May Fourth movement and the anti-feudal critiques made under the socialist regime. For most readers, the aesthetic and ideological appeal of the novel's lyric vision has overshadowed the impact of the conservative Confucian morals depicted in the Precious Mirror chapters. However, the thematic and numerical correspondences based on the number six that resonate throughout the sequence of chapters 5–6, 12, 17–18, 33, 36, and 65–66 strongly suggest that the Precious Mirror materials are much more carefully integrated into the novel than has been generally recognized. When read from a numerological perspective, these chapters, which share an unusually dense clustering of *yin* topoi, form a coherent narrative structure that shapes and frames the presentation of Grand Prospect Garden. Rather than being an earlier and cruder narrative kernel that Cao Xueqin needed to transcend stylistically and intellectually in order to write his masterpiece, the Precious Mirror materials should be read as an integral part of the novel's broad aesthetic vision in which contrasting views of desire are brought face to face.

That differing constructions of gender and desire are employed in these strands of the novel is a result of the divergent iconographies of orthodoxy and authenticity. The unusually monochromatic portraits of Wang Xifeng and the You sisters and the depiction of relations between the sexes as a crude life-and-death battle in the Precious Mirror chapters are paradigmatic expressions of orthodox rhetoric illustrating the dangers of desire. As attested by the Zhang Xinzhi commentary, this type of orthodox moral vision is embedded in a *yinyang*-influenced structural form that provides a stylistic and ideological counterpoint to the narrative *mise-en-scène* of *qing* in Baoyu's garden world. Perhaps because readers have been much more sympathetic to the lyric depictions of the characters clustered around Baoyu, they have been less able to acknowledge how the iconography incorporated in their characterizations is as conventional and clichéd as that used in the caricatures of lust and cruelty in the Precious Mirror chapters. Parallel to the dual reflections contained in Jia Rui's mirror, a full rendering of the shifting and contradictory meanings associated with the polysemous concept *qing* can be achieved only when the morally and aesthetically regenerative power of *qing* is recognized as simultaneous to and inseparable from its ability to threaten ritual order.

The multiple gender codes used in *Honglou meng* are integrally related to the shifting ideological and aesthetic meanings associated with desire. A variety of late imperial markers of idealized femininity, including physical beauty, emotional and aesthetic sensitivity, physical frailty, and modest purity, are appropriated as attributes of *qing* and lead to the feminization of all who live within the garden walls. In keeping with the aesthetics of the late Ming cult of *qing*, in which illusion, doubling, and inversions were prized, distinctions between male and female are repeatedly inverted and blurred. Similar to the troop of actresses who assume new genders at will, the masters also don gendered masks that enable them to perform their affinity for *qing*. The fluid gender roles and quick succession of bonds of affinity, culminating in a dazzling array of parallels and correspondences in the garden world, contrast sharply with the harsh and deadly relations between the sexes in the Precious Mirror chapters, in which the men are men and the women are dangerous ciphers of desire.

As will be seen in the following chapters, *Honglou meng* is not unusual for the way that multiple constructions of gender circulate simultaneously within the same text. Many works of fiction from this period reveal a similarly ambivalent yearning to achieve the social stability inherent in Confucian orthodoxy while allowing for the possibility of expressive and moral authenticity promised by the counterhegemonic values associated with *qing*.

Although Cao Xueqin's use of gender complementarity may be more complex than that of other eighteenth-century authors, his masterpiece suggests that there is no one way to "read" gender in late imperial fiction. As suggested by a close reading of *Honglou meng,* the subtle orchestration of gendered identities was one of the arsenal of techniques available to authors to shape both structure and thematic content of their fictional texts. That the texts woven from these various strands of meaning and structure resist simple analysis reveals the limitations of our own cultural and academic understandings of gender. *Honglou meng* had such a great impact on later Chinese literature that its ripples of influence can be felt everywhere. The chapters that follow analyze three later Qing novels from the context of themes raised in *Honglou meng* in an attempt to untangle their contradictory aesthetic and ideological visions.

CHAPTER FIVE

Expanding Orthodoxy: Narrative Excess and Expedient Authenticity in Yesou puyan

The least well known of the texts considered in this study, Xia Jingqu's 夏敬渠 (1705–87) *Yesou puyan* 野叟曝言 (A country codger's words of exposure), provides a fascinating counterexample to the idealization of the feminine in *Honglou meng* and the two later Qing novels discussed in the next chapter.[1] Even though *Yesou puyan* exploits many of the aesthetic conventions of the scholar-beauty romance, it shifts its construction of a utopic world to the *yang* end of the spectrum in its promotion of an orthodox Confucian vision. Although the novel was composed at roughly the same time as *Honglou meng, Yesou puyan* did not receive much attention until the 1880s, nearly a century after Xia's death, when it was brought out by at least three different publishing houses. This sudden interest in the novel in the late nineteenth century was likely due to its depiction of a muscular Confucianism leading a revival of Chinese cultural and political supremacy, a theme of obvious interest to readers witnessing the rapid dissolution of China's imperial dominance. Hence, although *Yesou puyan* fit the publishing and reading interests of late nineteenth and early twentieth century, it cannot be said to have influenced the development of Qing fiction.

One of the interpretive challenges presented by *Yesou puyan* is its defiance of so many of the generic conventions by which scholars have traditionally categorized and interpreted *xiaoshuo* fiction. The novel is remarkable for its length; at over 150 chapters, it is one of the longer, if not the longest, traditional Chinese novel. Two different versions of the Qing text are extant. Although the contents of the 152- and 154-chapter versions are so close that they do not properly constitute two different recensions, I will argue for the

1. The translation of the title is taken from McMahon's *Misers*.

aesthetic superiority of the 152-chapter version based on its use of *yinyang* numerological punning, even though that manuscript suffers from several lacunae and has been superseded by the 154-chapter version in all modern editions. Worth noting is that at least one twentieth-century editor thought the novel could be improved by pruning it to the canonical 100-chapter length; although this poorly edited abridgment was clearly produced for commercial reasons, its publishers, in contrast to Xia Jingqu, recognized the perceived cultural value of the 100-chapter format.[2]

Despite its commitment to reviving a Confucian social and political order, *Yesou puyan* exceeds the limits of orthodox restraint in more than just length. The novel contains passages that are strikingly pornographic. Indeed, one of the most unusual, and to many readers disturbing, aspects of *Yesou puyan* is its treatment of sexuality: rapacious sexual acts are used to portray the degenerate nature of the adherents of anti-Confucian groups, but the hero and, more surprisingly, several of the sympathetically portrayed female characters, including his future concubines, appear in a number of sexually graphic scenes. In most other late imperial texts, even a hint of illicit sexuality would immediately call into question any character's, especially a woman's, claims to a virtuous identity. *Yesou puyan* is unique in presenting itself as an orthodox text that treats uncoerced sexual contact between unmarried partners as unproblematic and frequently beneficial. Although some critics have suggested that this sexual content places the novel outside the mainstream of mid-Qing fiction, as I hope to show, it deserves a much more central position in the history of Qing fiction than it has been accorded, due

2. The novel continued to be of interest to Republican-era readers. A 100-chapter edition, entitled *Yuanzhu guben Yesou puyan* 原著古本野叟曝言 (Original, old-style *Yesou puyan*), preserved in the van Gulik collection, was published by the Shanghai Hao qingnian shudian in 1933. This text is a poor-quality abridgment of the longer novel and is of little literary interest. Although the publishing information on the back leaf states that this edition is the sixth reprint of a text originally published in Shanghai in September 1929, the claim is somewhat suspect. Appearing on the very last page is a table that compares the names used in the original *Yesou puyan* to those used in a novel entitled *Jiangu qinxin* 劍骨琴心 (Bones of sword, heart of zither). That this "Original, Old-Style *Yesou puyan*" was originally published as *Jiangu qinxin* is betrayed by the fact that the names of the characters in this early twentieth-century abridgment correspond to those listed in the *Jiangu qinxin* and that chapter 100 concludes with the formulaic closing line: "And here concludes my telling of the novel *Jiangu qinxin*." Since it was common practice during the late Qing for publishing houses to buy printing plates from one another and republish the book under a different title, this redaction may have been carried out much earlier than 1929.

to its engagements with thematic and aesthetic issues familiar to us from *Honglou meng* and *Jinghua yuan*.

Since much of the following analysis of the aesthetic patterning in the novel is based on its use of *yinyang* numerology, I need to engage the question of editions much more closely for *Yesou puyan* than has been necessary for any of the works discussed above. Two different published versions of the novel are extant: the 1881, 152-chapter woodblock Piling huizhenlou 昆陵彙珍樓 edition, which, as I describe below, seems to be an accurate copy of a damaged manuscript;[3] and two 154-chapter editions, the movable-type Shanghai Shenbao guan 申報館 edition, published in 1882, and a lithograph edition with a preface dated 1882 by the Woodcutter of the Eastern Min Mountains, Ximin shanqiao 西岷山樵. The publication information is missing from the last edition. The 152- and 154-chapter versions are very close and include identical chapter-summary comments by an anonymous commentator(s). The primary difference between the two versions is the inclusion of narrative materials missing from the 152-chapter version in the longer text; this material makes up part of the second chapter and the entirety of the third and fourth chapters in the 154-chapter version (thus, chapter 5 in the 154-chapter version is equivalent to chapter 3 in the 152-chapter version, chapter 6 to chapter 4, and so on).

A long-standing controversy exists as to the provenance of this material; the statement of editorial principles in the *fanli* 凡例 of the 152-chapter edition describes the incomplete state of the manuscript from which the woodblocks were carved and notes that this edition is faithful to that manuscript and "would not dare presume to add one word" (*bugan wangzeng yizi* 不敢妄增一字). Although one might expect a disclaimer of this sort for any unstable text, the *fanli* of the 154-chapter versions make no similar claim. This suggests that the editors of the 152-chapter woodblock version were aware of the extra materials and, for reasons they left unspecified, rejected them as spurious. The 152-chapter edition notes those places at which the source-

3. This woodblock edition was reprinted by Tianyi chubanshe in Taipei in 1985 and the Guji chubanshe (n.d.) in Shanghai. My references, unless otherwise noted, are to the 152-chapter Piling huizhenlou edition. For those chapters that are missing from the 152-chapter edition, references are to the 1993 reprint of the 154-chapter Shenbao guan edition with full chapter-summaries but no interlinear commentary published by the Renmin Zhongguo chubanshe in Beijing.

text was incomplete and provides a summary of the events between the end of chapter 2 and the beginning of chapter 3:

Following this was the flood, the flipping of the boat, the rescue of the young lady, the unearthing of the dragon, the capturing of the strange, the lodging in a temple, the swearing of the oath of sisterhood, the running into the hateful, the ambushing of the monk, the burning of the temple, the destroying of the wall, the releasing of the women, and so on. Since the world is without a complete manuscript, I've respectfully kept the original lacunae. 下有發水，覆舟，救妹，挖龍，擒怪，宿廟，結妹，逢兇，截僧，燒寺，破牆，放女等事。世無全稿，祇仍原缺.

The 154-chapter edition contains two extra chapters that faithfully narrate these events; it also supplies sections of chapters 132–36 that are missing in the shorter version.[4] Although I agree with others who have studied these texts that the material in chapters 3 and 4 of the 154-chapter version seems to be stylistically consistent with the rest of the novel, I question whether it should be inserted as two new chapters rather than treated as pages missing from chapters 2 and 3 of the original. Wang Qiongling has argued that this would make these chapters disproportionately long and busy, but there are reasons, in my opinion, for suggesting that these two extra chapters were not a part of the original design.[5] The recent discovery of a 154-chapter, hand-copied manuscript dated 1878 has shifted scholarly opinion toward accepting the extra material as integral to the text. Wang Qiongling has meticulously compared this manuscript with the extant published versions and has concluded that the 1878 manuscript represents the most authoritative version of the text extant.[6] According to her description, the manuscript represents a collation and correction of at least two sources. Like the 152-chapter version,

4. Ouyang Jian ("*Yesou puyan* banben bianxi") argues that the additions to the 154-chapter text are very close in spirit to Xia Jingqu's original text from which both versions are drawn. Joanna Kuriyama ("Confucianism in Fiction," pp. 211–12), however, notes a significant difference in content in the way these two versions handle the materials in chapters 132–36. The 152-chapter edition contains no references to Suchen's active involvement in orgiastic sexual activities, and he is represented throughout as a victim of sexual assaults. The extra materials in the 154-chapter edition describe Suchen as actively taking part in debauched sexual activities during the seven years of dementia he suffers after facing a roaring lion. Given the emphasis on Suchen's purity throughout the rest of the novel, his lapse into extreme moral debilitation is highly anomalous.

5. Wang Qiongling, *Qingdai sida caixue xiaoshuo*, p. 101.

6. Ibid., pp. 81–115.

the manuscript contains interlinear and chapter-summary comments (the two published 154-chapter editions have only the chapter-summary comments). The manuscript also contains a complete text until chapter 105 and lacks only the interlinear comments from chapters 3 and 4; starting with chapter 106, the manuscript has lacunae in both commentary and text.[7] There is nothing in the 152-chapter text that does not appear in the longer versions. The hand-copied manuscript corrects many of the wrong characters in the other versions, rearranges some of the chapter divisions, and changes or expands four of the chapter couplets.[8]

Although I do not dispute the editorial superiority of the 1878 manuscript, I believe that the textual issues may be more complicated than Wang's analysis allows. The first problem that needs to be addressed is that the table of contents in the 1878 manuscript omits the chapter couplets for chapters 3 and 4; Wang Qiongling explains this as an oversight on the part of the otherwise meticulous transcriber, who must have been working in part from a 152-chapter version and forgot to go back and fill in the blanks.[9] But it is also noteworthy that chapters 3 and 4 are the only ones before chapter 106 that do not contain interlinear commentary. Unfortunately, references in the chapter-summary commentaries to specific chapters by number do not provide clear evidence for either argument. Wang points to a comment at the end of chapter 9 of the 154-chapter version as evidence that the commentary was based on a 154-chapter version.[10] However, a number of other intratextual references she does not address work only for the 152-chapter length.[11] Several methodological problems limit the utility of this

7. This manuscript is housed in the rare books section of the Shehui kexue yanjiuyuan in Beijing. For more information on the manuscript, see Wang Qiongling's detailed discussion in *Qingdai sida caixue xiaoshuo*, pp. 85–86.

8. Based on their similar chapter divisions and chapter couplets, Wang Qiongling concludes that the two 1882 versions are based on the 1881 woodblock version, with the inclusion of missing materials. The Shenbao guan edition includes summary comments to chapters 2, 3–4, 65–68, 131–35, 138–39, and 148–51, all of which are missing from the woodblock version.

9. Wang Qiongling, *Qingdai sida caixue xiaoshuo*, pp. 103–4.

10. Ibid., pp. 101–2.

11. A comment appended to chapter 45 (p. 12a) about Suchen's disguise refers forward to chapter 53 in which Suchen's servants and concubines fail to recognize him (this incident can be found on 53.9b–10a). A comment appended to chapter 47 (p. 12b) refers specifically to Wen Suchen's anti-Daoist diatribe in chapter 57 (57.8b–10a); a second comment on 47.12b–13a refers specifically to the theme of dreaming introduced in chapter 46 (46.12a). Two references appear in chapter 115: the first (p. 15b) refers to a "demon-gazing mirror" in chapter 48,

approach to verifying the original length of the novel; since we do not know who wrote the commentary or when, it could have been written for either of the versions or perhaps started with one and filled in for the other. The facts that the often vague internal references do not work consistently for either version and that they appear in both the 152- and the 154-chapter texts suggest that all extant versions of *Yesou puyan* are corrupt to some degree. However, the majority of these internal references point to the 152-chapter length, and indeed one comment in chapter 47 runs: "If allowed to unfold, the story will run to 152 chapters and has not yet come to its climax" (放之則一百五十二回，而其勢方隆隆未已; p. 13a). The comments appear to have originally been written for a 152-chapter text. The one reference that supports the authority of the two extra chapters is placed early enough in the text (chapter 7 in the 152-chapter text and chapter 9 in the 154-chapter text) that it might have been added by whichever redactor (re)inserted the material.

Unfortunately, the evidence for either side of the argument is inconclusive and will likely remain so unless a more consistent text is found. The evidence does suggest, however, that there is something anomalous about the extra materials in chapters 3 and 4 of the longer version; neither table of contents, in the woodblock edition or the hand-copied manuscript, includes couplets for them. The table of contents in the 152-chapter edition is a reliable record of a complete text that existed at one point, for it lists the couplets for *all* the chapters, even those that it lacks but that appear in the 154-chapter edition. Moreover, since the *fanli* of both versions refer to the length of the novel rather imprecisely as 150-plus chapters (*yibai wushi yu hui* 一百五十餘回), it seems that even the early redactors were unwilling to state a precise figure for the length of the novel. These editorial inconsistencies, along with the evidence of *yinyang* numerological patterning introduced below, are enough to reopen the question of the intended length of the text.

Gender, as a manifestation of *yinyang* dualism, is a central thematic and structural device in *Yesou puyan*. However, even though the moral values it assigns to *yin* and *yang* are absolute, the novel's use of masculinity and femi-

---

the only reference to which is found in the chapter couplet to chapter 48 (chapter 50 in the 154-chapter version); the second (p. 16a) refers to a display of skill by two minor characters, Shemota 奢摩他 and Jingfu 精夫 in chapter 81. This reference does not work for either version; the two women show off their magic midway through chapter 80 of the 152-chapter edition (p. 9a) and chapter 82 of the longer version. As can be seen, the majority of intratextual references in the commentary work only for the 152-chapter edition.

ninity as symbolic terms is surprisingly fluid. In *Yesou puyan, yang* is unequivocally identified with the orthodox order and *yin* with heterodox threats to that order. Personifying *yin* excess are not shrews, as one might expect, but a loosely connected clique of Buddhists, Daoists, eunuchs, rogue monks, treasonous princes, and grotesque monsters who use sexual licentiousness and *yinyang* sorcery to attack and corrupt the empire. Women are sympathetically depicted as models of virtue and cultural achievement or as victims who are emblematic of the empire's moral collapse. Countering the heterodox challenge to Confucian dominance is Wen Suchen 文素臣, around whom the sprawling narrative is centered, and his mother, Lady Shui 水, the Confucian matriarch *par excellence*. Suchen, who literally embodies *yang*, is committed to activist Confucian ideals and spends much of the novel battling heterodox forces.

Honglou meng and *Yesou puyan* represent two opposing voices in an eighteenth-century conversation on the viability and appeal of orthodoxy. Unlike the feminine Baoyu, who resists the role of scholar-bureaucrat his family position thrusts on him in favor of a life defined by *qing*, Wen Suchen embraces his Confucian mission with such enthusiasm that he becomes a caricature of the scholar-activist ideal. Suchen's Confucian origins are evident in his name, the "unadorned minister," an allusion to Confucius' moniker "the unadorned king" (*suwang* 素王).[12] In the first chapter of the novel, Suchen declares his ambition to rid China of the dual evils of Buddhism and Daoism; after he takes leave of his mother and older brother on their modest family estate, he begins his tour of China, traveling in all five directions to eradicate heterodoxy (the fifth direction is the center, in this novel represented by the imperial court). In the process of restoring order, he or one of his followers quells rebellions in China's border regions and brings the known world as far as Ouluobazhou 歐羅巴洲, which includes the regions now defined as Europe and the Middle East, under the sway of Confucian rule. This reinstatement of orthodox dominance is a multifaceted process that involves the defense of the Confucian family, the restoration of the emperor's physical and moral health, a purge of treasonous officials and eunuchs, and full-scale military campaigns in China's border regions. By the end of the novel, the filial Suchen and his mother have been ensconced as the symbolic center of the Confucian order: the entire Wen family has established a residence in the imperial city, Suchen's children and grandchil-

12. See M. Huang, *Literati and Self-Re/Presentation*, pp. 15–16.

dren have married into the imperial family, foreign embassies arrive to celebrate Lady Shui's birthday, and Suchen and his mother are revered around the world as Confucian sages.

Interwoven into this narrative of Confucian triumphalism are a series of episodes that illustrate the moral corruption endemic to Buddhism and Daoism and the failure of the Confucian bureaucracy to stem the spread of these heterodox practices. The cabal of traitors who work to overthrow the Chenghua emperor (r. 1465–88), under the leadership of the eunuch Jin Ren 靳仁, divert the emperor's attention from governing by supplying him with a steady stream of beautiful women and girls kidnapped from all parts of China. Many of the dozens of women who become Suchen's allies, as well as his five concubines, come from among these displaced women. The shadowy army of monks and eunuchs who populate this fictional landscape are reminiscent of the soulstealing wanderers Philip Kuhn describes as inhabiting the imagination of China in 1768.[13]

Although the soulstealing scandal may have influenced Xia Jingqu's fictional representation of a dangerous underworld of traitorous necromancers, the novel differs from the incidents Kuhn describes in the sexualized twist given the characterizations. For example, in the opening chapter, Suchen's resolve to fight heterodoxy is motivated by a vignette of a magistrate who, rather than punish a monk who had broken into the home of a scholar and raped his wife, flogs the neighbors who had brought the monk to trial (1.9a–10a). One of the most unsettling scenes in the novel is Suchen's encounter with a swarthy monk who harvests fetuses for use in black magic. Suchen discovers the unclothed monk forcing a young naked woman, whom the monk had just magically impregnated, into a tub of steaming water to cause her to abort (12.12a). The association between monks and unbridled sexuality in the novel is so extreme that each time the loyalists raid a temple or traitor's stronghold they liberate dozens, if not hundreds, of naked women imprisoned in hidden dungeons.[14] Lecherous *yin* sexuality is the defining characteristic of the rebels; this, in conjunction with the fact that their social roles of transients, monks, and eunuchs place them outside the Confucian structures of family or state, encodes them as dangerously *yin*, despite the fact that the vast majority of traitors are biologically male.

13. Kuhn, *Soulstealers*.

14. See, e.g., 44.2b, 50.5a; and in the 154-chapter edition, chapter 5, p. 50, chapter 134, p. 1561, and chapter 137, p. 1619.

XIA JINGQU AND *YESOU PUYAN*

Few clues from Xia Jingqu's life shed light on his motivations for composing such a lengthy or provocative novel. He was born into a respected gentry family in the intellectually conservative county of Jiangyin in Jiangnan.[15] An uncle was mentioned in the local gazetteer for his learning, and his mother was noted for her filial service toward her mother-in-law.[16] Little is known about the specifics of Xia's life: he traveled widely, he failed to pass even the lowest level of the bureaucratic examinations, and a minor position as clerk that he obtained was transferred to him from his son. Xia Jingqu's patron was the official Yang Mingshi 楊名時 (1661–1736), a strong supporter of orthodox Cheng-Zhu Neo-Confucianism. As Stephen Roddy suggests, Xia Jingqu's rabid attacks on the School of the Mind in the novel may have been in part motivated by Xia's association with Yang. Yang Mingshi had recommended Xia for an editorial position on a historical project being compiled under Li Fu 李紱 (1675–1750), a proponent of Wang Yangming's School of the Mind. Xia's failure to obtain the position may have added fuel to his anti-idealist sentiments.[17] Despite Xia's lack of worldly success, local gazetteers refer respectfully to his treatises on history, medicine, the Classics, and poetry. In 1750, a prominent official invited him to lecture on the Neo-Confucian topic of nature and principle (*xingli* 性理).[18] According to the preface written by Xia's great-grand-nephew (dated 1890) to Xia's collected works, the *Huanyu xuanji* 浣玉軒集, this collection represents only one-tenth of Xia's writings. Although this no doubt is an exaggeration, it points to the revived interest in Xia's writings in the late nineteenth century.[19]

Xia followed the Qing literati practice of incorporating his intellectual interests into fiction by inserting discussions of poetry, history, mathematics and medicine into *Yesou puyan*.[20] One of the more extended of these is the

15. For biographical studies of Xia Jingqu, see Sun Kaidi, "Xia Erming yu *Yesou puyan*"; Zhao, "*Yesou puyan* yu Xiashi zongpu"; Kuriyama, "Confucianism in Fiction," pp. 23–45; and Roddy, *Literati Identity*, pp. 74–77.

16. Kuriyama, "Confucianism in Fiction," pp. 23–24.

17. Roddy, *Literati Identity*, pp. 75–77.

18. Zhao, "*Yesou puyan* yu Xiashi zongpu," p. 444.

19. Kuriyama, "Confucianism in Fiction," pp. 24–25.

20. See, e.g., chapters 5 and 6 (geometry and archery), chapters 8 and 36 (poetry), and chapters 19, 75, and 92 (medicine). As Wilt Idema ("Cannon, Clocks," p. 71) has suggested,

chapter-length discussion arguing that Chen Shou 陳壽 (233–97), the author of the *Sanguo zhi* 三國志, had supported the legitimacy of the state of Shu rather than Wei (chapter 78).[21] Xia Jingqu's support for Liu Bei 劉備 and the Shu-Han kingdom was not that unusual by the Qing; the Maos' commentary to the *Sanguo yanyi* followed Zhu Xi in granting political legitimacy to the Shu-Han state.[22] Many of the disquisitions Suchen delivers on poetic forms are surprisingly trite, given the enthusiasm with which the interdiegetic audience responds. According to his biography, Xia Jingqu was not prone to underestimate his own accomplishments; apparently when the Qianlong emperor toured southern China in 1786, Xia tried to present one of his historical works directly to him. The title of the novel derives from a proverb in the *Liezi* 列子, "yeren xianpu" 野人獻曝, "the rustic recommends resting in the sun to get warm," and refers to a simple farmer who desired to present some homespun advice to the emperor for a reward. This suggests that Xia regarded this novel as an offering he hoped would bring him recognition.[23]

One factor that may have prevented Xia Jingqu from gaining much recognition in his lifetime is his apparent lack of authorial skill and control, which must be considered when we assess the literary quality of the novel. The clumsy management of the closure of each chapter, a signature feature of Xia's style, argues against granting him too high a literary reputation. Although one feature of vernacular fiction is its mimicking of the oral storyteller's technique of ending each session on a note of suspense so as to hook the "audience" into staying for the next installment, Xia's use of this stylistic technique is often so heavy-handed that the reader quickly learns to discount the weird or wrenching events that appear in the last lines of a chapter.[24] Perhaps more than any other aspect of the text, these abrupt and

---

the list of 24 explanations for immaculate conception enumerated by Wen Suchen (*YSPY*, 75.54a–5a) may be a response to Christian teachings in China.

21. For a discussion of Xia's historical treatise on Chen Shou, see Kuriyama, "Confucianism in Fiction," pp. 42–43.

22. See Rolston, *Traditional Chinese Fiction*, pp. 56–57.

23. For the choice of title, see McMahon, *Misers*, pp. 153–54; and M. Huang, *Self-Re/Presentation*, pp. 109–11.

24. See, e.g., the one-line description of pandemonium when a fire breaks out at the end of chapter 35 and its immediate dismissal as an omen in the first lines of chapter 36; Suchen's tearful preparation to drown in the last paragraph of chapter 82 and his immediate rescue in the first line of chapter 83; and Suchen's death from shock when he hears that the crown

awkward narrative transitions reveal the limits of Xia Jingqu's skill as writer of fiction.[25] The narrative maintains an episodic and somewhat haphazard feel even into the final chapters, which introduce significant new characters without any lead-in. For example, in chapter 142 the heretofore unknown younger brothers of Lady Shui and the Empress Dowager abruptly present themselves at the imperial court to celebrate Lady Shui's hundredth birthday. Stephen Roddy has argued that these "accidental meetings" and "personal encounters are laden with fateful significance and determine both the individual's course in life and the broader moral and political aims of the literati as a whole."[26] Joanna Kuriyama has suggested that these digressions show the complexity of the real world and the breadth of intellectual resources needed to confront it.[27] Although I am less inclined to be as generous in this area, it is clear that Xia Jingqu took great care in editing the text for internal consistency. As Kuriyama has shown, many of the seemingly random digressions in the novel introduce themes and characters who later become significant to the plot. As she demonstrates, a number of minor characters stitch together the loosely woven narrative when they reappear dozens of chapters later in unrelated episodes.[28]

The sheer number of characters who surface more than once in the novel's many plots and subplots suggests that Xia Jingqu was a deliberate writer. We must then ask ourselves why Xia did not follow the established "canonical" format in his composition of the novel. By his time, many models existed to demonstrate the causal relationship between a fictional text's aesthetic complexity and the author's or editors' attempts to place it within an orthodox field of meaning. Like the contemporaneous 55- or 56-chapter

---

prince has been forced to hang himself at the end of chapter 102 and his immediate recovery in chapter 103 just in time to hear that it is a rumor.

25. Given the length of the novel and the number of play titles to which reference is made (see 72.2b–3a, 73.8a–b, 77.3a, 82.9a), it is puzzling that it includes so few intertextual references to other *xiaoshuo* novels. It is suggestive of influence from either *Jin Ping Mei* or, less likely, *Honglou meng* that the extended Wen household moves into an idyllic garden of Confucian delights in chapter 118, 100 chapters after the completion of the central garden worlds in those novels in chapter 18. An interlinear comment refers specifically to the grape arbor scene in *Jin Ping Mei* (60.9a) and the summary comments to chapters 65 and 67 compare the degree of obscenity in these chapters to that in *Jin Ping Mei* (preserved in the 154-chapter edition in chapters 67 and 69).

26. Roddy, *Literati Identity*, p. 149.

27. Kuriyama, "Confucianism in Fiction," p. 69.

28. Ibid., pp. 67–68.

Rulin waishi (depending on the edition), *Yesou puyan* fails to conform to the usual 40-, 100-, or 120-chapter length of most scholar novels. Not unexpectedly, readers of *Rulin waishi* have been similarly troubled by its lack of structural coherence, even though it is unified by its thematic exploration of "success, fame, riches, and rank" and its highly ironic use of figural density.

A number of other features, however, situate *Yesou puyan* firmly with elite publishing practices. All early editions, including the 1878 manuscript, are divided into 20 *juan*, each of which is labeled with a character. Read in order, these characters form the following couplet:[29]

> In brandishing weapons and wielding a brush, this virtuous knight is peerless under Heaven, 奮武撥文天下無雙正士
> In refining the Classics and reworking the histories, this is the world's number-one marvelous book. 鎔經鑄史人間第一奇書

Moreover, the number 100 runs as a leitmotif through the concluding chapters, as if to compensate for the text's awkward shape. The motif first appears in chapter 136 when the birth of Suchen's hundredth male descendant is announced as one of the auspicious indicators that sagely rule has been reestablished.[30] In chapter 137, immediately following the auspicious births of members of three generations of the Wen family on the same day, each province and foreign country submit poems in praise of the emperor's sagely rule, and Suchen collates them into a series of 100 linked poems and presents them to the emperor (137.5a–10a). Near the end of the novel, much is also made of the fact that the ages of ten of Suchen's grandsons add up to 100 (150.9b–10a).

The regulatory power of the number 100 is shown during the lengthy celebration of Lady Shui's centenary birthday in chapters 144 to 149. It is fitting that the structurally perfect number 100 be embodied by Lady Shui, for she provides the foundation for the revitalization of Cheng-Zhu orthodoxy.[31] The heart of her birthday celebration is a 100-act play performed by 100 actors and actresses, 50 boys and 50 girls from the "*yang*-identified" Miao 苗 territories of southwest China (discussed below). Lady Shui forbids the

29. The *juan* divisions in the 1878 manuscript differ from the published editions; see Wang Qiongling, *Qingdai sida caixue xiaoshuo*, pp. 83–84.

30. Other auspicious omens in the chapter are the success of Suchen's fifth son as a first-place imperial candidate and the arrival of the phoenix, the last of the four mythological beasts that appear only in times of peace and good government.

31. For a discussion of Lady Shui's centrality, see Roddy, *Literati Identity*, pp. 153–55.

performance of two scenes of questionable morality, making this perfectly structured "play-within-a-novel" a sanitized recapitulation of the major events in the narrative (144.3b).[32] Moreover, Lady Shui permits the play to be staged only on the condition that there be no improper contact between the actors and actresses and that they be given employment in proper professions once the performance is over. The chapter-end commentary reflects the ambivalence of the novel toward the effect of fiction and drama on audiences:

> How could Lady Shui's household teachings include such a thing as dramatic performances? But without the repetition of these hundred scenes, there would be nothing to link together (*gousuo*) the entire book, excite the blood, and move the spirit. Therefore Yu'er and the others [who are asking for permission to stage the performance] needed to check their hearts one hundred times to make sure that their emotions and reason both attained due measure before they could obtain one word of permission from Lady Shui; this is called "painstaking artistry." 水夫人家教豈有演劇之事？而非此百齣重題，無以鉤銷全書，而動盪血脈，流通精神。故必玉兒等百倍小心，情理俱至極處，然後得水夫人之一允也，是謂良工心苦。(144.14b)

Only in this dramatic recapitulation, transcribed and rectified by Lady Shui's efforts, does the unruly plot of *Yesou puyan* achieve orthodoxy of form and content.

In the face of the novel's extreme length and garrulous digressions, the commentary makes it a point to persuade readers of the text's tight narrative organization. Although most comments are little more than plot summaries followed by a declamatory "marvelous, marvelous" (*miao, miao* 妙，妙) or "extraordinary" (*qi* 奇), some illuminate structural patterns that a more casual reader might miss, and others compare passages to specific scenes in *Jin*

32. Curiously, in stating that the virtuoso sexual performance in chapter 67 (discussed later) is too obscene to bear repeating, the text once again foregrounds the material. "When Jinzhi and Wanxiang [two women who were originally kept in the harem in chapter 67, but now serve Suchen as retainers] saw that the playbill listed *Gazing at Flowers*, their faces turned bright red with embarrassment, but when they read that the script specified that all clothing would be kept fastened and no skin exposed, and that, moreover, there would be nothing of the sort of *extending the labia and distending the belly, or making sounds by striking the labia together*, it was as if a stone had rolled from their hearts" 金枝晚香見戲目有看花名目，把老臉暈得通紅，及看齣中註明紮縛衣褲，不露肌膚，又無翻牝做肚，擊牝作聲等事，心中一塊石頭方落下地 (144.3b; italics added).

Ping Mei and *Shuihu zhuan*.[33] The commentator highlights Xia's authorial control with comments such as one in chapter 115 that suggests that the appearance of two minor characters in chapter 81 was "entirely in order to put down roots for this scene" (*quan wei ci chu maigen ye* 全爲此處埋根也; 115.16a). The authority of the commentary is in part established by the fact that it is written in a terse classical prose, which implicitly influences the reader to perceive specific scenes as intentionally parallel. The following comment, for example, draws a stylistic connection between two retellings of the events surrounding Suchen's departure from the capital to suggest that the repetition of this minor incident was planned: "[The details concerning] the old man at Chongwen Gate were not narrated thirty-three chapters earlier when Suchen left the capital but are added to the narrative here; if [this incident] had been narrated earlier, it would have been wooden, but here it is lively" 崇文門口老蒼頭不敘於前三十三回素臣出京之時而補敘於此，敘前則呆板，敘此則靈活也 (41.10b–11a). Although this reader readily admits to growing impatience with what feels like an interminably long and overwritten novel, the fact that the commentator was able to point to such fine-stitching between distant scenes suggests that at least one traditional reader or editor (perhaps Xia Jingqu himself?) saw the novel as fitting within traditional fiction aesthetics.

All in all, however, literary judgment has not been kind to *Yesou puyan*. As Lu Xun wrote, "This book with its boasts and its insipid language should not really rank as literature; but from it we can learn a great deal about the psychology of scholars at the time."[34] One major task of recent scholarship has been to reclaim the novel as part of the mainstream of eighteenth-century literature. Although it is unlikely that Xia Jingqu knew of the *Shitou ji* manuscripts, which were in circulation during the period he was writing *Yesou puyan*, *Yesou puyan* can be read as a reaction against the same intellectual and aesthetic forces that inspired Cao Xueqin to compose *Honglou meng*.[35] Xia's response to the cultural malaise of the eighteenth century,

33. For references to these canonical novels, see 3.9a–b, 41.8b, 43.12a, 44.13a, 60.9a, and the summary comments to chapters 67, p. 770, and 69, p. 795, in the 154-chapter edition. The commentary also incorporates Jin Shengtan's expression "snake in the grass or [broken] chalk line" (*caoshe huixian fa* 草蛇灰線法) to refer to the repetition of a motif (see 7.7b and 137.10b).

34. Lu Xun, *A Brief History*, p. 303.

35. For readings of *Yesou puyan* in reference to *Honglou meng*, see McMahon, *Misers*, pp. 170–74 and *passim*; and M. Huang, *Self-Re/Presentations*, pp. 119, 123, and *passim*. McMahon de-

however, is a mirror opposite of Cao Xueqin's escapism. In structure, characterization, and theme, *Yesou puyan* rejects the ethics of *qing* celebrated in *Honglou meng*: even though Wen Suchen is described as a man of passion (*duoqing ren* 多情人), his and his friends' expressions of *qing* fuel their Confucian ambitions (*zhi* 志) rather than their escapist desires (see 7.7a and comment on 7.17a). Suchen has a passionate and unthinking commitment to a Confucian sense of justice. Unlike Baoyu, who prefers to stay within the feminizing and anti-ritualistic space of the garden, Suchen's peripatetic adventures parallel those of the sage-king Yu in re-establishing an orthodox political and moral order. Furthermore, each of Suchen's encounters with beautiful women, no matter how sexually explicit the description, becomes an opportunity for him to demonstrate his moral resolve as he substitutes a ritually sanctioned relationship for affective bonds. Even as the text absorbs the positive aspects of *qing* as a marker of authenticity, which in this case is equated with moral integrity, *Yesou puyan* demonstrates the superior regenerative power of ritual; by the end of the novel, Wen Suchen and his six wives have over 500 children and grandchildren.

As I shall discuss in more detail below, it is the structuralist use of *yinyang* iconography in *Yesou puyan* that provides the strongest defense of Xia Jingqu's artistic vision. Chapters 6, 66, and 136 foreground *yin* iconography, whereas the chapters clustered around chapter 90 contain a rare extended exploration of *yang* themes. For now, it will suffice to look at the treatment of desire in chapter 6 of *Yesou puyan*. A married couple named Liu 劉, whom Suchen has rescued, try to present him with their beautiful younger sister Xuangu 璇姑 as a concubine in order to show their gratitude; knowing that Suchen would refuse the match on moral grounds, they get him drunk and send Xuangu into his bed. When Suchen becomes aware of the ruse, he wraps himself in a blanket to protect both his own and the woman's honor. Only after she forces him to acknowledge that her chastity has already been compromised does he accept her as a secondary wife; true to his sense of propriety, however, he waits to obtain permission from his mother and primary wife before consummating the relationship with Xuangu, an event that does not occur until chapter 58. With the exception of Lady Tian 田, his primary wife, whose role is to manage the household and not to be an intel-

---

scribes the two novels as competing voices in a debate about the proper management of sexual and emotional relations in a polygamous household.

lectual or spiritual mate (*zhiji* 知己), each of Suchen's five concubines complements one of the many fields of knowledge he has mastered. Xuangu's talent is in mathematics, and chapter 6 is filled with tender descriptions of the couple lying chastely but intimately in bed, drawing geometric shapes on each other's torso and stomach as they calculate the circumferences and arcs of angles.[36]

Even though there is no external evidence that Xia Jingqu knew the *Shitou ji* manuscripts, it is tempting to read this chapter as an intentional rewriting of Baoyu's sexual awakening in chapters 5 and 6. The foregrounding of the Liu family in this chapter and the arithmetic-loving Xuangu and her brother, who is obsessed with marksmanship, shifts the emphasis of the *yin* associations of number six. Wen Suchen's refusal to engage in sexual activity with the beautiful Xuangu until he has received parental and spousal permission demonstrates his self-control, and the intellectual component of their relationship contrasts sharply with Baoyu's purely sensual attraction to Jianmei, "Two-in-One." The erotic references of the first line of the chapter couplet further indicate that Xia was consciously attempting both to evoke and to deconstruct the sexual connotations of the number "six." The couplet begins, "Neither clouds nor rain, infinitely surpassing a beautiful Wu Mountain dream" 非雨非雲絕勝巫山好夢.[37] Rather than lead to decadence, the events of chapter 6 culminate in the success of Xuangu's brother in mastering Suchen's lessons on the Confucian art of archery and in Suchen's return to his mother to ask for permission to marry.

Despite its quirky inconsistencies and digressions, *Yesou puyan* fits squarely within the eighteenth-century literary context of lengthy and episodic scholar novels about literati characters. In its broad inclusion of textual, historical, and philosophical references, it parallels other scholar novels, and like *Rulin waishi*, it combines aspects of scholar-beauty romances and knight-errant adventure stories, blending structural and thematic elements from both. And the sophistication of Xia Jingqu's extended thematic and structural development of *yinyang* iconography surpasses that of any Qing novel of which I am aware.

36. For a translation of this scene, see McMahon, *Misers*, pp. 158–59.

37. "Clouds and rain" is a common euphemism for sexual intercourse; Wu Mountain is the site of King Xiang of Chu's dreamed sexual encounter with a goddess.

YINYANG ICONOGRAPHY IN *YESOU PUYAN*

The most important structuring device in *Yesou puyan* is its extended development of *yinyang* iconography. From the very beginning of the novel, the *yinyang* symbolism is rooted in a system of morality that pits *yang*-associated orthodoxy against *yin*-associated heterodoxies. One of Suchen's earliest speeches lays out the oppositional values ascribed to the two terms:

> Mencius said: "All under Heaven endures by having order for every disorder." Thus the floodwaters overflowed during the age of Yao and Shun, and the wild beasts overran the world during the time of King Wu and the Duke of Zhou. The Way of Heaven and Earth parallels the interaction of *yin* and *yang*; it is impossible to have light without dark, spring without autumn, life without killing, the gentleman without the mean person. The Way of the Sages is thus: as phenomenal reality, it is bright; as a season, it is spring; as virtue, it is life; in action, it is the superior person. In contrast, Buddhism is obscurity, autumn, killing, and [the way] of the mean person. 孟子曰：『天下之生久矣，一治一亂。』故洪水横流於堯，舜之世，猛獸充塞於武，周之時。天地之道，陰陽倚伏，不能有明而無晦，有春而無秋，有生而無殺，有君子而無小人。聖人之道，在象爲明，在時爲春，在德僞生，在行爲君子；佛則晦也，秋也，殺也，小人也。(2.10a–b)

These analogical relationships, positive for *yang* and negative for *yin*, frame all of Suchen's subsequent battles against heterodoxy. In a later diatribe, Suchen refers to Daoism and Buddhism as "murderous *yin* ethers" 陰殺氣 (60.6a).[38] Lady Shui also reminds the readers of the moral value of *yin* and *yang* in chapter 136 when she lectures: "Change is based on the two hexagrams Qian and Kun; they illuminate the essence of *yin* and *yang*, the function of nine and six, and the paths of the superior person and mean person" 易於乾坤二卦，明陰陽之體，九六之用，君子小人之道 (chap. 138, p. 1633, 154-chapter ed.). Those heterodox characters in the novel who actively threaten the social and political stability are marked by stereotypical

38. Suchen's equation of "*yang* Confucianism, *yin* Buddhism" (*yangRu yinShi* 陽儒陰釋) is repeated so often it becomes a cliché. One of Suchen's sworn brothers comments that the embroidered picture of "spring breezes and a burning sun" illustrates Suchen's ambitions, "which are just like the sun rising, *yin* perversity being totally annihilated, *yang* sunlight shining everywhere, and the myriad things [existing] in a time of spring" 正如日出扶桑，陰邪悉滅，陽光遍照，萬物皆春 (7.7a). The interlinear comment describes the novel as arising from this picture.

yin desires for sexual gratification and power. Furthermore, only Lady Shui and Wen Suchen seem to be cognizant of the influence of larger *yinyang* patterns on the fate of the empire. The commentary ascribes this to their powers of moral discernment: "Lady Shui's excellent understanding and proper nature are so great that she alone has faith in [the divinatory powers] of *yin* and *yang*" 水夫人何等卓識，何等正性，乃猶信陰陽 (99.15a).[39]

As in other fictional texts, the *yin*-associated Double Three holiday is used to mark the loss of normative order. Reminiscent of *Shuihu zhuan*, the first date mentioned in *Yesou puyan* is the second day of the third month of the third year of the Chenghua reign period, the day Suchen sets off for Hangzhou on his mission to eradicate corrupt practices (1.13a). When Suchen arrives in Hangzhou, he is caught in a heavy downpour caused by the sorcery of the eunuch Jin Ren. The resultant flood on West Lake literally washes away the Confucian social structure of the city and dislodges hundreds of people from their families. Suchen spends the rest of the novel trying to undo the chaos wrought by the flood. Although the exact date of the flood is not stated, it is later referred to as having happened "early in the third month" (*sanyue tou* 三月頭; chap. 13, p. 150, 154-chapter ed.).[40] The displaced victims of the flood, women and boys alike, are kidnapped and sold into service around the empire as sexual slaves to the clique of monks and eunuchs who are attempting to usurp the throne. The especially beautiful boys caught in the flood are castrated and forced into sexualized service to a eunuch. The depiction of the flood makes full use of *yin* symbolic vocabulary, but divides destructive *yin* transgressors from sympathetic *yin* victims. Among the victims are a boatload of *six* people, including Su'e 素娥, who later marries Suchen, and the two sisters, Luanchui 鸞吹, who becomes a sworn sister of Suchen, and the younger Jinyu 金羽, who marries Suchen toward the end of the novel.[41]

The chaos of the flood is echoed in two later scenes when troops under the command of the rebels threaten to drive Suchen's wives from their home on the Double Three date. In the first example, Su'e and Xiangling 湘靈, the wife who specializes in poetry composition, narrowly escape being trans-

39. Suchen uses the *Yi jing* to divine in 41.4b, chapter 67, and 79.1a.

40. The first pages of chapter 11 are missing from the 152-chapter edition.

41. Four of Suchen's concubines are swept away by the flood. One of the subplots in the novel follows Suchen's attempts to track down all the people displaced during the flood and either return them to their families or integrate them into proper Confucian social roles.

ported to the capital to be trained in the occult arts (54.4b). The second use of the date occurs several years later when rebel troops raid the family estate and arrest Lady Shui and all the other women. In an attempt to humiliate the women, the soldiers threaten to expose the women's bare feet to public view (98.3a). In all three instances, the Double Three date functions as a site of rupture during which women or boys, who would normally be safely enclosed within family compounds, are shown to be especially vulnerable. These victims of the battle to overthrow the normative social and political order, especially the hundreds of naked women held in temple dungeons, are literally stripped of their respectability and converted into raw sexual capital.

As the narrative nears its conclusion, the Double Three date is used to signify the triumph of Neo-Confucian bureaucratic and domestic regulation, for the palace examination, whose final stage is conducted in the imperial presence, is held on this date. In each instance, the listing of examination successes is followed by a quick flurry of births to either Suchen or his sons or by other auspicious events (see 121.10b, 128.3a, 129.12a, 130.5b, and 139.1b). Since the palace examinations were normally held on the sixteenth day of the fourth month during the Qing dynasty,[42] the choice of the Double Three should be read as an intentional reinscription of the topos. Thanks to the revival of the Confucian order late in the novel because of the efforts of Suchen and Lady Shui, the Double Three no longer functions as a site of transgression but instead marks the successful harnessing of the dynamic and generative power of *yin* to further a new cycle of ideal government.

Although neither chapter 33 nor chapter 36 contains significant *yin* themes, the episode framed around chapter 66 surpasses every scene of which I am aware in its exploitation of *yinyang* imagery.[43] Throughout this pornographic episode, in which Wen Suchen is seduced by a harem of libidinous women, he functions as the literal embodiment of *yang*. A sudden cold spell in chapter 65 establishes a *yin* setting for the episode: just after Suchen arrives in Nanjing, normal life in the city is unexpectedly interrupted by a heavy snowfall. Nanjing is home to Li Youquan 李又全, a wealthy and powerful eunuch who has assembled a large harem in which he practices "Daoist" longevity techniques. Li kidnaps and drugs unusually virile men; after the women of his harem have induced them to ejaculate, Li drinks their semen (*xijing* 吸精; literally, "to suck their essence") in order to ingest their

42. See Miyazaki, *China's Examination Hell*, p. 71.

43. Significant sections of this chapter are translated in McMahon, *Misers*, pp. 161–65.

yang essence.[44] All his previous victims had literally had their life force sucked out of them. The eunuch runs a tavern in order to spy out men whose *yang* essence is particularly potent. A servant Li Youquan has stationed there catches sight of Suchen urinating into a bucket of snow, and her attention is immediately drawn by the quantity and heat of his urine, which melts all the snow in the bucket and sends up a billowing cloud of steam (65.4b–5a).[45] The eunuch then invites Suchen to his residence; when Suchen arrives there, he finds himself in a steamy hot tower filled with scantily clad servants.

The scene builds on the hot-cold imagery Zhang Zhupo identified as central to the aesthetics of *Jin Ping Mei*. The harem is kept in the Warm Jade Tower 煖玉樓, where steam billows up from a large kang (熱氣蒸蒸而出, 65.5b) despite the frigid temperatures outside.[46] Almost all details in the episode are drawn from *yinyang* iconography. Although eunuchs are typically pale and hairless, Li's large red nose and red beard are suggestive of his sexualized identity. The women in the harem are unusually sexual and aggressive: as part of their efforts to arouse Suchen, they stage a series of fantastic gymnastic and aural entertainments, which include manipulating their abdomens and labia in what seems to be a complicated form of belly dancing, inserting a toe or tongue into their own vagina, or blowing through the labia as a musical wind instrument to produce sounds as varied as silkworms eating leaves, water dripping, and babies nursing. Li Youquan comments that Suchen is "pure *yang*" (*chunyang* 純陽; 65.11b), a notion that is further confirmed by Suchen's age of 27 *sui*, a *yang* number. Moreover, during the scene in which the women attempt to extract his semen, Suchen's penis is consistently referred to as a "*yang* object" (*yangwu* 陽物) as opposed to a "cock" (*jiba* 雞巴), the preferred term used in the many dirty jokes and songs told and sung by the women in the harem.[47] The most sexually aggressive of the

44. A man's *yang* essence was believed to be stored in his bone marrow and released in his semen.

45. Heat is a clear sign of Suchen's *yang* potency. Moreover, in Ming-Qing literature, a man's urine often metonymically represents his semen; see Epstein, "Inscribing the Essentials."

46. The "jade" (*yu*) in the name of the tower no doubt invokes the common pun on desire (*yu*) and alludes to a common euphemism for the penis, the "jade stalk" (*yujing* 玉莖).

47. The second half of chapter 66, in which the women try to outdo each other with obscene jokes and songs, is a parody of a literati gathering. The generic "*jiba*" is used eighteen

women turns out to be a fox-spirit, and her true identity is revealed only after Suchen recognizes her nature and kills her.

At the heart of chapter 66 is a literal *mise-en-scène* of the Fu 復 hexagram. Fu ䷗ As we saw in the preceding chapter, this hexagram marks the end of *yin* dominance. In this chapter, the women drug Suchen and truss him up in such a way that the only part of his body that can move is his penis. Unable to avert his gaze or fend off the women's assault, Suchen does a mental divination of the *Yi jing* in order to keep his energy concentrated in his brain and thereby divert his *yang* essence away from his marrow. The hexagram he divines is Fu, "to return," and he gratefully recalls one of its commentaries, "On the seventh day comes return," for he realizes that if he can survive seven days in the tower, he will be rescued by some representative of *yin* (66.7b).[48] The Fu hexagram is constructed of a solitary *yang* line below five *yin* lines; the text visually puns on this image when five women enter the room one after another to try their luck at arousing Suchen (66.9a). It is truly a scene of dissolute *yin* assaulting an upright *yang*. Fortunately, for Suchen, his mental gymnastics are so successful at redirecting the flow of his essence that he emits a harmless stream of urine in place of semen. True to Suchen's divination, the episode concludes seven days later when Suchen is rescued by a female knight-errant (69.12a).

Just as a series of *yin* semes in *Honglou meng*, starting with Cook Liu in chapter 60, builds to the introduction of the You sisters, chapter 63 of *Yesou puyan* contains a number of *yin* motifs that lead toward chapter 66. In chapter 63, Suchen and his servant sail to Taiwan to look for one of his allies. Despite the historical importance of Taiwan as a base for Koxinga's (1624–62) loyalist resistance to the Manchus, Xia Jingqu depicts the island as an al-

---

times in their banter, whereas Suchen's penis is specifically referred to as a *yangwu* eight times. For the contrast, see especially 66.12b.

48. Worth noting is that the seasonal details of chapter 65 accord with the attached commentary to the Fu hexagram. "The winter solstice is the time when the *yin* principle commences its Return [begins to become quiescent]" (Lynn, *The Classic of Changes*, pp. 285–92). Zhang Zhupo also associates the Fu hexagram with the exhaustion of *yin* dominance. His comment to chapter 33 of the *Jin Ping Mei* reads: "Six is the *yin* number. Pan Liu'er and Wang Liu'er each match the number of the complete *yin*; *yang* is already completely exhausted, how could it not lead to death? When the Kun hexagram is exhausted, it becomes the Fu hexagram; the one *yang* line of the Fu hexagram must be quiescent in order to preserve itself" 六著，陰數也。潘六兒與王六兒合成陰之數，陽已全盡，安得不死？坤盡爲復，復之一陽，必須靜以保之方可(*JPM*, 33.503). Zhang also refers to the Fu hexagram in his prefatory comments to the same chapter.

legoric wilderness. Suchen and his servant sleep in a cave littered with human remains; in the middle of the night Suchen is awakened by a beautiful woman who pins him down with one hand and reaches into his pants with the other and begins to stroke his penis (*yangwu*, 63.4b). The yaksha (a female demon), for that is what she is, symbolically rapes him by using her enormously long and sharp tongue to lick his face; Suchen kills her by yanking her tongue out by the roots. This episode adumbrates several themes that are expanded three chapters later in the harem scene, the most important of which is Suchen's sexual victimization by a woman. In both instances, the female aggressor is denaturalized, here through the yaksha's lethal three-foot tongue, a curious phallic object transposed onto the body of a female demon. The cave setting, reminiscent of the many womblike caves, gourds, and containers in *Xiyou ji* and the many concealed chambers and dungeons in this novel, is an architectural reminder of the power of *yin* to entrap and encompass.[49] A similar cave setting is used in chapters 94–96 when Suchen does battle with the six pairs of *yin* pythons who terrorize the inhabitants of China's southwest. The Taiwan episode concludes with Suchen burying the remains of the yaksha's previous victims; this reinstatement of Confucian ritual foreshadows Suchen's lectures to the women in Li Youquan's harem on the importance of the "Four Female Virtues and the Three Subordinations" as well as the need to control their sexual desires (68.6b–10a).

A number of motifs established in the Taiwan episode are repeated later in the novel when two of Suchen's surrogates make a perilous sea voyage to the islands of Japan, the site of yet more sexual debauchery. In chapter 130, shortly after Suchen is afflicted with moral dementia, an expedition under the command of Wen Rong 文容 is sent to pacify Japan. The *yin* aspect of this episode is illustrated by the Japanese refusal to recognize Chinese sovereignty in either the political or the cultural realm. When the sexually perverted and depraved (*qiyin ji'e* 奇淫極惡) Japanese pirate Mu Xiu 木修 hears that Wen Rong, who had been castrated after being swept up in the flood in Hangzhou, is as beautiful as the ancient beauty Xi Shi 西施 (Wen Rong is one of the beautiful young boys who had been kidnapped and sold after being caught in the flood at West Lake), Mu Xiu has his retainers drug and strip him at a state banquet. The perversion of order in Mu Xiu's court

49. On the various containers used to entrap the pilgrims in *Xiyou ji*, see Plaks, *Four Masterworks*, p. 252*n*.

is shown in his failure to control either his own sexual urges or those of his wife. She permits her husband access to Wen Rong only if she gets Xiqin 奚勤, the second-in-command. When Wen Rong comes to after being drugged, he discovers that Mu Xiu is holding him on his lap and caressing his beautiful white body. Unlike Suchen, who decides to live on despite having been sexually violated, Wen Rong, whose masculinity is somewhat ambiguous to begin with, appropriately follows the woman's path by martyring himself in an attempt to assassinate the Japanese leader (chap. 132, pp. 1539–40, 154-chapter ed.). Wen Rong's death, one of the few acts of chaste suicide depicted in the novel, highlights the sexual decadence of the Japanese court.[50] When Xiqin and the queen die locked in a sexual embrace, Mu Xiu, rather than exhibiting shame, organizes a "lamaist" orgy in honor of this incarnation of the Joyful Buddha (Da huanxi Fo 大歡喜佛; chap. 133, pp. 1543–44, 154-chapter ed.).[51] In an after-ripple of this episode, the lascivious queen of Fusang 扶桑 also tries to force a handsome Chinese general to marry her (chap. 134, pp. 1562–63, 154-chapter ed.). Consistent with the iconography of heterodoxy used throughout the novel, the inability of the Japanese to regulate their sexual desires functions as a multivalent sign of their moral, cultural, and political resistance to Confucian norms. The obscene transgressions of order in Japan conclude with a striking example of the restoration of Confucian rites: shortly after the Japanese troops are defeated, ambassadors from China teach the Japanese to kowtow to them, provide Xiqin with a proper ritual burial, and convert the main Japanese Buddhist temple into a Confucian academy.[52]

The choice of Japan and Taiwan as allegorical sites for the rejection of Confucian values, which in *Yesou puyan* are consistently equated with sexual constraint, seems to be motivated by the fact that they are islands which can be reached only by a water crossing. The importance of water as a *yin* symbol in this novel is foregrounded not only in the flood in chapter 2 and these geographically *yin* settings but also in Suchen's inability to swim, expressed as "*bu shi shuixing*" 不識水性. This phrase suggests a fundamental difference

50. Several of the characters do choose suicide to demonstrate their rejection of a morally compromised situation (51.1a, 126.1a), but the majority of women live on to redeem themselves through returning to orthodoxy.

51. For references to the presence of similar Lamaist *yab-yum* statues in the Chinese court, see Gulik, *Sexual Life*, pp. 259–61.

52. See chap. 135, p. 1559, chap. 134, p. 1567, and chap. 137, p. 1662, in the 154-chapter edition.

between Suchen's essential *yang* male identity and women, those who are "watery natured" (*shuixing*).[53] (For a discussion of Lady Shui's unusual name, see below.) Suchen is described as having a "fiery nature" (*huoxing* 火性; 21.1a), which perhaps explains why he is so strikingly vulnerable to the water element. Remarkably able in other ways, he prepares for death when he is suddenly swept into bodies of water (see chapters 3 [154-chapter ed.], 61, 81, 109, and 127). Indeed, the most threatening attacks to Suchen's well-being are all *yin* identified: Suchen falls deathly ill after ingesting rainwater in chapter 15 and the *yin* ether (*yinqi*) from an oyster shell (113.12a), is almost killed by Li Youquan's harem (chapter 66), becomes paralyzed after coming into contact with the *yin* ether (*yinqi*) from the cave of the *yin* pythons (chapter 95; on which more below), and loses his mind after confronting a roaring lion at the imperial court (chapters 129–30; the roar of a lion was a common metaphor for the destructive energy of the shrew). The island settings of Taiwan and Japan fit well with the author's manipulation of *yin* sites and illustrate the degree to which the symbolic requirements of the narrative outweigh a desire for realism.

Pernicious *yin* energies are also blamed in chapter 85 for the weakening of the Chinese imperial court. Wen Suchen diagnoses the Chenghua emperor's illness as arising from "being too unbridled in his intimacy with women, which has resulted in an increase of *yin* and the decline of *yang*" 近女太驟，陰勝陽衰 (85.4a). Suchen instructs the emperor that in order to nurse his *yangqi* back to health, he must avoid the women's quarters, eat a simple diet of rice gruel, and sleep sandwiched between two robust boys. Moreover, in one of the many scenes in which he undertakes the "masculinization" of the emperor's polygamous household, Suchen suggests that two of his own male servants and their three wives should train the members of the imperial inner court and harem in martial arts in order to protect the emperor (85.4a–5a). To highlight the contrast between the emperor's *yang* deficiency and Suchen's *yang* potency, four of Suchen's wives give birth to four sons within the space of a fortnight in this same chapter.

The restoration of *yang* dominance in the imperial court in chapter 85 introduces an exploration of *yang* themes that parallels the narrative development of *yin* motifs in chapters 63 to 69. Although the *yang* themes appear in chapters 87–89, rather than in the 90s chapters, the unusual development of *yang* iconography in this section of the novel seems deliberately placed. It

53. On women as "watery natured," see McMahon, *Causality and Containment*, pp. 65–66.

may reflect the fact that in *xiaoshuo* aesthetics *yin* typography was much better and more widely developed than comparable *yang* imagery.[54] After advising the emperor that he needs to supplement his *yang* energy, Suchen sets off on an extended tour of China's southwest. Suchen arrives in a Miao region of Guangxi in time for the fifth day of the fifth month, the Festival of Correct Yang (Duanyang jiajie 端陽佳節), also celebrated as the Dragon Boat Festival. Although the date for this holiday was determined by the lunar calendar, in practice it had assimilated much of the symbolism associated with the summer solstice, the seasonal moment when *yin* and *yang* are in equilibrium before *yang* starts to cede ascendance to *yin*.[55] The holiday, as celebrated in the rough, masculinist Miao culture, rather than focus on the Qu Yuan story and watery symbolism of the dragon boats, features a number of *yang* semes, the most dominant of which are the color red, the bonfires and torches used to fight off the darkness of night, and displays of strength and military skills (88.12a). Running through this episode are references to the oppressive summer heat (88.7b–8a); when Suchen first arrives in a Miao village, he asks for more of the local brew, a "fire wine" 火酒 (*jiu* of course punning on the *yang* number nine), in order to "kill off the humidity" of the air (*sha yi sha shuiqi* 殺一殺水氣; 87.12a). The public celebration of the Duanyang festival is held at night in the blinding red of the Pomegranate Garden 石榴園, which is brilliantly illuminated by torches and fires:

> Entering the garden, in which grew only pomegranates, was like entering a brocade tent; there was an especially large and radiant one, it was like the red glowing clouds around the sun, or like fire or the [red] *tu* plant, it was extraordinarily brilliant. When [Suchen] took a closer look, he saw that the tree had hundreds of pomegranate flowers, and that each and every flower was measurably bigger than the peonies in Jiangnan. 進得園中，滿園純是榴花，如入錦幄，一棵大的，更是如火如荼，如霞如日，燦爛非常。近前看時，一樹開有數百朶榴花，每朶俱比江南牡丹，勺藥，更大一圍。(88.3b–4a)[56]

54. For example, despite the rich *yinyang* symbolism in *Xiyou ji*, chapter 99, a chapter that hammers home the significance of the number nine and is the site of the eighty-first and final trial, features yet another test by water rather than a more explicitly *yang* trial.

55. As discussed earlier, the Duanyang Festival is also a treated as a significant date in the heated chapter 30 of *Honglou meng*.

56. Kuihua dong 葵花峒, Sunflower Village, a second Miao community Suchen visits, incorporates many of the same *yang* details (chap. 90).

Highlighted in this section of the novel are Suchen's medical abilities, a *yang*-associated theme also exploited in *Jinghua yuan*.[57] However, unlike the medical discourse in *Honglou meng* and *Jinghua yuan*, which is based on a more complex five-element symbolism, many of the discussions in *Yesou puyan* use a *yinyang* conceptualization of disease.[58] One of Suchen's greatest medical successes is the curing of the Stone Maiden (*shinü* 石女), who suffers from an affliction of excessive *yin* that has retarded the proper development of her sexual organs: her body is unusually cold and pallid, her vagina is impenetrable (hence the name of the disease), she has never menstruated, and her breasts are smaller than Suchen's (94.9a). However, when the two are forced to share a bed, the *yangqi* from Suchen's body gradually "steams" (*zheng* 蒸) her and feeling slowly returns to her numb body.[59] The cure is completed when Suchen masturbates her, and she begins to menstruate (95.6b–7a). The *yinyang* underpinnings of this scene are raised explicitly in both commentary and text, which describe the Stone Maiden as pure *yin* (*chunyin* 純陰) and Suchen as pure *yang* (94.15a and 95.6a). Her subsequent birthing of 28 sons reveals Suchen's miraculous power to transform excessive and improperly managed *yin* into positive fecundity.

One of the most unusual uses of *yang* iconography in these chapters is the battle between Suchen and a sorcerer who uses heterodox *yang* black magic to attack him. What is atypical about the scene is that it is a false *yang* energy that is out of kilter rather than something explicitly *yin*. Suchen foils the sorcerer's first two attacks with the aid of a magical *yin* pearl shirt that allows him to disappear into the darkness of the shadows. The *yin* energy of the shirt had been demonstrated earlier when it was described as emitting a cooling breeze (89.4b). For his final onslaught, the sorcerer attacks Suchen with a blazing fireball; when Suchen puts out the fire by urinating on it, he

57. See *YSPY*, chaps. 89–92 and 94.

58. Although many of the cures Suchen effects do not include explicit *yinyang* terminology, the majority of ailments associated with Suchen or the emperor have an explicit *yin* basis. The most striking example is Suchen's prognosis, discussed earlier, that the emperor's wasting disease is caused by *yang* deficiency (chap. 85). In addition to the *yang*-enhancing remedies Suchen prescribes for the emperor, he later organizes a ritual to dispel the *yinqi* tainting the imperial court (115.8b).

59. Suchen's *yang* potency is also shown in the scene where the ghost of a female suicide explains that she chose a wet nurse to be her mouthpiece because the woman's natural excess of *yin* energy along with that woman's libidinous desires make her powerful enough to withstand the *yang* energy Suchen exudes (75.6a).

discovers that it was an illusion formed by the sorcerer's assistant "Red Boy," Honghaizi 紅孩子, who is covered in cinnabar and amulets (89.5a). The sorcerer who has falsely appropriated *yang* icons to attack Suchen is defeated by Suchen's urine, a pure *yang* substance.[60] The vital *yang* potency of Suchen's urine had been demonstrated earlier when one of Suchen's wives who was fatally ill was saved by ingesting it (18.11b) and when Suchen brought a dead man back to life by urinating on his straw-wrapped corpse (83.3a–b).[61]

The positive linking of masculinist *yang* characterizations with orthodoxy in *Yesou puyan* is developed most clearly in the example of the Miao people. The Miao are presented as having a crude but straightforward nature that is unlike the deviousness of the *yin* peoples, who are actively seeking to destroy the Chinese empire. The cultural backwardness of the Miao people is demonstrated by their ignorance of Confucian injunctions against the mixing of the sexes and their refusal to practice marital chastity. The Miao do not segregate the sexes: members of the opposite sex touch and embrace in public, and young people are free to choose their own marriage partner. As depicted in the novel, the Miao practice a form of delayed transfer marriage in which the woman moves into her husband's home only after she has become pregnant; until that time she is free to keep a lover (*yelang* 野郎; 88.10a–b). Yet, unlike the Japanese, who subscribe to the intricate forms of court ritual and are highly civilized to the point of decadence, the Miao enjoy a primitive, nonhierarchical culture that has a more natural and direct, even innocent, relationship to the body and sexuality. Their touching is depicted as inappropriate rather than immoral.[62] After contact with Suchen, however, the Miao adopt Confucian marriage practices (for example, see 92.6a–b) and accept Han Chinese political sovereignty. Moreover, the Miao are the only of

60. The interlinear commentary explains that Suchen "uses orthodox water to destroy heterodox fire" 以正水滅邪火 (89.5a). Similar examples can be found in the *Xiyou ji*: the *yang*-like attributes of the demons (especially those of Red Boy, Honghai 紅孩) at Flaming Mountain are ultimately treated as heterodox *yin* to the pilgrims' orthodox *yang* (*Xiyou ji*, chaps. 40–43). See also Campany, "Demons, Gods, and Pilgrims," p. 111.

61. The urine of boys is also used as a medicine in *Jinghua yuan* (29.2a); recall the patch from Tutor Chen's pants in the medicine used to resurrect Du Liniang in *Mudan ting*.

62. Suchen is twice taken aback by Miao attitudes toward the body. The grateful father of a girl Suchen has cured repeatedly suggests that Suchen strip off layers of clothing to cool down in the heat (91.7a); Suchen is also made uncomfortable by the Miao practice of greeting guests with a hug and a kiss (90.3a).

the non-Han Chinese peoples who are singled out for attention during the celebration of Lady Shui's hundredth birthday. (The 100 actors and actresses who re-enact the entire novel in a play of 100 scenes are grateful volunteers from Miao villages.)

Given that Ming and Qing attempts to subjugate the Miao were met by a series of fierce and bloody battles and uprisings, the tractability of the Miao in this novel is particularly noteworthy. Qing albums and fiction alike depict most Miao tribes as fierce and barely civilized.[63] Within the symbolism of this novel, however, apparently because they are culturally defined as a robust, *yang*-identified people, the Miao can represent no serious threat to the Chinese state.[64] In fact, their cultural position is akin to that of a rambunctious, slightly unruly, but promising son waiting to be refined through the acquisition of Confucian ritual. When the Miao boy Little Tiger, Hu'er 虎兒, pummels Suchen in the ribs for being in his way after running into his medicine bag, Suchen and everyone else present are pleased with the child's self-assertive aggressiveness. This sympathetic vision of the Miao is quite different from the equally masculinist depiction of the outlaws in the *Shuihu zhuan* in which the bandits take out much of their antisocial wrath on families and women. In *Yesou puyan*, the Miao, as representatives of an explicitly *yang* culture, are positively depicted as having a natural and vigorous sense of righteousness and honor. Like Suchen, they value straightforward, efficacious action over the rote performances of ritual. Appropriately enough, the Miao become Suchen's most important allies in quelling an insurrection led not by the Miao, as historical fact might lead one to expect, but by six pairs of phantasmic white pythons who have subjugated the Miao people.

The pythons, the major threat to the Chinese state in China's southwest, are a veritable pastiche of negative *yin* attributes. They resemble humans, except that their bodies are unusually long, their hair is white, they are covered in scales, and, like the Stone Maiden, their sexual organs are cold and numb (95.7b).[65] The pythons' energy is so noxious that Suchen is incapacitated by

63. See Diamond, "Defining the Miao." A violent Miao uprising appears in *Rulin waishi* (chapter 43); one of the major events of chapter 99 of *Xingshi yinyuan zhuan* is the outbreak of war among local tribes, likely Miao, in Sichuan.

64. Even the barbaric Yao 猺, who are depicted as being a fierce and highly militarized southern minority people little removed from animals, do not actually threaten Suchen or any other representatives of Han culture (chapter 102).

65. The couplet at the head of chapter 100 highlights the contrast between the negative and sterile *yin* qualities of the pythons and the prodigious fertility of the cured Stone Maiden.

the poisonous *yin* ether emitted from their cave (95.1a). Indeed, the pythons' *yin* force is so powerful that they produce a *yin*-dominated microcosm that encapsulates cold *yang* within cold *yin* (*lengyin lengyang qi* 冷陰冷陽氣); the only way for the Miao villagers to protect themselves against the unnatural cold is by drinking fire wine and taking *yang*-enhancing pills to bolster their own *yang* levels (95.7b). Even though their protective scales make them impervious to stone and metal weapons, the pythons are susceptible to various *yang* objects, such as anything red, fire, weapons made of fur and bamboo, and the oil of the paulownia tree (99.8a).

The characterization of the pythons incorporates the most pernicious aspects of *yin* typology. Reminiscent of the yaksha in the Taiwan episode, the pythons live underground in a cave at the foot of a large tree, and the corpses of their victims are scattered about the courtyard where they hold their orgies (94.11a). Interwoven into the narration of their illegitimate usurpation of political power in southwest China are the details of their sexual vampirism: the six python couples demand a regular tribute of Miao men and women, whom they brutally rape during their sexual orgies. (The pythons are tellingly referred to as "six couples" rather than twelve pythons.) As was the case for the Japanese pirates, the pythons do not distinguish gender roles in either public or private: husbands and wives alike participate in the orgies and the military campaigns. Their *yin* insurrection is eventually quelled, however, when Suchen and the loyalist Miao troops eventually destroy the pythons by means of fiery *yang* weapons in chapter 101.

The final battle between the *yin*-identified rebels and Suchen's *yang* loyalists takes place in the imperial palace, not insignificantly in chapters 104 to 106 (chapter 106 being another *yin* site). The rebellious Prince Jing 景王 has cast a spell that combines perverse sexuality with an attack on the Chinese state. Initially, the attack begins with a series of *yin* plagues: the imperial family suffers from malaria, the palace becomes unnaturally dark and cold, ice and snow fall, and when Suchen eventually manages to light a fire after everyone else has failed, it gives off no heat (chapter 104). Prince Jing then attacks the palace with an onslaught of heterodox *yang* and *yin* phantasmagoria: at first, the temperature rises and careening fireballs terrorize the imperial consorts. Then, piles of maggots and feces materialize and emit a terrible stench; daggers fly through the air; ghosts of dismembered people appear; and small dragons try to enter the anuses and vaginas of the imperial family and consorts (chapter 106). Suchen's presence seems to be the most effective means of combating Prince Jing's black magic: one scene has the crown prince and his consorts huddling on Suchen's blankets to protect themselves against the daggers that are stabbing them through the floors and beds (105.10b). Prince Jing's assault ends when, as did Ximen Qing in *Jin Ping Mei*, he takes an overdose of aphrodisiacs and "releases his *yang* and expires" (*zou yang er si* 走陽而死; 106.11b).

Suchen's explanation for the turmoil is founded on an elaborate metaphor based on *yinyang* images of light and dark; according to him, both the heir apparent and the empress, having been deluded by their faith in heterodox religions, are susceptible to black magic. Suchen, however, is immune to Prince Jing's spell because of his faith in Confucianism. "People's hearts are like the sun, and doubt is like a fog; heterodoxy is like a haze (*yinyi* 陰翳); if your heart is without doubt, then, like the red sun in an empty sky unobscured by any specks of cloud, it can destroy the haze" 人心如日，疑如雲霧；邪如陰翳之氣，心如一毫無疑，既如赤日當空，無纖微雲霧遮蔽一切陰翳之氣當之既滅 (chap. 108, p. 1240, 154-chapter ed.). As Suchen puts it, belief in Confucian orthodoxy is medicinal in its ability to strengthen a person's moral and physical constitution.

Parallel to this restitution of *yang* order in chapter 106, chapter 136 is filled with auspicious events that mark the juncture at which *yang* finally becomes dominant in the novel. The lecture that Lady Shui delivers on the *Yi jing* in chapter 136 is but one of the indicators that the period of *yin* imbalance that has been threatening the social and political order is drawing to a close. Lady Shui lectures on the two hexagrams Zhun 屯, "Difficulty at the Beginning," and Meng 蒙, "Youthful Folly," which follow immediately after Qian and Kun, respectively, in the sequence of hexagrams. The attached commentaries to these hexagrams reflect Suchen's struggles up until this point in the novel; as Lady Shui points out, they are both "precarious hexagrams" (*xian xiang* 險象) and warn that it is difficult for one to hold onto integrity (*nanzhen* 難貞; chap. 138, p. 1633, 154-chapter ed.). However, she continues, after a period of initial struggle, youthful integrity will prevail.

Zhun

Meng

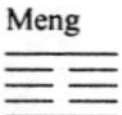

The main event of chapter 136 is the extended celebration of Lady Shui's seventieth birthday; it is her birthday, in place of an event explicitly connected to the political life of the empire, that provides the narrative motivation for representatives from the "myriad nations" (*wanguo* 萬國) to gather at the palace in a demonstration of the cultural sovereignty of Confucianism. The king of Arabia reports that although his people had practiced Islam since the Tang, since they began following Confucianism, they have rid their country of malevolent forces and are now blessed with the appearance of auspicious animals and plants (chap. 138, pp. 1638–39, 154-chapter ed.). Just when the foreign dignitaries are being received in the imperial gardens, a phoenix alights, and the hundred animals dance for the empress and Lady Shui in an enactment of one of the mythical signs of sagely rule (chap. 138, p. 1637, 154-chapter ed.). The flurry of marriages and examination successes of Suchen's *nine* sons in this same chapter is crowned by the birth of Suchen's hundredth male descendent. As Lady Shui points out, now that the murderous airs of Buddhism and Daoism have been eradicated, Suchen's prodigious fertility corresponds to the renewed vitality of the cosmos (*gan Tiandi zhi shengji* 感天地之生機; chap. 138, p. 1634, 154-chapter ed.). Regulative *yang* order has been reinstated.

The extended use of *yinyang* symbolism in *Yesou puyan*, particularly the placement of a *Yi jing*–based *yin* scene precisely in chapter 66, the exploration of *yang* themes leading to and throughout the 90s chapters, and the two final illustrations of the triumph of a *yang* Confucian order in chapters 106 and 136 strongly suggest an intentional structural design for the 152-chapter version of the text. Even though these numerological correspondences are thrown off in the 154-chapter version, weakening the links between the chapter numbers and yinyang symbolism detracts little from the importance of *yinyang* imagery to the semiotics of the novel. Despite the fact that the moral valence Xia Jingqu imposes on the *yinyang* iconography in the novel becomes numbingly predictable, his use of highly nuanced gender constructions goes well beyond a simple male-female dualism.

YESOU PUYAN AND THE MASCULINIZATION OF THE SCHOLAR-BEAUTY GENRE

One aspect of the appeal of scholar-beauty romances seems to lie in their ability to illustrate an "authentic" route to self-definition in place of the more rigid, externally defined self of orthodoxy. These romances explicitly challenge the norms of orthodox narratives in which the ideals valorized are achieved through self-sacrifice and adherence to duty. Scholar-beauty romances, like today's Harlequin® romances, promote the illusion that readers can best discover their true selves by going against societal norms and throwing themselves into passionately invigorating relationships. As we have seen, the genre of scholar-beauty romances produced a highly literary aesthetics of gender. The feminine became so widely associated with the lyric values linked to the authentic that in many scholar-beauty novels the male and female protagonists are in many ways indistinguishable. The liberating aspects of *qing* were conventionally staged in a "feminine" space, a garden, or the inner domestic section of the home, and the male protagonists were imbued with a host of feminizing attributes such as beauty, emotional sensitivity, physical frailty, and moral purity. *Honglou meng* and, as we shall see, *Jinghua yuan* and *Ernü yingxiong zhuan* illustrate how feminized variations on the "scholar theme" offer readers redemptive escapes from the spiritual, moral, and physical compromises demanded by more conventional Confucian roles.

The fictional exploits of the lovers or adventurers depicted in those novels promise a degree of autonomy, choice, sensual pleasure, and "authentic" self-expression (no matter how conventionally depicted), all largely independent of state and family control. It is possible to read the feminizing norms of scholar-beauty romances as a literati complement to the rhetoric of knight-errant fiction, which indulges many of the same fantasies of freedom from conventional society. Both genres depict their protagonists as somehow liberated, if only temporarily, from their obligations to family; this convention allows the protagonists the unreal luxury of choosing their primary affective attachments to either lovers or sworn brothers. In this sense, the bonds of righteousness (*yi* 義) of knight-errant fiction are a masculinist complement to the bonds of passion (*qing*). The protagonists of both genres resist conventional orthodox obligations in favor of more authentic forms of self-expression. In *Yesou puyan*, Xia Jingqu incorporates the positive claims to authenticity articulated in both scholar-beauty and knight-errant romances while avoiding their transgressive aspects. He achieves this by incorporating the discourse of authenticity into a narrative about the power and appeal of orthodoxy. The result is Wen Suchen the SuperRu, a superlative knight and soulmate (*zhiji*) to women.

One of the most remarkable aspects of *Yesou puyan* is the way it transposes the narrative conventions of the scholar-beauty novel so that the characterizations are shifted from the feminine to the masculine to accord with its orthodox message. The masculinization of scholar-beauty conventions is immediately apparent in Suchen's relationships with his six beautiful wives. Whereas most celebrated pairs of lovers in the Chinese tradition share an appreciation for the expressive arts, typically lyric poetry, painting, or music, Suchen's wives match him in the more scholarly pursuits of mathematics, medicine, the military sciences, and prosody;[66] passions that for a more sensual man might be expressed physically or aesthetically, in Suchen's case are translated into the intellectual sphere. As described above, Suchen's first night with Xuangu, the mathematical genius, is spent with each of them tenderly using the other's body to calculate circumferences and arcs of angles. Significantly, there is no lengthy exchange of poems with his wife Xiangling, the poetry expert, for it seems Suchen is interested more in the rules of composition than in the actual composition of poems. At one point, it seems that Xiangling will enjoy a poetically youthful demise, but on her deathbed she laments that her greatest regret is that she will not be able to fulfill her filial obligations to her parents. She then sighs that "the dead cannot come back to life" (*sizhe bu neng fusheng* 死者不能復生), as if to reject the regenerative power ascribed to *qing* in *Mudan ting* (39.3b), and thereupon allows herself to be cured. Su'e's medical abilities, discussed in more detail below, are the equal of Suchen's. The fourth of the concubines, Hongdou 紅豆, is Suchen's match in outspoken rectitude, as seen in her fearless remonstrations with the emperor when she serves at the imperial court. Nan'er 難兒, a sworn sister to the empress, is the least well developed of Suchen's wives, but she seems to be an appropriate mate to Suchen because of her near-royal status.

The gathering of Suchen's beautiful wives in an idyllic estate is a remarkable reworking of the garden topos. The placement of this scene in chapters 55 to 61 invites comparison to the garden celebration at the midpoint of *Honglou meng* when all semblance of hierarchical order implodes with the introduction of new cousins into Grand Prospect Garden. In *Yesou puyan*, the entire Wen family, including servants and retainers, moves into a stunning garden provided for them by a friend who has just become a *jinshi*. The garden is a true utopia, with magical fungi, a mountain and stream filled with game and fish, and flowers that bloom in all four seasons. Unlike

66. The unusual nature of these pairings in *Yesou puyan* is highlighted by a comparison to the marriage between Scholar Chu, a young man interested only in poetry, and Miss Lu, who disdains poetry in favor of eight-legged essays in *Rulin waishi* (chapter 11). The humor in this unlikely match would be lost if the couple's interests were reversed, for the joke depends on the reader's expectations that women are not supposed to be passionate about serious knowledge.

Grand Prospect Garden, however, no hint of artificiality or interest in illusion is allowed, for the narrative pointedly insists on the authenticity of the mountain and stream: "The mountains are real mountains; the water is real water" (*shan shi zhenshan, shui shi zhenshui* 山是眞山，水是眞水; 57.7a).[67]

Rather than inspire the usual gathering of poetic talent, however, the lush garden setting is used to stage a display of Confucian regimentation. Throughout the novel, one of the primary criticisms leveled against Buddhism is the perversity of its injunctions against marriage and procreation; shortly after the Wen household's arrival in the garden, Lady Shui arranges marriages for all the unmarried members of the household, including the servants, Suchen's many retainers, and three of Suchen's concubines.[68] Each of the couples is matched according to class status and education in such a way that social hierarchies are preserved.[69] As part of her Confucianization of the household, Lady Shui rectifies the servants' names by converting any Buddhist names into more suitable equivalents (55.9a–b). Fearing that family members will be corrupted by living in such a sumptuous environment, Lady Shui also arranges detailed schedules so that each person divides his or her day between study and household responsibilities (58.7b–8a). The most striking transformation of the garden trope is the substitution of contests of strength and military skills for the more usual poetry competitions (chapter 58). Several of the newly married male and female servants compete against each other, and the women outdo the men in sword dancing, weightlifting, archery, and jousting competitions (58.9a–14b). Rather than practice needlework or engage in poetry composition or painting, Suchen's female retainers work on their mastery of martial arts (60.7b–8a). In chapters 59 and 60, the maids and female retainers engage in more conventional contests of matching wits in a lengthy discussion of riddles, rebuses, mathematical puzzles, and medical knowledge. But in keeping with the utilitarian nature of

67. Another similarity to *Honglou meng* is that the name of each garden pavilion corresponds to the name of the character who resides there, although there is no attempt to match the architectural details with the personality of its occupant.

68. Suchen is adamant that it is a filial responsibility of all his retainers to marry and reproduce. In the most clearly articulated of these scenes, he convinces the female knight who had just rescued him from Li Youquan's harem that filiality, here synonymous with procreation, is more important than chivalry (69.13b).

69. In one case, Lady Shui pairs up the kidnapped daughter of a good family and gives her to one of the family slaves; when he complains that she is "second-hand goods" (*erhun huo* 二婚貨), Lady Shui scolds him and reminds him of his servile status (57.2a).

Suchen's relationships with his beautiful wives, these exchanges are more scholarly than the playful repartee recorded in either *Honglou meng* or *Jinghua yuan*. Moreover, in the midst of this gathering of beauties, Suchen and his mother lecture the entire household on the superiority of Cheng-Zhu Confucianism. In a delightfully moral parody of the voyeurism in the grape arbor scene in chapter 27 of *Jin Ping Mei*, the mistresses eavesdrop on their maids as they debate the virtues of Confucianism and Buddhism under a grape arbor (60.9a).[70]

A further indication of how far *Yesou puyan* has shifted away from the sentimental and feminizing conventions of the scholar-beauty genre is its treatment of women warriors. Unlike *Jinghua yuan* and *Ernü yingxiong zhuan*, in which the women are eventually domesticated and cloistered, the female acrobats and warriors in *Yesou puyan* keep their martial prowess and public roles even after they marry. These women warriors are matched with men who are their physical equals and fight alongside them in husband-and-wife teams.[71] There is no hint of any impropriety when these women appear in public, however, and in pointed contrast to the pythons and the Japanese pirates who also fight as couples, the Chinese women warriors never usurp their husbands' role as leaders. Many of these women fight in single-sex troops, although this arrangement is humorously shown to have a drawback when one battalion of 200 women is thrown into chaos when their opponents, Miao troops under the command of the pythons, come prepared to do battle wearing nothing more than their weapons (99.7a).[72] Military activism seems to be a higher goal than the universal sequestering of women.

Although Suchen, with his remarkably fair skin, seems to be modeled after the beautiful young scholars of scholar-beauty romances, he is never feminized or sexualized. In contrast, Baoyu, much as would a woman, often receives preferential treatment because of his unusual beauty.[73] Suchen's fair complexion sets him off from the swarthy monks in the novel and seems to indicate his moral purity rather than sensuousness. His beauty, however, is not foregrounded, for throughout much of the novel Suchen travels in a

70. An interlinear comment refers specifically to *Jin Ping Mei* (60.9a).

71. See, e.g., 85.7a and 118.1a–b.

72. Female warriors also appear in chaps. 85, 109, 117, and 124.

73. The quick friendship between Baoyu and the handsome Prince of Beijing seems to be based, in part, on the Prince's appreciation for Baoyu's striking looks (see *HLM*, 14–15.141–43 and 85.48–49).

disguise that gives his body a purplish, unattractive complexion.[74] The reader comes to know of Suchen's beauty incidentally, through comments made by other characters rather than through the narrator. Moreover, lest the reader think that Suchen is a coddled son of a wealthy household, his characterization incorporates the bravado and strong stomach for alcohol typical of more masculine *haohan* figures.[75] The depiction of Suchen, as military and civil leader, is perfected in his eldest son, Dragon, Long'er 龍兒, who becomes a *jinshi* at the inconceivably young age of eight by recycling one of Suchen's unsuccessful examination essays as his own.[76] This precocious start allows Long'er to establish himself as a sage-magistrate by the time he reaches the perfect *yang* age of nine (chapter 126). Even Suchen's long-lost sister is given a masculine twist. At first mistaken for his double when she presents herself at court, this "beautiful male" (*mei nanzi* 美男子) is described as being identical to her brother (116.15a).

Like *Honglou meng*, gender depictions in *Yesou puyan*, rather than being directly representative of a *yinyang* binary, occur along a continuum in shifting pairs. Thus, Suchen's masculine qualities contrast most sharply with the femininely beautiful Wen Rong, whose characterization, more so than any character in the novel, is most closely derived from the aesthetics of *qing*. Not only is Wen Rong's delicate beauty enough to incite desire in those who see him, he himself is susceptible to passion in unlikely settings.[77] Much to the derision of Suchen's personal servant, who has just captured the woman warrior Sai Guanyin 賽觀音 in battle, Wen Rong is immediately smitten by

74. When Suchen tries to ransom two of his future wives while in disguise, the man overseeing the transaction says to their father, "You shouldn't have picked such an ugly son-in-law; you bragged that your son-in-law is talented and widely learned, but when I see this kind of appearance, he hardly resembles someone with talent or learning" (54.5a). For the role of physical beauty in distinguishing dashing romantic heroes from their cruder *haohan* brothers, see McMahon, *Causality and Containment*, pp. 54–55.

75. For examples of Suchen's arrogance, see 16.2a–3a and 32.10b–11a; for his taste for wine, see 13.9a and 87.12b. Unlike the *haohan* characters in the *Shuihu zhuan*, however, when Suchen gets carried away with passion, it is to insist on his absolute loyalty to Confucian values and never to act on personal or petty loyalties.

76. As Martin Huang (*Literati and Self-Re/Presentation*, p. 127) notes, Suchen's overachieving sons and grandsons should be read as extensions of his character. Each of Suchen's five oldest sons masters a branch of knowledge: the oldest military knowledge, the next civil affairs, the third astronomy, the fourth geography, and the last poetry (see *YSPY*, chap. 121).

77. In addition to being kidnapped and castrated because of his beauty, Wen Rong is almost raped in two separate scenes (49.2a–b and chap. 132).

her beauty and pleads on the battlefield that her life be spared so that he can marry her (51.9a–10a, 52.2a–b). They marry, but Sai Guanyin maintains her military identity. A variation on the gender inversion represented by this couple is the marriage between the woman warrior "Flying Maid," Feiniang 飛娘, and her equally martial mate "Red Beard," Hongxu Ke 紅鬚客.

Even though the iconography of the novel shifts the characterizations of the positive characters toward the masculine, many enemies of the Confucian state have masculine physical attributes, such as the beards, swarthy complexions, and stocky builds of the monks. Despite their masculine markings, which are frequently associated with crudeness, these characters take on the role of the destabilizing *yin* agents. Not only do they manipulate the empire so that it suffers from obvious signs of *yin* excess (including the flood, Li Youquan's harem, the most effective of whom is a fox-spirit, and the six pairs of white pythons), but they embody the destructive potential of *yin* in their direct attacks on Suchen and the Confucian state. Those women who are Suchen's allies, even his beautiful wives, are aligned with the rectifying power of *yang*, as demonstrated by their physical strength, their prodigious fertility, and their commitment to Confucian pursuits, not the least of which is the martial arts.

Lady Shui's positioning along the *yinyang* continuum may seem somewhat unclear. Although her surname, "water," suggests that she should be read as the embodiment of *yin* to complement Suchen's embodiment of *yang*, this symbolic meaning is nowhere developed in the novel. In fact, this interpretation contradicts the incessant and explicit equation of *yin* with virulent forms of heterodoxy. Instead, it seems more likely that the "water" of Lady Shui's name is meant to evoke other philosophical associations of the element. The first definition of water in the *Shuowen jiezi* is as a standard (*zhun* 準), a carpenter's level, which as Sarah Allan has shown, was extended to mean a moral standard.[78] Allan has suggested that water, more than being a source of imagery or analogy in classical Confucian rhetoric, was taken as physical proof of certain moral principles. As she explains, in the Confucian *Analects* (VI.22), water is a source of knowledge; in *Mencius* (VIA.2), flowing water is admired as being an unending source, that, like the *Dao*, moves unceasingly in predictable directions. As Mencius put it, "The people's turning to humaneness is like water flowing downward or animals' running to the

78. Allan, *The Way of Water*, p. 34.

wilds" (IVA.9).[79] When water comes to a standstill, it forms into mirroring pools (*jian* 鑒, or in its earlier form without the metal radical, 監), another standard by which to reflect and judge moral behavior, found, for example, in Sima Guang's 司馬光 (1019–86) famous *Zizhi tongjian* 資治通鑑 (Comprehensive mirror for aid in government).[80]

It is these positive qualities of nurturing and providing foundational ethics that are associated with Lady Shui, not the *yin* threat of transgression of which the "watery-natured" *pofu* is emblematic. Other positively depicted parents, especially fathers, have watery names, such as Lin Daiyu's father, who is named Ruhai 如海 "Like the Sea" in *Honglou meng*;[81] An Ji's 安驥 father in *Ernü Yingxiong zhuan*, who is named Xuehai 學海, "Study the Seas," and has the style of Shuixin 水心, "Water Heart"; and Tang Ao 唐敖 of *Jinghua yuan*, who comes from "River Source" county (Heyuan 河源) in "Abundant Seas" prefecture (Haifeng 海豐). This strongly suggests that Lady Shui's name is derived from this conventional association of water with the nurturing love of a parent rather than from the highly moralistic *yinyang* symbolism in *Yesou puyan*.

The foregrounding of Lady Shui as the symbolic center of the novel's Confucian world is another important reversal of scholar-beauty conventions. As mentioned above, the plot of most romances is dependent on the absence of the parents, a device that resolves the tension between filial obligation and romantic desire by freeing the protagonists to choose their own lovers. Suchen manages to be a paragon of filial devotion even while he selects his secondary wives. The tension between mother, or primary wife, and the son's/husband's erotic partners is an almost universal theme in Chinese fiction; yet it is conspicuously absent in *Yesou puyan*. Although Suchen meets his five concubines while away from his mother and all but consummates a physical relationship with several of them, he insists on obtaining Lady Shui's permission before agreeing to any of the matches. His primary wife, Lady Tian, the only one of his wives who does not share an intellectual pursuit with Suchen (she is, however, an ideal wife as demonstrated by her careful and impartial management of the household), seems a shadow of Lady Shui in her dispassionate interest in Suchen's fertility.

79. Ibid., pp. 22 and 42.

80. Ibid., p. 51.

81. Cf. Zhang Xinzhi's comment that "the sea being in the southeast" is a *yang* element (*SJPB*, p. 4).

The primacy of filiality in the Wen household can be seen in Suchen's decision to keep his mother company in her chambers after he is reunited with his family following a long separation, even though he has yet to see his first child, a son born in his absence. He joins his wife, Lady Tian, after several nights, but only when ordered to do so by his mother. Even after his mother has chosen an auspicious date for him to marry two of his concubines, Suchen at first tries to sleep in his mother's antechamber. He then tries to delay consummation of his marriages by arguing that he should observe proper hierarchy by spending the first night with Lady Tian, but she angrily forces him to join his new wives (47.8a). This scene of Suchen as reluctant bridegroom, preferring filial devotion to sexual passion, is repeated twice (55.10a, 56.2a).[82] Within this idealized Confucian household, conjugal love and sexuality are public arrangements that countenance no individual or private desires. Moreover, although Suchen's deference to his mother and primary wife in the careful management of his sexuality might seem parodic, Suchen's regimen of releasing semen only once each month with each wife (see 86.2b) results in a phenomenal level of fertility. Suchen fathers 24 sons, and by the end of the novel has over 500 descendants.[83]

By the end of the novel, the entire empire, and indeed world, has joined Suchen and the imperial family in elevating Lady Shui to the center of a cult of filial piety. Foreign delegations arrive to pay homage to Lady Shui and celebrate Chinese cultural dominance on the occasion of her seventieth and hundredth birthdays (chapters 136 and 142). Several Miao counties erect shrines to honor her and Suchen (149.7a–b). The novel concludes with a triumphant dream vision in which Lady Shui is inducted into the assemblage of Confucian matriarchs (*sheng mu* 聖母) and Wen Suchen joins the pantheon of Confucian sages. This dream sums up the orthodox bent of the novel's Neo-Confucian politics. A dispute breaks out among the sage-matriarchs when the mother of Lu Xiangshan 陸象山 (1139–93), a contemporary of Zhu Xi whose idealist theories opposed Cheng-Zhu dualism, protests that her son does not receive the same degree of respect as Zhu Xi or the Cheng brothers and that Suchen has destroyed her son's writings. The mother of Emperor Yao, 堯母, dismisses her plaint, pronounces Lu Xiangshan's emphasis on enlightenment as heterodox, and commands the

82. See Chapter 3 for a similar depiction of a filial son who prefers to keep his mother company rather than join his wife in *Xingshi* (49.531–32).

83. Chapter 141 contains a complete genealogy of Suchen's children and grandchildren.

humiliated woman to kowtow to Lady Shui in acknowledgment of her own and her son's guilt (152.5b).

Even though Lady Shui is identified as the center of the novel's moral vision, her narrative importance derives from Xia Jingqu's construction of filial piety as the definitive expression of Confucian orthodoxy rather than from an extended description of her actions. Lady Shui's role as symbolic figurehead to the state cult of filial piety opens the possibility for Suchen's own aggrandized expressions of filiality. To put it bluntly, the creation of a pure object of devotion, in this case the mother, is a necessary prop to the creation of the filial son, a theme that is central to the novel's vision of Confucian heroism. As Alan Cole has pointed out in his recent study of filiality in Chinese Buddhism, the conventional iconography of mother-son filiality contains a heroics of filial piety that is largely absent from narratives of father-son filiality.[84] In this sense, Lady Shui in no way dilutes the masculinist bent of the novel; in fact, her presence, as a nurturing source of authority, informs it just as the cult of the chaste lady gave coherence to the highly masculinist medieval European code of chivalry.

EXPEDIENCY, *QING*, AND THE ETHICS OF SEXUALITY

Although *Yesou puyan* largely conforms to Qing fictional standards, its iconoclastic treatment of sexual material has created an interpretive problem for readers. When explaining what feels off about the novel, readers and critics of *Yesou puyan* most often cite the uneasy balance between the sexually explicit scenes, which frequently borrow the language and imagery of pornography, and the conservative homilies on Confucian morality. Although it is not unusual for traditional Chinese fiction to combine morality and explicit descriptions of sexual behavior, the two are usually represented by separate groups of characters; what is unsettling about *Yesou puyan* is that Wen Suchen repeatedly moves between displays of sexually questionable behavior and expressions of Confucian values and, more pointedly, is implicated in the most obscene chapters of the novel rather than having a secondary character fill in for him. The literary practice of defaming a character by ascribing a sexually predatory or weak nature to him or her has a long and respectable history dating back to the *Zuo zhuan* and the *Shi ji*. In this sense,

84. Cole, *Mothers and Sons*, esp. pp. 57–64.

whereas Xia Jingqu's prurient obsession with sexuality may distinguish him from other proponents of Confucian orthodoxy, his use of sexually explicit material differs from other writers in degree rather than concept. Even though the crude and often violent depictions of sexuality typical of late Ming fiction had given way to a more allusive and sentimentalized treatment of desire by the eighteenth century, the tradition of associating transgressive sexual acts with certain groups not contained by the strictures of Confucian family regulation, especially monks, eunuchs, and the six categories of bawds (*liu po* 六婆), who serve as go-betweens, midwives, and nuns, had continued uninterrupted into the sentimental fiction of the late Qing.[85] In *Yesou puyan*, however, the sexual violence that is largely implicit in more sentimental novels becomes a dogmatic rule.

The unusual emphasis on denaturalized sexual behavior in *Yesou puyan* has disturbed some readers' sense of generic propriety to such an extent that rather then stretch their definition of the *xiaoshuo* novel to accommodate *Yesou puyan*, they have rationalized the novel's unusual depiction of sexual themes as a reflection of quirks in Xia Jingqu's psychology. In the 1930s, the scholar Han Lü was the first to suggest that Xia Jingqu was slightly unbalanced; in the 1970s, Hou Jian went one step further and dismissed the novel as the product of a deranged mind. As Hou Jian wrote in "The Perverse Psychology of *Yesou puyan*," Suchen's exaggerated reverence for his mother in conjunction with the frequent descriptions of aberrant sexuality and scatological details suggest that the author was psychologically unsound and suffered from an Oedipus complex.[86] More recently, Martin Huang has interpreted the creation of Suchen's fantastic career as an act of "self-healing" on the part of Xia Jingqu in order to compensate for his own failed career.[87]

85. *Chanzhen yishi* 禪眞遺史 is an example of an early Qing novel in which illicit sexuality is associated with the figure of a monk in long and almost loving detail; see McMahon, "Two Late Ming Vernacular Novels." One could say that transgressive sexuality was an accepted, and even expected, theme in *xiaoshuo* fiction so long as it was properly distanced by being attributed to one of these conventionally asocial characters.

86. Han Lü, "Tan *Yesou puyan*"; Hou Jian, "*Yesou puyan* de biantai xinli." Wang Qiongling ("*Yesou puyan* yanjiu," p. 17) has estimated that descriptions of sexual encounters constitute approximately 5 percent of the novel.

87. M. Huang, *Literati and Self-Re/Presentation*, pp. 112–13. In keeping with the author-centered focus of Chinese literary studies, Sun Kaidi ("Xia Erming yu *Yesou puyan*") and Zhao Jingshen ("*Yesou puyan* yu Xiashi zongpu") have identified autobiographical content in the novel as seen through parallels between the lives of Xia Jingqu and Wen Suchen: each lost his father early, was raised by his mother, and had one older brother and one younger

Rather than interpret the novel according to psychological criteria, a task that is limited by our lack of understanding of psychic norms for eighteenth-century Han literati, I believe Xia's use of sexual material can be meaningfully contextualized not only within the conventions of fiction writing but also within eighteenth-century philosophical debates on Confucian activism.

Throughout the novel, Suchen is tempted or threatened by other people's sexual advances. As discussed above, the use of sexualized encounters to define both political and ethical boundaries was well established in Chinese literature. The ecstatic voyages away from the political center in the *Chuci* and narrative Han-dynasty *fu* poetry posit sexual union with a goddess as the ultimate sign of the shaman or ruler's moral worth. Within this topos, the goddess's giving herself to a male representative of the Chinese state provides divine proof of his charismatic political and moral legitimacy. Confucian ethics taught that the ruler, or shaman, should assert his moral superiority by refusing the goddess.[88] As we have seen, Suchen is repeatedly presented with opportunities for improper sexual pleasure, and he repeatedly demonstrates his virtue by rejecting it. The novel presents Suchen's ability to regulate his own sexuality as well as that of the empire as one of the definitive contributions of Confucian orthodoxy. Throughout the novel, Suchen confronts two types of sexual encounters. There are those that threaten his physical well-being and metonymically the integrity of the empire and that take place in key *yin* chapters, and there are those that show him prioritizing other Confucian values over physical purity.

Recent discussions of the Confucian values represented in late imperial fiction have focused on the contrast between expedient, or pragmatic, action (*quan* 權) and the ideal expression of orthopraxy (*jing* 經).[89] This interest in expediency may have been in part a reflection of the open acknowledgment by Qing scholars that the implementation of orthodox practices was not always a straightforward process.[90] The philosophical tradition had long been aware of the frequent dissonance between the ideal ritual response to a situation, as defined by canonical texts, and the reality of what was possible

sister. Moreover, many of Xia's poems and some sections from his historiographical essays are inserted into the novel.

88. See W. Y. Li, *Enchantment*, pp. 4–33.

89. See McMahon, *Misers*, pp. 165–67; M. Huang, *Literati and Self-Re/Presentation*, pp. 120–22; and Kuriyama, "Confucianism in Fiction," pp. 44, 109–32.

90. An example of this was the Qing debate of whether and how to resurrect the defunct descent-line system (discussed in Chow, *The Rise of Confucian Ritualism*, pp. 115–28).

in a complex and uncontrollable environment. Classical Confucian discourse had developed the concept of expedient action to deal with these contingencies; although expedient action might conflict with the ideal, the end was thought to justify the means. What is important for the present analysis is that discussions of expedient action were framed in sexualized terms in the earliest sources; the *locus classicus* for the debate on expediency is the passage in which Mencius argues that despite the ritual injunction forbidding men and women not married to each other to touch, it is permissible for a man to use his discretion (*quan*) to reach out a hand to save a sister-in-law from drowning.[91] The controversy about the propriety of expedient action became particularly intense in Neo-Confucian thought after Cheng Yi insisted that the ritual ideal should never be compromised and that suicide was preferable to losing one's virtue.

As has been pointed out in other studies of *Yesou puyan*, many of the trials undergone by Wen Suchen illustrate the difficulty of leading a Confucian life in a less than orthodox world.[92] It is striking that many of these moral tests contain a sexual component. For example, early in the novel, in a direct enactment of the Mencian discussion on expediency, Suchen rescues Luanchui, the daughter of an official, from the flood at Lake Xihu. As night falls, the narrator poses the question, "If at dawn this lone man and unaccompanied woman spending the night outside here were seen by someone, it would really be inconvenient. But given these circumstances, what would be best?" 倘竟露宿在此，狐男寡女。天明了，被人看見，更不方便，這卻如何是好? (chap. 3, p. 33, 154-chapter ed.). Suchen carries Luanchui, whose feet are bound, to a nearby shrine, where he dries their clothes by a fire. Luanchui, out of gratitude to Suchen and fear of gossip, argues that they should marry, but Suchen successfully persuades her that they should continue to treat each other as brother and sister. In a similar scene in which Suchen rescues a woman, who then wants to marry him, he refers to the same passage from the *Mencius* to explain why marriage would be inappropriate for them. Suchen chides the woman that she must adapt to changing circumstances: "Every situation is different depending on whether the circumstances are constant or changing; preserving the orthodox and acting expediently are extensions of the same principle" 處常處變，事各不同；守經行權，理無二致 (75.7a). The crown prince also refers to the same passage

91. *Mengzi*, 4A.17; this passage is also discussed in McMahon, *Misers*, p. 166.

92. McMahon, *Misers*, p. 166; Kuriyama, "Confucianism in Fiction," pp. 109–32.

from *Mencius* in defense of expediency when convincing Suchen to write talismanic characters directly on the chests of the women in the imperial harem to protect them against black magic (chap. 108, p. 1243, 154-chapter ed.).[93] The heroine, Shui Bingxin 水冰心, of the late Ming, early Qing romance *Haoqiu zhuan* 好逑傳 (The fortunate union), also refers to the Mencian defense of expediency when arguing that a young scholar should be allowed to recuperate in her house, even though no proper chaperon is present.[94] In both *Haoqiu zhuan* and the later *Ernü yingxiong zhuan*, however, any potentially compromising intimacy between a young man and woman is neutralized by having the characters marry. *Yesou puyan* has a much more tolerant attitude toward women's sexual purity, as demonstrated by the fact that Luanchui goes on to marry a highly successful scholar who never questions her sexual purity. A more unusual treatment of the topos of expediency is Suchen's cure of the Stone Maiden, which involves sexually stimulating her in order to activate her *yang* energy and bring on her menses (95.6b–7a). The woman's prodigious fertility after she marries an appropriate husband is proof that Suchen's "expedient" means were justified: the woman miraculously gives birth to 28 sons, which, as the text points out, is equal to the full number of constellations (100.12b).[95]

Among the most troubling illustrations of Suchen's use of expediency are the entrances of three of Suchen's secondary wives into the narrative. Because these scenes compromise the perceived purity of women in his own household, they come close to undermining the orthodox ideals concerning the separation of men and women. The early stages of his relationship with Xuangu, with whom Suchen shared intimate geometry lessons, has already been discussed. Suchen meets another of his secondary wives, Xie Xiangling, when called to the home of an official to attend to Xiangling's sister. While ministering to the sister, Suchen abruptly reaches toward Xiangling and rips off her shirt; the text voyeuristically adds: "That girl's upper body was exposed, and two soft breasts popped out" 那女子精著半身出兩隻嫩乳

93. For other discussions of the propriety of expediency versus orthodoxy, see 40.3b and 142.4a.

94. *Haoqiu zhuan*, 6.153. McMahon discusses a similar scene in chapter 54 of *Chanzhen houshi* 禪眞後史 (Later tales of the true way) in *Causality and Containment*, p. 118.

95. The chapter-end commentary develops the analogy that Suchen's massaging of her vagina is analogous to Pan Gu's mythical "boring open of Chaos" (*zaokai Hundun* 鑿開), and the delivery of 28 sons is equivalent to "Chaos transforming itself into order" (*Hundun wei wenming* 混沌爲文明; chap. 102, p. 1178, 154-chapter ed.).

(17.4b). This unexpectedly sexual detail forces the reader initially to question the propriety of Suchen's actions, even though the text later takes great pains to justify them. As explained by the narrator, Suchen's medical acumen is such that he recognizes signs of disease on Xiangling's otherwise healthy face; tearing off her shirt shocks her system into producing enough adrenaline to ward off what would otherwise be imminent death. Similar to the style of Jin Shengtan and Zhang Zhupo, the interlinear commentary shifts the readers' attention from this shocking lapse of propriety to aesthetic concerns. At first the commentator blandly comments, "This business is extremely strange," 那間 [*sic*] 事奇極, a refrain that is twice repeated. After the description of how the girl's "two soft breasts popped out," the commentator hurriedly anticipates Suchen's own defense by explaining, "This is extremely distressing; but after all, life has priority [over propriety]" 不堪極矣，然究係人命爲重 (17.4b). Suchen later uses this same justification of the primacy of life. Not unexpectedly, the next comment turns to aesthetic issues and the "marvelous" (*miao*) descriptions; thereafter, the majority of comments busily and unnecessarily identify the shifts in point of view as the narrative records each character's reactions to the scene.[96]

The initial stages of Suchen's relationship with Su'e also seem to contravene ritual ideals. Su'e is the servant of Luanchui, the woman Suchen saved from the flood. Although the shared character "Su" in their names suggests that they are predestined marriage partners, the difference in status between her and Suchen's other wives makes the match seem unsuitable. Before they publicly announce their betrothal, Su'e, who is highly skilled in medicine, nurses Suchen through a raging fever by using herself as a human compress and alternately heating and chilling her naked body to bring him some relief. Soon after he recovers, she mistakenly ingests an aphrodisiac concocted by that same monk who was impregnating women in order to obtain their fetuses and is overcome by uncontrollable sexual desires. In what amounts to a mimicry of sexual intercourse, Suchen stabilizes her condition by thrusting his leg between her thighs, massaging her and stopping up her mouth with his tongue (15.2a). The reader's questions about the propriety of these unorthodox cures is reinforced by the suspicions of Luanchui, through whose eyes the scene is focalized: when Luanchui sneaks in the following morning to check why their room is so quiet, she immediately jumps to the conclu-

96. The commentary similarly directs the readers' attention to stylistic issues during the pythons' orgy (95.9a–12a).

sion that they have engaged in illicit sexual activity (15.4a). Luanchui is made even more disquieted by the sight of Su'e's silk red undergarments lying in a heap behind their feet. Although the purity of Suchen's actions is later vindicated in court, the reader is left wondering why Xia Jingqu felt it necessary to push this episode to the furthest limits of propriety by weaving in so many sexually suggestive details. Curiously, Xia seems ultimately more concerned with clearing away the taint of Su'e's low social status than with defending her moral reputation. Shortly after they are betrothed, Su'e dispels any doubts about her origins when she reveals that her father had been a renowned Confucian medical expert and that she had been sold into servitude by an uncle after she was orphaned at age nine (19.3b).

More than illustrating the importance of expediency as a legitimate and life-saving form of action, these scenes reject Neo-Confucian notions of chastity. Within Suchen's value system if not that of Xia Jingqu, rigid codes of sexual purity are less important than the fulfillment of other Confucian obligations. Thus, when Suchen deliberates on whether to commit suicide after being sexually violated by Li Youquan's harem, he reassures himself that he should live because he was an innocent victim and is still able to serve his country and his aged mother. "How could I preserve the minor principles (*xiaojie*), which are like ditches or channels, and forget the canonical paths of loyalty and filiality?" 我豈可守溝瀆之小節而忘忠孝之大經乎? (65.10b–11a). After exposing Xiangling's body, Suchen repeatedly justifies his actions, saying "All I was doing was giving priority to life" 正以人命爲重 (17.7b). Clearly to Suchen, the end does justify the means, no matter how far from orthodoxy he veers. Most striking in Xia Jingqu's exploration of Confucian activism, given the number of female suicides represented in the fiction, morality texts, and gazetteers of this period, is the number of women in the novel who go on to lead proper married lives after having been sexually defiled. Several characters in the novel do choose suicide to demonstrate their rejection of a morally compromising situation, but the vast majority live on to redeem themselves through adherence to orthodoxy.[97]

Suchen's choice of expediency (*quan*) over a narrower and stricter definition of orthodoxy is his way of expressing authenticity. In this novel, authenticity continues to be based on an affinity for *qing*. Suchen is a "man of passion" (*duoqing ren*), and it is this *qing* that infuses his passionate loyalty to

97. For examples of virtuous suicides, see 51.1a, 126.1a, and chap. 132, pp. 1539–40 (154-chapter ed.).

orthodoxy, his appreciation of the women who become his intellectual "soulmates" (*zhiji*), and his ability to recognize the merits of the unconventional men, women, and supernatural creatures who become his sworn allies. As Joanna Kuriyama has pointed out, Suchen's passionate engagement with life does not meet with his mother's approval.[98] From the perspective of Lady Shui (and the commentator), Suchen's excessive willingness to take up the causes of other people leads him to reckless self-endangerment and the relinquishing of his filial obligation to preserve his body. In response to the rejoinder that not to act would be to imitate the early philosopher Yang Zhu 楊朱 (who took self-preservation to the extreme in claiming that he would not be willing to save the world if it meant having to pluck a hair from his arm), Lady Shui likens Suchen to Mozi 墨子, who did not recognize the Confucian hierarchy of relationships (54.2b–3a). She further accuses Suchen of having studied in vain, since he does not understand that the proper Confucian path lies in being able to judge appropriate action. She ends her lecture by threatening to disown Suchen if he fails to "focus his energies on following the upright [moderate and orthodox] path of the sages" 專力於聖人中正之道(54.23a–b).

The commentator concurs with Lady Shui and notes that Suchen's earlier illness was a result of his recklessness and that "the heterodox only know how to act without focusing their spirit and are therefore neither moderate nor orthodox" 異端只爲作弄，精神不收斂，故不中不正耳(54.3a). The chapter commentary has high praise for the way Lady Shui's lecture draws a parallel between the philosophies of Yang Zhu and Mozi and Suchen's unthinking heroics. It concludes by saying that "with a mother like this, I have never heard of the son not being a sage" (54.12b). In an earlier homily, when two of the concubines question Lady Shui about her equanimity after hearing that Suchen had been sentenced to death, Lady Shui answers by saying that when the emotions are restrained, they will achieve their proper expression, "but if one follows his or her private emotions and forgets heavenly principle" (若徇私情，忘天理), then the emotional expression will be inappropriate (38.6b). Since in this instance Suchen had risked his life for a politically appropriate goal (he had remonstrated against the emperor's misguided goals of promoting Buddhism and Daoism), Lady Shui is able to resign herself to her loss without undue grief.

98. Kuriyama, "Confucianism in Fiction," pp. 103–8.

In her own dealings, Lady Shui scrupulously avoids resorting to expedient action. Only in one instance is she persuaded to follow expediency (*congquan* 從權), even though she calls the situation "counter to ritual in the extreme" (*shu fei li* 殊非禮). She gives her implicit consent for the women in her household to stage a phony wedding ceremony to protect those still unmarried from being selected for the imperial harem (40.2b). Ultimately, however, she disavows this decision to compromise her moral standards and expresses regret that she allowed her family to submit to expedient means (142.4a).[99] Tellingly, in a later scene, when faced by a humiliating order to appear barefoot in public, an action that would jeopardize their claims to absolute sexual integrity, Lady Shui and all the women of the household resolve to commit suicide rather than acquiesce to the command (98.3a).

Even while honoring Lady Shui's unwavering commitment to the highest level of orthodox restraint, the narrative implicitly promotes Suchen's style of passionate activism. For example, despite the suggestions that he had taken to heart his mother's lecture on the necessity of moderating his heroism, Suchen goes on to risk his life many more times. More pointedly, in one of the most trenchant clashes between expediency and orthodoxy, expediency clearly wins out. When Lady Shui lies near death, one of Suchen's sons prepares a broth from his own flesh in order to revive her. As Wen Long argues to himself, although cutting his flesh (*gegu* 割股) is counter to orthodox ritual (*fei zheng li* 非正禮), it is permissible to resort to expediency during a crisis (129.2b). Remarkably enough, Lady Shui declares the soup delicious and has an immediate and miraculous recovery. Hearing this, Suchen's wives and several of the female servants join Wen Long in organizing a ten-day rota among themselves to prepare fresh batches of soup. When Lady Shui discovers the reason for the bandages on their arms, she scolds them for their ignorant filiality (*yuxiao* 愚孝), which no true Confucian would adopt 但愚孝之爲君子不取 (129.7b). Despite Lady Shui's stern disapproval, the immediate efficacy of the unorthodox cure proves its value as a filial act. The ultimate proof of the propriety of Wen Long's choice of expediency is that his prayers for an end to the lengthy drought (which had afflicted Beijing since the onset of Lady Shui's illness) are answered with a heavy snowfall that lasts several days.[100]

99. See ibid., p. 115.

100. Interestingly, the commentary is ambivalent whether these filial actions are proper (129.16b).

In keeping with the masculinist bent of the novel, even as Suchen's passionate (*duoqing*) heroic nature is celebrated, more conventional expressions of *qing* are denigrated. Sentimentalized views of love are repeatedly dismissed as childish and selfish. Rather than signaling innocence or purity, shyness and embarrassment about discussing betrothal plans are dismissed as "childish conceits" (*haizi qi* 孩子氣, 4.15a) or as "childish reticence" or "immature deportment" (兒女私情，兒女態; 10.7b, 13.12a, 38.6b, 99.1b). The scornful attitude toward sexual passion is revealed in one of the rare illustrations of it in this novel with the ludicrous description of Wen Rong flirting with Sai Guanyin on the battlefield. As modeled by Xue Baochai in *Honglou meng*, marriage is a matter of family obligation and responsibility, not private emotions.

The difference in characterization between Suchen and his mother points to the gendered politics of orthodoxy implicit in the novel. Suchen is given license to transcend the strictures of orthodox behavior in ways his mother is not. As a male, he embodies the regulatory powers of *yang* and is thus able to bring order through the mere presence of his body. Lady Shui, like many chaste and virtuous women of the late imperial period, invokes a much more rigid and absolute definition of Confucian orthodoxy that is not subject to negotiation. Even though the prominence of Lady Shui anchors the fictional world in orthodox values, without Suchen's heroics there would be no story worth telling. Lady Shui's unbending integrity protects the Confucian tone of the novel from being unduly undermined by Suchen's unconventional antics.

Although many readers have clearly felt that *Yesou puyan* stretches the definition of orthodoxy beyond meaningful limits, its emphasis on the dissemination of Confucian practices throughout the known world suggests that Xia Jingqu was trying to appropriate the unconventional but redemptive power of *qing* into a largely orthodox narrative. Not only is the startling use of sexuality in *Yesou puyan* an outgrowth of the classical vocabulary used to discuss the legitimacy of expediency, it also resonates with the novel's equation of filiality with sexual restraint. Throughout the novel, the adoption of Confucian marriage practices is symbolic of the willingness of foreign peoples to accept Chinese sovereignty: those peoples, such as the Miao and the Europeans who are willing to be incorporated in the Han Chinese cultural sphere, eagerly take to arranged marriages and the segregation of the sexes in order to manage their local sexual economies. It is these peoples whose participation is foregrounded in the celebration of Lady Shui's birthdays. The intractable *yin*-identified groups, such as Buddhists, Daoists, and the Japanese, demonstrate their resistance to Chinese sovereignty through decadent and threatening sexual practices.

The decentering of sexual chastity as an essential definition of morality, particularly for women, fits well with Xia Jingqu's rejection of the intellectual, quietist aspects of Neo-Confucian self-cultivation in favor of an activist definition of Confucianism. Since the problematic of desire was an important component of the Neo-Confucian discourse on self-cultivation, it is not surprising that it disappears from *Yesou puyan* as a major thematic concern. Like the nineteenth-century works taken up in the following chapter, *Yesou puyan* narrates the process of regulating an unbalanced society through the reuniting of families, the curing of diseases, the combating of corrupt powers, and the regulating of floods. These works, even those novels directly influenced by *Honglou meng,* were no longer focused on Neo-Confucian self-cultivation. In none of these novels is desire treated as problematic. It was no doubt Xia Jingqu's anticipation of themes that became dominant in later fiction that rescued his eccentric novel from complete obscurity.

CHAPTER SIX

Masterful Women and Deficient Men in Jinghua yuan *and* Ernü yingxiong zhuan

The two nineteenth-century novels *Jinghua yuan* and *Ernü yingxiong zhuan* are remarkable for their depictions of elite women who assume the roles of scholars, statesmen, and knights-errant. Although the women in *Honglou meng* were "ten times" better than the men, their ambitions are still limited to the domestic sphere. In these two later novels, both of which were influenced by *Honglou meng* and indeed allude to it, women literally displace men from traditionally male activities. In many ways, the characterizations of these active female protagonists are derived from the beautiful and frail women who dominated the imaginary of the late Ming and achieved their fullest expression in *Honglou meng*; however, rather than functioning as icons of self-expressive or lyric authenticity, a value that we have seen to be potentially subversive of orthodox social structures, the beautiful women in *Jinghua yuan* and *Ernü* reclaim the Confucian ideal of social engagement with an enthusiasm and ease their male counterparts seem incapable of mustering.

Unlike *Honglou meng*, these novels do not treat the symbolic feminine as a place of resistance to the often demoralizing demands of institutionalized orthodoxy; instead, they cast sympathetic female characters as successful figures who are privileged to engage in a variety of public pursuits. Moreover, in both novels the women's participation in traditionally masculine pursuits somehow redeems career aspirations that had become politically and morally corrupt. The male characters, in contrast, are deeply ambivalent about their own engagement in the literati occupations of learning and public service. *Jinghua yuan* and *Ernü* use the authenticating power of the feminine to restore dignity and integrity to these traditional male routes to identity; in these fictional worlds, the problem no longer lies in the individual's inability to conform to Neo-Confucian ideals of behavior but in a bureaucratic infrastructure that has become morally bankrupt. The two novels end conventionally with the redemption of the Confucian meritocracy; however, the decaying imperial system is salvaged only through the fantasy of feminine purity.

THE RULE OF WOMEN IN *JINGHUA YUAN*

Critical response to Li Ruzhen's 李汝珍 (ca. 1763–1830) *Jinghua yuan* 鏡花緣 (Flowers in the mirror) has been mixed. Although particular episodes have received critical attention for their depiction of women, their reflection of mid-Qing literati values including popular Daoism, or their brilliant use of allegory and satire, twentieth-century scholarly opinion is unanimous in judging the 100-chapter novel as flawed because of its rambling episodic structure.[1] Indeed, the novel's structural integrity is so weak that most scholarship has focused on discrete episodes or themes, rather than on the novel in its entirety. Those rare studies that attempt to do justice to the entire novel likewise resort to breaking it down into episodes, without elaborating the narrative logic that connects or unifies the parts. The novel splits into two roughly equivalent halves: the first section narrates the maritime voyage of the unsuccessful scholar Tang Ao 唐敖 through mythic lands to seek out and bring together the most important of the 100 flower-spirits who have been exiled to earth (chapters 7–48). The second half takes place in China, where the full complement of 100 girls takes the special examination for women and then gather in an enclosed garden to engage in various genteel pursuits, such as telling stories, playing word games, composing poetry, painting, and discussing mathematics (chapters 58–93). As we shall see, however, the episodic structure of the novel is informed and unified by a broad *yinyang* allegorical framework.

1. On *Jinghua yuan* as a feminist text, see Hu Shi, "A Chinese Declaration"; Evans, "Social Criticism"; Brandauer, "Women in the *Ching-hua yüan*"; Bao Jialin, "Li Ruzhen de nannü pingdeng sixiang"; and Q. Y. Wu, *Female Rule*, pp. 82–87, 90–97, and *passim*. On the celebration of literati culture, see Hsia, "The Scholar Novelist"; and Roddy, *Literati Identity*, pp. 200–206. For treatment of allegory, see H. C. Chang, *Allegory*; and H. S. Kao, *Li Ju-chen*. On Daoist content, see Wang Jiwen "*Jinghua yuan*"; Yue Hengjun, "Penglai guixi"; and L. T. H. Chan, "Religion and Structure." For a reading of the novel as an anti-Manchu political allegory, see You Xinxiong, "*Jinghua yuan* de zhuzhi." Translations of the novel have focused on either episodes from the voyage or the epilogue: see T. Y. Lin's heavily abridged *Flowers in the Mirror*; and the translations by H. C. Chang of chapters 32–37 in idem, *Chinese Literature*, pp. 405–60, and chapters 96–100 in idem, *Allegory*, pp. 39–71.

Li Ruzhen's uses of the feminine are a crucial aspect of the aesthetic patterning in *Jinghua yuan*. The novel is set during the Zhou dynasty 周 (C.E. 690–705), the fifteen-year interregnum when Wu Zetian 武則天 (624–705) usurped the throne from the ruling Tang dynastic line and established herself as empress. Women are the primary focus of the novel, as goddesses, rulers, the cultured elite, and adventurers, and men are literally displaced from the center of power. The central male protagonist, Tang Ao, whose name reveals his symbolic association with the Tang dynasty, does not return to China after he achieves enlightenment. Most studies of the treatment of women in the novel have followed Hu Shi's lead in reading it as motivated by feminist concerns, even if only to put forward the idea that women could be the intellectual equals of men.[2] However, since, as we have seen, the idealizing of beautiful and talented young women and girls had become a common trope inspired by the cult of *qing*, *Jinghua yuan* is not atypical in its idealization of women and the feminine.

If we shift our attention from the question of Li Ruzhen's feminist intent, we then confront the question of how to resolve the contradictory meanings associated with the feminine in the characterizations of the historical figure Empress Wu Zetian and the period of internal tumult (*neiluan* 内亂) associated with her rule and the idealized 100 talented beauties. In *Honglou meng*, the disjuncture between the sympathetic depiction of the girls and the destructive shrews goes straight to the heart of that novel's paradoxical views of desire; in *Jinghua yuan*, Li Ruzhen makes use of the same gendered vocabulary to explore issues of literati engagement in late Qing systems of power and knowledge. The flower-spirits, although not expressive of the passions and desires associated with the cult of *qing*, nonetheless function as feminine emblems of the authentic. If *Honglou meng* is a celebration of the values associated with the interior lyric self, *Jinghua yuan* attempts to recapture the apolitical integrity of the late imperial institutions of power and knowledge that had been undermined through their association with the examination system.[3] Although female characters serve as icons of literati culture in both novels, the feminine no longer functions as a utopic symbolic space accessible to men. The women's takeover of traditional male preserves is less a

2. See Ono, "*Kyōka gen* no sekai."

3. As Stephen Roddy (*Literati Identity*, pp. 201–2) has recently argued, the cynical ambiguity in *Jinghua yuan* toward pure intellectualism may be a critique of the late Qing institutionalization of evidential studies.

feminist call for expanding women's access to exclusively male avenues of power, as has been widely argued, than a reflection of a yearning to reinvest these elite male pursuits with a sense of dignity and ethical purity they had lost. Sadly, the women's joyful celebration of literati culture is shut off to men.

More so than the novels discussed above, *Jinghua yuan* depicts the position of scholar-bureaucrat as diminished in authority. Like other Qing works, especially *Rulin waishi*, *Jinghua yuan* treats ascension to official status, one of the crowning achievements in a scholar's life, with as much trepidation as joy. This lack of enthusiasm for Confucian engagement is, no doubt, one of the factors that has led some critics to read *Jinghua yuan* as a Daoist work. Indeed, the sympathetic treatment of popular Daoism and the pursuit of immortality exemplifies the novel's escapist fantasies. However, although a Daoist fate seems predicted by the character Ao 敖 in Tang Ao's name, which is suggestive of *aoyou* 遨遊, "to roam," the free and easy travel sought by Daoist sages, he is as ambivalent about his Daoist interests as his Confucian ambitions. He pursues Daoist enlightenment seriously only when all other doors have been closed. Despite his connection to the Tang loyalists, which should preclude participation in Empress Wu's illegitimate government, Tang takes the examination under her and wins the coveted third-place *tanhua* 探花 status. He abandons scholarly pursuits only after Wu Zetian discovers his alliance with the Tang loyalists and demotes him to the lowest-level status of licentiate.

As C. T. Hsia and Stephen Roddy have suggested, the novel can be read more successfully as a celebration of Qing intellectual pursuits, of which popular Daoism is just one thread. As Roddy further points out, however, literati culture in this novel has been separated from its moral purpose and has been trivialized into a brilliant and entertaining "play of form."[4] The novel's spatial organization reveals the dangers of this excessive reliance on aesthetics over ethics. The scattering and dispersal of China's political center outside China's borders, where the voyagers learn that all values are relative, seems to be emblematic of literati fears of displacement and marginalization during the long period of political and cultural decline of the early nineteenth century. Since Li Ruzhen was working on the novel only decades before the outbreak of the Opium War in 1839 and the Taiping uprising in

4. See ibid., pp. 200–206.

1851,[5] one is tempted to read his depiction of the scattering of the Tang court as prescient of the turmoil that was soon to expose the limits of Chinese imperial power and systems of knowledge.

Gender, Structure, and Yinyang *Patterning*

Although modern readers and critics are often apologetic about the novel's length and episodic structure, the work was a great success among nineteenth-century readers. Indeed, the steady demand for it resulted in the publication of multiple editions of varying quality.[6] The popularity of *Jinghua yuan* may in part be due to its rich intertextual weaving of elements from earlier masterpieces of the classical and vernacular canon, as well as the erudite knowledge culled from Li's own research in phonetics.[7] The encyclopedic range of allusions to the Classics, vernacular fiction, popular Daoism, and recondite knowledge in *Jinghua yuan*, though daunting and often frustrating to the modern reader who is accustomed to reading for narrative development, would have appealed to the tastes of traditional readers trained in the pleasures of identifying intertextual resonances and structural patterning. The thematic climax, the 30-chapter gathering of the 100 flower-spirits banished to earth as talented girls, is a clear attempt to outdo the poetry gatherings of the twelve flower-spirits in *Honglou meng*.[8] In fact, one of

5. Li Ruzhen wrote the novel over ten-plus years; he seems to have completed it in 1817, and it was first printed in 1818. He continued to revise the novel several times between the appearance of the earliest edition in 1818 and the illustrated 1828 Jiezi yuan 芥子園 edition; most changes involved minor linguistic substitutions or the strengthening of the characterization of the central female character, Tang Guichen, by assigning other characters' speeches to her; see Sun Jiaxun, *"Jinghua yuan" gong'an bianyi*, pp. 37–48. In contrast to Sun Kaidi (*Zhongguo tongsu xiaoshuo*, p. 178), who identified the earliest extant text as the 1828 Jiezi yuan edition, Sun Jiaxun (pp. 48–49, 133) has tentatively pushed back the date of this text to 1818 and identified the place of publication as Suzhou. My page references are to the reprint of the illustrated 1888 Shanghai Dianshi zhai 點石齋 edition, entitled *Huitu Jinghua yuan* 繪圖鏡花緣 (Beijing: Zhongguo shudian, 1985).

6. The Beijing Library alone houses ten editions, dated 1830, 1842, 1858, 1877, 1888, Guangxu 光緒 (1875–1908), 1890 (2), 1895, and 1897.

7. Li compiled a study of phonology called the *Yin jian* 音鑒. Chapter 17 of *Jinghua yuan* contains a discussion of historical changes in pronunciation, and chapter 31 diagrams a phonetic system to record contemporary pronunciation.

8. The gathering in *Jinghua yuan* is an extended celebration of high Qing literary culture. The girls discuss card games (74.1b–2b), *go* and other chess games (74.2b–3a), quoits and archery (74.3a–3b, 79.1a–2a), swinging (74.3b–4a), and drinking games (78.1a–1b). The

the girls self-consciously remarks on the historical uniqueness of this gathering of 100 girls (71.3a).

Although the sentimental *Jinghua yuan* idealizes the feminine, it borrows structural motifs from the violent and often misogynist *Shuihu zhuan*. In chapter 48, 100 jade tablets list the names of the 100 flower-spirits; as in *Shuihu*, the tablets are inscribed in the "tadpole" (*kedou* 蝌蚪) calligraphic style, which only Tang Guichen 唐閨臣 (literally, Lady Minister of the Tang), the leader of the flower-spirits, is able to read. The gradual accumulation of the full complement of girls, accomplished only in chapter 69, is reminiscent of the gathering of the Liangshan heroes in chapter 70 of *Shuihu zhuan*. Also similar to *Shuihu zhuan* is the discussion of the seating arrangements for the 100 successful examination candidates, which serves as an opportunity to record the name of each girl.[9] By setting the novel during the Tang dynasty, Li Ruzhen ensured that Tang Ao's voyage through many of the lands listed in the mythic *Shanhai jing* 山海經 (Classic of the mountains and seas) would evoke both that Han geographical classic and the fictional *Xiyou ji*.[10] In a fashion similar to the allegoric structure of *Xiyou ji*, Tang Ao's quest brings geopolitical order to the countries he passes through and culminates in his own enlightenment. The conclusion, the architectural rendering of the allegory of the four vices of excess (*sitan* 四貪; chapters 94–100), is similar to Dong Yue's *Xiyou bu* in the way the protagonists become physically entrapped in their own desires.

Li Ruzhen's seemingly exhaustive attempts at intertextual inclusion produced a text that almost defies a unified reading. Yet there are clear indications that Li was cognizant of some of the structural features of the canonical novel and used them to shape his sprawling text, on which he worked for over ten years. In accordance with novelistic conventions, *Jinghua yuan* opens with a supernatural frame story that motivates the action of the main plot. Although the work does not divide into ten-chapter units, it follows the normative structural pattern of the 100-chapter novel by dividing neatly into

---

brilliant drinking poem that spans chapters 82 to 87 is a phonetic *tour de force* of rhyme and alliteration.

9. A further allusion to *Shuihu zhuan* may be the huntress Luo Hongqu 駱紅渠, one of the twelve central flower-spirits, who appears in chapter 10 camouflaged in a tiger skin. Unlike Li Kui 李逵, whose battle with a tiger leads to his mother's death, Luo Hongqu hunts tigers in order to avenge her mother.

10. In addition to culling details from the *Shanhai jing*, Li also borrowed from the *Bowu zhi* 博物志, *Huainanzi* 淮南子, and *Shenyi ji* 神異記; see Wang Jiwen, "*Jinghuan yuan*," pp. 7–11.

two narrative hemispheres at the midway point and in using chapters that numerically mirror each other to establish a series of structural frames.

A number of thematic patterns are used to set off the contrasts between the two halves. The first section, set largely outside China in a geographically dispersed space vaguely referred to as "overseas" (*haiwai* 海外), architecturally mirrors the second half, which takes place in China, mostly in the enclosed space of a garden. The focus of the two halves is demarcated by gender, with male adventurers in the first half and female flower-spirits in the second. More interestingly, the six-chapter prologue narrates Wu Zetian's rise to power, and the six-chapter epilogue describes her defeat at the hands of the Tang loyalists. In Chapters 7–8, Tang Ao prepares to leave China; the loyalist forces begin to assemble at this exact point in the second half of the novel in chapters 57–58. In terms of tone, the two halves of the novel also contrast with each other. The biting satires on all forms of hypocrisy in the first half give way to the enthusiastic celebration of literati arts in the garden.

Although the novel clearly divides into two halves, there is some ambiguity about which narrative moment represents the midway point. In chapters 49 and 50, the exact numerical midpoint, the two most important of the girls descend from the mountain on Little Penglai Island, a utopian Daoist fairyland replete with magical plants, waterfalls, and numinous aura, and begin the voyage back to China. The structural importance of chapter 50 as a "centering" chapter is heightened by the voyagers' return to Two-Faced Country, Liangmian guo 兩面國, a country they had first visited in chapter 25. However, an equally strong caesura falls in chapter 48, in which the girls learn their true identities as flower-spirits from the 100 jade stelae on Little Penglai Island and Tang Ao achieves Daoist enlightenment. Tang Ao's enlightenment is echoed in chapter 95 when his daughter, the reincarnation of the Fairy of the Hundred Flowers (Bai hua xianzi 百花仙子), returns to this same island for her own enlightenment. The repetition on Little Penglai Island of many of the places named in the mythological prologue further suggests the thematic and structural importance of this chapter. A final reason for reading chapter 48 as structurally significant is that it is divisible by six.

The *yin* number six is exploited repeatedly in the structuring of *Jinghua yuan*. The novel is unusual in that, despite its 100-chapter length, the structural patterns are based on the number six rather than on the more usual complements of five or ten. The importance of the *yin* number six to the structure corresponds to the novel's thematic exploration of a *yin*-dominated cosmos in which men are eclipsed by women in both the heavenly and political spheres. In the six-chapter prologue, the 100 flower-spirits are exiled to earth as punishment for blooming out of season. On earth, this celestial disruption is matched by Wu Zetian's usurpation of the Tang throne and her establishment of the Zhou dynasty, the scattering of the Tang loyalists, and Wu Zetian's forcing of her garden to bloom in the dead of winter. In the six-chapter epilogue, the cycle of karmic retribution is brought to a close when Tang Ao's daughter reverts to her celestial identity, Wu Zetian is defeated by an army of Tang loyalists, and the male Tang dynasty is reinstated.

Women and topics related to the feminine are foregrounded in the six-chapter prologue. The novel begins with a brief discussion of proper behavior for women—the "four virtues" of feminine virtue, speech, demeanor, and work, as laid out in Ban Zhao's *Instructions for Women* (1.1a).[11] The narrative that follows this didactic warning to women pointedly illustrates what happens when women do not respect their proper social roles. All the goddesses gather at Mount Kunlun to celebrate the birthday of the Daoist figure Xiwangmu, Mother-Queen of the West, on the third day of the third lunar month. As in *Xingshi*, *Honglou meng*, and *Yesou puyan*, this use of the double-three date initiates a period of chaos that, in this instance, does not conclude until the epilogue, when the Tang loyalists choose the third day of the third lunar month as the date to begin their uprising against Wu Zetian (96.1a). Further repetitions of the doubled-three highlight the *yin* associations of the motif: for example, the episode in the Country of Women (Nü'er guo 女兒國) begins in chapter 33; and in chapter 65, perhaps in anticipation of the *yin* chapter 66, a group of the girls inconclusively debate the significance of the coincidence that 33 of them are gathered together, that the apricot flowers have 33 petals, and that they have drawn a divination stick with three-three written on it (65.3a–4a).

The prologue is set during a period of *yin* ascendancy. As the goddesses gather for Xiwangmu's birthday banquet, one of them points out how unusual it is that no male deities are present. Stranger yet is that the god of the literary examinations has been transformed into female form. The Fairy of

11. Opening with a token nod toward this classic for women may have been a defensive move designed to mitigate the political dangers of writing a novel about usurpation under Manchu rule. Wu Qingyun (*Female Rule*, pp. 95–97) argues that the reference to Ban Zhao's *Instructions for Women* is an ironic subversion of the four feminine virtues.

the Hundred Grasses (Bai cao xianzi 百草仙子) explains that this and a number of other *yin* portents signal the future dominance of women in the literary sphere (1.1b). Ironically, since Ban Zhao's exhortations to female modesty directly precede the celebration of Xiwangmu's birthday, the major theme of the party is the perversion of the proper political and seasonal order. Chang'e 嫦娥 is the central character in the scene. Rather than develop the more common and sympathetic aspect of the Chang'e myth, in which she is portrayed as a divine and lonely beauty, this narrative draws out the subversive aspect of the myth, the story of a wife who was banished to the moon for deceiving her husband and stealing the elixir of life.

At the banquet, Chang'e imperiously tries to force all the flowers to bloom simultaneously. The Fairy of the Hundred Flowers refuses, explaining that each flower should bloom according to its proper season, that to tamper with this would reverse the proper hierarchy of *yin* and *yang* (*diandao yinyang* 顛倒陰陽; 2.1b), and that she would prefer to be exiled to earth rather than commit such an infamy. Chang'e eventually tricks the flowers into blooming, and consequently the 100 flower-spirits are banished to earth.[12] This indignant vow of the Fairy of the Hundred Flowers to uphold the natural order exposes the fundamental disjuncture in the novel between the sympathetic female characters, who would uphold propriety, and those rebellious women, who subvert the "natural" order of *yin* and *yang*. The gathering of the flower-spirits on earth is the result of Chang'e's disruption of the natural order; it is not something to be emulated. This inversion of the *yinyang* order is reminiscent of the events in the town of Mingshui just before the catastrophic flood in *Xingshi*.

The political analogue to this heavenly disturbance is the reincarnation of the Heart-Moon Fox (Xinyue hu 心月狐) as Empress Wu Zetian, an event that is described as disrupting the *yinyang* balance (*cuo luan yinyang* 錯亂陰陽; 3.1b). The name of the Heart-Moon Fox derives from a common rebus for the character *qing* 情 and evokes the violent sexuality frequently associated with Wu Zetian.[13] The Heart-Moon Fox chooses to descend to earth on the *Taiyin* 太陰 day, the coldest part of the winter, when *yin* is at its peak (3.1b). When Wu Zetian re-enacts Chang'e's transgression by creating an

12. It may be significant that Chang'e's deception is carried out with the help of heavy *yin* clouds, which cause the Fairy of the Hundred Flowers to be absent (2.2b).

13. The name of the character Little Moon King, Xiaoyue Wang 小月王, is used as a rebus for *qing* 情 in *Xiyou bu*.

artificial summer at the height of winter, the trees have interlocking branches, and the flowers bloom with double calyxes. As one of the witnesses interprets it, these "doubled signs are *yin* portents, and *yin* is the symbol of women" (5.2a.) In an earlier fictional treatment of this scene in the 1695 novel *Sui Tang yanyi* 隋唐演義 (The romance of the Sui and Tang), the blooming of the flowers occurs in autumn rather than the height of winter;[14] the change of season in *Jinghua yuan* suggests a conscious heightening of *yin* symbolism. A second innovation, the description of Wu Zetian as drunk when she orders the flowers to bloom (the word alcohol, *jiu*, is repeated seven times in the opening lines of chapter 4), subtly reinforces the notion of Wu Zetian's decadence. *Yin* iconography links the prologue to the abrupt introduction of Tang Ao in chapter 7, when he is described as coming from the watery-sounding "Plentiful Seas," Haifeng 海豐, prefecture and "River Source," Heyuan 河源, county.

Mirroring the *yin* symbols in the prologue are the *yang* terms in the six-chapter epilogue in which the male loyalist troops gather to overthrow Wu Zetian. The auspicious double-*yang* holiday (*chongyang jiqi* 重陽吉期) on the ninth day of the ninth month marks the beginning of the epilogue (94.2b).[15] As mentioned above, the loyalists begin their uprising on the double-three date. The rise of *yang* forces in this section is further suggested by the discussion by some of the Tang loyalists of a medicine that is able to cure a disease of the *jueyin* 厥陰 artery (95.2b); the artery can be glossed as a pun for *jueyin* 絕陰, "cutting off the yin." At the end of that same chapter, the unnecessary repetition of the word *taiyang* 太陽 (sun) in a pair of military poems mirrors the *taiyin* in Chapter 5.[16] The epilogue concludes with the restoration of the Tang court and the return of the flower-spirits to their proper domestic roles within China.

Yin themes also dominate chapters 33–37, the key *yin* chapters of the novel and probably the most extensively discussed episode in the work. Chapter 36, which is set in the Country of Women, exploits the symbolic connections among women, flooding, and transgressive behavior that are so important to the aesthetics of *Xingshi* and *Yesou puyan*. The most immediate

14. *Sui Tang yanyi*, 73.562.

15. For a discussion of the *yang* Double Nine Festival as parallel to the *yin* Double Three Festival, see Aijimer, "Chong-Yang and the Ceremonial Calendar," p. 180.

16. The mention of the foundational Qian and Kun hexagrams in the second poem also suggests a direct connection to the cosmic order.

literary source for this episode is the Land of Women at Xi Liang (Xi Liang nü guo) 西梁女國 episode in chapters 54 and 55 of the *Xiyou ji*. Again, the source materials are revised to heighten a sense that excessive *yin* is actively subverting the *yang* order. Whereas the Land of Women in *Xiyou ji* is inhabited only by women, the *Jinghua yuan* version inverts male and female gender roles so that the Country of Women functions as a microcosm of China under Wu Zetian's rule. In this country, not only are men under the political control of women, but they also are forced to bind their feet, are sequestered within the house, and spend their time doing needlework and raising children, while women enjoy the freedoms usually reserved for men. As in the Land of Women episode in *Xiyou ji*, improper sexual desires lead to political abuses. In *Jinghua yuan*, the licentious female "king" is smitten with Lin Zhiyang 林之洋, the most handsome of Tang Ao's fellow travelers. Reminiscent of Sujie's violent feminization of Xichen, palace retainers kidnap Lin, imprison him, bind his feet, and pierce his ears in preparation for making him the "queen." Parallel to this unbridled *yin* inside the palace walls, floodwaters threaten the inhabitants of the Country of Women. The king, however, is too preoccupied by her desire for Lin Zhiyang to care about the flood. Lin's fellow travelers right these imbalances when Tang Ao dredges the river using scrap metal from the ship's hold in return for Lin's release.

A number of changes in the *Xiyou ji* material foreground the *yinyang* symbolism in this episode. The chief minister of the government is surnamed Kun 坤, and the name of the "crown prince" is the feminine Yin Ruohua 陰若花 (Yin like a flower). Although H. C. Chang may be correct that the flood in chapter 36 reflects Li Ruzhen's interest in flood control, the placement of the flood, an emblematic expression of *yin* excess, precisely in this key *yin* chapter suggests that Li was working with a structural design.[17] The *yinyang* symbolism in the episode is further brought out in Tang Ao's success in dredging the river, which he accomplishes through his access to metal, a *yang* element so rare in the Country of Women that the law forbids the fashioning of it into tools (36.1a). The numerological punning in chapter 36

17. H. C. Chang (*Chinese Literature*, pp. 411–13) traces Li Ruzhen's interest in flood control to his appointment in 1801 as assistant magistrate in a county of Henan where the Yellow River had flooded, as well as to the treatise on water conservation written by his father, Li Jieting. Li's experiences in flood control are also discussed in Sun Jiaxun, *"Jinghua yuan" gong'an bianyi*, pp. 7–11.

is echoed in chapter 66 when characters from the Country of Women reappear quite abruptly and arbitrarily.

Although *yang* motifs are comparatively poorly developed in *Jinghua yuan*, they provide a thematic complement to the *yin* iconography. The most obvious is the association of the normative political order with male rule and the re-establishment of the Tang court in chapter 100. Moreover, chapters 9 and 27–30, chapters that are sites for *yang* themes in *Honglou meng* (the schoolroom scene and the period of intense summer heat), suggestively refer to medical lore, a theme that is explicitly linked to *yang* regulatory power in *Yesou puyan*. During the first stop on the travelers' voyage in chapter 9, Tang Ao takes his first steps toward enlightenment on an island that is covered with a variety of magical plants and animals. In a satire of the style of preparation required for the examination system in which scholars cram down as many texts as they can, Tang Ao ingests a grass that purges him of all the useless material he has memorized; after an impressive bout of flatulence, he realizes he can only recall one-tenth of the essays and poetry he had memorized (9.3b). Medical lore is again foregrounded in chapters 27–30, where the remedies and prescriptions offered by Tang Ao and the helmsman Duo Jiugong 多九公 (Master Plentiful Nines) are called ways "to save the world" (*jishi* 濟世; 27.4a, and chapter couplet to chapter 29). Significantly, a *yang* setting is established for this section when the travelers sail past a volcano (*huoshan* 火山; literally, "fire mountain") in chapter 27. The only other reference to medicine occurs in the epilogue when the loyalists discuss the *jueyin* artery.[18]

That Duo Jiugong, a former licentiate who abandoned his life as a scholar, has the greatest knowledge of medicine again suggests the *yang* associations of the theme. The gruff and practical Duo Jiugong is the most robust and self-reliant of the male characters in the novel; the presence in *Ernü yingxiong zhuan* of a similarly practical older man, Deng Jiugong 鄧九公, Deng Master Nine, who is equally impatient with the overrefinement of literati culture, makes it tempting to read them both as positive emblems of *yang* vigor.[19] In chapter 29, Duo uses boys' urine, a *yang* substance, in medicines to

18. Medical cures are discussed in 26.3b–4a, 27.1a, 27.3b–4a, 29.1b–3b, 30.1a–2a, and 95.1b–2b.

19. For a translation of a scene in which Duo Jiugong becomes impatient with the overly academic approach to philology of two girls from Black Teeth Country (Heichi guo 黑齒國), see Roddy, *Literati Identity*, p. 188.

cure the crown prince and his consorts in Forked Tongue Country (Qisheguo 岐舌國) in exchange for a phonetic table; worth noting in this episode is the implicit connection drawn between the overly developed intellectualism of the inhabitants of Forked Tongue Country and a threat to virility. The laws against letting outsiders learn their complex phonological system are so strict that offenders are punished with lifelong celibacy or castration (28.3b).

Admittedly, the accumulation of *yang* themes grouped around chapters 27–30, though suggestive, is inconclusive evidence of structural patterning. However, as we saw in *Yesou puyan*, the themes of restoring order by containing errant or excessive *yin* through the acts of regulating the government (*zhizheng* 治政) by combating traitors, regulating the family (*zhijia* 治家) by returning women to their homes, curing sickness (*zhibing* 治病), and regulating floodwaters (*zhishui* 治水) are central to *yang* iconography. The specific forms of statecraft that are foregrounded in both *Jinghua yuan* and *Yesou puyan* illustrate the extent to which pragmatic activism had become an ideal of the late imperial literati. Fictional texts depict only a small number of topics covered in actual treatises on statecraft; these handbooks covered a wide spectrum of issues, including problems with overpopulation, taxation methods, military defense, agriculture, and the financing and building of granaries. In contrast, *Jinghua yuan* and *Yesou puyan* foreground precisely those forms of statecraft that are most deeply rooted in *yinyang* symbolism, namely the defeat of traitors (who are defined in *yin* terms), flood control, medicine, and the ordering of the family as represented by the returning of displaced women to their proper kinship and inner domestic positions.[20]

In traditional fiction, the abduction or displacement of women from the home commonly signals the breakdown of the social and moral order.[21] The scattering of the 100 flower-spirits in *Jinghua yuan* reflects larger Qing debates about the status and education of women. Susan Mann has suggested that the widespread interest in controlling women's lives in the eighteenth century can be read as a metonym for regulating the social order. "By fixing the place of wives within the domestic sphere, they [the literati] sought to fix the fluidity of social change that threatened to erode the boundaries of their

20. This pattern is also true of *Lao Can youji*, in which the Confucian hero returns kidnapped girls to their families, amazes others with his medical expertise, and battles political and social corruption.

21. See McMahon, *Causality and Containment*, pp. 25–28.

own respectability."[22] This anxiety about the breakdown of the normative social order is clearly illustrated in the basic plot of *Jinghua yuan*.

Many parallels are drawn between Tang Ao and the paradigmatic figure of the activist sage-king Yu, who regulated the floodwaters.[23] The descriptions of all but two of the 31 countries Tang Ao visits are drawn from the *Shanhai jing*, traditionally thought to have been written by Yu and his assistant Yi 益 as they traveled over the earth to dredge the floodwaters.[24] When Tang Ao dredges the floodwaters of the Country of Women, he explicitly takes Yu as his model (35.4a); and when the inhabitants of that country witness Tang Ao's diligence in dredging the river basins, they erect a shrine to him (36.2b). Late imperial writers drew on the myth of Yu, the ideal Confucian sage activist, to depict flood control as an individual struggle against the forces of disorder, a battle that depended on moral purity and courage, rather than as the bureaucratic ability to organize large numbers of people and resources.

When Yu dredged the river basins, he simultaneously regulated the floodwaters and extended China's civilizing influence to the far reaches of the earth. Tang Ao's tour of the lands outside China, like Wen Suchen's travels in *Yesou puyan*, also mimics Yu in the way he extends the limits of the social and natural order and reaffirms China's position as the political center: in addition to regulating the flood, Tang Ao returns a number of girls who have been scattered overseas to their proper "inner" (*nei*) position in China. The first girl he encounters is the filial daughter of the poet Luo Binwang 駱賓王, who was executed for rebelling against Wu Zetian (chapter 10). The travelers come upon her while she is hunting tigers to avenge her mother's death. The next girl they rescue dives for pearls in order to support her widowed mother (chapter 13). After this they meet Tang Ao's teacher, who had fled China after submitting a memorial asking Empress Wu to uphold the way of women and return the throne to a man (15.2a), and the sons of the four most important of the Tang loyalists. Like floodwaters, which are out of place because of the blockage of proper channels, each of these filial and loyal characters has been displaced from her or his

22. Mann, "Grooming a Daughter for Marriage," p. 205.

23. For studies of Yu, see Maspero, "Legendes"; and Gu, *Gushi lunwenji*, 2: 143–52.

24. Li Ruzhen's two independent creations are Two-Faced Country and the Country of Excellent Wisdom (Zhijia guo 智佳國).

proper place in China.[25] The similarity between the Confucian activist ideals of flood control (*zhishui*), regulation of the family (*zhijia*), medicine (*zhibing*), and government (*zhizheng*) is that each is based on the ability to restore order to a skewed *yinyang* imbalance. It is likely for this symbolic reason that these forms of statecraft are foregrounded in Qing fiction.

Orthodox Discourse in Jinghua yuan: *The Gendering of Order*

In *Jinghua yuan*, the *yin* world of female rule is counterposed to the *yang* world of the Tang loyalists. The narrative progresses from the initial disruption of normative order with Wu Zetian's usurpation of the throne to an idealized period of *yin* ascendancy and finally to the reinstatement of a *yang*-identified meta-order. During the *yin* phase of the cycle, China's center is literally "scattered" to the margins. Only during the later *yang* phase are these elements "centered" in their rightful places: the 100 girls are initially contained within the garden and eventually settled in appropriate marriages to the Tang loyalists, and these same men are returned to power at the imperial center. It is this process of centering (*zhong* 中) that ritually defines the Chinese state.[26] No matter how idealized the gathering of the 100 flower-spirits might be, it still represents a rupture of the proper ritual and political order.

The main representatives of *yin* disorder in *Jinghua yuan* are the insubordinate Chang'e, Wu Zetian the fox-spirit, and the libidinous "king" of the Country of Women. These three *yinfu* form a figural chain: Chang'e initiates cosmic transgression at the birthday party of Xiwangmu, Wu Zetian subverts the proper political order, and the king abuses her power to pursue a sexual relationship with Lin Zhiyang rather than attend to her responsibilities as ruler. Although the transgressive aspects of Chang'e's and Wu Zetian's actions are not as well developed as those of the king, the three can be read together as a composite character, motivated by uncontrolled arrogance, desire for power, and lust, who appears at specific structural moments to subvert the normative order. Since the degree of transgression depicted in *Jinghua yuan* is understated compared with that found in other Qing novels, readers might gloss over the significance of the *yinfu*; however, many of the

25. For an extended analysis of images of stagnation and blockage as metaphors for frustration with the breakdown of the imperial bureaucracy, see Roddy, *Literati Identity*, pp. 176–79.

26. I am borrowing Zito's ("Silk and Skin," p. 105) definition of the verb *zhong* "to center," a ritualized process of self-creation through "the correct separation of upper and lower, the correct bounding of inner and outer."

understated details of their characterization take on more serious implications when read against the intertextual stereotype of the shrew.

One of the surprising features of *Jinghua yuan* is the muted depiction of Wu Zetian, which differs from the cruel and pornographic image of her prevalent in other works of fiction.[27] No acts of murder or sexually explicit details color her rule in court; in fact, the closest *Jinghua yuan* comes to showing Wu Zetian's moral decadence is the description of her drunken state when she arrogantly orders all the flowers to bloom in the dead of winter and the mention of two of her ministers, Zhang Yizhi 張易之 and Zhang Changzong 張昌宗, who are made infamous in other sources as her lovers (100.2b). The thoroughly Confucian twelve-point decree she promulgates in chapter 40, instituting honors and protections for virtuous wives and daughters, even lends her a positive image.[28] Although Wu Zetian is not vilified in *Jinghua yuan*, it could be assumed that readers' perceptions of her would be informed by her popular image as a symbol of political and sexual transgression.[29] The popular association between Wu Zetian and illicit sexuality is so immediate that her mirror is one of the first erotic objects mentioned in Qin Keqing's boudoir (*HLM*, 5.47).

One of the most notorious depictions of Wu Zetian may be the pornographic sixteenth-century *Ruyi jun zhuan*.[30] This pseudo-biography in an an-

27. Wu Zetian was a favorite symbol of both sexual and political transgression. She appears in *Ruyi jun zhuan*, *Sengni niehai* 僧尼孽海 (Monks and nuns in a sea of sins), *Sui Tang yanyi*, and *Chanzhen houshi*, as well as the late eighteenth-century *Xue Gang fan Tang* 薛剛反唐 (Xue Gang revolts against the Tang), *Wu Zetian sida qi'an* 武則天四大奇案 (The four strange cases of Wu Zetian), and *Lü mudan* 綠牡丹 (The green peony).

28. These decrees reward the chaste and filial as well as women who are kind to their sisters-in-law; they institute that those girls who serve in the court shall be married by age 20; they provide dowries, medical care, and old-age support for poor women and stipends for widows to help them maintain their chastity; and they provide burial assistance so that the corpses of poor women shall not be exposed to public view.

29. The lack of sexually explicit material in *Jinghua yuan* may be a result of its genealogical links to the sentimental scholar-beauty genre; the novel may also have been conceived of, and marketed as, suitable for women of good families, as suggested by the fact that it begins with a short exposition on Ban Zhao's *Instructions for Women* and that at least one fine edition, the *Huitu Jinghua yuan*, contained prefatory lyric *ci* 詞 by female readers.

30. Although the earliest extant edition of this rare text is dated 1763, it was in circulation by at least 1540 when it received its first bibliographic notice in Huang Xun's 黃訓 (1491–1540) *Dushu yide* 讀書一得 (published 1562). My pagination refers to a reprint of the edition stored in the Tokyo Tōyō bunka kenkyūjo, with a preface by Huayang sanren 華陽散人,

nals format covers the period from her entrance into Tang Taizong's 唐太宗 (r. 626–49) harem at fourteen *sui* and her incestuous investiture as empress by his son, Tang Gaozong 唐高宗 (r. 649–83), to her founding of the Zhou dynasty. The bulk of the text narrates her erotic liaisons with various of her high ministers, several of whom appear by name in *Jinghua yuan*. The title of the biography is based on the apocryphal story that she named the four-month reign period Ruyi (the fifth to the eighth month of 692) after her well-endowed lover, Xue Aocao 薛敖曹, the eponymous "Lord as You Like It" (p. 21). Although the fictional Wu Zetian outlives two emperors, she remains girlishly young by means of the *yang* energy she absorbs from her many male lovers. Woven through the descriptions of her sexual conquests in *Ruyi jun zhuan* is the political narrative of her usurpation of the throne and her banishment of the heir apparent.

Wu Zetian also appears in the many historical novels recounting the history of the Tang dynasty, the best-known of which is the *Sui Tang yanyi*.[31] In contrast to *Ruyi jun zhuan*, these novels foreground Wu Zetian's political rise to power. Although some of the events in *Jinghua yuan*, such as the blooming of the flowers and the unsuccessful uprising of Li Jingye 李敬業[32] and Luo Binwang in 684, are most likely drawn from this earlier material, Li Ruzhen glossed over Wu Zetian's reputation for ruthless killing by leaving out the scenes that implicate her in the murder of Empress Xiao 蕭 or the murder of her own daughter in order to blame it on her rival Empress Wang 王.[33] Although Wu Zetian does not murder in cold blood in *Jinghua yuan*, the deadly passes that trap a number of the Tang loyalists, the kidnapping of Lin Zhiyang by the king of the Country of Women, and the usurpation of power by Chang'e and Wu Zetian are suggestive of the political ruthlessness and sexual vampirism that define her in the broader cultural imagination. Her reputation for obscene transgression is no doubt why no real justification is given for the loyalist uprising against her in *Jinghua yuan*; despite the positive accomplishments attributed to Wu Zetian's reign in the novel,

---

dated Jiaxu 甲戌, tentatively identified as either 1634 or 1754; see Ōta and Iida, *Chūgoku hiseki sōkan*, p. 14.

31. For the sources of this hundred-chapter novel, see Hegel, "*Sui T'ang yen-i*," pp. 126–31.

32. Both *Sui Tang yanyi* and *Jinghua yuan* mistakenly refer to the historical figure Li Jingye as Xu 徐Jingye.

33. Both events are recorded in *Sui Tang yanyi*, 70.542 and 71.551.

readers would still understand and assume the moral obligation to remove her from office.

Counterposed to the transgressive *yin* usurpers are the male Tang loyalists, who are metonymically associated with the *yang* meta-order. The men in the novel, however, are largely flawed or ineffectual. Although Tang Ao's fortunes are intertwined with the fate of the exiled Tang court, he is curiously uninterested in the political ideals of loyalty or service. Even after the Tang loyalists return to power, he does not seek a life of meaningful political or social engagement. His brother-in-law, the calculating and somewhat lustful Lin Zhiyang, presents a model of moral deficiency that foreshadows the inability of the Tang loyalists to control their desires and ambitions in the epilogue.

In a relatively playful reworking of the narrative of desire so central to *Xingshi yinyuan zhuan*, Lin Zhiyang's victimization at the hands of the "king" of the Country of Women is initiated by his own lack of self-mastery. Lin's inclination toward desire is first suggested by his fair complexion and delicate beauty.[34] As Lin admits, his initial willingness to be left behind in the Country of Women sets in motion his misfortunes in this episode (36.2b). When Lin first enters the palace to sell cosmetics, he breaks one of the cardinal rules of gender segregation, a fundamental tenet of Confucian sexual protocol, by approaching the female "king." Rather than see her in her roles of ruler (as Tang Ao does) or potential consumer of his cosmetics, his supposed purpose in entering the palace, Lin notices only her beauty (*se* 色). As he sees it, "although the king is over thirty years old, her fair complexion and red lips give her a most beautiful appearance" (33.1a). The narrative order of the scene, in which the description of Lin Zhiyang's lustful gaze precedes the king's desire for him, strongly suggests that it is Lin's desire that sets in motion his eventual fall.

Nor is this the first time Lin's desires have been shown to be easily aroused, with potentially deadly consequences. After leaving Black Teeth Country (Heichi guo 黑齒國), where the three travelers had been humiliated (Tang Ao and Duo Jiugong because the girls there knew more about philology than they, and Lin Zhiyang because the dark-complected people cared more for scholarship than his cosmetics), they pass through a mulberry wood, where they see some beautiful women wrapped in red silk.

34. It is tempting to read the characters Zhiyang 之洋 in Lin Zhiyang's name as an intentional pun on "approaching Yang" 至陽.

Some of the women are eating mulberry leaves, others are spinning silk from the threads they spit from their mouths. Lin's reaction is that he would like to take several of the beautiful women home as concubines since, as he explains, they can weave silk and have sons. Duo Jiugong creates a perfect metaphor for the dangers of female sexuality when he explains to Lin how these women bind their male victims in silk cocoons and then kill them (20.1a).

Although Lin Zhiyang escapes these women without incident, he eventually meets a similar fate when he is captured, stripped, and bound by the retainers of the king of the Country of Women. "Without discussion, they all grabbed hold of Lin Zhiyang's clothing and stripped him bare. As these ladies-in-waiting had boundless strength, it was just like a hawk nabbing a finch, how could he be master of the situation?" 不由分說七手八腳，把林之洋內外衣服脫得乾乾淨淨。這些宮娥力大無窮，就如鷹拿燕雀一般，那裏又他作主? (33.1a). The ladies-in-waiting then bind Lin Zhiyang's feet and pierce his ears. By the end of this episode, in an epiphany worthy of *Xingshi*, Lin learns to master his easily aroused desires and recognizes the dangers of the king's beauty. On their wedding night, Lin "saw that although the king was young and attractive, he felt that a lethal energy emanated from her beautiful face. Although he had not seen her kill anyone, her type of gentle demeanor actually seemed to be more fierce than a knife" 看那國王，雖是少年美貌，只覺從那美貌之中透出一般殺氣。雖不見他殺人，那種溫柔體態倒像比刀還覺利害 (36.2b–3a). After this enlightenment, Lin Zhiyang is rescued and assumes a more appropriate and active male role when he leads the rescue of the crown prince in chapter 37.

Lin Zhiyang's imprisonment in the Country of Women prefigures the entrapment of the Tang loyalists in the four allegorical mazes of the epilogue. The names of the "self-exterminating" formations are rebuses for the four traditional vices of alcohol 酉水 (*youshui*), anger 无火 (*wuhuo*), sex 巴刀 (*badao*), and wealth 才貝 (*caibei*). The troops who enter each trap are immediately caught up in illusory microcosms, and several perish. One loyalist, Zhang Hong 章葒, volunteers to enter the wealth formation and is immediately so dazzled by the huge coin blocking the road that he ignores the crowds of people gambling, fighting, and stealing at its base and climbs up a ladder to pass through the hole in the middle of the coin. There he enters a world of opulence in which he only needs to think of a luxury for it to appear. He quickly forgets his military mission and passes 60 years immersed in pleasure. Not until his eightieth-birthday celebration does Zhang realize that he has been deluded. When he attempts to escape, he gets stuck in the eye of the cash through which he first entered and dies (99.1a–4a). The allegorical passes serve as a moral litmus test for the loyalists, who are able to re-establish the Tang dynasty only after they have passed through them. The men repeatedly show themselves to be dependent on the 100 women, who are by now established as their sisters and wives, to survive these deadly tests. The women obtain protective talismans and foods that allow the male troops to pass through the passes unharmed; the women also establish a separate women's military encampment from which they lead successful attacks against Wu Zetian's black magic. Despite the help from the women, the men's moral frailty almost undermines their joint efforts. One example is that the amulets against drunkenness prove to be useless until the men realize they must refrain from drinking for 24 hours prior to entering the maze (chapter 97).

The metanarrative about the loss and reinstatement of order in *Jinghua yuan* makes use of a *yinyang* symbolic vocabulary that includes gendered oppositions and numerological punning on the *yin* number six. Even though this highly conventional metanarrative is overshadowed by more unusual narrative materials for which the novel is justly famed, it nonetheless provides the structural frame around which the narrative is organized. As discussed below, this structure, which treats *yin* dominance as a rupture of normative order, suggests Li Ruzhen was working with multiple constructions of the feminine.

Aesthetics and Ambivalence

One cannot read *Jinghua yuan* without being struck by the contrast between the ambiguous position of the male characters in relation to the centers of power and knowledge and the certainty and ease with which the female flower-spirits step into these traditionally male preserves. On one level, the oppositional complementarity between the loyalists and the flower-spirits reflects the novel's use of gender as part of its formal patterning. However, the stark contrast between the men's cynicism toward their own participation in the examination system and the women's unabashed enthusiasm for it suggests an unresolved ambivalence toward everything that the examination system represents. The flower-spirits' uniform success—all 100 pass—resurrects the ideal of the Confucian bureaucracy as a system that recognizes and rewards merit; this is a possibility all the male characters reject. It is as if Li Ruzhen's nostalgia for the ideal can be maintained only when it is refracted through a gendered lens that somehow prettifies and sentimentalizes the process.

As is broadly reflected in Qing fiction, many literati were capable of taking a cynical view of the arduous examination preparation not as a meaningful form of intellectual and moral discipline but as an instrumental step toward pursuing a bureaucratic career that was itself suspect.[35] The intellectual integrity of philology, which earlier presented an alternative to the institutionalization of Confucian knowledge, was undermined by the late eighteenth century when it, too, was incorporated into the examination curriculum.[36] *Jinghua yuan* betrays an anxiety that the pursuit not only of a bureaucratic career but also of knowledge, and philology in particular through its connections to the examination system and networks of patronage, had become so inextricably intertwined with ambition that scholarship was becoming ethically tainted.[37] By having young women, who culturally were kept pure of taint from ambitions for power or success, perform the role of scholar, the novel makes possible the illusion that throwing oneself into these prescripted career paths could be a meaningful form of self-expression rather than a self-serving pursuit of ambition. Reassuringly, none of the girls is asked to compromise her moral or intellectual beliefs, and none is demoted, exiled, or executed. This fantasy of the 100 flower-spirits who unproblematically achieve the intellectual and career ambitions of any late imperial scholar is clearly dependent on the association of the feminine with the authentic. Like Tang Xianzu and Cao Xueqin, Li Ruzhen presents the feminized space of the garden as a site of cultural redemption. Unlike the male characters in *Mudan ting* and *Honglou meng*, however, those in *Jinghua yuan* are excluded from this ideal space. Perhaps the possibility of literati returning to a society in which their hard-earned knowledge and skills could bring them recognition without moral compromise is a fantasy as unachievable as capturing the reflection of "the moon in water," or "flowers in a mirror."

The wit of the intellectual play in the second half of the novel masks a

35. See Ropp, *Dissent*, pp. 91–101.

36. Elman, "Changes," pp. 135–40, 142.

37. See Stephen Roddy's (*Literati Identity*, pp. 197–99) argument that the loyalists' search for philological knowledge ("knowledge of name") "is overpowered by, and subsumed under, the desire for fame" (*ming*).

change in the value placed on learning and study. As Stephen Roddy has so insightfully pointed out, the traditional hierarchy of knowledge, based on the premise that certain forms of learning have an ethical function, has been erased, and this erasure leads to the trivialization of knowledge in *Jinghua yuan*. He comments that orthodox learning in the novel "is embedded within the context of games that make no distinction between classical erudition and trivia, scatological jokes, puns, riddles and other amusements."[38] Within the discourse of authenticity, as we have seen in *Mudan ting* and *Honglou meng*, lyric self-expressive language is presented as the ethical equivalent of orthodox learning; in *Jinghua yuan*, as Roddy suggests, form displaces ethical content.[39] The girls' equalizing of all branches of knowledge, here in the format of a vast game of wit, is analogous to the cultural decentering of China in the first half of the novel. The voyagers are repeatedly confounded by the societies that challenge their conventional expectations. The dark-skinned girls of Black Teeth Country are morally and intellectually superior to the beautifully dressed but illiterate and arrogant people of White People Country (Baimin guo 白民國; chapters 21–22), and the self-righteous hypocrisy of the rigidly Confucian inhabitants of the Country of Noble Gentlemen (Shushi guo 淑士國; chapters 22–24) is outdone only by the people of Two-Faced Country (chapter 25).

Within this tapestry of cultural relativism, China itself appears as just another variation on a theme, rather than the moral, intellectual, and political center it is in other travel narratives such as *Xiyou ji* or *Yesou puyan*. This collapse of a strongly defined ethical vision in favor of aesthetic patterning perhaps further explains why the moral aspect of the loyalists' struggle to oust the usurper Wu Zetian is so muted in comparison to other novels from the period. If Stephen Roddy is correct that Li Ruzhen modeled *Jinghua yuan* after *Lü mudan* 綠牡丹 (The green peony; earliest extant edition dated 1800), a novel in which the opposition to Wu Zetian is central to the plot and in which an army of young women joins the male loyalists, then the minimizing of the theme of political loyalism in *Jinghua yuan* is a significant aesthetic choice.[40]

38. Ibid., p. 174.

39. Ibid., p. 204.

40. For the possible influence of *Lü mudan* on *Jinghua yuan*, see ibid., p. 282n6. *Wu Zetian sida qi'an* is another late eighteenth-century novel in which the overthrow of Empress Wu is a major narrative theme; see Idema, "The Mystery."

The unmooring of learning from its foundation in ethics may also provide an explanation for the troubled relationship between literati culture (*wen*) and the male protagonists.[41] The satirical image of the flatulent Tang Ao purging himself of useless scholarly clutter illustrates just how trivial the examination curriculum could be made to appear. All that remains after the laxative is Tang Ao's practical knowledge of medicine, flood control, and philology. Despite Li Ruzhen's own interest in phonetics and philology, his fictional treatment of them is ambivalent. Tang Ao's training in philology is shown to be deficient under the questioning of the girls in Black Teeth Country, and Duo Jiugong is impatient with it as a purely intellectual exercise. For Duo, philology is of interest only as a practical tool that can enhance the ability to communicate with other peoples. The odd punishment of castration in Forked Tongue Country for the repeated offense of disseminating the phonological table hints at a danger of emasculation associated with overly developed intellectualism. As we shall see, the notion that an overly refined culture is detrimental to orthodox masculinity is repeated more forcefully in *Ernü yingxiong zhuan*. Moreover, the most self-possessed and effective of the male characters, Duo Jiugong, has gone the furthest in rejecting institutionalized knowledge in favor of more practical but less refined skills; this points to the limitations of the intellectually dazzling, but morally empty, world of the garden. The extended display of literati culture, especially the linguistic games, is attractive when staged by 100 beautiful girls in an apolitical utopia but smacks of aestheticized decadence when read against the Confucian imperative to "regulate names" (*zhengming*) and use language as an ethical standard.

Even though the values projected onto the feminine in *Jinghua yuan* are highly ambiguous, there is no question that an influential number of nineteenth- and twentieth-century readers have focused on the novel's positive and empowering depictions of women as a form of resistance to traditional Chinese prohibitions against women entering male spheres. The appeal of these feminist readings, however, must not be allowed to influence the debate about Li Ruzhen's feminist intent. In composition at least, this 100-chapter novel is less about the lives of, or possibilities for, actual women and girls than a highly patterned fantasy in which the gender complementarity builds on the contradictory meanings associated with the symbolic feminine. Balancing the admiring depictions of beautiful and talented flower-spirits in

41. For a lengthy discussion of this, see Roddy, *Literati Identity*, pp. 184–85.

the novel is an anxiety about the dissolution of the systems of power and knowledge from which the literati drew their identity. Given the novel's ambivalence about Wu Zetian's usurpation of the throne and the achievements of the male protagonists, it is difficult not to question the status of *Jinghua yuan* as a "manifesto" for women's empowerment.

ERNÜ YINGXIONG ZHUAN: PLAYING WITH GENDER/GENRE

The witty use of gender inversions in the otherwise conventional *Ernü yingxiong zhuan* 兒女英雄傳 (A tale of heroic lovers; hereafter *Ernü*), makes this little-studied late Qing romance a fitting complement to the preceding analyses of gender in *Honglou meng, Yesou puyan,* and *Jinghua yuan.*[42] *Ernü,* which fantasizes a masculinist solution to the breakdown of elite society, promotes Confucian domestic values even while it reverses the gender roles of the scholar and the beauty. The first half of the 40-chapter novel casts the beauty, He Yufeng 何玉鳳, in the role of a knight-errant; in contrast, the scholar, An Ji 安驥, the only son of a Manchu bannerman, is repeatedly described in feminizing terms. This first half, which is based on the masculinizing norms of the military romance, presents Yufeng as Thirteenth Sister, Shisan Mei 十三妹. She is an educated young woman who lives in the murky world of outlaws in order to avenge her father. He was a high official from the Solid Yellow Banner who had died while being held on trumped-up charges after refusing to betroth his daughter to the unworthy son of his superior. Despite her delicate beauty, Thirteenth Sister is so strong and so

42. The novel is frequently translated into English as *The Gallant Maid,* based on a 1906 Shanghai lithograph edition entitled *Xianü qiyuan* 俠女奇緣 (a 1980 two-volume edition published by the Guangxi renmin chubanshe also appeared under this title).

I consulted the Huandu woshu shi laoren 還讀我書室老人 "The Old Man of Rereading My Books Studio" commentary edition at the Academia Sinica in Taipei. As listed on the title page, this edition is called the *Huitu pingdian Ernü yingxiong zhuan* 繪圖評點兒女英雄傳; it has 40 chapters (*hui*) and one introductory chapter, divided into 6 *zhuan,* and was published by the Feiying guan 蜚英館 printers in Shanghai in 1888. "Huandu woshu laoren" was a pseudonym used by Dong Xun 董恂 (1807–92), a high official who rose to the position of president of the Board of Revenue and who was officially recognized for his services in foreign affairs (see *ECCP,* pp. 789–91). This edition has been reprinted as the *Huandu woshu shi zhuren ping Ernü yingxiong zhuan* (Ji'nan: Qi Lu shushe, 1989). All references are to this edition. I also examined the much more poorly printed 1879 Shenbao guan *Ernü yingxiong zhuan* 兒女英雄傳 edition housed at Taiwan Normal University.

skilled in the martial arts that the other outlaws, all male, respect and fear her. Early in the novel, she plans to rob the timid An Ji, who is transporting a large load of silver to ransom his own father, but after learning of his filial motivations, she becomes his protector. The novel concludes as a conventional scholar-beauty romance: An Ji celebrates a double marriage to He Yufeng (Jade Phoenix) and the identically beautiful Zhang Jinfeng 張金鳳 (Golden Phoenix), passes the highest-level examination, and is given an official position, and the two women give birth to sons. Thirteenth Sister so overshadows An Ji as the source of narrative interest that most popular dramatic versions of the story focus on her character as a righteous outlaw and either leave out or rewrite the events after the marriage.[43] This composite of the female protagonist as both virtuous outlaw and chaste beauty marks a new height in the literary trend of constructing girls as the bearers and preservers of Confucian culture, even as they defy the conventional ritual behaviors that defined women's proper social roles, and of depicting the male protagonists as either somehow lacking or disenfranchised.

The basic plot of *Ernü* seems to borrow from the widely circulated seventeenth-century moralistic scholar-beauty romance *Haoqiu zhuan*, in which both the scholar and the beauty are dedicated to righting the corrupt imperial bureaucracy in order to avenge their fathers. In *Haoqiu zhuan*, the beauty, Shui Bingxin, is unrelentingly stern in her commitment to Confucian morality (see especially chapters 8 and 16). The scholar Tie Zhongyu 鐵中玉, who is unusually strong and daring compared with other characters of his type, rescues her from her boorish uncle, who is plotting to marry her against her will to the dissolute son of a powerful official. Before going to take the examination, Tie Zhongyu stays under the same roof as Shui Bingxin, and the uncle spreads rumors that call into question her chastity. After Tie Zhongyu passes the metropolitan examination in first place, he and Bingxin marry, but she refuses to consummate their relationship be-

43. Of the sixteen dramatic spinoffs listed in the *Jingju jumu cidian* 京劇劇目詞典, only three center on events after their marriage. One of these changes the plot so that Thirteenth Sister leads a campaign to avenge her father's death after she has married. Zhang Henshui 張恨水 used Thirteenth Sister as a prototype for a proletariat woman knight-errant in his 1930 novel *Tixiao yinyuan* 啼笑姻緣 (see Borthwick, "*Fate in Tears and Laughter*," pp. 257, 258, 260). The title was also borrowed for a revolutionary play *Xin Ernü yingxiong zhuan* written in 1949 by Kong Jue and Yuan Jing (see Hegel, "Making the Past Serve the Present," pp. 210–14). An opera entitled *Shisan Mei* continues to be performed and has been produced for television in Taiwan.

cause of the rumors. The eighteen-chapter romance concludes with the emperor ordering the empress to oversee a physical examination that proves Bingxin's virginity. The emperor then punishes the guilty and rewards the loyal, and Zhongyu and Bingxin finally consummate their marriage.

In *Ernü*, even though the female protagonist continues to be the voice of conventional Confucian values, particularly concerning the necessity of examination preparation and government service, it is the scholar who needs to be rescued. The scene in which a group of bandit monks abduct An Ji, tie him up, and expose his "white, tender breast" (*bai nennende xiongbu* 白嫩嫩的胸脯) in preparation for disemboweling him (5.102) recalls the figurally linked scenes of the binding, stripping, and eviscerating of Yan Poxi 閻婆惜, Pan Jinlian, and Pan Qiaoyun 潘巧雲 in *Shuihu zhuan*.[44] In *Ernü*, Thirteenth Sister miraculously appears out of nowhere to save the innocent and terrified victim.

The scant information we have about the author, Wen Kang 文康, is of little help in contextualizing the gender inversions in the novel. Wen Kang's seeming confidence in Confucian sociopolitical values as a means to right political injustices is more than slightly perplexing, given the turbulent times through which he lived. According to the Ma Congshan 馬從善 preface, dated 1879, Wen Kang was active during the Daoguang reign period (1821–50).[45] Wen Kang was from a prominent Manchu family that belonged to the Bordered Red Banner. Among its most famous members was Wen Fu 溫福 (1717–97), a general and grand secretary honored by the Qianlong emperor,[46] and Lebao 勒保 (1740–1819), Wen Kang's grandfather, who had also served as a general and grand secretary.[47] A second cousin of Wen Kang's generation, Wen Qing 溫慶 (1796–1856, *jinshi* 1822), administered three sets of provincial examinations and eventually rose to the position of grand secretary. Although the clan managed to continue producing prominent statesmen such as Wen Qing into the nineteenth century, not all branches were uniformly successful. Wen Kang himself never seems to have had any success in the official examinations; he served in the capital as official compiler and editor in 1824–25 and in 1842 was sent to Tianjin as intendant for two

44. *SHZ*, 21.395, 25.504, 45.860–861.

45. For a partial translation of the Ma Congshan preface, see Lu Xun, *A Brief History*, p. 355.

46. See entry under A-kuei in *ECCP*, pp. 6–8.

47. See ibid., pp. 444–46.

years. He served as second-class sub-prefect in Anhui in 1851–54. He likely began to compose the novel after this period. According to the Ma Congshan preface, Wen Kang was appointed imperial agent to Lhasa, but illness prevented him from going. This last detail is not confirmed in any gazetteers or official documents, but Ma Congshan provided it as evidence to argue that the novel was partially autobiographical.[48]

The earliest extant edition of *Ernü* is the 1879 Shenbao guan edition. Based on internal evidence and the little that is known about Wen Kang's life, scholars agree that the novel was composed between 1851 and 1879.[49] This would place the composition of the novel after China's humiliating defeat in the Opium War (1839–42) and either during or after the devastations of the Taiping Rebellion (1850–64).[50] This was a dark period of Chinese history when those who dared look beneath the façade of continued imperial glory could not help but be struck by the realities of China's military weakness and bureaucratic corruption. Wen Kang's clan and bureaucratic connections would have made it impossible for him to be oblivious to the signs of political decay around him. Yet little of this disturbing reality is reflected in this novel set during the Qing dynasty; it seems that Wen Kang's primary interest was in reworking and parodying fictional conventions rather than reflecting the political or social environment of the mid-nineteenth century.[51] Wen Kang's gesture of loyalty to "our great Qing Dynasty" (*wo da*

48. Near the end of the novel, An Ji is horrified when he hears that he has been appointed as a consultant (*canzan* 參贊) to Wuliyasitai, Mongolia (40.985–86). Much to his and his family's relief, the order is rescinded, and the novel ends happily with An Ji receiving a much more comfortable posting in Shandong.

49. Internal evidence discussed in more detail below, based on a reference to the novel *Pinhua baojian* 品花寶鑑 written during the Xianfeng period (1851–62), sets the earliest possible date as 1851; see Hu Shi, "*Ernü yingxiong zhuan* xu," p. 497. Peng Caizhu ("Wen Kang yu *Ernü*," pp. 53–56) suggests that Wen Kang could not have written the novel until after he left office in 1853.

50. The sole reference to Europeans that I noted is in An Shuixin's dismissal of an admiring comment about the accuracy of Western astronomical predictions; he says that the Chinese of ancient times were just as skilled (34.799).

51. Despite his prominent political position and diplomatic connections with foreign missions, the commentator Dong Xun, too, was primarily interested in the novel for its literary qualities rather than its content; his commentary makes frequent references to literary techniques and intertextual allusions. It uses such critical terms as: the historian's technique (*shifa* 史法; 8.158), "the marvelous technique of white clouds dotted [across the sky]" (*bai yundian zhi miao* 白雲點之妙; 19.384); "the style of writing like passing cloud, flowing water, and falling rain that leave the sky empty" (*biyi yiru xingyun liushui, yuguo tiankong* 筆意亦如行雲流水，

Qing 我大清) appears when the narrator ironically compares Qing bandits, whom he claims steal only out of desperation, taking money not lives and never harming women or girls, to the outlaws in *Sanguo* and *Shuihu* (21.428). In chapter 21, the community of bandits is so touched by Thirteenth Sister's filial example that they decide to stop stealing in order to support their mothers more honorably.

Although scholars of the novel have tried to fit *Ernü* into the mold of autobiographical fiction written by a frustrated scholar to compensate for his own lack of success, they have gleaned little meaningful information from this approach.[52] At least one character in the novel seems to be based on a historical figure: Ji Xiantang 紀獻唐, the abusive official in the novel responsible for the death of Thirteenth Sister's father, has been identified as Nian Gengyao 年羹堯.[53] Hu Shi claimed to have evidence that the characterization of An Ji's concubine Changjie'er 長姐兒 was based on a real person, but since she is a minor and unexceptional figure, this piece of information adds little to our understanding of the text.[54]

One autobiographically linked question that must be asked concerns the degree of Wen Kang's self-identification as Manchu and of his sinicization and how these influenced his attitudes toward women and gender roles in the creation of Thirteenth Sister.[55] The Manchu banner status of the An family is treated as a matter of fact in the novel; on several occasions, An Ji and his father, An Shuixin 安水心, are the only ones able to understand the

---

雨過天空; 31.687); and adumbration, "painting in the background with ornamental detail [to give shape to the real subject]" (*hongtuo xuanran* 烘托絢 [sic] 染; 33.740). The commentary also refers explicitly to Cao Xueqin and Shi Nai'an (6.106, 31.691). The heavy-drinking gallant Deng Jiugong 鄧九公, Deng Master Nine, is described as having the highest level of character (*shangshang renwu* 上上人物; 15.281) in the manner of Jin Shengtan's ranking of the Liangshan heroes.

52. See the entry under Wen Qing in *ECCP*, pp. 852–53. Very little else is known about Wen Kang's life and background. Hu Shi and Lu Xun both argued that the novel is somewhat autobiographical. Hu Shi ("*Ernü yingxiong zhuan* xu," p. 498) suggested that An Ji's career could be a composite of positions held by various family members. Lu Xun (*A Brief History*, p. 369) described the scholar An Ji as an idealized rendering of the author or one of his sons. The Ma Congshan preface also treats the fiction as autobiographical.

53. See Miao Tianhua, "*Ernü yingxiong zhuan* kaozheng," p. 2. Nian was a governor of Sichuan and Shanxi who abused his power and was ordered by imperial command to commit suicide in 1725.

54. Hu Shi, "*Ernü yingxiong zhuan* xu," p. 498.

55. Zhou Zuoren ("*Ernü yingxiong zhuan*," in *Zhou Zuoren wenxuan*, pp. 478–80) suggests that Wen Kang's Manchu identity was an important factor in his creation of Thirteenth Sister.

Manchu spoken by court officials.[56] Historically, the Manchus, like other inhabitants of the nomadic steppes, were more tolerant of physically robust women than the Han Chinese. For the most part, garrisoned Manchus did not bind women's feet, although they did replace the traditional practice of levirate marriages with the Confucian ideal of widow chastity.[57] Although the women around Wen Kang were likely to have been fully sinicized, it is not unlikely that images of horse-riding women from the steppes formed some part of his consciousness of, and perhaps pride in, his Manchu identity.[58] However, the repeated bans against the binding of Manchu women's feet suggest that at least some Manchus were adopting the practice. In *Ernü*, although Lady An has natural feet, she reassures An Ji's second wife, Jinfeng, that she does not need to unwrap her feet, much to the relief of Jinfeng and An Ji, since, as the mother explains, many women in the family have adopted the Han style of binding (12.224). All the young women in the novel seem to have bound feet; Thirteenth Sister's "two- to three-inch golden lotuses" probably reflect the general cultural fantasy of female beauty and may not be indicative of a specific ethnic identity.[59]

It is entirely conceivable that the characterization of Thirteenth Sister evolved directly from the long tradition of female knights in Chinese fiction without specific Manchu influence.[60] Since the Tang dynasty, female knights and warriors had made frequent cameo appearances in fiction and drama;[61] the 100-chapter Qing novel *Nüxian waishi* was among the earliest

56. The use of Manchu is mentioned on 40.1010, 1021, and 1039. For this last entry, the 1888 Feiying guan edition staggers the placement of the characters in the transliteration of the Manchu and provides the Chinese translations as an interlineal gloss beside it.

57. Crossley, *Orphan Warriors*, pp. 80–81.

58. For example, there are accounts of Manchu women and girls who helped defend Hangzhou against the Taiping rebels; see ibid., p. 129.

59. Thirteenth Sister's feet were bound at age seven (14.253).

60. On literary treatments of female knights-errant, see F. P. Chen, "Female Warriors"; and Edwards, "Woman Warriors." A tradition of female military leaders also existed during the Ming: see the biographies of Tang Sai'er 唐賽兒 (fl. 1420) in *DMB*, pp. 1251–52, and Qin Liangyu 秦良玉 (d. 1648) and Shen Yunying 沈雲英 (1624–61) in *ECCP*, pp. 168–69. My thanks to Ellen Widmer for this point. The military exploits of Tang Sai'er were immortalized in *Nüxian waishi*.

61. Some examples from the Tang are "Shanghai zhuan" 上海傳, "Xie Xiao'e zhuan" 謝小娥傳, "Nieyin niang" 聶隱娘, "Hongxian zhuan" 紅線傳, "Chezhong nüzi" 車中女子, "Pan Jiangjun" 潘將軍, and "Jiaren qi" 賈人妻. Song examples include "Zhang xun qi" 張訓妻, "Xia furen" 俠婦人, "Jing Shisan niang" 京十三娘, and "Cuo zhan Cui Ning" 錯斬崔寧. Ming examples are "Xianü sancai xunjie" 俠女散財殉節, "Houguan xian lienü jianchou"

full-length *xiaoshuo* to focus on a female warrior.[62] Curiously, many of the more unconventional courtesans of the late Ming were labeled *nüxia*, female knights-errant, in recognition of their independent spirits. The heroism of these historical women, however, seems to have been related more to their ability to take charge of their own lives and sexual relations than to physically daring exploits.[63] The abundant pre-Qing literary sources for the characterization of Thirteenth Sister make it unnecessary to find precise Manchu roots for her. As we shall see, Wen Kang manipulated literary conventions in every aspect of the composition of the novel; the fluid gendering of Thirteenth Sister is but one of the narrative elements he exploited for aesthetic and entertainment value.

Ernü as Literary Parody

Until recently, *Ernü* has received little critical attention in Western-language scholarship.[64] Lu Xun and Hu Shi pioneered investigation into the textual history of *Ernü*, and probably because of their disparaging remarks about the author's "corrupt" feudal mentality, little serious attention has been paid to the novel since.[65] Both Lu Xun and Hu Shi dismissed the novel because of what they perceived as an inconsistency between Thirteenth Sister's roles as outlaw and as wifely paragon. Moreover, because *Ernü* ultimately confirms traditional Confucian values and betrays no hint of desire for political or social reforms despite its late date of composition, many other critics have also rejected it as a conventional, shallow, and tiresome piece of writing. Literary historians who read through the corpus of mid- and late Qing fiction looking for psychological realism or reformist political satire, in anticipation of those values that dominated May Fourth aesthetics, cannot fail to be disap-

---

侯官縣列女殲仇, "Cheng Yuanyu diansi daichangqian" 程元玉店肆代償錢, and "Shiyi niang Yun'gang zongtanxia" 十一娘雲崗縱譚俠.

62. The author, Lü Xiong 呂熊 (ca. 1640–1722), was a Ming loyalist who wrote the novel as a criticism of the Yongle usurpation. The earliest extant edition was published in 1711, but the novel was likely finished by 1702; see *DMB*, pp. 1251–52.

63. See W. Y. Li, "The Late Ming Courtesan," pp. 60–63.

64. For its treatment of polygamy, see McMahon, *Misers*, pp. 265–82. On its complex use of narrative voices, see Rolston, *Traditional Chinese Fiction*, pp. 304–11. For a discussion of heroism and love, see D. Wang, *Fin-de-siècle Splendor*, pp. 156–64.

65. For defenses of *Ernü* against charges of shallowness and pedantry, see Zhou Zuoren, "*Ernü yingxiong zhuan*," in idem, *Zhou Zuoren wenxuan*, pp. 479–80; and Hou Jian, "*Ernü yingxiong zhuan* shiping."

pointed by the novel. *Ernü*, however, does demonstrate many of the signature attributes of the intentionally constructed literati novel: the 40-chapter novel is tightly, self-consciously, and symmetrically structured, and it alludes to a wide range of *xiaoshuo* texts, including fiction criticism.[66] Whatever one makes of the literary merit of the novel, its cultural value is assured because of the enduring popular appeal of the figure of the female knight-errant.

The novel divides into a number of units variously based on eights, tens, and twelves.[67] *Ernü* breaks down into five narrative sections, each of which concludes with a gathering of characters and an explicitly named *tuanyuan* 團圓 (a dramatic term describing a reunion of characters on stage and used to mark a dramatic climax) and a variation of the phrase "This is conclusion no. __ for *Ernü yingxiong zhuan*" 正是兒女英雄傳的第__番結束 (see 12.231, 20.415, 28.624, 36.862, and 40.1043). The novel ends with the following comment in the voice of the storyteller about the efforts of the fictionalized author, Yanbei xianren 燕北閒人, "The Capital Man of Leisure."

> This Yanbei xianren, sitting by an oil lamp that is almost burnt out, gripping a tattered brush—who knows how much sweat he has expended for the sake of this book? How futile it is. Dear reader, the storyteller, after relating the story from beginning to end, has covered everything. Is it not marvelous to conclude with a "grand finale"? 這燕北閒人，守著一盞殘燈，拈一枝禿筆，不知爲這部書出了幾身臭汗，好不冤枉。列公，說書的話，交代到這裏，算通前澈後。交代過了。做個收場，豈不妙哉 (40.1043)

66. As David Rolston (*Traditional Chinese Fiction*, p. 311) has commented, *Ernü* "represents the most completely developed example of an author's decision to react to fiction commentary by incorporating it into his text." Both the fictionalized author and the narrator make frequent references to the novel's structure and list the narrative units by chapter number (see, e.g., 25.538, 28.614, 29.629, and 37.894). Novels referred to by name include *Honglou meng* (34.786); *Xiyou ji* (10.181); *Pingyao zhuan* 平妖傳 and *Suoyun nang* 鎖雲囊 (8.149); *Sanguo yanyi* and *Shuihu zhuan* (21.428); and *Fengshen yanyi* (38.920). The *haohan* character, Deng Jiugong, has *Sanguo yanyi, Shuihu zhuan, Lü mudan*, the recently published *Shi gong'an* 施公案, and *Yu gong'an* 于公案 on his table (39.959; *Shi gong'an* is also referred to in 32.715). Thirteenth Sister thinks of Pu Songling's story "Qingmei zhuan" 青梅傳 when she finds herself kowtowing to her new in-laws (28.602), and both An Ji and a servant refer to the *Guwen guanzhi* 古文觀止 anthology (30.663). Finally, An Ji's father watches scenes from an unnamed play about the Hegemon of Western Chu (39.966).

67. Structural units based on tens and twelves seem to be equally important in *Ernü* and may likely be an attempt to mimic the multilayered structural patterns of *Honglou meng*. The use of eight-chapter narrative units allows breaks at both chapter 12 and the midway point of the novel in chapter 20.

"Grand finale" (*shouchang* 收場) is another term borrowed from drama to refer to the final gathering of all the characters on stage.

Each of the sections has a different thematic focus. Thirteenth Sister's chivalrous exploits dominate the first twelve chapters. The attempt to discover Thirteenth Sister's true identity provides the suspense for the traditional crime-case mystery (*gong'an* 公案) in the second section (chapters 13–19); the mystery is not solved until chapter 19 when He Yufeng reveals her true name and An Ji's father discovers that the families have been connected for several generations. In chapter 20, the exact midpoint of the novel, all the major characters gather together and prepare for the marriage between An Ji and Yufeng. Chapter 20 marks an abrupt shift in genres from military knight-errant adventure to civil scholar-beauty romance. The family heirlooms, An Ji's inkstone and Yufeng's bow, which they had first exchanged in chapter 10, are used as emblems of the union of military (*wu*) and civil (*wen*) to bridge the two halves of the novel. "Starting from this chapter 21, I shall write a 'carved bow precious inkstone, separations ending in reunion' story, to create a beautiful tale of a pair of phoenixes singing together" 從這二十一回起，就要作一篇雕弓寶硯，已分重合的文章，成一段雙鳳齊鳴的佳話(21.418).

As shall be discussed in greater detail below, although *qing* is a major theme of chapters 21–28, it is contained and consecrated through larger communal rituals. In this third section of the romance, An Ji and Zhang Jinfeng join Yufeng in donning mourning for Yufeng's deceased mother and the An family recognizes Thirteenth Sister as their benefactor (*enren* 恩人) for saving the lives of An Ji and Zhang Jinfeng. This third section concludes with the long-awaited marriage between An Ji and Yufeng. Chapter 29 begins with an announcement of An Ji's formal biography (*zheng zhuan* 正傳), and chapter 36 concludes with the celebration of An Ji's success in the metropolitan examination, which he passes as the third-place *tanhua*. The four-chapter epilogue illustrates the renewal of the moral and social order: An Ji's father, An Shuixin, a relatively undistinguished Manchu bannerman, reenacts a scene from the Confucian *Analects*; An Ji becomes a *jinshi* while still in his twenties and is given the prestigious position of overseer of local customs and morals in Shandong, the center of the cult of Confucius; and An Ji's two wives give birth to sons within their first year of marriage. The redemption of the An family fortunes is mirrored in a number of clichéd omens that indicate the return of sagely rule: auspicious clouds, fungi, and a *qilin* unicorn appear, and the Yellow River runs clear. An ideal harmony has returned to both the micro- and macrocosmic levels of the Confucian imperium.

The hybrid text is woven together from a pastiche of literary genres and styles. It brings the exaggeratedly feminized characterizations of *chuanqi* drama and the gruff military figures of Peking opera onto the same stage; it interweaves fiction with fiction criticism; and it plays the authorial persona of Yanbei xianren against the oral style of the unnamed but loquacious and highly intrusive storyteller-narrator.[68] In dismissing *Ernü* as an example of uninspired and formulaic writing, Lu Xun and Hu Shi overlooked the novel's witty sophistication in its use of voice, characterizations, and self-referential textuality. It is from within this consciously literary context that we should try to make sense of its striking use of gender.

More so than the other texts discussed above, *Ernü* uses gendered patterning as an aesthetic device rather than as an ideological tool. Although the narrative makes use of some details based on *yinyang* iconography, there is no clearly identified *yin* threat to the cosmic or social order. It is suggestive that the story begins with a series of floods that highlight bureaucratic corruption (chapters 1–2). When An Shuixin, a recent *jinshi* and official, realizes that the flooding has been caused by years of official peculation and incompetence, he becomes a threat to those in power. They not only block his conscientious efforts to limit flood damage but also imprison him on trumped-up charges. Although flooding initiates the main storyline, it quickly fades from focus. Thirteenth Sister is born on the third day of the third month, a date that elsewhere marks a critical juncture in the *yinyang* seasonal balance and presages the rise of *yin*, but once again, a provocative detail is not exploited to any narrative purpose. Her *yin* birthdate is balanced by the fact that Thirteenth Sister was born in the auspicious year of the dragon (the most *yang* horoscope sign) during the *chen* 辰 hours (correlating to the dragon). This conjunction of *yang* signs seems to position her as equally balanced in terms of *yin* and *yang*, which might presage her later role as a female warrior. The numerological placement of certain episodes is strongly suggestive of a manipulation of *yinyang* structural patterns: An Ji is most endangered precisely in chapters 5 and 6 and substitutes filial devotion for

68. Wang Hailin (*Zhongguo wuxia xiaoshuo*, pp. 111–12) follows Lu Xun in arguing that the skillful use of the narrator's voice mimicked the *zidi shu* 子弟書 oral storytelling style performed by Manchu bannermen in the capital. For a detailed discussion of the multilayered use of authorial and storyteller voices in *Ernü*, see Rolston, *Traditional Chinese Fiction*, pp. 304–11.

romantic passion because he is too preoccupied with saving his father to spare any energy for thinking about marriage in chapter 9; He Yufeng gains an enlightened understanding that marriage (*chujia* 出嫁) is a higher filial calling than entering a religious life (*chujia* 出家) in chapter 27; and most strikingly, the ninetieth birthday of the gruff old soldier Deng Jiugong falls in chapter 39. As we shall see below, Wen Kang was extremely conversant with the conventions of fiction; his casual use of these *yinyang* details may indicate just how conventional some of these topoi were.

Wen Kang's knowledge of fiction and fiction commentary was so sophisticated that he used a meta-commentary about narrative conventions to propel the plot. In the following speech, Thirteenth Sister explains to Zhang Jinfeng and An Ji why she has suddenly changed her mind and decided to leave them.

"First of all, I want to see how you two feel about this. Second, I want to test your courage. Third, the details of the case (*gong'an* 公案) today are too complex, and there has been too much idle talk. What if at some later date someone wants to compile it into a book? He won't find a place to tie this chapter together, and the digressions (*huitou* 回頭) are too long. For these reasons, just now when I got done speaking, I got up and was about to go so as to bring this scene to conclusion (*zuoge shouchang* 作個收場), to provide the writer a chance to rest his brush and the storyteller a chance to wet his throat. Doesn't that make sense to you?" (9.162).[69]

In this next passage, the intrusive and long-winded narrator justifies Yanbei xianren's use of chapter 12 to recapitulate the events without advancing the plot.

Dear reader, after listening to this chapter, doesn't it seem verbose and muddleheaded to you that [the author Yanbei Xianren] has just taken the events of the last couple of chapters and rewritten them? Well, it is not that way. When I tell a story, it is no more than looking at a script and developing a narrative (*zhaoben yanshuo* 照本演說); but writing has its own particular difficulties. Although these unofficial histories can't be compared to official histories, neither can they skimp on the structural principles (*jieggou* 結構) of foreshadowing and reflecting back (*fuying* 伏應) or direct and indirect descriptions (*xushi* 虛實). Otherwise, it would be the same

69. For other examples of how characters justify their actions in terms of literary structure or devices, see 16.313, 16.317, and 37.893.

as Song Zijing's 宋子京 compiling of historical annals;[70] as soon as these events were written into a book, even if it were an official history (*zheng shi* 正史), it would become a laughingstock. As for those listening to the story, how could all of them listen from the very beginning (*kaizong mingyi* 開宗明義)?[71] If it were not for this recapitulation, it would not form a [properly] ordered composition. It is not at all that he [the author] was wasting time and ink, but because chapter 12 has a small reunion (*xiao tuanyuan* 小團圓), it marks the first narrative climax (*jieshu* 結束) of *Ernü yingxiongzhuan*. (12.231)[72]

The anonymous storyteller embarks on an even more detailed discussion of the concessions he has to make to structural principles in another passage.

Dear reader, just be patient and stop fretting. It isn't that I as storyteller (*shuoshu de*) am determined to have it this way; it's just that even though these unofficial histories are trifles (*wanyi* 頑意), they still have their [compositional] rules, which are the same as those for writers. First, you have to make distinctions between the main biography (*zhengzhuan* 正傳) and the secondary biographies (*fuzhuan* 附傳), the "host" (*zhuwei* 主位 [main protagonist]) and the "guest" characters (*binwei* 賓位), foreshadowing and reflection, indirect and direct descriptions, and only then will you have a solid structure. For example, this passage is the formal biography of Thirteenth Sister, so she is the "host," Old Master An is the "guest," and [characters] such as Deng and Zhu can't even be considered as "guests," they just count as "extras" (*xiaoxiang* 小相). (16.318)

Clearly, this was a novelist who enjoys playing with the conventions of fiction. Wen Kang also used the narratorial voices to engage in exuberant digressions to retard the action at moments of great suspense. For example, chapter 5 ends with the description of a monk's hand poised with a knife pointed at An Ji's exposed chest and an acolyte kneeling with a bowl to catch the blood and entrails. Suddenly there is a yell and a thump of someone falling. The storyteller shamelessly inserts himself into the action for over a page: he first reassures the audience (*ting dao zheli de* 聽到這裏的) that it could not have been An Ji who fell, since he was tied up to a pillar, before digressing into a discussion of storytelling techniques. He rounds off his ora-

70. Song Qi 宋祁 (998–1061) was a historian involved in compiling the *Xin Tangshi* 新唐史 (The new history of the Tang dynasty) who was known for his terse style. Annals list information in chronological order without any narrative to link them together.

71. This term comes from the chapter heading of the opening chapter of the *Xiaojing* 孝經 (Classic of filial piety).

72. For other comments by the storyteller on Yanbei xianren's technique, see 25.538, 28.614–15, 29.654, and 37.894.

tion with a host of extraneous details before returning the impatient readers to the scene of the murder.[73]

In one scene Wen Kang uses intertextuality to outstanding ironic effect when he has the brusque man of action Deng Jiugong step into the sensuously decadent world of a romance. After Deng visits a theater near the southern walls of Beijing, he disgustedly recounts to Old Master An the intimate conversations he overheard between the actresses and their elite admirers. One level of humor comes from the fact that An Shuixin and the readers are fully aware that the actresses who so offended Deng are actually *xiaodan* actors who specialize in female roles (32.710–716). That several of the *xiaodan* actors whom Deng names are from Chen Sen's 陳森 (fl. 1823–49) highly urbane novel *Pinhua baojian* 品花寶鑒 (Precious mirror of flower registers), a work that glamorizes the homoerotic demimonde of Beijing theater culture, only adds to the humor of the scene. In addition to the improbable mixing of genres, which allows us to see the urban and highly refined male beauties of *Pinhua baojian* through the eyes of a blunt, unsophisticated *haohan* character, Wen Kang has Deng unwittingly make a number of sophomoric puns on the names of these characters. The corpulent Xu Duxiang 徐度香 becomes Duxiang 肚香, "Fragrant Belly," and Yuan Baozhu 袁寶珠 becomes Yuan Baozhu 元寶豬, "Silver Tael Pig." Deng's indignation over the decadent mixing of actresses and officials is undermined when An Shuixin, who is himself from the capital, laughs and slyly asks Deng if he is jealous because none of the actors had flirted with him (32.713–4). The playing off of Thirteenth Sister's tough businesslike manner against An Ji's fainthearted naïveté surely reflects a similar pleasure in genre-bending.

Heroic Confucianism: Activism and Domestic Rituals

Ernü paradoxically foregrounds a female knight-errant while promoting conservative Confucian values. How can a young woman from an elite family who lives on the fringes of society be construed as a savior of Confucian values? The 100 beauties in *Jinghua yuan* indicate the extent to which uncon-

73. Dong Xun's commentary compares the narrative linking between chapters 5 and 6 to that achieved by Shi Nai'an and Cao Xueqin (6.106). For other examples of the storyteller's teasingly interrupting the narrative at moments of high suspense, see 3.57, 4.78, 5.88–89, and 16.318–9.

ventional depictions of women had lost a counterhegemonic edge by the late Qing and indeed seem to have become a conventional feature of fiction aesthetics. Thirteenth Sister's split personality, of knight-errant and capable wife, goes to the heart of Wen Kang's aesthetic and ethical vision. Just as Tang Xianzu used Du Liniang to represent the contradictory values of sensuous passion and wifely virtue in *Mudan ting* (admittedly not very successfully in that instance either), the military and civil aspects of Thirteenth Sister's character encompass the Confucianized definition of *qing* used in *Ernü*.

Initially, the beautiful Thirteenth Sister seems akin more to the masculine *haohan* models of authenticity found in the *Shuihu zhuan* than to a conventional heroine. She is a shadowy, marginal outlaw who actively threatens An Ji. She stalks him in order to rob him and pay for her mother's funeral expenses. Unlike other beauties, Thirteenth Sister is not encumbered by fantasies of delicacy: she can gulp down seven steamed buns and wolf four and a half bowls of rice in a flash (9.174), she is enormously strong, and her speech can be gruff and aggressive. She is also willing to kill even when not physically threatened (7.139). Most female knights, such as those from Pu Songling's *Liaozhai* and Li Ruzhen's *Jinghua yuan*, never seem to lose their feminine charms; Thirteenth Sister has enough bravado to fit in with the male outlaws.

Curiously, no aspect of her gender inversion is presented as either subversive or transgressive. Despite the fact that Thirteenth Sister's appropriation of a masculine role breaks many of the taboos for female behavior by exposing her to public view and forcing her to mix with men without a chaperone, all this is excused within the logic of the narrative because it is motivated by her filiality. The girl knights-errant in *Jinghua yuan* are also motivated by their filiality, and this suggests that for unmarried women, as in the case of Mulan or Xie Xiao'e 謝小娥 of the *Xin Tang shi*, filial expediency was a higher ethical calling than the injunction to maintain a clear boundary between the inner female and the outer male spheres. Thirteenth Sister does maintain certain aspects of Confucian propriety regarding the separation of the sexes; for example, she insists that she should sit apart from the male outlaws not only because she is a woman but also because she is in mourning (16.307). Her expedient choice to live among men as an outlaw, however, never seems to compromise her reputation for sexual purity or social gentility. In *Jinghua yuan*, by way of comparison, the women, with the exception of the usurper Wu Zetian, maintain a careful segregation of the sexes—witness their all-female military encampment.

Wen Kang exploited the gender inversions in *Ernü* to portray the full complementarity of the lovers. He went beyond the conventions of scholar-beauty romances, in which the male and female protagonists are androgynously interchangeable, and assigned the two protagonists reversed gender roles. As is conventional in romances, He Yufeng and An Ji are prized only children of literati families. Yufeng, however, is raised as a son with an education in both the Classics and the martial arts, whereas An Ji gets all the delicate, feminine traits that are usually assigned to beautiful girls. He is a beautiful and fragile boy who has lived his whole life sequestered in his family's home; his only contacts as a child are with his parents, his wet nurse, and the maids who care for him. An Ji is remarkably innocent and pure; he is often unable to understand the speech of those not in his family, and when he meets a new girl, he blushes and is at even more of a loss than she.[74] He also has a propensity to break into tears.

Thirteenth Sister is the mirror opposite of An Ji; she travels widely on her own in the male world of outlaws and innkeepers. She is single-minded in her pursuit of avenging her father's death. The first twenty chapters of the novel are set in a landscape of roadside inns, remote temples, and small communities hidden deep within forests, settings more appropriate to *Shuihu zhuan* than a scholar-beauty romance. The narrator compares Thirteenth Sister favorably to Luosha nü 羅刹女 of *Xiyou ji* and Aunt Gu 顧大嫂 of *Shuihu zhuan* (10.181). In contrast to An Ji, she is tremendously capable and independent; within the space of the first ten chapters, Thirteenth Sister has killed five bloodthirsty monks and one of their female cohorts and has rescued An Ji as well as the three members of Zhang Jinfeng's family. She is also endowed with superhuman strength, which terrifies An Ji when he watches her place a huge millstone by his door without breaking into a sweat.

During the first half of the novel, the incongruities between the capabilities of An Ji and Thirteenth Sister are highlighted in ways that make An Ji a parody of the inept scholar. The first time the predestined lovers meet, An Ji is transporting 2,500 taels of silver to ransom his father from jail. The family steward accompanying him suddenly suffers a strange paralysis and sends An Ji on with these words of warning: "If you meet anyone, just tell them

74. For An Ji's inability to understand the speech of outsiders, see 1.13, 4.77, and 5.87–88.

three parts of the truth. You mustn't let them know everything" 逢人只說三分話，未可全拋一片心 (3.62). An Ji hires two dubious locals, White-faced Wolf (Bai lian'er lang 白臉兒狼) and Dumb Dog (Sha gou 傻狗), as porters. As soon as the two realize what easy prey he is, they steal their wages and abandon him. An Ji makes it to an inn, but when the porter tries to tempt him with a prostitute, An Ji "does not understand a word he says, but figures that it probably wasn't proper" 一套話公子一字兒也不懂，聽去大約不是甚麼正經話 (4.77). He overhears the porter talking to a young woman but is again unable to understand a word. Thirteenth Sister enters An Ji's room and secures his door with a huge millstone, which even two burly men cannot budge. She then reverses their roles by seating herself in his room, taking the role of host, and inviting An Ji, the guest, to join her. When she asks An Ji his name, where he is from, and where he is going, he is thrown into a quandary trying to decide exactly what three-tenths of the truth would be. "Think about it, if I reveal only three parts of my name 'An' 安, how should I split it? Which is better, to say my name is 'Baotou' 寶頭 [the top element of the character Bao, i.e., 宀] or to say my name is 'Nü' 女?" 想了想，我這『安』字說三分，可怎麼樣的分法兒呢？難道我說我姓寶頭兒，還是說我姓女不成？(5.88).[75] When he is done talking, Thirteenth Sister sees through his naïve ruse and scoffs, "How could a person like you study the Classics in vain and not understand the real world?" 你這人怎生的這等枉讀詩書，不明世事？ The most striking reversal of their gender roles occurs in chapter 5 when she rescues An Ji from the hands of outlaw monks who are about to murder him. An Ji is completely helpless and dependent.

Although the gender inversions add narrative interest to what would otherwise be a highly conventional plot, they also function as a marker of authenticity. Unconventional behaviors round out each character's personality and, like Li Yu's use of ironic twists, imbue the conventional orthodoxy of the conclusion with a freshness it might otherwise lack. As the narrative states, actions should arise from *qing* and come to rest in ritual (*fa hu qing, zhi hu li* 發乎情，止乎禮; 9.171 and 34.787); unconventional gender signals authentic *qing*. Thirteenth Sister's passionate and exceptional filiality is portrayed through her masculine role, and An Ji's femininity denotes his purity and self-sacrificing dedication. More important, An Ji's feminine qualities

75. This form of riddling in which characters are split into their constituent parts is called *chaizi* 拆字.

never bleed over into sensuousness; his girlishness functions as a sign of his childlike moral purity and his lack of a corrupting ambition. Living within the protective walls of his family's estate has insulated An Ji from anything that might taint or compromise his integrity.

The colorful, mysterious Thirteenth Sister, the social outsider willing to commit acts of daring, contrasts sharply with the depiction of He Yufeng, the name she resumes after agreeing to marry An Ji. In the second half of the novel, Yufeng withdraws into the domestic quarters of the household, and her former identity as righteous knight is supplanted by her role as wife; she spends her days quietly embroidering and urging her husband to study. She begins to experience a "lover's tenderness" (*ernü rouchang* 兒女揉腸; 20.410), and her "chivalric spirit completely disappears" (*xiaqi quanxiao* 俠氣全消; 27.575). Although critics and later redactors alike have chafed at the artificiality of this transformation in personality, Yufeng's primary character trait in both roles is consistently her filiality. Her willingness to help An Ji, rather than rob him, arises from her admiration for his filiality (8.156). And her decision to become an outlaw had been dictated by expediency, since there is no other way to avenge her father.

Even in her role as filial outlaw, she subordinates her personal loyalties to a higher good. She refrains from killing the official who persecuted her father because he is still an important official serving the empire, and "she cannot harm the affairs of state for the sake of a personal vendetta" 他是朝廷重臣，國家正在用他建功立業的時候，不可因我一人私仇壞國家的大事 (8.150). After learning that the official has already been executed by imperial command, Thirteenth Sister tries to commit suicide because her life's ambition has been accomplished (18.373). She agrees not to only after An Shuixin persuades her that she can best honor her parents by living in order to tend their graves and continue their ancestral line. Fortunately for the readers, her heroism is not completely lost in her transcription into ideal wife, even though she loses her truly unconventional qualities of being a tough-talking, tough-acting swordswoman who is able to cast aside the four virtues for women. During the marriage celebrations, Yufeng discovers four thieves breaking into the house, and she captures one of them before the men take over (31.688–89).

The equation of *qing* with filial piety and marital devotion provides Wen Kang's rationale for the abrupt break at the exact midpoint of the novel. The narrative rupture marks the transition between these two expressions of *qing*.

The first twenty chapters, written in the style of knight-errant fiction, and the last half, which follows the conventions of a scholar-beauty romance, allow the female protagonist to embody the dual aspects of *qing* through her complementary personae as Thirteenth Sister and He Yufeng. The inversion of the two lovers' gender roles in the first half of the novel foregrounds the uniqueness of their moral qualities, her passion and his purity, rather than call orthodox ideology into question. For this reason it does not seem incongruous that the second half of *Ernü* should reproduce many of the popular didactic passages from morality books and household instructions. As An Shuixin lectures his daughters-in-law, marriage is the foundation of the cosmic and social order: "The Way of Qian forms man, the Way of Kun forms woman. When Qian and Kun are fixed, earth is peaceful, and Heaven is complete" 乾道成男，坤道成女。乾坤定而後地平天成 (25.530). In case they, or the readers, miss the point, An Ji's mother reminds the two brides their most important tasks are to establish their husband's career and produce children (28.603–4), a point reinforced when An Shuixin twice quotes Ban Zhao's *Instructions for Women*, the same text with which *Jinghua yuan* begins, to instruct the new brides that a wife's duty is to serve her husband and parents-in-law (28.622),[76] and that a wife should not keep private goods (*sihuo* 私貨) or have private relationships (*siyu* 私與; 33.752).[77] He later quotes from the *Doctrine of the Mean*: "The Way of the gentleman originates in the husband-wife relationship" 君子之道造端乎夫婦 (37.890). Much of the second half of the novel reads like a primer on the proper deportment for wives in its demonstration of how the two women transform An Ji into a serious scholar by threatening to ignore him until he becomes more diligent in his studies (30.673) and how they become dedicated and conscientious managers of the domestic finances (33.749).[78]

76. Thirteenth Sister had earlier dismissed the tension between bride and mother-in-law: she says she cannot understand why most girls fear their in-laws, since they are just like their own parents and should be loved as such (14.258).

77. There is also a brief aside on the four womanly virtues (27.575).

78. Repeated throughout the novel is the sentiment that admonitions from a parent cannot compete with the pressure exerted by a wife (see 12.223, 28.603–4, and 30.671–76). This seems to be a common didactic theme reproduced in other scholar-beauty romances: Shui Bingxin of *Haoqiu zhuan* persuades her husband to devote himself to his studies, and in *Honglou meng* it is Daiyu, Baochai, and Xiren who exert rather halfhearted pressure on Baoyu to study.

The threat of female jealousy, a favorite topos of fiction, is raised and reassuringly dismissed. Just before Yufeng and An Ji marry, Yanbei xianren delivers a long and clichéd disquisition on jealousy. He divides jealous wives into two categories: those who "can eat vinegar" and those who do not know how to eat vinegar properly. ("Eating vinegar" is a common expression for jealousy.) The highest category of woman is the saintly wife who runs all aspects of the family; when she realizes she is unable to have children, she arranges for the purchase of several concubines and cares for the children better than their natural mothers could. She is jealous only of other women's fertility, not of their presence. The worst kind of wife is as stupid as she is ugly. She does not care if there are no sons and will not allow her husband to take a concubine, even if the new woman is more stupid and ugly than she. She is so jealous and possessive that she would rather kill her husband than have him mention the word "concubine" (27.575–77). Naturally, Yufeng and Jinfeng get along without a trace of jealousy or friction; they even agree that An Ji should take a maid along as his concubine to accompany him to his official post since they are pregnant and unable to travel.[79]

The finale to this hybrid romance about heroic lovers is the enactment of a scene from the *Analects* with An Shuixin, the Manchu bannerman, taking the role of Confucius.[80] Shuixin travels to Shandong, the birthplace of Confucius, where he meets descendants of the four disciples Zilu 子路, Zeng Xi 曾皙, Ranyou 冉有, and Gongxi Hua 公西華 who are continuing their forefathers' famous discussion of how they would like to fulfill their ambitions if given an opportunity to serve in government.[81] Traditionally, there has been no consensus among commentators on how to interpret Confucius' enigmatic responses to the disciples; most have agreed that Confucius approved of the modest *qin*-playing Zeng Xi, who voiced an am-

79. Despite An Shuixin's reiteration that family tradition allows a man to take a concubine only if he is still childless at 50 (23.488 and 40.1007), the novel ultimately glorifies the practice of polygamy in the extended and idealized depiction of An Ji's triple marriage.

80. Because of this scene, Hou Jian ("*Ernü yingxiong zhuan* shiping," p. 67) argues that An Shuixin is actually the novel's focal character and that the biographies of An Ji and Yufeng are of subsidiary importance; rather than the children's courage bringing redemption to the political world of the father, An Ji's successes should be read as a karmic reward for Shuixin's life of virtue. Even though An Shuixin is a minor character in terms of plot, the narrator indicates his symbolic centrality in describing him as "the essence of the sun, the energy of the moon, the root of wood, and the origin of water" (29.629).

81. *Lunyu*, XI.26.

bition to observe the spring equinox ritual according to ancient practice. Confucius smiled ambiguously when the impulsive Zilu answered that he would right all the problems of a war-torn state in three years. This smile has historically been interpreted as a sign of the Master's displeasure with Zilu's brashness.

However, in Wen Kang's nineteenth-century pragmatist rewriting of the scene, Shuixin explains that Confucius' silence after Ranyou, Gongxi Hua, and Zeng Xi had spoken indicated that they had answered as he had expected. His smile after Zilu spoke was not derisive, but an indication of Confucius' approval that Zilu had jumped in with his response rather than wait for the others, who were older than he, to speak first. Although Confucius had praised Zeng Xi more than the others for his modesty, Shuixin explains that in actuality Confucius valued activism over pure ritual. An Shuixin then chastises the four young men for having been too influenced by Zhu Xi's metaphysical interpretations (*Zhu zhu* 朱註) and for having lost a sense of true Confucianism. After his speech, the four disciples, who had originally looked down on Shuixin as a bannerman, toast him as their teacher (39.968–73). In the final chapter, Deng Jiugong leads An Shuixin on a pilgrimage to climb Taishan, the same mountain Confucius once climbed, and then takes him to meet Kong Jiyao 孔繼遙, a direct descendant of Confucius. Wen Kang's activist and pragmatic interpretation of the *Analects* reproduces a mainstream Qing intellectual impatience with Cheng-Zhu metaphysics and introspection in favor of a more vigorous engagement in society and politics.

It is Thirteenth Sister, however, who is the most successful and unambiguous model of activist Confucianism in the novel, even more so than the gruff and militaristic character Deng Jiugong, who, like the independent Duo Jiugong of *Jinghua yuan*, has turned away from the corrupting influence of bureaucratic institutions in order to avoid relinquishing his own ideals. Deng Jiugong embodies a number of *yang* qualities: he has a red face; is easily angered (anger being a hot emotion); loves to drink alcohol (*jiu*), which in addition to being a *yang* substance also puns with the number nine *jiu* in his name; and, although over 80, looks like a fit man in his sixties. Deng's spirit is untrammeled: the first time he meets An Shuixin, he is angered that someone dares to intrude on him in his home, and despite the fact that Master An is an official, he yells that he is the master (*zhu* 主, 15.279). As mentioned above, Deng celebrates the miraculous coincidence of his ninetieth birthday and the birth of his first son in chapter 39. Deng Jiugong, like Duo Jiugong, excels in practical details and is impatient with the details of book-learning and social etiquette. Duo Jiugong turned to navigation after he failed in the official examinations, is knowledgeable in practical learning (*shixue* 實學), and disdains Tang Ao's evidential learning. In Deng Jiugong's case, despite the fact that his practicum in the military examination was outstanding, he ruined his chance at a military position when he miswrote two characters in the essay and then refused to bribe the examiners to overlook the mistakes.

These two self-confident and independent men represent an autonomous and "authentic" manhood uncompromised by the often corrupting and demeaning demands of the examination system and official service. Their spontaneous and vigorous Confucian instincts are a direct critique of institutionalized Neo-Confucian quietist practices. Unlike expectant examination candidates or officials who are dependent on the favor of those above them for success, neither Deng nor Duo is cast in a *yin* position of service. Nor, unlike the literati, are they forced to turn to emasculating feminine metaphors of purity in order to express their loyalty to the state. In chapter 39, An Shuixin honors Deng with a biography as the first righteous knight (*yishi* 義士) he has met outside the pages of historical and literary texts. Deng Jiugong, who lives in Shandong, the center of the Confucian cult, introduces An Shuixin to the four Confucian disciples and initiates the union of the military and the civil traditions, the Manchu and the Confucian. This ideal of a robust and ethical masculinity fits in well with what Prasenjit Duara has described as an effort by the Qing state to promote a virile Confucianism.[82] However, although Deng Jiugong embodies an activist and rigorous Confucianism, to the end he remains marginalized from the institutions of the state. Only the feminine An Ji, after marrying Yufeng and allowing himself to be cajoled into sitting for the official examinations, is rewarded with the successful career trajectory denied An Shuixin, Deng Jiugong, and Yufeng's father. As in *Jinghua yuan*, it seems that real men can no longer find a place for themselves in the imperial bureaucracy and that the hope for systemic redemption and reinvigoration is dependent on the fantasy of feminine purity.

82. Duara, "Superscribing Symbols," p. 784.

Revising Honglou meng *and Rectifying* Qing

The gender depictions in *Ernü* make most sense when interpreted within the context of *Honglou meng*, *Jinghua yuan*, and other Qing novels that idealize the feminine. In fact, *Ernü* repeatedly asks to be read as a response to *Honglou meng*. Wen Kang's pseudonymously written Guanjian wozhai 觀鑒我齋 preface, spuriously dated 1734, borrows a citation from the Confucian *Analects* to compare the moral level of *Ernü* favorably with the canonical novels *Xiyou ji*, *Shuihu zhuan*, *Jin Ping Mei*, and *Honglou meng*;[83] although those earlier works may have had good didactic intentions, the preface claims they are flawed because they rely on improper means to express their messages.

> Those who think deeply about it, [understand] that although these several books claim to be based in correct behavior, self-cultivation, and good governance, they actually entrust their message to the strange (*guai* 怪), to physical exploits (*li* 力), to decadence (*luan* 亂), and the supernatural (*shen* 神). *Xiyou ji* has its supernatural and strange, *Shuihu zhuan* has its physical exploits, *Jin Ping Mei* has its decadence, and *Honglou meng* clearly entrusts its message to feelings (*qing*) and is filled with concealed desires; these are the strange, physical exploits, decadence, and supernatural. (Preface, p. 2)[84]

The Guanjian wozhai preface singles out *Honglou meng* as the focus of its attacks for "using false words to express what is true" 托假言以談眞事 and for the fault of "when talking of emptiness and form, half of the talk spreads licentiousness" 談空談色，半是宣淫 (Preface, pp. 1–2).[85] The brief second preface, dated 1794 and signed Wuliao weng 吾了翁 "The Old Man I Know," fabricates a textual history for the manuscript, as if to create for the novel a ready-made historical pedigree. Wuliao weng claims to have found a manuscript entitled *Zhengfa yancang wushisan can* 正法眼藏五十三參 (Fifty-three chapters of the True Law hidden from sight). According to

83. Lu Xun (*A Brief History*, p. 338) and Hu Shi ("*Ernü yingxiong zhuan* xu," p. 497) dismiss the two prefaces dated 1734 and 1794 as forgeries written by Wen Kang himself. Not only is the style of the prefaces similar to that of the novel, reference is made to them in the mythical prologue. Furthermore, the dating of the prefaces is implausible: even though they predate widespread knowledge of *Honglou meng*, both mention and criticize it.

84. This passage alludes to an oft-quoted line in the Confucian *Analects*: "The Master [Confucius] never spoke of the strange, physical exploits, disorder, or the supernatural" (VII.20).

85. For criticisms of *Honglou meng* within the body of the text, see 26.558 and 34.786.

this preface, Wuliao weng initially assumed that this was a Buddhist text, but he soon realized the true value of the novel and edited it under the name *Ernü yingxiong zhuan pinghua*.[86]

The narrator twice makes explicit comparisons between *Ernü* and *Honglou meng*.[87] In chapter 26, the narrator lists the symbolic objects associated with each character and comments that unlike the love tokens used in *Honglou meng* (several of which he fabricates or derives from dramatic versions of the story), the objects in *Ernü* are family heirlooms. His eclectic list from *Honglou meng* includes Xue Baochai's empathy for Baoyu, Shi Xiangyun's golden kylin (a mythical animal), the maid Hongyu's longing for the handkerchief dropped for her by Jia Yun, Xiren's crimson cummerbund, You Erjie's jade dragon pendant, Siqi's 司棋 pornographic purse, the character *qiang* 薔 scratched out in the dirt by the actress Zhuangling 椿齡, and everything about Mingyan 茗烟 (Tealeaf in Hawkes's translation, Baoyu's closest male

86. No scholarship I have seen questions this title, and most scholars follow the claim of this preface that the last thirteen manuscript chapters were lost before it fell into Wuliao weng's hands. If one assumes for a moment that Wuliao weng is someone other than Wen Kang and that he had done all the editing necessary to make the 40-chapter structure as integrated and coherent as it is, it would be surprising that he did not mention the amount of time and effort that went into editing the manuscript. A note in the manuscript copy explains that with the addition of the prologue chapter, the 53-chapter novel would require 54 chapter-title couplets, a total of 108 sentences (*EN*, p. 10*n*). As David Rolston (*Traditional Chinese Fiction*, p. 304*n*) comments, this is "an abbreviated way of imitating Jin Shengtan's listing of the chapter titles at the end of his new prologue for the *Shuihu zhuan*." The number 108 of course evokes the 108 heroes of the *Shuihu zhuan*, and the title *Fifty-three Chapters of the True Law* suggests that *Ernü*, like *Honglou meng*, might preach Buddhist detachment from the world. As we shall see, the novel translates many Buddhist messages from *Honglou meng* into calls for engagement with the world. However, the 40-chapter novel is so tightly and symmetrically structured with internal cross-references to chapter numbers that it is unlikely that the original manuscript could have been any other length.

Other alternative titles mentioned in the body of the novel are *Jinyü yuan* 金玉緣 (The predestined marriage of gold and jade; Prologue, p. 1, and 40.1042), a title also used for *Honglou meng*; and *Rixia xinshu* 日下新書 (A new book for all under the sun; Prologue, p. 1, and 37.894). The artifice of supplying variant titles within the body of the text was probably inspired by *Honglou meng*.

87. Further gestures to *Honglou meng* include the narrator's explanation that *Ernü* is set during the Qing dynasty and not some distant historical period (1.11) and the description of the An family garden in which the buildings are used for study, martial arts practice, meditation, and the family shrine. In an obvious comparison to Grand Prospect Garden, the narrator comments, "It can't be said that it resembles one of those painted paradises or dream visions of a sage's grotto talked about in novels (*xiaoshuo*)" 道不得像小說部中說的那樣畫裏天宮，神仙洞府的夢境夢話 (24.500).

servant). These objects, the narrator states, are completely different from the heirlooms in *Ernü*.

The narrator also claims that the treatment of human relations, the central theme of the novel, is also an improvement over that found in other novels.

Moreover, the majority of novels waste a lot of brush and ink talking about lascivious desires (*yinyu*), but this *Ernü yingxiong zhuan pinghua* borrows the [same] topics to write about "human nature and emotions" (*xingqing*). From its entirety, extending to each chapter, each sentence, and each word, all is written in the style of Sima Qian. How could there be any infelicities? 況且諸家小說，大半是費筆墨，談淫慾，這兒女英雄傳平話，卻是借題目寫性情。從通部以至一回，乃至一句一字，都是從龍門筆法來的，安得有此敗筆？ (26.558).

In chapter 10, when An Ji and Thirteenth Sister exchange bow and inkstone, they substitute public, political signs in place of the private, shifting meanings associated with the gold and jade pairings that mark desire and desirability in *Honglou meng*.[88] There are no puns here on desire and jade; instead the character "Jade" (Yu 玉) in Yufeng's name becomes the "Thirteen" 十三 in her name. The recounting of Thirteenth Sister's first-year ritual, when she picks out weapons as if she were a "Hua Mulan" (19.390), must be read in contrast to the description of Baoyu's choice of cosmetics and other objects used by girls at a similar rite (*HLM*, 2.19).

More pointedly in chapter 34, the narrator enumerates the faults of many members of the Jia household. The list begins with Baoyu, who, although he comes from a more advantaged background than An Ji, finds the thought of the provincial examination unbearable and shows no interest in establishing a name for himself through the examination system. According to the narrator, only one fundamental difference distinguishes the two youths: "In comparing Young Master An to Young Master Jia, the basic issue is the correctness of their nature and emotions" (本來就獨得性情之正; 34.787). Jia Zheng is hypocritical; he pretends to orthodoxy (*zheng er buzheng* 正而不正), associates with a group of social-climbing and deceitful men, and fails to

88. A third object, an agate cup (*ma'nao bei* 瑪瑙杯), assigned by the family to be Zhang Jinfeng's token, is also given a public rather than an intimate meaning. The characters for agate pun on *ma'nao* 馬鬧, literally "a horse makes trouble," and are jokingly alluded to as the problems An Ji's family has had with him, their "wild horse" (*yema* 野馬; the character Ji, in An Ji's name means "stallion").

educate his son properly.[89] As for Lady Wang, she shows her deceitfulness by favoring her own niece Baochai and showing no concern for Daiyu, who is Jia Zheng's niece. The symbolic double union of Daiyu and Baochai with Baoyu is marred by the jealousy of both girls that eventually causes Daiyu's death. The narrator smugly points out that in *Ernü*, not only are He Yufeng and Zhang Jinfeng as beautiful and clever as Daiyu and Baochai, they are united in their love and concern for An Ji. The narrator even compares the two maids Xiren and Changjie'er: "Similarly, the two had served their masters since childhood and are both two years older than their masters, but I have never heard of [An Ji] noticing how striking she [Changjie'er] was and naming her Hua Xiren, or of her testing out any 'cloud-rain passion' with Longmei [An Ji]" 也是一樣的從幼服侍公子，一樣的公子大得兩歲，卻不曾聽得他照那襲而取之的花襲人，一般同安龍媒初試過甚麼雲雨情(34.786–87).

The final comparison in this section is saved for Cao Xueqin. Even though *Honglou meng* is acknowledged as stylistically superior, the narrator berates Cao for writing such a decadent work.

> Since people pay scant attention to the familiar and attend to what is anomalous and dislike the old and take pleasure in the new, it's unavoidable that reading Yanbei xianren's tired and laughable *Ernü yingxiong zhuan* cannot compare with reading Cao Xueqin's alluring and passionate *Honglou meng*. That could just be where Cao Xueqin went too far. When Cao Xueqin was writing that book, I don't know what unbreakable curse he placed on the Jia household so that he left that family without one complete person or uttering one good word. When Yanbei xianren was writing this book, his heart was totally pure; how could you induce him to express such abhorrent and destructive words? (34.787)

Unlike *Honglou meng*, which concludes with the disbanding of the Jia family, each person to follow his or her cold and empty fate, *Ernü* concludes triumphantly with the restoration of activist Confucian values, the redemption of the official bureaucracy, and the blessings of virile fecundity.

Wen Kang also has a response to Cao Xueqin's use of Buddhist themes. In *Honglou meng*, Baoyu's sudden decision to leave behind the world of the senses to become a monk hinges on his sudden understanding of the paradox concerning the illusory nature of form, or perceived reality (*se*), that

89. The narrator mentions Shan Pinren 單聘仁 and Cheng Rixing 程日興 by name. These two minor characters appear several times as Jia Zheng's cronies and as friends of the dissolute Xue Pan.

"form is emptiness, emptiness is synonymous with form" 色即是空，空既是色. In the final chapters of *Honglou meng*, we are to believe that Baoyu has finally grasped the vanity of his fascination with illusion. In what can only be read as an exegesis on this theme, Thirteenth Sister sees a couplet: "Emptiness arises from the illusion of form, but form is not empty" (*kong you se huan, se fei kong* 空由色幻，色非空; 27.587). After studying the couplet, Thirteenth Sister decides against becoming a nun. One of the tragedies of Baoyu's world is that all the girls must eventually leave the Jia household, either to marry (*chujia* 出嫁) or to enter a religious order (*chujia* 出家). Thirteenth Sister deliberates between the two ways of "leaving home"; she had originally vowed never to marry in order to devote her life to tending her parents' graves, but she comes to realize that both meanings of *chujia* are synonymous and that she can best enact her filiality by marrying (27.587). Marriage for her is not an act of passion but an expression of filial duty.

At the core of Wen Kang's critique of *Honglou meng* is his conviction that Baoyu's obsession with *qing* leads him to abdicate his parallel responsibilities toward family and state. Although Wen Kang eliminated almost all the transgressive aspects of *qing* from *Ernü*, it was still such a powerful term that he had to circumscribe its ambiguous meanings radically. His strategy was to incorporate *qing* into his definition of heroism by narrowly equating *qing* with filial love. *Qing* in this novel is no longer pulled between the poles of destructive desire and socially redemptive compassion; it is treated as synonymous with the objectively defined human nature (*renqing tianli* 人情天理). The Prologue to *Ernü* mimics many of the great and controversial masterpieces of late Ming and Qing fiction by extolling the multifaceted qualities of *qing*. As the reader quickly discovers, however, it is a case of false advertising, since the term appears only infrequently throughout the rest of the novel and then only in combinations that neutralize any selfish or sexual connotations of the word, such as "Heavenly principle and human emotions" (*tianli renqing*) and "the affective nature" (*xingqing* 性情). The *qing* celebrated here does not inspire transgressive acts of passion. The style of individualism inspired by *qing* in *Ernü* is largely equivalent to the chivalry motivated by righteousness (*yi*) and filiality in other works.

This narrow definition of *qing* becomes Wen Kang's foundation for a sentimentalized and authentic expression of conventional Confucian roles. The Prologue begins:

What makes a lover/child (*ernü*), son or daughter, is nothing but Heavenly endowed nature,	兒女無非天性
What makes a hero does not lie outside human emotions.	英雄不外人情
Most precious are those who are both hero and lover/child,	最憐兒女又英雄
For they alone are the "dragons and phoenixes" among people.	才是人中龍鳳

The Prologue continues to exploit the semantic slippage of the ambiguous term *ernü* to refer to boys and girls both as sons and daughters and as lovers.

Most people now divide the expression "lover-hero" (*ernü yingxiong*) into two categories of people, two different concepts. They erroneously take those who get up their mettle to engage in battle or who fight against the rapacious as heroes and take those who mix rouge and powder their faces or who "cut their sleeves and share peaches" [male homosexuals] as lovers (*ernü*). Therefore, as soon as they open their mouths, they start to talk about the limited aspirations of such and such a hero, the depth of some lover's passion, or the inconstancy of such and such a lover and the fortitude of some hero. Many do not realize that the perfected nature of the hero is a prerequisite for having the constitution of a lover / filial child (*ernü*). Only when you have the true emotions of a lover / filial child, can you perform the true work of a hero. For example, when people set their ambitions on being loyal ministers, this is their heroic heart. There are no loyal ministers who do not love (*ai* 愛) their lords; loving one's lord is their lover's / filial child's heart (*ernü xin* 兒女心). When people set their ambitions on being a filial child (*xiaozi* 孝子), this is their heroic heart. There are no filial children who do not love (*ai*) their parents; this is their *child's* heart (*ernü xin*). As for the word "righteousness" (*jieyi* 節義), it is this heart and principle and no other that is extended from the relationships with lord and parents to siblings, spouses, and friends. Without this heart, there would be none of the countless loyal ministers and martyrs from past and present who have died for the sake of written remonstrances and military battle. (Prologue, p. 5).

The use of the term "the lover/child's heart" (*ernü xin*) in this passage invokes the late Ming concept of the "childlike mind" (*tongxin*), which refers to the idealized innate moral understanding (*liangzhi*) available to those whose judgment has not been clouded or corrupted. This passage reveals how Wen Kang, like Xia Jingqu in *Yesou puyan*, desexualized the concept of lover. By using the same term *ernü* to refer to a filial child and romantic lover, he elided the difference between the love a child feels for his or her parents, the love that an official feels for his lord, and the passion a lover feels for his or her beloved. Tellingly, the first two examples of the *ernü* heart provided in the next paragraph are Nüwa's 女媧 selfless repairing of the sky and the Sakyamuni Buddha's conversion of the Brahmans (Prologue, pp. 5–6). No examples of powdered or sensual *ernü* appear. This connection between *qing* and heroism can be traced to the late Ming figure Zhou Quan 周銓, whose essay "On the Limits of the Hero" ("Yingxiong qiduan shuo" 英雄氣短說) argues precisely the same point; namely "that what makes heroes heroes is that they love in greater measure than others."[90]

By truncating the definition of *qing* to exclude its most common association with desire, Wen Kang was able to claim that the emotions are so fundamental to human nature that they can be used as a standard to guard against hypocrisy.

> In dealing with others, even if they are loyal, filial, virtuous, or righteous, there will be some deceit. Only in dealing with oneself are the four [emotions], of liking and disliking, grief and joy, true and reliable and without deceit. When these four [emotions] have not yet been expressed, then this is heavenly nature (*tianxing*); after they have been expressed and found their true measure, they are then human emotions (*renqing*). 打交道，那怕忠孝節義。都有假的。獨有自己合自己打起交道來，這喜怒哀樂四個字，是個貨眞假實的生意，斷假不來。這四個字含而未發，便是天性；發皆中節，便是人情。 (17.342)

The ideal of Wen Kang's sentimentalized Confucianism is no longer just to conform to ritual practice but to ensure that ritual is imbued with authenticating *qing*. Moreover, the emotions are so powerful and essential to human nature that they cannot be repressed, *even* by sages. As Zhang Jinfeng thinks to herself while contemplating a marriage with An Ji:

> Even if one were to meet a person on a par with Pan An or Cao Zhi [two famous male beauties], one must still begin in *qing* and come to rest in ritual. But resting in ritual is something everyone can do; as for not allowing things to arise from *qing*, then even sages, virtuous people, immortals, or Buddhas could not do it. 縱然遇見

90. Zhou Quan's essay can be found in Wei Yong's 衛泳 late Ming prose anthology *Bing xue xi* 冰雪攜 (Shanghai, 1935), II, pp. 144–45, and is translated by Lin Yutang as "On Heroes and Women" in his *Importance of Understanding* (Cleveland: World Publishing Company, 1960), pp. 117–18 (cited from Hanan, *Chinese Vernacular Story*, p. 221n). An earlier opposition between *qing* and boldness can be found in the following sixth-century description of Zhang Hua 張華 (232–300), found in Zhong Rong's 鍾嶸 (fl. 502–19) *Shipin* 詩品: "I [Rong] especially regret that his poetry was too sentimental (*qing duo* 情多) and insufficiently heroic."

潘安，子建，一流人物，也只好發乎情，止乎禮。但是止乎禮，是人人有發兒的；要說不准他發乎情，雖是聖仙佛也沒發兒。 (9.171)[91]

As in Feng Menglong's *Anthology of Qing*, *qing*, rather than moral principle, is posited as the foundation of moral action. In fact, one minor character who does not realize that the emotions are prior to ritual and that "the Way of Kings is rooted in human emotions" 王道本乎人情 (35.815) is singled out for criticism. This point is reiterated when An Shuixin lectures his two daughters-in-law that a person's basic disposition (*xingqing*) is the basis of human relations (37.890). The word *qing* displaces both ritual and principle in Wen Kang's moral vocabulary; it has become so divested of any potentially disruptive or dangerous aspects that there is no hint that it is related to the simultaneously self-deluding and self-fulfilling passions explored in other novels.

Both *Jinghua yuan* and *Ernü yingxiong zhuan* build on the aesthetic and ideological vocabulary of authenticity found in *Honglou meng*. However, these two nineteenth-century works use gender to very different ends, even though they superficially mimic *Honglou meng* in depicting young women as somehow better than their male equivalents. On a structural level, each is based on a cycle in which *yin* dominance (either positively or negatively identified) gives way to the return of a normative *yang*-identified order. *Honglou meng* presents Baoyu's *yin* world of lyric authenticity as a powerful alternative to an orthodox life of duty. In *Jinghua yuan* the feminized world of genteel and apolitical intellectualism is more attractive than other options, but ultimately it reveals itself to be a superficial diversion from the primary business of restoring proper government. Of the three, *Ernü yingxiong zhuan* goes furthest in romanticizing activist Confucian values, but only as associated with the beautiful and virtuous Thirteenth Sister. What ties it more closely to *Honglou meng* than *Yesou puyan*, despite its explicit rejection of the lyric sensuality of the former, is that *Ernü* continues to exploit the feminine as an unproblematic site of authenticity, even as it redefines *qing* as synonymous with filiality and political loyalty.

The strikingly positive depictions of the feminine in the three novels may be less about actual women's lives or aspirations for women than reflections of the male authors' feelings about their own place in society. Common to *Honglou meng*, *Jinghua yuan*, and *Ernü yingxiong zhuan* is a deep cynicism con-

91. The importance of starting in *qing* and concluding in ritual is repeated in 34.787.

cerning the actual functioning of the imperial bureaucracy. Even Jia Zheng of *Honglou meng,* despite his deep faith in the system, is almost destroyed through his involvement with it. Baoyu, Tang Ao, Duo Jiugong, and Deng Jiugong all opt out of the bureaucratic order as if it were somehow demeaning and would make them less than who they are. Baoyu seeks authenticity by moving first into the feminine world of *qing* and then into Buddhist enlightenment. Tang Ao retreats into a private world of Daoist enlightenment. Deng and Duo find alternatives to official service that never force them to compromise their principled activist ideals. *Ernü* ends triumphantly; An Ji becomes a *jinshi* on his first attempt. The examiners right the inequities in the examination system by overlooking his poor calligraphy and ranking him third rather than eighth. (This scene refers back to the injustice of Deng Jiugong's disqualification from the military examination because of his miswritten characters.) But despite the ease with which he succeeds, even An Ji is wary of official service. When he hears that his first posting will be in Outer Mongolia, he is described as feeling as helpless as he did when he first met Thirteenth Sister or when he was abducted by the monks (40.985–86).

It may be that an underlying ambivalence toward the viability and appeal of the bureaucratic institutions makes it unproblematic for women to displace men as the representatives of Confucian engagement in both *Jinghua yuan* and *Ernü.* Unlike the female or feminized characters in other texts who represent a counterhegemonic alternative to orthodoxy, the heroines of these two novels construct a sentimentalized orthodoxy. These female scholars and knights live in a Confucian fantasy world untroubled by cynicism or moral compromise; unlike their male counterparts, their ambitions are fulfilled through their public roles. The men, in contrast, face a constant threat of emasculation, both literal and symbolic. It is as if literati institutions had become so constraining for mature men such as Duo Jiugong, Deng Jiugong, and An Shuixin that only women and immature youths could blossom within the roles provided by those institutions. In fact, Lin Zhiyang makes this point in *Jinghua yuan* when he compares the pain of having his feet bound to the constriction of sitting for an examination (*JHY,* 33.2b).[92] Perhaps this is why the childishly feminine An Ji is the only male character who truly succeeds in the Confucian bureaucracy.

The sentimentalized orthodoxy of *Jinghua yuan* and *Ernü yingxiong zhuan* makes possible a fantasy in which the literati no longer have to compromise

92. Discussed in Roddy, *Literati Representation,* pp. 176–77.

their ideals to participate in the Confucian bureaucracy. By feminizing this exclusively male institution, both texts are able to invest bureaucratic careers with the positive associations of *qing*: the ethical qualities of passionate virtue and authentic self-expression and the equally important aesthetic qualities of novelty (perhaps even transgression) and beauty. These female actors of male roles are charming enough that they allow both authors and readers to overcome the cynicism and malaise they might have felt toward the institutionalization of their public identities and thereby reinvest these literati identities with their traditional patina of glory and prestige.

CONCLUSION
From the Symbolic to the Political

My original interest in reading gender in late imperial fiction was to make sense of the omnipresent gender fluidity that is clearly transgressive when read against Confucian norms. However, I found that my efforts to locate these representations of gender in theoretical models of resistance quickly fell apart, not only because of the broad and often contradictory meanings projected onto the sexual during this period but also because of the rapidity and ease with which Confucianism was able to incorporate competing value systems into itself. Moreover, it quickly became clear that writers were using more than one construction of gender. In an attempt to understand the meanings and genealogies of these different discourses on gender, I found it necessary to isolate various rhetorical strategies. However, anyone who has read this far is as aware as I am that my identification of the two discourses of "authenticity" and "orthodoxy" is a heuristic artifice, and my use of the terms is meaningful only insofar as it describes certain narrative features rather than categorizes content. *Xingshi yinyuan zhuan,* the most orthodox of the texts I discuss in terms of rhetoric, is filled with such grotesque imagery that its content is anything but orthodox; however, its didactic frame and use of *yinyang* symbolism unequivocally illustrate the Neo-Confucian precept, spelled out in the *Great Learning,* of the necessity of regulating self and family. This anxiety about losing control over self and society is projected onto the *yin* figure of the shrew, and order is associated with the regulatory power of *yang.* The other novels discussed, those that make use of the rhetoric of *qing,* construct the feminine as a sympathetic and empowering alternative to the dominant ideological culture.

Underlying the gendered meanings traced in this study of Ming-Qing fiction is a tension between two potentially oppositional ideological stances: one is a deeply conservative desire for social stability, which I have associated with cultural orthodoxy; the other is an equally compelling desire for individual expressive freedom, here identified with the authentic. The interplay between these two ideological poles has long informed and inspired the development of Chinese culture in both political and aesthetic terms: historically, the two poles were typically expressed through the opposition between Confucian communitarian definitions of self and Daoist- or Buddhist-identified forms of individualism. For the most part these two subject positions were treated as complementary and mutually sustaining, as exemplified by those officials who fulfilled their bureaucratic and familial obligations in their performance of their public roles and then retreated into a private Daoist microcosm within the confines of their studio or garden.

The late Ming cult of *qing*, like the Neo-Daoist movement of the Six Dynasties period (220–589), represented a tipping of the philosophical balance toward individualist values; the writings from both periods are filled with polemical attacks on core Confucian values and practices.[1] Since Daoism was historically one of the major philosophical counterweights to Confucianism, it should not be surprising that the late Ming cult of *qing* borrowed from it its anti-Confucian vocabulary of naturalism, anti-hierarchical pluralism, rejection of the conventional, and, of greatest concern for my study, the appropriation of the feminine and a nexus of values associated with it as somehow superior to hegemonic Confucian values. The aesthetic movement inspired by the philosophic search for moral authenticity went even further in turning orthodox values on their head by substituting the ephemeral, the emotive, the excessive, and the flawed for the pragmatic, solid, and measured propriety of Confucian ritualism.

The period of sharp opposition between orthodox values and the cry for an authentic subjectivity was relatively brief, but its echoes can be heard in mainstream Qing materialist philosophy and the aesthetics of *qing*, which quickly established itself as a dominant mode of fictional discourse. The frustration expressed by these late Ming figures was a legitimate cry against the unprecedented reach of state institutions of orthodoxy, from village-level recitations of the Grand Proclamations to the examination curriculum, and the increasingly precarious balance of bureaucratic rewards and sanctions. This state-sponsored intensification and rigidification of Neo-Confucian thought, as the distillation of orthodox values, had little effect on the cor-

1. This is especially true of post-Han Neo-Daoism; see Y. S. Yü, "Individualism and the Neo-Taoist Movement"; and Mather, *A New Account*.

ruption and breakdown of government, a process that was particularly acute during the lengthy Jiajing and Wanli reign periods. This irony was not lost on a broad range of literati whose allegiances spanned the Taizhou and Donglin schools. Yet it cannot be stated too strongly that even the most alienated of these late Ming critics, unlike some of their Neo-Daoist forebears, never rejected the power of Confucian rituals or the necessity of social engagement. In large part, they were rebelling against what they saw as a misguided, or at worst hypocritical, manipulation of Confucian forms that was leading neither to moral regeneration nor to institutional strength.

The fact that writers of fiction were quick to assimilate the self-expressive rhetoric of *qing* into conventional and didactic orthodox narratives, thereby blurring the boundaries between the two, should not prevent us from seeing that the two discourses, the orthodox and the authentic, were originally oppositional. The forcible reconciliation of Du Liniang's world of passion with her father's expressions of duty and reason in the final scene of *Mudan ting* does not blunt the antagonistic relationship between the two value systems illustrated throughout the body of the drama. Despite the inherent opposition between the two, Feng Menglong's *Anthology of Qing* is much more typical of the way the discourse of *qing* was incorporated into narratives promoting the conventional values of chastity, fidelity, filiality, and loyalty in ways that reinvest them with new levels of authenticity. Although the adversarial edge of the aesthetics of *qing* was quickly dulled, it continued to circulate as a mode of expression that was somehow more genuine and impassioned.

By incorporating this aesthetics of resistance into conventional didactic frames, writers of *xiaoshuo* fiction created dynamic, heteroglossic texts that simultaneously voice the desire to reject a corrupt form of Confucianism and to return to a redeemed Confucian status quo. To reject the orthodox frames of novels such as *Honglou meng* and *Jinghua yuan* as packaging superfluous to the author's message, as many critics do, is to ignore the ability of orthodox rhetoric to energize itself by absorbing competing value systems. Although my use of the word "orthodox" threatens to expand the term beyond any meaningful intelligibility within the late imperial context, the tendency in English to posit the Orthodox as an unchanging monolith also misrepresents the term. Any ideological or aesthetic system, in order to remain vibrant, must be able to respond to changing cultural and political contexts. My use of the English word "orthodoxy" is an attempt to reflect the verbal aspect of the term *zheng* in Chinese, an unceasing process of regulating and recentering. As interpreted by Wen Kang in *Ernü yingxiong zhuan*, orthodoxy is akin to the ability to "arise from *qing* and come to rest in ritual" (發乎情止乎禮; *EN*, 9.171, 34.787). Rather than interpret the *xiaoshuo* novels discussed here as resisting Confucian norms, particularly in terms of their superficially transgressive constructions of gender, we could equally plausibly consider them as products of a flexible and expansive Confucianism.

Not only did the symbolic meanings projected onto gender and the sexual expand dramatically during the late imperial culture wars, but they became greatly intensified. (This can be seen by making a quick comparison with Six Dynasty writings; although these earlier texts deal with many of the same underlying cultural tensions, they do not foreground gender.) As I have argued, the increased ideological importance of gender in late imperial fiction is to a greater or lesser degree derived from the centrality of the bias against desire and the emotions in Neo-Confucian dualistic metaphysics. Because "the desires" had historically been identified as *yin*, the feminine became appropriated as a symbolic locus of resistance to the perceived excesses of Neo-Confucian teachings and practices. The foundational importance of *yinyang* symbolism to Confucian cosmological thinking made gendered depictions a rich and polysemous source for aesthetic patterning; furthermore, because of the associative nature of dualistic Chinese *yinyang* symbolism, any term could be implicitly gendered. For these reasons, even as the philosophical importance of *yinyang* metaphysics waned, the manipulation of gendered *yinyang* symbolism in fiction composition and interpretation became increasingly complex. Gender was, and continues to be, a pivotal node at which a number of ideological and aesthetic concerns intersect and expose unresolved hermeneutic tensions.

Discussions of gender in Ming-Qing fiction can be, and often are, reduced to a discussion of the feminine. Feminist readings of Qing fiction tend to see the celebration of women in these texts as a change in the status of women; although there is no doubt that novels such as *Honglou meng* and *Jinghua yuan* did enlarge the possibilities for women's lives, especially during the May Fourth period, these political readings do not adequately explain the fascination with the feminine. Whether cast in the role of the dangerous "other," capable of destroying normative, patriarchal order, or of idealized self, the female characters in the novels we have examined reflect a spectrum of male literati concerns related to issues of personal and social power. By reading these fictional women as products of male minds, projections that serve to direct the reader's gaze away from masculine agency in such a way that renders the masculine transparent and normative, we can reverse the process and focus on the male literati self, which I believe to be the real subject of these novels.

In the development of the vernacular novel, the ideological meanings attached to gender were quickly overshadowed by the aesthetic. Gendered *yinyang* pairings became a central feature of Ming-Qing *xiaoshuo* aesthetics. The encyclopedic patterns of characterization in traditional novels allow for a greater variety of gendered subject positions than a simple male-female duality: the continuum between the socially destructive *yin* "Liu" characters and the positive *yang* "Jiugong" characters encompasses a fluid range of gender positions, including feminized male beauties, activist female outlaws, idealized *yang*-identified matriarchs, and lecherous *yin* traitors and shrews. All of these take on different meanings as they are arranged in different pairings. As is five-elements symbolism, these evolving gendered patterns are essential to the dynamic structure of the traditional novel. Although it is a matter of judgment whether, or in what ways, any particular depiction of gender challenges orthodox norms, it is clear that as writers began adopting the rhetoric and iconography of *qing* as a means to reinvest more conventional values with a sense of authenticity and passion, gender reversals lost much of their transgressive edge. By the same token, the ensuing representations of conventional Confucian values no longer seemed so constraining or rigid.

With the collapse of traditional Confucian society and the crisis of making the empire into a modern nation, it was no longer possible to treat gender as an aesthetic flourish. The need to engineer new gender roles, appropriate to citizens of a republic, transformed the symbolic into the political and rigidified the connections among biological sex, social power, and gender. As the masculine became more clearly and positively associated with power and control and the feminine with passivity, subjugation, and victimization, it was no longer empowering for male intellectuals to appropriate a feminine subject position as a place from which to resist and critique the dominant political structure. Largely in response to the gender codes of Western imperialism, the masculine has become the charged symbolic site of modernization in China. Each of the modernizing political regimes, nationalist, Maoist, and now post-socialist, has identified the regeneration of social health with the masculinization of society; even Maoism, which went further than any other ideology in promoting women's rights and equality, did so along masculinist lines.[2] (One need only conjure up an image of the brawny Iron Girl Brigades of the Cultural Revolution to understand how much the Maoist construction of the feminine differs from late imperial ideals.) The shift of interest to the masculine in no way reduced the symbolic burden on the feminine in twentieth-century literature and film; it merely underscores the increased importance of the masculine as a site of ideological contestation.[3]

It is likely that the modernist association of masculinity, power, and the redemption of society, more so than its fantasy of international cultural dominance, motivated the sudden interest in *Yesou puyan* in the late nineteenth century. As discussed in Chapter 5, although *Yesou puyan* was written during the late seventeenth century, the work languished until the 1880s when it rapidly appeared in multiple editions. The publishing house that brought out the earliest extant edition of the masculinist *Ernü yingxiong zhuan* in 1879, the Shenbao guan of Shanghai, also published an edition of *Yesou puyan* three years later, in 1882. Although literary interest in the novel was never high, it inspired at least one sequel, the *Xin Yesou puyan* 新野叟曝言 (The new *Yesou puyan*) by Lu Shi'e 陸士諤 (n.d.), published in 1909,[4] as well as a popular 100-chapter abridgment and dramatic and television versions entitled *Wen Suchen*.[5] The omission of all episodes set outside China from the 100-chapter abridgment suggests that the novel's masculinist vision may have been even more powerful than its imperialist message to Republican-era readers. The publishing information in this 1933 edition, the *Yuanzhu guben Yesou puyan* 原著古本野叟曝言 (Original, old-style *Yesou puyan*), claims that it is the sixth reprint of a text originally published in 1929.[6]

Although this poorly edited but visually pleasing edition seems to have been published largely for commercial reasons, changes to the narrative reveal an editorial interest in reshaping the text's construction of sexual and

2. Even feminist writers such as Ding Ling 丁玲 (1904–86) and Zhang Ailing 張愛玲 (1921–95), who sought to include women as well as men as agents in the liberating project of modernization, rejected the image of traditional male scholar as too passive.

3. For a history of attempts to masculinize Chinese culture after the Taiping Rebellion, see Morris, "Cultivating the National Body."

4. Lu Shi'e also wrote a sequel to Zeng Pu's 曾樸 *Niehai hua* 孽海花 (A flower in an ocean of sin) entitled the *Xin Niehai hua*, published in 1910.

5. See Wang Qiongling, *Qingdai sida caixue xiaoshuo*, p. 91.

6. For more on this edition, see note 2 to Chapter 5, p. 200.

gender norms to accord more with contemporary European practices. Of interest in the revised text is its demonization of male homosexuality, a theme that is entirely absent from the parent text. Although the monks in the revised version continue to kidnap and rape hundreds of women, they come in for particular condemnation for preying on boys. The result is that male homosexuality displaces the sexual mistreatment of women as the ultimate sign of moral perversion in the *Yuanzhu guben Yesou puyan*.[7] The threat of invasion by Japanese pirates (chap. 67, p. 187), the only mention of foreign peoples in the abridged text, is immediately overshadowed by an interpolated and lengthy discussion of how the southern (*min* 閩, Fujianese) taste for money (literally coin holes, *qianyan* 錢眼, a metonymic expression referring to the hole in the center of traditional cash) is second only to the predilection for "bumholes" (*piyan* 屁眼; chap. 64, pp. 191–94; chap. 65, pp. 202–3). One man is so indignant that the degenerate local customs have forced him to pay his young houseboy to stay out of his bed that he proposes beheading everyone in the province to eradicate homosexual practices (chap. 64, p. 194). This pathologization of male homosexuality is entirely absent from the earlier text and strongly suggests the influence of European sexological and gender categories that were being imported into Japan and China during the 1910s.[8]

The characterization of the Wen Suchen character, Zhu Ming 朱明 as he is called in the revision, emphasizes the male protagonist's leadership and autonomy.[9] As discussed, Lady Shui is central to the moral vision of Xia Jingqu's novel at both the state and the familial levels. Zhu Ming's mother is largely absent from the rewritten text, likely because her presence would only diminish the son's agency and authority. Rather than being a Confucian hero, marked by a filial willingness to subordinate himself to his mother, Zhu Ming is a military hero who displays his superior physical strength.[10] In

7. See *Yuanzhu guben Yesou puyan*, chap. 11, p. 145; chap. 62, p. 166; chap. 64, pp. 191–94; chap. 65, pp. 202–3; chap. 78, p. 147; and chap. 79, p. 167.

8. Krafft-Ebbing's *Psychopathia Sexualis*, published in 1886, was first translated into Japanese around 1912; see Sang, "The Emerging Lesbian," p. 91*n*.

9. The names of all the major characters are changed in the rewritten abridgment. Wen Suchen's name is an obvious anti-Manchu reference to Han loyalism. Zhu Ming also goes by the name Quan Shiying 全士英, a transparent pun on "hero for the whole world" 全世英.

10. Zhu Ming twice expresses his filiality toward his mother: first when he regrets that he will not live on to serve her when he is on the verge of drowning (chap. 76); and again when

contrast to Suchen, who avoids direct conflict when possible, Zhu Ming is more than willing to engage in fistfights (chap. 2, p. 28; chap. 14, p. 187; chap. 23, p. 91). The abridgment cuts out most of the domestic scenes, which highlight Lady Shui as head of household, to focus on Zhu Ming's military exploits.

One of the most surprising changes to the revision is found in the conclusion. In place of the multitiered dream in which Lady Shui and Suchen are canonized as Confucian sages, the abridgment ends with Zhu Ming receiving imperial recognition for his defeat of the malevolent pythons in China's southwest. The very last paragraph of the novel, however, adds a surprising sexual dimension to Zhu Ming's adventures. This interpolated passage voyeuristically takes us into the bedroom on the wedding night of Zhu Ming and a concubine in order to record their conversation and murmurs of pleasure. Only the continued use of Zhu Ming's name connects this short and unexpected paragraph to the preceding narrative. The placement of this scene as a coda to the rest of the novel suggests that this sanctioned sexual conquest is the ultimate reward and perhaps even the proof of Zhu Ming's heroism.

In traditional fiction, the portrayal of sexual intimacy between married couples is the stuff of pornography; sentimental texts might refer to the long-awaited pleasures of the wedding night but then demurely pass over the event in silence so as not to undermine the wife's claims to respectability. In the parent text of *Yesou puyan*, sensual contact between Suchen and his concubines is described openly before they are properly betrothed, but even that voyeuristic narrator does not violate the sanctity of the wedding chamber. It is likely that the shift from promoting the Confucian values of sexual regulation and restraint in the eighteenth-century text to illustrating sexual enjoyment in the final scene of this edition can be linked to early modernist attempts to reform Chinese attitudes toward gender roles and sexuality.[11] The 1920s were precisely a period when sexual agency was being recuperated as a privileged aspect of modern (masculine) identity in place of both the

---

he is distraught that he cannot kowtow to his mother on her birthday because his legs have become numb (chap. 90, p. 80).

11. The Hao qingnian bookstore (好青年書店), which published the *Yuanzhu guben Yesou puyan*, was likely associated with the Hao qingnian tushuguan (好青年書圖書館), which published an anthology of writings in 1929 by the Chinese sexologist Zhang Jingsheng 張競生, popularly known as "Dr. Sex," entitled *Aiqing dingze lunwenji* 愛情定則討論集. I have been unable to find any other texts published by this press.

traditional emphasis on sexual restraint as an index of self-cultivation and the negative association of sexuality with a matrix of feminizing *yin* symbols.[12] The striking lack of interest in reproducing the original fantasy of Chinese international dominance in this revised edition points to the salience that the modernist reconfiguring of masculine identities must have held for non-elite Shanghai readers. The publication of *Yesou puyan* and works inspired by it may have served to provide traditional Chinese roots for these radically new constructions of modern masculinity.

Although the intensification and increasing politicization of meanings projected onto the sexual may be a defining feature of modern identity, the use of the sexual as a symbolic arena through which to figure human identity and experience is in no way unique to the modern period. The sexual, a category that includes and conflates sexual desire, biological sex, and gender, was as compelling a source of ideological and aesthetic meanings for late imperial writers as it was throughout the twentieth century. I hope to have shown that the gendered meanings recent scholarship has begun to "discover" in traditional *xiaoshuo* fiction are not merely a product of the contemporary feminist sensibilities and politics we bring to our readings, but were critical to the composition and traditional reception of these texts. It is my hope that modern readers of traditional fiction will become more attuned to the symbolic and aesthetic connotations of gendered depictions in the late imperial imaginary. Although I have intentionally limited my readings of gender in *xiaoshuo* fiction to the discursive in order to disrupt the modern tendency to read representations of gender against our own sexual politics, the real question for me remains how the Ming-Qing textual fascination with the poetics of gender reflected and affected the lives of real men and women at different levels of society. The more we come to appreciate how deeply informed *xiaoshuo* fiction is by discursive conventions, the more pressing it is that we return to the basic issue of the relation between representation and reality.

12. See Dikötter, *Sex, Culture and Modernity*, pp. 1–3, 62–69.

Reference Matter

Bibliography

ABBREVIATIONS

Periodicals

CLEAR	*Chinese Literature: Essays, Articles, Reviews*
HJAS	*Harvard Journal of Asiatic Studies*
HLMXK	*Honglou meng xuekan* 紅樓夢學刊
JAOS	*Journal of the American Oriental Society*
JAS	*Journal of Asian Studies*
LIC	*Late Imperial China*
MS	*Ming Studies*
PEW	*Philosophy East and West*
TP	*T'oung Pao*

Collections of Articles, Publications Series, and Collectanea

Body, Subject and Power	*Body, Subject and Power in China*, ed. Angela Zito and Tani Barlow. Chicago: University of Chicago Press, 1994.
Cao Xueqin	*Cao Xueqin yu Honglou meng* 曹雪芹與紅樓夢, ed. Yu Yingshi 余英時 and Zhou Cezong 周策縱. Taipei: Liren, 1985.
Chinese Approaches	*Chinese Approaches to Literature*, ed. Adele Rickett. Princeton: Princeton University Press, 1978.
Chinese Narrative	*Chinese Narrative: Critical and Theoretical Essays*, ed. Andrew H. Plaks. Princeton: Princeton University Press, 1977.

Education	*Education and Society in Late Imperial China, 1600–1900,* ed. Benjamin A. Elman and Alexander Woodside. Berkeley: University of California Press, 1994.
HLMJ	Yisu 一粟, ed. *"Honglou meng" juan* 紅樓夢卷. Shanghai: Zhonghua shuju, 1963.
How to Read	*How to Read the Chinese Novel,* ed. David L. Rolston. Princeton: Princeton Universtity Press, 1990.
Neo-Confucian Education	*Neo-Confucian Education: The Formative Stage,* ed. Wm. Theodore de Bary and John W. Chaffee. Berkeley: University of California Press, 1989.
Orthodoxy	*Orthodoxy in Late Imperial China,* ed. Kwang-ching Liu. Berkeley: University of California Press, 1990.
Self and Society	*Self and Society in Ming Thought,* ed. Wm. Theodore de Bary. New York: Columbia University Press, 1970.
Unfolding	*The Unfolding of Neo-Confucianism,* ed. Wm. Theodore de Bary. New York: Columbia University Press, 1975.
Women	*Women in Chinese Society,* ed. Margery Wolf and Roxane Witke. Stanford: Stanford University Press, 1975.

SOURCES

Adshead, S. A. M. "The Seventeenth-Century General Crisis in China." *Asian Profile* 1 (1973): 271–80.

Ahern, Emily Martin. "The Power and Pollution of Chinese Women." In *Women,* pp. 193–214.

Ahern, Emily Martin, and Hill Gates, eds. The *Anthropology of Taiwanese Society.* Stanford: Stanford University Press, 1981.

Aijmer, Göran. "Chong-Yang and the Ceremonial Calendar in Central China." In *An Old State in New Settings: Studies in the Social Anthropology of China in Memory of Maurice Freedman,* ed. Hugh Baker and Stephan Feuchtwang, pp. 178–96. Oxford: JASO, 1991.

Allan, Sarah. *The Way of Water and Sprouts of Virtue.* Albany: SUNY Press, 1997.

Allen, Joseph, R. "Dressing and Undressing the Chinese Woman Warrior." *Positions* 4, no. 2 (1996): 343–79.

Anderson, Marston. *The Limits of Realism: Chinese Fiction in the Revolutionary Period.* Berkeley: University of California Press, 1990.

Andres, Mark F. "Ch'an Symbolism in *Hsi-yu Pu*: The Enlightenment of Monkey." *Tamkang Review* 20, no. 1 (1989): 24–44.

Arkush, David. "Orthodoxy and Heterodoxy in Twentieth-Century Chinese Peasant Proverbs." In *Orthodoxy*, pp. 311–31.

Atwell, William, S. "From Education to Politics: The Fu-she." In *Unfolding*, pp. 39–66.

Bai Xianyong 白先勇. "Jia Baoyu de suyuan: Jiang Yuhan yu Hua Xiren—Jianlun *Honglou meng* de jieju yiyi" 賈寶玉的俗緣：蔣玉函與花襲人—兼論紅樓夢的結局意義. *Lianhe wenxue yuekan* 聯合文學月刊 5 (1986): 25–30.

Bao Jialin 鮑家麟. "Li Ruzhen de nannü pingdeng sixiang" 李汝珍的男女平等思想. In *Zhongguo funü shi lunji*, ed. idem (q.v.), pp. 221–38.

———. "Yinyang xueshuo yu funü diwei" 陰陽學說與婦女地位. *Hanxue yanjiu* 漢學研究 5, no. 2 (Dec. 1987): 501–12.

Bao Jialin 鮑家麟, ed. *Zhongguo funü shi lunji* 中國婦女史論集. Taipei: Daoxiang chubanshe, 1988.

Barlow, Tani E. "Theorizing Woman: *Funü, Guojia, Jiating.*" In *Body, Subject and Power*, pp. 253–89.

Bell, Catherine. *Ritual Theory, Ritual Practice.* New York: Oxford University Press, 1992.

Birge, Bettina. "Chu Hsi and Women's Education." In *Neo-Confucian Education*, pp. 325–67.

Black, Alison H. "Gender and Cosmology in Chinese Correlative Thinking." In *Gender and Religion: On the Complexity of Symbols*, ed. Caroline Walker Bynum et al., pp. 166–95. Boston: Beacon, 1984.

———. *Man and Nature in the Philosophical Thought of Wang Fu-chih.* Seattle: University of Washington Press, 1989.

Bloom, Irene. *Knowledge Painfully Acquired, The "K'un-chih chi," by Lo Ch'in-shun.* New York: Columbia University Press, 1987.

Bodde, Derk. *Festivals in Classical China.* Princeton: Princeton University Press, 1975.

Borthwick, Sally. "Translator's Preface to *Fate in Tears and Laughter.*" *Renditions* 17–18 (1982): 255–61.

Brandauer, Frederick P. "Women in the *Ching-hua yüan*: Emancipation Toward a Confucian Ideal." *JAS* 36, no. 4 (1977): 647–60.

Bray, Francesca. *Technology and Gender: Fabrics of Power in Late Imperial China.* Berkeley: University of California Press, 1997.

Brokaw, Cynthia J. *The Ledgers of Merit and Demerit: Social Change and Moral Order in Late Imperial China*. Princeton: Princeton University Press, 1991.

———. "Tai Chen and Learning in the Confucian Tradition." In *Education*, pp. 257–91.

Brooks, Timothy. "Funerary Ritual and the Building of Lineages in Late Imperial China." *HJAS* 49, no. 2 (1989): 465–99.

Busch, Heinrich. "The Tung-lin shu-yuan and Its Political and Philosophical Significance." *Monumenta Serica* 14 (1949–55): 1–163.

Butler, Judith. *Bodies That Matter: On the Discursive Limits of "Sex."* New York: Routledge, 1993.

———. *Gender Trouble: Feminism and the Subversion of Identity*. New York: Routledge, 1990.

Cahill, James. *The Compelling Image: Nature and Style in Seventeenth-Century Chinese Painting*. Cambridge: Harvard University Press, 1982.

———. *Fantastics and Eccentrics in Chinese Painting*. New York: Asia Society, 1967.

Cahill, Suzanne. "Performers and Female Taoist Adepts: Hsi Wang Mu as the Patron Deity of Women in Medieval China." *JAOS* 106, no. 1 (1986): 155–68.

Campany, Robert F. "Demons, Gods, and Pilgrims: The Demonology of the *Hsi-yu ji*." *CLEAR* 7, no. 1/2 (1985): 95–115.

Cao Xueqin 曹雪芹 and Gao E 高鶚. *Honglou meng bashihui jiaoben* 紅樓夢八十回較本. Hong Kong: Zhonghua shuju, 1985.

Carlitz, Katherine. "Desire, Danger, and the Body: Stories of Women's Virtue in Late Ming China." In *Engendering China: Women, Culture, and the State*, ed. Christina K. Gilmartin et. al., pp. 101–24. Cambridge, Mass.: Harvard University Press, 1994.

———. *The Rhetoric of "Chin P'ing Mei."* Bloomington: University of Indiana Press, 1986.

———. "The Role of Drama in the *Chin P'ing Mei*." Ph.D. diss., University of Chicago, 1978.

———. "The Social Uses of Female Virtue in Late Ming Editions of *Lienü zhuan*." *LIC* 12, no. 2 (1991): 117–52.

Chan Hok-lam. *Li Chih, 1527–1602, in Contemporary Chinese Historiography*. New York: M. E. Sharpe, 1980.

Chan, Leo Tak-hung. "Religion and Structure in the *Ching-hua yüan*." *Tamkang Review* 20, no. 1 (Autumn 1989): 46–66.

Chan Ping-leung. "Myth and Psyche in *Hung-lou meng*." In *Critical Essays on Chinese Fiction*, ed. Winston L. Y. Yang and Curtis P. Adkins, pp. 165–79. Hong Kong: Chinese University Press, 1980.

Chan, Wing-tsit. *Chu Hsi: Life and Thought*. Hong Kong: Chinese University Press; New York: St. Martin's Press, 1987.

———. "How Buddhistic Is Wang Yang-ming?" *PEW* 7 (1962): 203–16.

———. "The Evolution of the Neo-Confucian Concept *Li* as Principle." *Tsinghua Journal of Chinese Studies* 4, no. 2 (1964): 123–49.

———. "Neo-Confucianism: New Ideas in Old Terminology." *PEW* 17 (1967): 15–36.

Chan, Wing-tsit, comp. and trans. *A Source Book in Chinese Philosophy*. Princeton: Princeton University Press, 1973.

Chan, Wing-tsit, trans. *Reflections on Things at Hand, by Chu Hsi and Lü Tsu-ch'ien*. New York: Columbia University Press, 1967.

Chang, H. C. *Allegory and Courtesy in Spenser: A Chinese View*. Edinburgh: Edinburgh University Press, 1955.

———. *Chinese Literature: Popular Fiction and Drama*. Edinburgh: Edinburgh University Press 1973.

Chang, K'ang-i Sun. *The Late-Ming Poet Ch'en Tzu-lung: Crises of Love and Loyalism*. New Haven: Yale University Press, 1991.

Chaves, Jonathan. *Pilgrim of the Clouds—Poems and Essays by Yüan Hung-tao and His Brothers*. New York: Weatherhill, 1978.

Cheang, Eng-chew. "Li Chih as a Critic: A Chapter of the Ming Intellectual History." Ph.D. diss., University of Washington, 1973.

Chen Bingzao 陳炳藻. "Pu Songling ye shi Xi Zhou sheng ma?" 2 pts. 蒲松齡也是西周生嗎? *Zhongbao yuekan* 中報月刊, no. 69 (1985): 64–70; no. 70 (1985): 45–48.

Chen Dongyuan 陳東原. *Zhongguo funü shenghuo shi* 中國婦女生活史. Reprinted—Taipei: Shangwu, 1967.

Chen Fan Pen. "Female Warriors, Magic and the Supernatural in Traditional Chinese Novels." In *The Annual Review of Women in World Religions*, vol. 2, *Heroic Women*, ed. Arvind Sharma and Katherine K. Young, pp. 91–109. Albany: SUNY Press, 1992.

Chen Qinghao 陳慶浩, ed. *Xinbian Shitou ji Zhiyan Zhai pingyu jijiao zengding ben* 新編石頭記脂硯齋評語輯校增訂本. Taipei: Lianjing, 1986.

Chen Sen 陳森. *Pinhua baojian* 品花寶鑑. Beijing: Renmin chubanshe, 1993.

Chen Shih-hsiang and Harold Acton, trans. *The Peach Blossom Fan*. Berkeley: University of California Press, 1976.

Chen Wanyi 陳萬益. "Shuo Jia Baoyu de 'yiyin' he 'qingbuqing'—zhiping tanwei zhiyi" 說賈寶玉的 « 意淫 » 和 « 情不情 » —脂評探微之一. In *Cao Xueqin*, pp. 205–48.

Chen Xizhong 陳曦鍾, Hou Zhongyi 侯忠義, and Lu Yuchuan 魯玉川, eds. *Shuihu zhuan huiping ben* 水滸傳會評本. Beijing: Beijing daxue, 1981.

Chen Xizhong 陳曦鍾, Song Xiangrui 宋祥瑞, and Lu Yuchuan 魯玉川, eds. *Sanguo yanyi huiping ben* 三國演義會評本. Beijing: Beijing daxue, 1986.

Cheng Chung-ying. "The Constancy and Meaning of the Four-Sentence Teaching in the *Ming Ju Hsueh-an*." In idem, *New Dimensions* (q.v.), pp. 481–503.

———. "*Li-ch'i* and *Li-yü* Relationships in Seventeenth Century Neo-Confucian Philosophy." In idem, *New Dimensions*, pp. 504–36.

———. *New Dimensions of Confucian and Neo-Confucian Philosophy*. Albany: SUNY Press, 1991.

———. "Reason, Substance, and Human Desires in Seventeenth-Century Neo-Confucianism." In *Unfolding*, pp. 469–509.

Cheng Chung-ying, trans. *Tai Chen's Inquiry into Goodness: A Translation of the "Yuan shan," with an Introductory Essay*. Honolulu: East and West Press, 1971.

Cheng Hao 程顥. *Mingdao wenji* 明道文集. In *Er Cheng quanshu* 二程全書. Baogao tang ed., n.d.

Cheng Peikai. "Reality and Imagination: Li Chih and T'ang Hsien-tsu in Search of Authenticity." Ph.D. diss., Yale, 1980.

Ch'ien, Edward. *Chiao Hung and the Restructuring of Neo-Confucianism in the Late Ming*. New York: Columbia University Press, 1986.

Ching, Julia, trans. *The Records of Ming Scholars*. Honolulu: University of Hawaii Press, 1987.

Chou Chih-p'ing (Zhou Zhiping) 周質平. *Gong'an pai de wenxue piping ji qi fazhan* 公安派的文學批評及其發展. Taipei: Shangwu, 1986.

———. "*Ping Gong'an pai zhi shilun*" 評公安派之詩論. *Zhongwai wenxue* 中外文學 12, no. 10 (1984): 70–94.

———. *Yüan Hung-tao and the Kung-an School*. New York: Cambridge University Press, 1988.

Chow Kai-wing. "Discourse, Examination, and Local Elite: The Invention of the T'ung-ch'eng School in Ch'ing China." In *Education*, pp. 183–219.

———. *The Rise of Confucian Ritualism in Late Imperial China: Ethics, Classics, and Lineage Discourse*. Stanford: Stanford University Press, 1994.

Chu Hung-lam. "The Debate Over Recognition of Wang Yang-ming." *HJAS* 48, no. 1 (1988): 47–70.

———. "Intellectual Trends in the Fifteenth Century." *MS* 27 (Spring 1989): 1–33.

———. Review of Carney T. Fisher, *The Chosen One: Succession and Adoption in the Court of Ming Shizong* (Sydney: Allen and Unwin, 1990). *HJAS* 54, no. 1 (1994): 266–77.

Clunas, Craig. *Fruitful Sites: Garden Culture in Ming Dynasty China*. Durham, N.C.: Duke University Press, 1996.

———. *Superfluous Things: Material Culture and Social Status in Early Modern China*. Urbana: University of Illinois Press, 1991.

Cole, Alan. *Mothers and Sons in Chinese Buddhism*. Stanford: Stanford University Press, 1998.

Crawford, Robert. "Chang Chü-cheng's Confucian Legalism." In *Self and Society*, pp. 367–413.

Crossley, Pamela Kyle. *Orphan Warriors: Three Manchu Generations and the End of the Qing World*. Princeton: Princeton University Press, 1990.

Dai Bufan 戴不凡. *"Honglou meng" zhuzuo quan lunzheng ji* 紅樓夢著作權論爭集. Taiyuan: Shanxi renmin chubanshe, 1985.

Dardess, John W. *Confucianism and Autocracy: Professional Elites in the Founding of the Ming Dynasty*. Berkeley: University of California Press, 1983.

de Bary, Wm. Theodore. "Individualism and Humanitarianism in Late Ming Thought." In *Self and Society*, pp. 145–247.

de Bary, Wm. Theodore, and and Irene Bloom, eds. *Principle and Practicality: Essays in Neo-Confucianism and Practical Learning*. New York: Columbia University Press, 1979.

de Groot, J. J. M. *Les fêtes annuellement célébrées à Emoui*. 2 vols. Trans. C. G. Chavannes. Paris: Leroux, 1886.

Deng Zhicheng 鄧之誠. *Gudong suoji quanbian* 骨董瑣記全編. Beijing: Sanlian, 1955.

Despeux, Catherine. *Immortelles de la Chine ancienne: Taoïsme et alchimie féminine*. Puiseax: Paides, 1990.

Diamond, Norma. "Defining the Miao: Ming, Qing and Contemporary Views." In *Cultural Encounters on China's Ethnic Frontiers*, ed. Stevan Harrell, pp. 92–116. Seattle: University of Washington Press, 1995.

Dikötter, Frank. *Sex, Culture and Modernity in China: Medical Science and the Construction of Sexual Identities in the Early Republican Period*. Honolulu: University of Hawaii Press, 1995.

Dimberg, Ronald G. *The Sage in Society: The Life and Thought of Ho Hsin-yin*. Honolulu: University of Hawaii Press, 1974.

Ding Naifei. *Obscene Objects, Intimate Politics: On the "Jin Ping Mei."* Durham. N.C.: Duke University Press, forthcoming.

———. "Tears of *Ressentiment*, or, Zhang Zhupo's *Jin Ping Mei*." *Positions* 3 (1995): 663–94.

Dong Yue 董說. *Xiyou bu* 西遊補. Reprint of 1641 ed. Taipei: Shijie shuju, 1962.

Dong Zhongshu 董仲舒. *Chunqiu fanlu zhuzi suoyin* 春秋繁露逐字索引, ed. D. C. Lau. Hong Kong: Commercial Press, 1994.

Duan Yucai 段玉裁. *Shuowen jiezi zhu* 說文解字注. Changsha: Shangwu yinshuguan, 1936.

Duara, Prasenjit. "Superscribing Symbols: The Myth of Guandi, Chinese God of War." *JAS* 47 (1988): 778–95.

Dudbridge, Glen. *The "Hsi-yu chi": A Study of Antecedents to the Sixteenth-Century Novel*. Cambridge, Eng.: Cambridge University Press, 1970.

———. "A Pilgrimage in Seventeenth-Century Fiction: T'ai-shan and the *Hsing-shih yin-yüan chuan*." *TP* 77, no. 4/5 (1991): 226–52.

Eberhard, Wolfram. "Ideas About Social Reform in the Novel *Ching-hua yüan*." In idem, ed., *Moral and Social Values of the Chinese*, pp. 413–21. Taipei: Cheng-wen, 1971.

Ebrey, Patricia Buckley. *Chu Hsi's Family Rituals*. Princeton: Princeton University Press, 1991.

———. *Confucianism and Family Rituals in Imperial China: A Social History of Writing About Rites*. Princeton: Princeton University Press, 1991.

———. *The Inner Quarters: Marriage and the Lives of Chinese Women in the Sung Period*. Berkeley: University of California Press, 1993.

Edwards, Louise. "Gender Imperatives in *Honglou meng*: Baoyu's Bisexuality." *CLEAR* 12 (1991): 69–81.

———. "Women in *Honglou meng*: Prescriptions of Purity in the Femininity of Qing Dynasty China." *Modern China* 16, no. 4 (1990): 407–29.

———. "Woman Warriors and Amazons of the Mid Qing Texts *Jinghua yuan* and *Honglou meng*." *Modern Asian Studies* 29, no. 2 (1995): 225–55.

Elman, Benjamin A. "Changes in Confucian Civil Service Examinations from the Ming to the Ching Dynasty." In *Education*, pp. 111–49.

———. *From Philosophy to Philology: Intellectual and Social Aspects of Change in Late Imperial China*. Cambridge, Mass.: Harvard University Press, 1984.

———. "Philosophy (*I-li*) Versus Philology (*K'ao-cheng*): The *Jen-hsin Tao-hsin* Debate." *TP* 64 (1983): 175–222.

Elvin, Mark. "Female Virtue and the State of China." *Past and Present*, no. 104 (Aug. 1984): 111–52.

Eno, Robert. *The Confucian Creation of Heaven*. Albany: SUNY Press, 1990.

Epstein, Maram. "Confucian Imperialism and Masculine Chinese Identity in the Novel *Yesou puyan*." Unpublished paper.

———. "Inscribing the Essentials: Culture and the Body in Ming-Qing Fiction." *MS* 41 (1999): 6–36.

Evans, Nancy. "Social Criticism in the Ch'ing: The Novel *Ching-hua yüan*." *Harvard Papers on China* 23 (1970): 52–66.

Farmer, Edward L. "Social Regulations of the First Ming Emperor: Orthodoxy as a Function of Authority." In *Orthodoxy*, pp. 103–25.

———. *Zhu Yuanzhang and Early Ming Legislation: The Reordering of Chinese Society Following the Era of Mongol Rule*. Leiden: E. J. Brill, 1995.

Fausto-Sterling, Anne. "The Five Sexes." *The Sciences* (1993): 20–25.

Feng Menglong 馮夢龍. *Qingshi* 情史. In *Feng Menglong quanji* 馮夢龍全集, vol. 20. Shanghai: Guji chubanshe, 1993.

———. *Xingshi hengyan* 醒世恒言. Beijing: Renmin wenxue chubanshe, 1986.

Feuerwerker, Albert. *Rebellion in Nineteenth-Century China.* Ann Arbor: Michigan Papers in Chinese Studies, 1975.

———. *State and Society in Eighteenth-Century China: The Ch'ing in Its Glory.* Michigan Papers in Chinese Studies. Ann Arbor: University of Michigan, Center for Chinese Studies, 1976.

Fingarette, Herbert. *Confucius—The Secular as Sacred.* New York: Harper and Row, 1972.

Fisher, Carney T. *The Chosen One: Succession and Adoption in the Court of Ming Shizong.* Sydney: Allen and Unwin, 1990.

Fung Yu-lan. *A History of Chinese Philosophy.* 2 vols. Trans. Derk Bodde. Princeton: Princeton University Press, 1983.

Furth, Charlotte. "Androgynous Males and Deficient Females: Biology and Gender Boundaries in Sixteenth and Seventeenth-Century China." *LIC* 9, no. 2 (Dec. 1988): 1–31.

———. "Blood, Body, and Gender: Medical Images of the Female Condition in China, 1680–1850." *Chinese Science* 7 (1986): 53–65.

———. "The Patriarch's Legacy: Household Instructions and the Transmission of Orthodox Values." In *Orthodoxy*, pp. 187–211.

Gardner, David K. *Learning to Be a Sage: Selections from the Conversations of Master Chu, Arranged Topically.* Berkeley: University of California Press, 1990.

Gilmartin, Christine K.; Gail Hershatter; Lisa Rofel; and Tyrenne White, eds. *Engendering China: Women, Culture, and the State.* Cambridge, Mass.: Harvard University Press, 1994.

Goodrich, L. Carrington. *The Literary Inquisition of Ch'ien-lung.* Rev. ed. Reprinted—New York: Paragon, 1966.

Goodrich, L. Carrington, and Chao-ying Fang, eds. *Dictionary of Ming Biography.* 2 vols. New York: Columbia University Press, 1976.

Goyama Kiwamu 合山究. "*Honglou meng* de nü xing chongbai sixiang ji qi yuanliu" 紅樓夢的女性崇拜思想及其源流. Trans. Fujishige Noriko 藤重典子. *HLMXK* 1987, no. 2: 103–23.

Graham, A.C. "The Background to the Mencian Theory of Human Nature." *Tsing Hua Journal of Chinese Studies*, n.s. 6 (Dec. 1967): 215–71.

Gu Jiegang 顧頡剛. *Gushi lunwenji* 古史論文集. Beijing: Zhonghua shuju, 1988.

Guisso, R. W. L. "Thunder on the Lake: The Classics and the Perception of Woman in Early China." In *Women in China: Current Directions in Historical Scholarship*, ed. idem and S. Johannesen, pp. 47–61. Youngstown, N.Y.: Philo Press, 1981.

———. *Wu Tse-t'ien and the Politics of Legitimation in T'ang China.* Program in E.A.S., vol. 11. Bellingham: Western Washington University, 1978.

Gulik, Robert H. van. *Sexual Life in Ancient China.* Leiden: Brill, 1974.

Guo Changhe 郭昌鶴. "Jiaren caizi xiaoshuo yanjiu" 佳人才子小說研究. 2 pts. *Wenxue jikan* 1, no. 1 (Jan. 1934): 194–215; 1, no. 2 (Apr. 1934): 303–23.

Han Huiqiang 韓慧強. "*Honglou meng* zhong de xing guannian ji wenhua yiyi" 紅樓夢中的性觀念及文化意義. *Beijing daxue yanjiusheng xuekan* 北京大學研究生學刊 1 (1988): 77–82.

Han Lü 悍膂. "Tan *Yesou puyan*" 談野叟曝言. *Taibai yuekan* 太白月刊 1, no. 12 (1935): 594–99.

Hanan, Patrick. *The Chinese Short Story*. Cambridge, Mass.: Harvard University Press, 1973.

———. *The Chinese Vernacular Story*. Cambridge, Mass.: Harvard University Press, 1981.

———. *The Invention of Li Yü*. Cambridge, Mass.: Harvard University Press, 1988.

———. "Sources of the *Chin P'ing Mei*." *Asia Major*, n.s. 10, no. 2 (1963): 23–67.

———. "The Text of the *Chin P'ing Mei*." *Asia Major*, n.s. 9, no. 1 (1962): 1–57.

Handlin, Joanna F. *Action in Late Ming Thought: The Reorientation of Lü K'un and Other Ming Dynasty Scholar Officials*. Berkeley: University of California Press, 1983.

———. "Lü K'un's New Audience: The Influence of Women's Literacy on Sixteenth-Century Thought." In *Women*, pp. 13–38.

Hanshu 漢書. Beijing: Zhonghua shuju, 1962.

Haoqiu zhuan 好逑傳. Taipei: Shuangdi guoji chuban, 1995.

Hawkes, David. "The Translator, the Mirror and the Dream—Some Observations on a New Theory." *Renditions* 13 (1980): 5–20.

Hawkes, David, and John Minford, trans. *The Story of the Stone*. 5 vols. Harmondsworth, Eng.: Penguin, 1973–86.

Hegel, Robert E. "Making the Past Serve the Present in Fiction and Drama: From the Yen'an Forum to the Cultural Revolution." In *Popular Chinese Literature and Performing Arts in the People's Republic of China 1949–1979*, ed. Bonnie S. McDougall, pp. 197–223. Berkeley: University of California Press, 1984.

———. *The Novel in Seventeenth Century China*. New York: Columbia University Press, 1981.

———. *Reading Illustrated Fiction in Late Imperial China*. Stanford: Stanford University Press, 1998.

———. "*Sui T'ang yen-i* and the Aesthetics of the Seventeenth-Century Suchou Elite." In *Chinese Narrative*, pp. 124–59.

Hegel, Robert E., and Richard Hessney, eds. *Expressions of Self in Chinese Literature*. New York: Columbia University Press, 1985.

Henderson, John B. *The Development and Decline of Chinese Cosmology*. New York: Columbia University Press, 1984.

Hessney, Richard. "Beautiful, Talented and Brave: Seventeenth-Century Chinese Scholar-Beauty Romances." Ph.D. diss., Columbia University, 1979.

Hevia, James L. *Cherishing Men From Afar: Qing Guest Rituals and the Macartney Embassy of 1793*. Durham, N.C.: Duke University Press, 1995.

Ho Ping-ti. *The Ladder of Success in Imperial China, Aspects of Social Mobility, 1368–1911*. New York: Columbia University Press, 1980.

———. "The Salt Merchants of Yang-chou: A Study of Commercial Capitalism in Eighteenth-Century China." *HJAS* 14 (1954): 130–68.

———. *Studies in the Population of China, 1368–1953*. Cambridge, Mass.: Harvard University Press, 1959.

Holmgren, Jennifer. "The Economic Foundations of Virtue: Widow-Remarriage in Early and Modern China." *Australian Journal of Chinese Affairs* 13 (Jan. 1985): 1–28.

Holzman, Donald. *Poetry and Politics: The Life and Works of Juan Chi*. Cambridge, Eng.: Cambridge University Press, 1976.

Hong Qiufan 洪秋藩. *Du "Honglou meng" suibi* 讀紅樓夢隨筆. Chengdu: Ba Shu shushe, 1984.

"Honglou meng" sanjia pingben 紅樓夢三家評本. Shanghai: Guji chubanshe, 1988.

Hou Jian 侯健. "*Ernü yingxiong zhuan* shiping" 兒女英雄傳試評. In idem, *Zhongguo xiaoshuo bijiao yanjiu* 中國小說比較研究, pp. 55–75. Taipei: Dongda tushu, 1983.

———. "*Yesou puyan* de biantai xinli" 野叟曝言的變態心理. In *Zhongguo gudian wenxue luncong* 中國古典文學論叢, ed. Wang Meng'ou 王夢鷗, 3: 97–112. Taipei: Zhongwai wenxue, 1975.

Hsia, C. T. *The Classic Chinese Novel*. New York: Columbia University Press, 1968.

———. "The Military Romance: A Genre of Chinese Fiction." In *Studies in Chinese Literary Genres*, ed. Cyril Birch, pp. 339–90. Berkeley: University of California Press, 1974.

———. "The Scholar-Novelist and Chinese Culture: A Reappraisal of *Ching-hua yüan*." In *Chinese Narrative*, pp. 249–90.

———. "Time and the Human Condition in the Plays of T'ang Hsien-tsu." In *Self and Society*, pp. 249–90.

Hsu Pi-ching. "Celebrating the Emotional Self: Feng Meng-lung and Late Ming Ethics and Aesthetics." Ph.D. diss., University of Minnesota, 1994.

Hu Shi (Hu Shih) 胡適. "A Chinese Declaration of the Rights of Women (The *Ching-hua yüan* of Li Ju-chen)." *Chinese Social and Political Science Review* 8, no. 2 (1924): 100–109.

———. *Dai Dongyuan de zhexue* 戴東原的哲學. Shanghai: Shangwu, 1932.

———. "*Ernü yingxiong zhuan* xu" 兒女英雄傳序. In idem, *Hu Shi wencun* (q.v.), 3: 497–513.

———. *Hu Shi wencun* 胡適文存. Taipei: Yuandong, 1969.

———. "*Jinghua yuan* de yinlun" 鏡花緣的引論. In *Hu Shi wencun* (q.v.), 2: 400–433.

———. "Yan Li xuepai de Cheng Tingzuo" 顏李學派的程廷祚. In *Hu Shi xuanji* 胡適選集, vol. 107, *Renwu* 人物, pp. 111–58. Taipei: Wenxing, 1966.

———. "*Xingshi yinyuan zhuan*" *kaozheng* 醒世姻緣傳考證. In *Hu Shi wencun* (q.v.), 4: 329–84.

Hu Yinglin 胡應麟. *Shaoshi shanfang bicong* 少室山房筆叢. Beijing: Zhonghua shuju, 1959.

Huang, Martin W. *Literati and Self-Re/Presentation: Autobiographical Sensibility in the Eighteenth-Century Novel*. Stanford: Stanford University Press, 1995.

Huang Qifang 黃啓方. "*Shuihu zhuan* de zhongyao nüxing" 水滸傳的重要女性. In *Zhongguo gudian wenxue yanjiu congkan* 中國古典文學研究叢刊, ed. Ke Qingming 柯慶明 and Lin Mingde 林明德, pp. 49–87. Taipei: Juliu, 1977.

Huang, Ray. *1587: A Year of No Significance*. New Haven: Yale University Press, 1981.

Huang Zongxi 黃宗羲. *Mingru xue'an* 明儒學案. Taipei: Shijie shuju, 1961.

Hucker, Charles O. "The Tung-lin Movement of the Late Ming Period." In *Chinese Thought and Institutions*, ed. John K. Fairbank, pp. 132–62. Chicago: University of Chicago Press, 1957.

Hummel, Arthur W., ed. *Eminent Chinese of the Ch'ing Period*. 2 vols. Washington, D.C.: U.S. Government Printing Agency, 1943.

Hung Ming-shui. "Yüan Hung-tao and the Late Ming Literary and Intellectual Movement." Ph.D. diss., University of Wisconsin, 1974.

Idema, Wilt L. "Cannon, Clocks and Clever Monkeys: Europeana, Europeans and Europe in Some Eighteenth Century Chinese Novels." In *White and Black: Imagination and Cultural Confrontations*, ed. M. Schipper, W. L. Idema, and H. M. Leyton, pp. 55–81. Amsterdam: Royal Tropical Institute, 1990.

———. "The Mystery of the Halved Judge Dee Novel: The Anonymous *Wu-tse-t'ien ssu-ta ch'i-an* and Its Partial Translation by R. H. van Gulik." *Tamkang Review* 8 (1977): 155–70.

Jingju jumu cidian 京劇劇目詞典. Beijing: Zhongguo xiju chubanshe, 1989.

Jin Ping Mei cihua 金瓶梅詞話. Hong Kong: Wenhai chubanshe, 1963.

Kao, Hsin-sheng C. *Li Ju-chen*. Boston: Twayne Publishers, 1981.

Kao, Karl S.Y., ed. *Classical Chinese Tales of the Supernatural and the Fantastic*. Bloomington: Indiana University Press, 1985.

Kao Yu-kung. "The Lyric Vision in Chinese Narrative Tradition: A Reading of *Hung-lou meng* and *Ju-lin wai-shih*." In *Chinese Narrative*, pp. 227–65.

Kelleher, Theresa M. "Back to Basics: Chu Hsi's *Elementary Learning* (*Hsiao-hsüeh*)." In *Neo-Confucian Education*, pp. 219–51.

Ko, Dorothy. *Teachers of the Inner Chambers: Women and Culture in Seventeenth-Century China*. Stanford: Stanford University Press, 1994.

Kuhn, Philip A. *Soulstealers: The Chinese Sorcery Scare of 1768*. Cambridge, Mass.: Harvard University Press, 1990.

Kuriyama, Joanna Ching-yuan Wu. "Confucianism in Fiction: A Study of Hsia Ching-chü's *Yeh-sou p'u-yen*." Ph.D. diss., Harvard University, 1993.

Kutcher, Norman A. *Mourning in Late Imperial China: Filial Piety and the State*. Cambridge, Eng.: Cambridge University Press, 1999.

Laqueur, Thomas. *Making Sex*. Cambridge, Mass.: Harvard University Press, 1990.

Lau, D. C. trans. *The Analects*. Harmondsworth, Eng.: Penguin, 1979.

———. *Mencius*. Harmondsworth, Eng.: Penguin, 1970.

Lau Wing-Chung, Clara. "A Study of the Concepts of Women's 'Talent' and 'Virtue' During the Early and High Ch'ing Periods." M.A. Phil. thesis, Hong Kong University, 1987.

Legge, James, trans. *The Chinese Classics*. 5 vols. Oxford University Press, 1865–95. Reprinted—Hong Kong: Hong Kong University Press, 1961.

———. *Li Chi, Book of Rites*. 2 vols. Sacred Books of the East. Oxford: Oxford University Press, 1885. Reprinted—New York: University Books, 1967.

Lévy, André. "About the Date of the First Printed Edition of the *Chin P'ing Mei*." *CLEAR* 1, no. 1 (1979): 43–47.

——— *Le conte en langue vulgaire du XVIIe siècle*. Paris: Biblioteque de l'Institut des hautes études chinoises, vol. 25, 1981.

——— "Un document sur la querelle des anciens et des modernes *more sinico*." *TP* 54 (1969): 251–74.

——— "Pour une clarification de quelques aspects de la problematique du *Jin Ping Mei*." *TP* 66, no. 4/5 (1980): 183–98.

Lévy, Jean. "Le renarde, la morte et la courtisane dans la Chine classique." *Etudes mongoles* 15 (1984): 111–39.

Li ji 禮記. In *Shisan jing* 十三經. Shanghai: Kaiming shudian, 1935.

Li Ruzhen 李汝珍. *Huitu Jinghua yuan* 繪圖鏡花緣. Facsimile reprint of the 1888 illustrated Shanghai Dianshi zhai 點石齋 ed. Beijing: Zhonghua shudian, 1985.

Li, Wai-yee. *Enchantment and Disenchantment: Love and Illusion in Chinese Literature*. Princeton: Princeton University Press, 1993.

———."The Late Ming Courtesan: Invention of a Cultural Ideal." In *Writing Women in Late Imperial China*, ed. Ellen Widmer and Kang-i Sun Chang, pp. 46–73. Stanford: Stanford University Press, 1997.

Li Yu (Li Yü) 李漁. *Li Yu quanji* 李漁全集. Hangzhou: Zhejiang guji chubanshe, 1991.

———. *Silent Operas*. Ed. Patrick Hanan. Hong Kong: Renditions, 1990.

———. *Wusheng xi* 無聲戲. Ed. Helmut Martin. Reprint of edition held in the Sonkeikaku Library. Taipei: Zhengwen chubanshe, 1970.

Li Zhi 李贄. *Cangshu* 藏書. Beijing: Zhonghua shuju, 1974.

———. *Lishi fenshu, Xu fenshu* 李氏焚書續焚書. Kyoto: Zhongwen chubanshe, 1971.

———. *Xu cangshu* 續藏書. Beijing: Zhonghua shuju, 1962.

Lienü yanyi 列女演義. Microfilm of late Ming edition in the Rare Books Room of the Taipei Central Library.

Lin Shuen-fu. "Ritual and Narrative Structure in *Ju-lin wai-shih*." In *Chinese Narrative*, pp. 244–65.

Lin Shuen-fu and Larry Schulz, trans. *The Tower of Myriad Mirrors*. Berkeley: Asian Humanities Press, 1978.

Lin Tai-yi, trans. *Flowers in the Mirror*. Berkeley: University of California Press, 1965.

Liu, James J. Y. *The Chinese Knight-Errant*. London: Routledge and Kegan Paul, 1967.

———. *Chinese Theories of Literature*. Chicago: University of Chicago Press, 1975.

Liu Ts'un-yan. *Buddhist and Taoist Influences on Chinese Novels*. Wiesbaden: Otto Harrassowitz, 1962.

———. *Chinese Popular Fiction in Two London Libraries*. Hong Kong: Lung-men, 1967.

———. "Introduction: 'Middlebrow' in Perspective." *Renditions* 17–18 (1982): 1–40.

Liu Xie 劉勰. *Wenxin diaolong zhu* 文心雕龍注. Annot. Fan Wenlan 范文蘭. Hongkong: Shangwu, 1960.

Lo, Andrew Hing-bun. "*San-kuo yen-i* and the *Shui-hu chuan* in the Context of Historiography: An Interpretive Study." Ph.D. diss., Princeton University, 1981.

Lu Kan 路侃. "Shi lun Mingdai wenyi lilun zhong de 'zhuqing' shuo" 試論明代文藝理論中的"主情"說. *Wenxue lunji* 文學論集 7 (1984): 165–180

Lu, Sheldon Hsiao-peng. *From Historicity to Fictionality: The Chinese Poetics of Narrative*. Stanford: Stanford University Press, 1994.

Lu Xun. *A Brief History of Chinese Fiction*. Trans. Hsien-yi and Gladys Yang. Beijing: Foreign Languages Press, 1959.

Lü Kun 呂坤. *Guifan tushuo* 閨範圖說. Kangxi ed., ca. 1613.

———. *Shenyin yu* 呻吟語. Ed. Kōda Rentarō 公田連太朗. Tokyo: 1956.

Lunyü yinde 論語引得. Harvard-Yenching Institute Sinological Index Series. Taipei, 1966 reprint.

Lynn, Richard John. *The Classic of Changes: A New Translation of the "I Ching" as Interpreted by Wang Bi*. New York: Columbia University Press, 1994.

———. "Orthodoxy and Enlightenment: Wang Shih-chen's Theory of Poetry and Its Antecedents." In *Unfolding*, pp. 217–69.

———. "Tradition and the Individual: Ming and Ch'ing Views of Yüan Poetry." *Journal of Oriental Studies* 15, no. 1 (1977): 1–19.

Mann, Susan. "'Fuxue' (Women's Learning) by Zhang Xuecheng (1738–1801): China's First History of Women's Culture." *LIC* 13, no. 1 (1992): 40–62.

———. "Grooming a Daughter for Marriage: Brides and Wives in the Mid-Ch'ing Period." In *Marriage and Inequality in Chinese Society*, ed. Ruby Watson and Patricia Ebrey, pp. 204–30. Berkeley: University of California Press, 1991.

———. *Precious Records: Women in China's Long Eighteenth Century*. Stanford: Stanford University Press, 1997.

Martinson, Paul. "Pao, Order, and Redemption: Perspectives on Chinese Religion and Society Based on a Study of the *Chin P'ing Mei*." Ph.D. diss., University of Chicago, 1973.

Maspero, Henri. "Legendes mythologiques dans le *Chou King*." *Journal asiatique* 204 (1924): 11–100.

Mather, Richard B., trans. *Shih-shuo hsin-yü: A New Account of Tales of the World*. Minneapolis: University of Minnesota Press, 1976.

Mathieu, Rémi. "Aux origines de la femme-renarde en Chine." *Etudes mongoles* 15 (1984): 83–109.

———. *Etude sur la mythologie et l'ethnologie de la Chine ancienne*. 2 vols. Mémoires de l'Institut des hautes études chinoises, vol. 22. Paris: Collège de France: Institut des hautes études chinoises, 1983.

McMahon, R. Keith. "A Case for Confucian Sexuality: The Eighteenth-Century Novel *Yesou Puyan*." *LIC* 9, no. 2 (1988): 32–55.

———. *Causality and Containment in Seventeenth-Century Chinese Fiction*. Leiden: E. J. Brill, 1988.

———. "The Classic 'Beauty-Scholar' Romance and the Superiority of Women." In *Body, Subject and Power*, pp. 227–52.

———. "Eroticism in Late Ming, Early Qing Fiction: The Beauteous Realm and the Sexual Battlefield." *TP* 73 (1987): 217–64.

———. *Misers, Shrews, and Polygamists: Sexuality and Male-Female Relations in Eighteenth-Century Chinese Fiction*. Durham, N.C.: Duke University Press, 1995.

———. "Two Late Ming Vernacular Novels: *Chan zhen yishi* and *Chan zhen houshi*." *MS* 23 (1987): 21–47.

McMorran, Ian. "Wang Fu-chih and the Neo-Confucian Tradition." In *Unfolding*, pp. 413–67.

Mengzi yinde 孟子引得. Harvard-Yenching Institute Sinological Series. Taipei, 1966 reprint.

Miao Tianhua 繆天華. "*Ernü yingxiong zhuan* kaozheng" 兒女英雄傳考證. In Wen Kang 文康, *Ernü yingxiong zhuan* 兒女英雄傳, pp. 1–3. Taipei: Sanmin shuju, 1976.

Miyazaki, Ichisada. *China's Examination Hell: The Civil Service Examinations of Imperial China*. Trans. Conrad Schirokauer. New York: Weatherhill, 1976.

Monschein, Ylva. *Der Zauber der Fuchsfee: Entstehung und Wandel eines "Femme-fatale"—Motivs in der chinesischen Literatur*. Frankfurt: Haag und Herchen, 1988.

Morris, Andrew David. "Cultivating the National Body: A History of Physical Culture in Republican China." Ph.D. diss., University of California, San Diego, 1998.

Mote, Frederick W. "The Intellectual Climate in Eighteenth-Century China." *Chinese Painting Under the Qianlong Emperor: The Symposium Papers*, vol. 1, pp. 17–55. Tempe: Arizona State University, College of Fine Arts, School of Art, 1988.

———. *Intellectual Foundations of China*. New York: Knopf, 1971.

———. "The T'u-mu Incident." In *Chinese Ways of Warfare*, ed. Frank A. Kierman, Jr., pp. 243–72. Cambridge, Mass.: Harvard University Press, 1974.

Mote, Frederick W., and Denis Twitchett, eds. *The Cambridge History of China*, vol. 7, pt. I. *The Ming Dynasty, 1368–1644*. Cambridge, Eng.: Cambridge University Press, 1988.

Mowry, Hua-yuan Li. *Chinese Love Stories from Ch'ing-shih*. Hamden, Conn.: Anchor Books, 1983.

———. "*Ch'ing-shih* and Feng Meng-lung." Ph.D. diss., University of California, Berkeley, 1976.

Munro, Donald. *Images of Human Nature: A Sung Portrait*. Princeton: Princeton University Press, 1988.

Murray, Julia K. "Didactic Art for Women: The *Ladies' Classic of Filial Piety*." In *Flowering in the Shadows: Women in the History of Chinese and Japanese Painting*, ed. Marsha Weidner, pp. 27–53. Honolulu: University of Hawaii Press, 1990.

Naquin, Susan. *Shantung Rebellion: The Wang Lun Uprising of 1774*. New Haven: Yale University Press, 1981.

Naquin, Susan, and Evelyn S. Rawski, eds. *Chinese Society in the Eighteenth Century*. New Haven: Yale University Press, 1987.

Needham, Joseph. *Science and Civilisation in China*, vol. 2, *History of Scientific Thought*. Cambridge, Eng.: Cambridge University Press, 1956.

Ng, On-cho. "*Hsing* (Nature) as the Ontological Basis of Practicality in Early Ch'ing Ch'eng-Chu Confucianism: Li Kuang-ti's (1642–1718) Philosophy." *PEW* 44, no. 1 (1994): 79–109.

Nivison, David. *The Life and Thought of Chang Hsüeh-ch'eng*. Stanford: Stanford University Press, 1966.

Nü xiaojing 女孝經. Baibu congshu jicheng. n.d.

Ōba Osamu 大庭脩, ed. *Hakusai shomoku* 舶載書目. Fukita-shi: Kansai daigaku, Tozai gakujutsu kenkyūjo, 1972.

Ono Kazuko 小野和子. "*Kyōka en* no sekai: Shinchō kōshōgakusha no yutopia zō" 鏡花緣の世界：清朝考証学のユートピア象. *Shisō* 721 思想 (1984:7): pp. 40–55.

Ōta Tatsuo 太田辰夫 and Iida Yoshirō 飯田吉郎. *Chūgoku hiseki sōkan* 中國秘書叢刊. Tokyo: Kyūko shōin, 1987.

Ouyang Jian 歐陽健. "*Yesou puyan* banben bianxi" 野叟曝言版本辨析. *Ming Qing xiaoshuo yanjiu* 明清小說研究 1 (1988): 181–95.

Overmyer, Daniel L. *Precious Volumes: An Introduction to Chinese Sectarian Scriptures from the Sixteenth and Seventeenth Centuries*. Cambridge, Mass.: Harvard University Asia Center, 1999.

———. "Values in Chinese Sectarian Literature: Ming and Ch'ing *Pao-chuan*." In *Popular Culture in Late Imperial China*, ed. David Johnson, Andrew J. Nathan, and Evelyn S. Rawski, pp. 219–54. Berkely: University of California Press, 1985.

Owen, Stephen. *Traditional Chinese Poetry and Poetics: Omen of the World*. Madison: University of Wisconsin Press, 1989.

Peng Caizhu 彭彩珠. "Wen Kang yu *Ernü yingxiong zhuan*" 文康與兒女英雄傳. M.A. thesis, Wenhua University, Taiwan, 1986.

Perdue, Peter C. *Exhausting the Earth: State and Peasant in Hunan, 1500–1850*. Cambridge, Mass.: Harvard University, Council on East Asian Studies, 1987.

Peterson, Willard J. *Bitter Gourd: Fang I-chih and the Impetus for Intellectual Change*. New Haven: Yale University Press, 1979.

———. "Making Connections: Commentary on the Attached Verbalizations of the *Book of Changes*." *HJAS* 42 (1982): 67–116.

———. Review of Kwang-ching Liu, ed., *Orthodoxy in Late Imperial China*. *HJAS* 53, no. 1 (1994): 249–68.

Plaks, Andrew. H. "After the Fall: *Hsing-shih yin-yuan chuan* and the Seventeenth-Century Chinese Novel." *HJAS* 45 (1985): 543–80.

———. *Archetype and Allegory in the Dream of the Red Chamber*. Princeton: Princeton University Press, 1976.

———. *The Four Masterworks of the Ming Novel*. Princeton: Princeton University Press, 1987.

———. "Full-length *Hsiao-shuo* and the Western Novel: A Generic Reappraisal." *New Asia Academic Bulletin* 1 (1978): 163–76.

———. "The Problem of Incest in *Jin Ping Mei* and *Honglou meng*." In *Paradoxes of Traditional Chinese Literature*, ed. Eva Hung, pp. 123–46. Hong Kong: Chinese University Press, 1994.

———. "Terminology and Central Concepts." In *How to Read*, pp. 75–123.

Plaks, Andew H., trans. "[Zhang Xinzhi on] How To Read the *Dream of the Red Chamber*." In *How to Read*, pp. 323–40.

Pomeranz, Kenneth. "Power, Gender, and Pluralism in the Cult of the Goddess of Taishan." In *Culture and State in Chinese History: Conventions, Accommodations, and Critiques*, ed. Theodore Huters, R. Bin Wong, and Pauline Yu, pp. 182–204. Stanford: Stanford University Press, 1997.

Porter, Deborah. "Setting the Tone: Aesthetic Implications of Linguistic Patterns in the Opening Section of the *Shui-hu chuan*." *CLEAR* 14 (1992): 51–76.

Powers, Martin J. *Art and Political Expression in Early China*. New Haven: Yale University Press, 1991.

Pratt, Leonard, and Su-hui Chiang, trans. *Six Records of a Floating Life*. London: Penguin Books, 1983.

Pu Songling 蒲松齡. *Liaozhai zhiyi* 聊齋志異. Ed. Zhang Youhe 張友鶴. Shanghai: Guji chubanshe, 1978.

Rawski, Evelyn S. *Education and Popular Literacy in Ch'ing China*. Ann Arbor: University of Michigan Press, 1979.

Rickett, Allyn W. *Guanzi*. Princeton: Princeton University Press, 1985.

Robertson, Maureen. "Voicing the Feminine: Constructions of the Gendered Subject in Lyric Poetry by Women of Medieval and Late Imperial China." *LIC* 13, no. 1 (1992): 63–110.

Roddy, Stephen J. *Literati Identity and Its Fictional Representations in Late Imperial China*. Stanford: Stanford University Press, 1998.

Rolston, David. *Traditional Chinese Fiction and Fiction Commentary: Reading and Writing Between the Lines*. Stanford: Stanford University Press, 1997.

Rolston, David, ed. *How To Read the Chinese Novel*. Princeton: Princeton University Press, 1990.

Ropp, Paul S. *Dissent in Early Modern China: "Ju-lin wai-shih" and Ch'ing Social Criticism*. Ann Arbor: University of Michigan Press, 1981.

———. "The Seeds of Change: Reflections on the Condition of Women in the Early and Mid-Ch'ing." *Signs* 2 (1976): 5–23.

Rou putuan 肉蒲團. Hong Kong: Lianhe, n.d.

Rowe, William T. "Women and the Family in Mid-Qing Social Thought: The Case of Chen Hongmou." *LIC* 13, no. 2 (1992): 1–41.

Roy, David, T. "Chang Chu-p'o's Commentary on the *Chin P'ing Mei*." In *Chinese Narrative*, pp. 115–23.

———. "Translator's Commentary." *Renditions* 24 (1985): 18–24.

Roy, David T., trans. "[Zhang Zhupo on] How to Read the *Chin P'ing Mei*." In *How to Read*, pp. 202–43.

———. "[Mao Zonggang on] How to Read *The Romance of the Three Kingdoms*." In *How to Read*, pp. 152–95.

———. *The Plum in the Golden Vase, or Chin P'ing Mei*, vol. 1. Princeton: Princeton University Press, 1993.

Ruyi jun zhuan 如意君傳. Reprint of edition held in the Tokyo Tōyō bunka kenkyūjo. N.p., n.d.

Sakai, Tadao. "Confucianism and Popular Educational Works." In *Self and Society*, pp. 331–66.

Sang Tze-lan, Deborah. "The Emerging Lesbian: Female Same-Sex Desire in Modern Chinese Literature and Culture." Ph.D. diss., University of California, Berkeley, 1996.

Sangren, Steven P. *History and Magical Power in a Chinese Community*. Stanford: Stanford University Press, 1987.

———. "Orthodoxy, Heterodoxy, and the Structure of Value in Chinese Rituals." *Modern China* 13, no. 1 (1987): 63–89.

Saussy, Haun. "Reading and Folly in *Dream of the Red Chamber*." *CLEAR* 9, no. 1/2 (1987): 23–47.

Schutskii, Iulian K. *Researches on the I Ching*. Trans. William L. MacDonald. Princeton: Princeton University Press, 1979.

Scott, Mary E. "Azure from Indigo: *Hong Lou Meng*'s Debt to *Jin Ping Mei*." Ph.D. diss., Princeton University, 1989.

Seaman, Gary. "The Sexual Politics of Karmic Retribution." In *The Anthropology of Taiwanese Society*, ed. E. M. Ahern and Hill Gates, pp. 383–96. Stanford: Stanford University Press, 1974.

Shen Fu 沈復. *Fusheng liu ji* 浮生六記. Taipei: Jinfeng, 1986.

Shih, Vincent Yu-chung, trans. *The Literary Mind and the Carving of Dragons*. Taipei: Zhonghua shuju, 1960.

Shisan jing 十三經. Shanghai: Kaiming shudian, 1935.

Sieber, Patricia. "Corporeality and Canonicity: A Study of Technologies of Reading in Early Modern *Zaju* Drama." *Graven Images* 2 (1995): 171–82.

Sishu jizhu 四書集注. Taipei: Shijie, 1968.

Soulliere, E. F. "Palace Women in the Ming Dynasty." Ph.D. diss., Princeton University, 1987.

Spence, Jonathan D., and John E. Wills, eds. *From Ming to Ch'ing: Conquest, Region, and Continuity in Seventeenth-Century China*. New Haven: Yale University Press, 1979.

Struve, Lynn. *Voices from the Ming Cataclysm: China in Tiger's Jaws*. New Haven: Yale University Press, 1993.

Su Shufang 蘇淑芳. "*Jinghua yuan* yanjiu" 鏡花緣研究. M.A. thesis, Dongwu University, Taiwan, 1978.

Sui Tang yanyi 隋唐演義. Taipei: Shijie shuju, 1962.

Sun Jiaxun 孫佳迅. *"Jinghua yuan" gong'an bianyi* 鏡花緣公安辨疑. Ji'nan: Qi Lu shushe, 1984.

Sun Kaidi 孫楷第. "Xia Erming yu *Yesou puyan*" 夏二銘與野叟曝言. In idem, *Cangzhou houji* 滄州後集. Beijing: Zhonghua shuju, 1985.

———. *Zhongguo tongsu xiaoshuo shumu* 中國通俗小說書目. Taipei: Fenghuang chuban she, 1974.

Tain Tzuey-yueh. "Tung Chung-shu's System of Thought: Its Sources and Influences on Han Scholars." Ph.D. diss, UCLA, 1974.

Tang Xianzu 湯顯祖. *Mudan ting* 牡丹亭. Ed. Xu Shuofang 徐朔方 and Yang Xiaomei 楊笑梅. Taipei: Liren shuju, 1986.

T'ien Ju-k'ang. *Male Anxiety and Female Chastity: A Comparative Study of Chinese Ethical Values in Ming-Ch'ing Times.* T'oung Pao, monograph no. 14. Leiden: E. J. Brill, 1988.

Tu Ching-i. "The Chinese Examination Essay: Some Literary Considerations." *Monumentica Serica* 31 (1977): 393–406.

Tu Wei-ming. *Neo-Confucian Thought in Action: Wang Yang-ming's Youth (1471–1509).* Berkeley: University of California Press, 1976.

———. "Yen Yuan: From Inner Experience to Lived Concreteness." In *Unfolding,* pp. 511–44.

Twitchett, Denis C. "Chinese Biographical Writing." In *Historians of Japan and China,* ed. E. G. Pulleyblank and W. G. Beasely, pp. 95–114. London: SOAS, 1961.

———. "Problems of Chinese Biography." In *Confucian Personalities,* ed. Arthur Wright, pp. 24–39. Stanford: Stanford University Press, 1962.

Vallette-Hémery, Martine. *Yuan Hongtao: théorie et practique littéraires.* Paris: Presses Universitaires, 1982.

Vinograd, Richard. *Boundaries of the Self: Chinese Portraits, 1600–1900.* New York: Cambridge University Press, 1992.

Volpp, Sophie. "The Discourse on Male Marriage: Li Yu's 'A Male Mencius' Mother.'" *Positions* 2, no. 1 (1994): 113–32.

———. "The Male Queen: Boy Actors and Literati Libertines." Ph.D. diss., Harvard University, 1995.

Wakeman, Frederic, Jr. *The Great Enterprise: The Manchu Reconstruction of Imperial Order in Seventeenth-Century China.* Berkeley: University of California Press, 1985.

Wang Anshi 王安石. *Wang Linchuan quanji* 王臨川全集. Taipei: Shijie shuju, 1961.

Wang Chi-chen, trans. "*Marriage as Retribution.*" Trans. of selections from *Xingshi yinyuan zhuan. Renditions* 17–18 (1982): 41–94.

Wang Chong 王充 (27–ca. 100). *Lunheng jijie* 論衡集解. Ed. Yang Jialuo 楊家駱. Taipei: Shijie shuju, 1962.

Wang, David Der-wei. *Fin-de-siècle Splendor: Repressed Modernities of Late Qing Fiction, 1849–1911.* Stanford: Stanford University Press, 1997.

Wang Fuzhi 王夫之 (1619–92). *Chuanshan yishu* 船山遺書. Taiping yang edition, n.d.

Wang Guowei 王國維. "*Honglou meng* pinglun" 紅樓夢評論. In *HLMJ,* pp. 244–65.

Wang Hailin 王海林. *Zhongguo wuxia xiaoshuo shilüe* 中國武俠小說史略. Taiyuan: Beiyue chubanshe, 1988.

Wang Jide 王驥德. *Qulü* 曲律. Hunan: Renmin chubanshe, 1983.

Wang Jiwen 王季文. "*Jinghua yuan* shenhua guo du yanjiu" 鏡花緣神話國度研究. M.A. thesis, Furen University, Taiwan, 1979.

Wang, John C. Y. "The Chih-yen-chai Commentary and the *Dream of the Red Chamber*: A Literary Study." In *Chinese Approaches*, pp. 189–220.

Wang, John C. Y., trans. "[Jin Shengtan on] How to Read the *Fifth Book of Genius*." In *How to Read*, pp. 131–45.

Wang Liqi 王利器. *Yuan Ming Qing, sandai jinhui xiaoshuo xiqu shiliao* 元明清三代禁毀小說戲曲史料. Rev. ed. Shanghai: Shanghai guji, 1981.

Wang Qiongling 王瓊玲. *Qingdai sida caixue xiaoshuo* 清代四大才學小說. Taipei: Shangwu yinshuguan, 1997.

———. "*Yesou puyan* yanjiu" 野叟曝言研究. M.A. thesis, Dongwu University, Taiwan, 1986.

Wang Rumei 王汝梅. "Zhang pingben dui Cao Xueqin chuangzuo de yingxiang" 張評本對曹雪芹創造的影響. In idem, "*Jin Ping Mei*" *tansuo* 金瓶梅探索, pp. 83–85. Changchun: Jilin daxue, 1990.

Wang Rumei 王汝梅, Li Zhaoxun 李昭恂, and Yu Fengshu 于鳳樹, eds. *Zhang Zhupo piping Jin Ping Mei* 張竹坡批評金瓶梅. Ji'nan: Qi Lu shushe, 1991.

Wang Shouyi 王守義. "*Xingshi yinyuan zhuan* de chengshu niandai" 醒世姻緣傳的成書年代. *Guangming ribao* 光明日報, May 28, 1961.

Wang Shumin 王叔岷. *Zhuangzi jiaoquan* 莊子校詮. Taipei: Zhongyang yanjiu yu lishi yanjiusuo, 1988.

Watson, James L. "Of Flesh and Bones: The Management of Death Pollution in Cantonese Society." In *Death and the Regeneration of Life*, ed. Maurice Bloch and Jonathan Parry, pp. 155–86. Cambridge, Eng.: Cambridge University Press, 1982.

———."The Structure of Chinese Funerary Rites: Elementary Forms, Ritual Sequence, and the Primacy of Performance." In *Death Ritual in Late Imperial and Modern China*, ed. idem and Evelyn Rawski, pp. 3–19. Berkeley: University of California Press, 1990.

Watson, Rubie, and Patricia Ebrey, eds. *Marriage and Inequality in Chinese Society*. Berkeley: University of California Press, 1991.

Wen Kang 文康. *Huandu woshu shi zhuren ping Ernü yingxiong zhuan* 還讀我書室主人評兒女英雄傳. Ed. Er Gong 爾弓. Ji'nan: Qilu shushe, 1989.

Widmer, Ellen. "The Epistolary World of Female Talent in Seventeenth-Century China." *LIC* 10, no. 2 (1989): 1–43.

———. *The Margins of Utopia: "Shui-hu hou-chuan" and the Literature of Ming Loyalists*. Cambridge, Mass.: Harvard University, Council on East Asian Studies, 1987.

———. "Xiaoqing's Literary Legacy and the Place of the Woman Writer in Late Imperial China." *LIC* 13, no. 1 (1992): 111–55.

Widmer, Ellen, and K'ang-i Sun Chang, eds. *Writing Women in Late Imperial China.* Stanford: Stanford University Press, 1997.

Wilhelm, Richard W. *Change: Eight Lectures on the "I Ching."* Trans. Cary F. Baynes. Princeton: Princeton University Press, 1973.

Will, Pierre-Etienne. "Un cycle hydraulique en Chine: la province du Hubei du 16ième au 19ième siècles." *Bulletin de l'Ecole française d'Extrême Orient* 68 (1980): 261–87.

Wittfogel, Karl. *Oriental Despotism.* New Haven: Yale University Press, 1957.

Wong Siu-kit. "*Ch'ing* in Chinese Literature." Ph.D. diss., Oxford University, 1967.

———. "*Ch'ing* and *Ching* in the Critical Writings of Wang Fu-chih." In *Chinese Approaches,* pp. 121–50.

Wong, Timothy. *Wu Ching-tzu.* Boston: Twayne Publishers, 1978.

Wu Jingzi 吳敬梓. *Rulin waishi* 儒林外事. Taipei: Heluo tushu, 1981.

Wu, Pei-yi. *The Confucian's Progress: Autobiographical Writings in Traditional China.* Princeton: Princeton University Press, 1990.

———. "Education of Children in the Sung." In *Neo-Confucian Education,* pp. 307–24.

———. "The White Snake: The Evolution of a Myth in China." Ph.D. diss., Columbia University, 1969.

Wu Qingyun. *Female Rule in Chinese and English Literary Utopias.* Syracuse: Syracuse University Press, 1995.

Wu Shih-ch'ang (Wu Shichang) 吳世昌. *"Honglou meng" tanyuan waibian* 紅樓夢探源外編. Shanghai: Guji chubanshe, 1980.

———. *On the Red Chamber Dream.* Oxford: Clarendon Press, 1961.

Wu, Yenna. *The Chinese Virago: A Literary Theme.* Cambridge, Mass.: Harvard University, Council on East Asian Studies, 1995.

———. "The Inversion of Marital Hierarchy: Shrewish Wives and Henpecked Husbands in Seventeenth-Century Chinese Literature." *HJAS* 48, no. 2 (1988): 363–82

———."Marriage Destinies to Awaken the World: A Literary Study of *Xingshi yinyuan zhuan.*" Ph.D. diss., Harvard University, 1986.

Xia Jingqu 夏敬渠. *Yesou puyan* 野叟曝言. Facsimile reprint of 152–chapter 1881 Piling huizhenlou 毘陵彙珍樓 woodblock print ed. Taipei: Tianyi chubanshe, 1985.

———. *Yesou puyan* 野叟曝言. 154–chapter ed. Beijing: Renmin Zhongguo chubanshe, 1993. (154–chapter edition)

Xie Zhaozhe 謝肇淛. *Wu zazu* 五雜俎. Ca. 1600. Reprinted—Taibei: Xinxing shuju 1971.

Xingshi yinyuan zhuan 醒世姻緣傳. Facsimile reprint of Qing ed. Taipei: Tianyi chuban she, 1985.

Xingshi yinyuan zhuan 醒世姻緣傳. Beijing: Renmin Zhongguo chubanshe, 1993.

Xinke xiuxiang piping Jin Ping Mei 新刻繡像批評金瓶梅. Hong Kong: Xianglian shudian, 1990.

Xu Shuofang 徐朔方. "*Honglou meng* he *Jin Ping Mei*" 紅樓夢和金瓶梅. *Honglou meng yanjiu jikan* 紅樓夢研究集刊, 7th series (1981): 143–62.

———. *Lun Tang Xianzu ji qita* 論湯顯祖及其他. Shanghai: Shanghai guji, 1983.

Xu Xialing 徐夏岭. "*Xingshi yinyuan zhuan*" *zuozhe he yuyan kaolun* 醒世姻緣傳作者和語言考論. Ji'nan: Qilu shushe, 1993.

Xunzi yinde 荀子引得. Taipei: Chinese Materials and Research Aids Service Center, 1966.

Yan Yuan 顏元. *Yan Yuan ji* 顏元集. Beijing: Zhonghua shuju, 1987.

Yang Jialuo 楊家駱, ed. *Lunheng jijie* 論衡集解. Taipei: Shijie shuju, 1962.

Yao Mingda 姚名達. *Cheng Yichuan nianpu* 程伊川年譜. Shanghai: Shangwu yinshu guan, 1937.

Yee, Angelina. "Counterpoise in *Honglou meng*." *HJAS* 50 (1990): 613–50.

———. "Self, Sexuality, and Writing in *Honglou meng*." *HJAS* 55 (1995): 373–407.

Yen, Alsace. "*Shang-ssu* Festival and Its Myths in China and Japan." *Asian Folklore Studies* 34, no. 2 (1975): 45–86.

Ying Bicheng 應必城. "*Honglou meng* yu *Ernü yingxiong zhuan*" 紅樓夢與兒女英雄傳. In *Cao Xueqin*, pp. 100–121.

Yisu 一粟, ed. "*Honglou meng*" *juan* 紅樓夢卷. Shanghai: Zhonghua shuju, 1963.

———. "*Honglou meng*" *shulu* 紅樓夢書錄. Shanghai: Shanghai guji, 1981.

You Xinxiong 尤信雄. "*Jinghua yuan* de zhuzhi ji qi chengjiu" 鏡花緣的主旨及其成就. *Li Ruzhen yanjiu ziliao* 李汝珍研究資料, ed. Zhu Chuanyu 朱傳譽, pp. 31–33. Taipei: Tianyi chubanshe, 1981.

Yu, Anthony, C. *Rereading the Stone: Desire and the Making of Fiction in Dream of the Red Chamber*. Princeton: Princeton University Press, 1997.

Yu, Anthony, C. trans. "[Liu Yiming on] How to Read *The Original Intent of the Journey to the West*." In *How to Read*, pp. 299–315.

———. trans. *The Journey to the West*. 4 vols. Chicago: University of Chicago Press, 1977–83.

Yu, Pauline. *The Reading of Imagery in the Chinese Poetic Tradition*. Princeton: Princeton University Press, 1987.

Yu Pingbo 俞平伯. "*Honglou meng*" *yanjiu* 紅樓夢研究. Hong Kong: Tangdi chubanshe, 1953.

———. "Yingyin *Zhiyan Zhai chongping Shitou ji* shiliu hui houji" 影印脂硯齋重評石頭記十六回後記. *Zhonghua wenshi luncong* 中華文史論叢 (1962): 314–317.

Yu Yingshi 余英時 (Yü Ying-shih). "Cao Xueqin de Hanzu rentonggan bulun" 曹學芹的漢族認同感補論. In idem, *"Honglou meng" de liangge shijie* (q.v.), pp. 197–210.

———. "Cong Song Ming ru lixue de fazhan lun Qingdai sixiang shi" 從宋明儒理學發展論清代思想史. *Zhongguo xueren* 中國學人 (1970): 19–41.

———. *"Honglou meng" de liangge shijie* 紅樓夢的兩個世界. Taipei: Lianjing chuban she, 1978.

———. "Individualism and the Neo-Taoist Movement in Wei-Chin China." In *Individualism and Holism: Studies in Confucian and Daoist Values*, ed. Donald J. Munro, pp. 121–55. Ann Arbor: University of Michigan, Center for Chinese Studies, 1985.

———. "The Intellectual World of Chiao Hung Revisited." *MS* 25 (Spring 1988): 24–66.

——— *Lun Dai Zhen yu Zhang Xuecheng—Qingdai zhongqi xueshu sixiangshi yanjiu* 論戴震與章學誠—清代中期學術思想史研究. Hong Kong: Longmen, 1976.

———. *Shi yu Zhongguo wenhua* 士與中國文化. Shanghai: Shanghai renmin chubanshe, 1987.

———. "Some Preliminary Observations on the Rise of Ch'ing Confucian Intellectualism." *Tsing-hua Journal of Chinese Studies*, n.s. 11, no. 2 (1975): 105–46.

Yu Zhengxie 俞正燮 (1775–1840). *Guisi leigao* 癸巳類稿. Taipei: Shijie shuju, 1960.

Yuan Hongdao 袁宏道. *Yuan Zhonglang quanji* 袁中郎全集. Taipei: Shijie shuju, 1964.

Yuan Mei 袁枚. *Xiaocang shan fang chidu* 小倉山房尺牘. Hong Kong: Baixin tushu wenju gongsi, 1959.

———. *Xiaocang shan fang wenji* 小倉山房文集. 1850.

———. *Zi bu yu quanji* 子不語全集. Hebei: Hebei renmin chubanshe, 1987.

Yuan Tsing. "Urban Riots and Disturbances." In *From Ming to Ch'ing: Conquest, Region, and Continuity in Seventeenth-Century China*, ed. Jonathan D. Spence and John E. Wills, pp. 279–320. New Haven: Yale University Press, 1993.

Yuanzhu guben Yesou puyan 原著古本野叟曝言. Shanghai: Hao qingnian shudian, 1933.

Yue Hengjun 樂蘅軍. "Penglai guixi—Lun *Jinghua yuan* de shijie guan" 蓬萊詭戲—論鏡花緣的世界觀. In idem, *Gudian xiaoshuo sanlun* 古典小說散論. Taipei: Chun wenxue chuban she, 1976, pp. 167–86.

Zeitlin, Judith T. *Historian of the Strange: Pu Songling and the Chinese Classical Tale*. Stanford: Stanford University Press, 1993.

———. "Shared Dreams: The Story of the Three Wives Commentary on *The Peony Pavilion*." *HJAS* 54 (1994): 127–79.

Zhang Qingji 張清吉. *"Xingshi yinyuan zhuan" xinkao* 醒世姻緣傳新考. Zhengzhou: Zhengzhou guji chubanshe, 1991.

Zhang Zai 張載. *Zhang Zai ji* 張載集. Beijing: Zhonghua shuju, 1978.

Zhao Jingshen 趙景沆. "*Yesou puyan* yu Xiashi zongpu" 野叟曝言與夏氏宗譜. In idem, *Zhongguo xiaoshuo congkao* 中國小說叢考, pp. 433–47. Ji'nan: Qilu shushe, 1980.

Zhou Kangxie 周康燮. *Yan Li xuepai yanjiu congbian* 顏李學派研究叢編. Hong Kong: Datong shuju, 1978.

Zhou Ruchang 周汝昌. *"Honglou meng" xinzheng* 紅樓夢新證. Beijing: Renmin wenxue chubanshe, 1976.

———. "*Honglou meng* yu qing wenhua" 紅樓夢與情文化. *HLMXK* 1993, no. 1: 67–78.

———. *"Honglou meng" yu Zhonghua wenhua* 紅樓夢與中華文化. Taipei: Dongda, 1989.

———. "*Honglou meng* yuanben shi duoshao hui?" 紅樓夢原本是多少回？In *Honglou meng ziliao ji* 紅樓夢資料集, 2: 168–73. Hong Kong: Zhongguo xueshu ziliao, 1983.

Zhou Zuoren 周作人. *Zhou Zuoren wenxuan* 周作人文選. Taipei: Hongfan, 1983.

Zhu Xi 朱熹. *Zhuzi yulei* 朱子語類. Ed. Li Jingde 黎靖德. Beijing: Zhonghua shuju, 1986.

Zhu Xi 朱熹 and Lü Zuqian 律祖謙. *Jinsi lu jizhu* 近思錄集注. Siku shanben congshu ed.

Zhu Yanjing 朱燕靜. "*Xingshi yinyuan zhuan* yanjiu" 醒世姻緣傳研究. M.A. thesis, Taiwan Normal University, Taipei, 1978.

Zito, Angela. *Of Body and Brush: Grand Sacrifice as Text/Performance in Eighteenth-Century China*. Chicago: University of Chicago Press, 1997.

———. "Ritualizing *Li*: Implications for Studying Power and Gender." *Positions* 1, no. 2 (1993): 321–48.

———. "Silk and Skin: Significant Boundaries." In *Body, Subject and Power*, pp. 103–30.

Index

Harvard East Asian Monographs
(* out-of-print)

*1. Liang Fang-chung, *The Single-Whip Method of Taxation in China*
*2. Harold C. Hinton, *The Grain Tribute System of China, 1845–1911*
3. Ellsworth C. Carlson, *The Kaiping Mines, 1877–1912*
*4. Chao Kuo-chün, *Agrarian Policies of Mainland China: A Documentary Study, 1949–1956*
*5. Edgar Snow, *Random Notes on Red China, 1936–1945*
*6. Edwin George Beal, Jr., *The Origin of Likin, 1835–1864*
7. Chao Kuo-chün, *Economic Planning and Organization in Mainland China: A Documentary Study, 1949–1957*
*8. John K. Fairbank, *Ching Documents: An Introductory Syllabus*
*9. Helen Yin and Yi-chang Yin, *Economic Statistics of Mainland China, 1949–1957*
*10. Wolfgang Franke, *The Reform and Abolition of the Traditional Chinese Examination System*
11. Albert Feuerwerker and S. Cheng, *Chinese Communist Studies of Modern Chinese History*
12. C. John Stanley, *Late Ching Finance: Hu Kuang-yung as an Innovator*
13. S. M. Meng, *The Tsungli Yamen: Its Organization and Functions*
*14. Ssu-yü Teng, *Historiography of the Taiping Rebellion*
15. Chun-Jo Liu, *Controversies in Modern Chinese Intellectual History: An Analytic Bibliography of Periodical Articles, Mainly of the May Fourth and Post–May Fourth Era*
*16. Edward J. M. Rhoads, *The Chinese Red Army, 1927–1963: An Annotated Bibliography*
17. Andrew J. Nathan, *A History of the China International Famine Relief Commission*
*18. Frank H. H. King (ed.) and Prescott Clarke, *A Research Guide to China-Coast Newspapers, 1822–1911*
19. Ellis Joffe, *Party and Army: Professionalism and Political Control in the Chinese Officer Corps, 1949–1964*
*20. Toshio G. Tsukahira, *Feudal Control in Tokugawa Japan: The Sankin Kōtai System*
21. Kwang-Ching Liu, ed., *American Missionaries in China: Papers from Harvard Seminars*
22. George Moseley, *A Sino-Soviet Cultural Frontier: The Ili Kazakh Autonomous Chou*
23. Carl F. Nathan, *Plague Prevention and Politics in Manchuria, 1910–1931*

*24. Adrian Arthur Bennett, *John Fryer: The Introduction of Western Science and Technology into Nineteenth-Century China*
25. Donald J. Friedman, *The Road from Isolation: The Campaign of the American Committee for Non-Participation in Japanese Aggression, 1938–1941*
26. Edward LeFevour, *Western Enterprise in Late Ching China: A Selective Survey of Jardine, Matheson and Company's Operations, 1842–1895*
27. Charles Neuhauser, *Third World Politics: China and the Afro-Asian People's Solidarity Organization, 1957–1967*
28. Kungtu C. Sun, assisted by Ralph W. Huenemann, *The Economic Development of Manchuria in the First Half of the Twentieth Century*
*29. Shahid Javed Burki, *A Study of Chinese Communes, 1965*
30. John Carter Vincent, *The Extraterritorial System in China: Final Phase*
31. Madeleine Chi, *China Diplomacy, 1914–1918*
*32. Clifton Jackson Phillips, *Protestant America and the Pagan World: The First Half Century of the American Board of Commissioners for Foreign Missions, 1810–1860*
33. James Pusey, *Wu Han: Attacking the Present through the Past*
34. Ying-wan Cheng, *Postal Communication in China and Its Modernization, 1860–1896*
35. Tuvia Blumenthal, *Saving in Postwar Japan*
36. Peter Frost, *The Bakumatsu Currency Crisis*
37. Stephen C. Lockwood, *Augustine Heard and Company, 1858–1862*
38. Robert R. Campbell, *James Duncan Campbell: A Memoir by His Son*
39. Jerome Alan Cohen, ed., *The Dynamics of China's Foreign Relations*
40. V. V. Vishnyakova-Akimova, *Two Years in Revolutionary China, 1925–1927*, tr. Steven L. Levine
*41. Meron Medzini, *French Policy in Japan during the Closing Years of the Tokugawa Regime*
42. Ezra Vogel, Margie Sargent, Vivienne B. Shue, Thomas Jay Mathews, and Deborah S. Davis, *The Cultural Revolution in the Provinces*
*43. Sidney A. Forsythe, *An American Missionary Community in China, 1895–1905*
*44. Benjamin I. Schwartz, ed., *Reflections on the May Fourth Movement.: A Symposium*
*45. Ching Young Choe, *The Rule of the Taewŏngun, 1864–1873: Restoration in Yi Korea*
46. W. P. J. Hall, *A Bibliographical Guide to Japanese Research on the Chinese Economy, 1958–1970*
47. Jack J. Gerson, *Horatio Nelson Lay and Sino-British Relations, 1854–1864*
48. Paul Richard Bohr, *Famine and the Missionary: Timothy Richard as Relief Administrator and Advocate of National Reform*
49. Endymion Wilkinson, *The History of Imperial China: A Research Guide*
50. Britten Dean, *China and Great Britain: The Diplomacy of Commercial Relations, 1860–1864*
51. Ellsworth C. Carlson, *The Foochow Missionaries, 1847–1880*
52. Yeh-chien Wang, *An Estimate of the Land-Tax Collection in China, 1753 and 1908*
53. Richard M. Pfeffer, *Understanding Business Contracts in China, 1949–1963*
54. Han-sheng Chuan and Richard Kraus, *Mid-Ching Rice Markets and Trade: An Essay in Price History*

Harvard East Asian Monographs

55. Ranbir Vohra, *Lao She and the Chinese Revolution*
56. Liang-lin Hsiao, *China's Foreign Trade Statistics, 1864–1949*
*57. Lee-hsia Hsu Ting, *Government Control of the Press in Modern China, 1900–1949*
58. Edward W. Wagner, *The Literati Purges: Political Conflict in Early Yi Korea*
*59. Joungwon A. Kim, *Divided Korea: The Politics of Development, 1945–1972*
*60. Noriko Kamachi, John K. Fairbank, and Chūzō Ichiko, *Japanese Studies of Modern China Since 1953: A Bibliographical Guide to Historical and Social-Science Research on the Nineteenth and Twentieth Centuries, Supplementary Volume for 1953–1969*
61. Donald A. Gibbs and Yun-chen Li, *A Bibliography of Studies and Translations of Modern Chinese Literature, 1918–1942*
62. Robert H. Silin, *Leadership and Values: The Organization of Large-Scale Taiwanese Enterprises*
63. David Pong, *A Critical Guide to the Kwangtung Provincial Archives Deposited at the Public Record Office of London*
*64. Fred W. Drake, *China Charts the World: Hsu Chi-yü and His Geography of 1848*
*65. William A. Brown and Urgrunge Onon, translators and annotators, *History of the Mongolian People's Republic*
66. Edward L. Farmer, *Early Ming Government: The Evolution of Dual Capitals*
*67. Ralph C. Croizier, *Koxinga and Chinese Nationalism: History, Myth, and the Hero*
*68. William J. Tyler, tr., *The Psychological World of Natsume Sōseki*, by Doi Takeo
69. Eric Widmer, *The Russian Ecclesiastical Mission in Peking during the Eighteenth Century*
*70. Charlton M. Lewis, *Prologue to the Chinese Revolution: The Transformation of Ideas and Institutions in Hunan Province, 1891–1907*
71. Preston Torbert, *The Ching Imperial Household Department: A Study of Its Organization and Principal Functions, 1662–1796*
72. Paul A. Cohen and John E. Schrecker, eds., *Reform in Nineteenth-Century China*
73. Jon Sigurdson, *Rural Industrialism in China*
74. Kang Chao, *The Development of Cotton Textile Production in China*
75. Valentin Rabe, *The Home Base of American China Missions, 1880–1920*
*76. Sarasin Viraphol, *Tribute and Profit: Sino-Siamese Trade, 1652–1853*
77. Ch'i-ch'ing Hsiao, *The Military Establishment of the Yuan Dynasty*
78. Meishi Tsai, *Contemporary Chinese Novels and Short Stories, 1949–1974: An Annotated Bibliography*
*79. Wellington K. K. Chan, *Merchants, Mandarins and Modern Enterprise in Late Ching China*
80. Endymion Wilkinson, *Landlord and Labor in Late Imperial China: Case Studies from Shandong by Jing Su and Luo Lun*
*81. Barry Keenan, *The Dewey Experiment in China: Educational Reform and Political Power in the Early Republic*
*82. George A. Hayden, *Crime and Punishment in Medieval Chinese Drama: Three Judge Pao Plays*

*83. Sang-Chul Suh, *Growth and Structural Changes in the Korean Economy, 1910–1940*
84. J. W. Dower, *Empire and Aftermath: Yoshida Shigeru and the Japanese Experience, 1878–1954*
85. Martin Collcutt, *Five Mountains: The Rinzai Zen Monastic Institution in Medieval Japan*
86. Kwang Suk Kim and Michael Roemer, *Growth and Structural Transformation*
87. Anne O. Krueger, *The Developmental Role of the Foreign Sector and Aid*
*88. Edwin S. Mills and Byung-Nak Song, *Urbanization and Urban Problems*
89. Sung Hwan Ban, Pal Yong Moon, and Dwight H. Perkins, *Rural Development*
*90. Noel F. McGinn, Donald R. Snodgrass, Yung Bong Kim, Shin-Bok Kim, and Quee-Young Kim, *Education and Development in Korea*
91. Leroy P. Jones and II SaKong, *Government, Business, and Entrepreneurship in Economic Development: The Korean Case*
92. Edward S. Mason, Dwight H. Perkins, Kwang Suk Kim, David C. Cole, Mahn Je Kim et al., *The Economic and Social Modernization of the Republic of Korea*
93. Robert Repetto, Tai Hwan Kwon, Son-Ung Kim, Dae Young Kim, John E. Sloboda, and Peter J. Donaldson, *Economic Development, Population Policy, and Demographic Transition in the Republic of Korea*
94. Parks M. Coble, Jr., *The Shanghai Capitalists and the Nationalist Government, 1927–1937*
95. Noriko Kamachi, *Reform in China: Huang Tsun-hsien and the Japanese Model*
96. Richard Wich, *Sino-Soviet Crisis Politics: A Study of Political Change and Communication*
97. Lillian M. Li, *China's Silk Trade: Traditional Industry in the Modern World, 1842–1937*
98. R. David Arkush, *Fei Xiaotong and Sociology in Revolutionary China*
*99. Kenneth Alan Grossberg, *Japan's Renaissance: The Politics of the Muromachi Bakufu*
100. James Reeve Pusey, *China and Charles Darwin*
101. Hoyt Cleveland Tillman, *Utilitarian Confucianism: Chen Liang's Challenge to Chu Hsi*
102. Thomas A. Stanley, *Ōsugi Sakae, Anarchist in Taishō Japan: The Creativity of the Ego*
103. Jonathan K. Ocko, *Bureaucratic Reform in Provincial China: Ting Jih-ch'ang in Restoration Kiangsu, 1867–1870*
104. James Reed, *The Missionary Mind and American East Asia Policy, 1911–1915*
105. Neil L. Waters, *Japan's Local Pragmatists: The Transition from Bakumatsu to Meiji in the Kawasaki Region*
106. David C. Cole and Yung Chul Park, *Financial Development in Korea, 1945–1978*
107. Roy Bahl, Chuk Kyo Kim, and Chong Kee Park, *Public Finances during the Korean Modernization Process*
108. William D. Wray, *Mitsubishi and the N.Y.K, 1870–1914: Business Strategy in the Japanese Shipping Industry*
109. Ralph William Huenemann, *The Dragon and the Iron Horse: The Economics of Railroads in China, 1876–1937*
110. Benjamin A. Elman, *From Philosophy to Philology: Intellectual and Social Aspects of Change in Late Imperial China*
111. Jane Kate Leonard, *Wei Yüan and China's Rediscovery of the Maritime World*
112. Luke S. K. Kwong, *A Mosaic of the Hundred Days:. Personalities, Politics, and Ideas of 1898*

113. John E. Wills, Jr., *Embassies and Illusions: Dutch and Portuguese Envoys to K'ang-hsi, 1666–1687*
114. Joshua A. Fogel, *Politics and Sinology: The Case of Naitō Konan (1866–1934)*
*115. Jeffrey C. Kinkley, ed., *After Mao: Chinese Literature and Society, 1978– 1981*
116. C. Andrew Gerstle, *Circles of Fantasy: Convention in the Plays of Chikamatsu*
117. Andrew Gordon, *The Evolution of Labor Relations in Japan: Heavy Industry, 1853–1955*
*118. Daniel K. Gardner, *Chu Hsi and the "Ta Hsueh": Neo-Confucian Reflection on the Confucian Canon*
119. Christine Guth Kanda, *Shinzō: Hachiman Imagery and Its Development*
*120. Robert Borgen, *Sugawara no Michizane and the Early Heian Court*
121. Chang-tai Hung, *Going to the People: Chinese Intellectual and Folk Literature, 1918–1937*
* 122. Michael A. Cusumano, *The Japanese Automobile Industry: Technology and Management at Nissan and Toyota*
123. Richard von Glahn, *The Country of Streams and Grottoes: Expansion, Settlement, and the Civilizing of the Sichuan Frontier in Song Times*
124. Steven D. Carter, *The Road to Komatsubara: A Classical Reading of the Renga Hyakuin*
125. Katherine F. Bruner, John K. Fairbank, and Richard T. Smith, *Entering China's Service: Robert Hart's Journals, 1854–1863*
126. Bob Tadashi Wakabayashi, *Anti-Foreignism and Western Learning in Early-Modern Japan: The "New Theses" of 1825*
127. Atsuko Hirai, *Individualism and Socialism: The Life and Thought of Kawai Eijirō (1891–1944)*
128. Ellen Widmer, *The Margins of Utopia: "Shui-hu hou-chuan" and the Literature of Ming Loyalism*
129. R. Kent Guy, *The Emperor's Four Treasuries: Scholars and the State in the Late Chien-lung Era*
130. Peter C. Perdue, *Exhausting the Earth: State and Peasant in Hunan, 1500–1850*
131. Susan Chan Egan, *A Latterday Confucian: Reminiscences of William Hung (1893–1980)*
132. James T. C. Liu, *China Turning Inward: Intellectual-Political Changes in the Early Twelfth Century*
133. Paul A. Cohen, *Between Tradition and Modernity: Wang T'ao and Reform in Late Ching China*
134. Kate Wildman Nakai, *Shogunal Politics: Arai Hakuseki and the Premises of Tokugawa Rule*
135. Parks M. Coble, *Facing Japan: Chinese Politics and Japanese Imperialism, 1931–1937*
136. Jon L. Saari, *Legacies of Childhood: Growing Up Chinese in a Time of Crisis, 1890–1920*
137. Susan Downing Videen, *Tales of Heichū*
138. Heinz Morioka and Miyoko Sasaki, *Rakugo: The Popular Narrative Art of Japan*
139. Joshua A. Fogel, *Nakae Ushikichi in China: The Mourning of Spirit*
140. Alexander Barton Woodside, *Vietnam and the Chinese Model.: A Comparative Study of Vietnamese and Chinese Government in the First Half of the Nineteenth Century*
141. George Elision, *Deus Destroyed: The Image of Christianity in Early Modern Japan*

142. William D. Wray, ed., *Managing Industrial Enterprise: Cases from Japan's Prewar Experience*
143. T'ung-tsu Ch'ü, *Local Government in China under the Ching*
144. Marie Anchordoguy, *Computers, Inc.: Japan's Challenge to IBM*
145. Barbara Molony, *Technology and Investment: The Prewar Japanese Chemical Industry*
146. Mary Elizabeth Berry, *Hideyoshi*
147. Laura E. Hein, *Fueling Growth: The Energy Revolution and Economic Policy in Postwar Japan*
148. Wen-hsin Yeh, *The Alienated Academy: Culture and Politics in Republican China, 1919–1937*
149. Dru C. Gladney, *Muslim Chinese: Ethnic Nationalism in the People's Republic*
150. Merle Goldman and Paul A. Cohen, eds., *Ideas Across Cultures: Essays on Chinese Thought in Honor of Benjamin L Schwartz*
151. James Polachek, *The Inner Opium War*
152. Gail Lee Bernstein, *Japanese Marxist: A Portrait of Kawakami Hajime, 1879–1946*
153. Lloyd E. Eastman, *The Abortive Revolution: China under Nationalist Rule, 1927–1937*
154. Mark Mason, *American Multinationals and Japan: The Political Economy of Japanese Capital Controls, 1899–1980*
155. Richard J. Smith, John K. Fairbank, and Katherine F. Bruner, *Robert Hart and China's Early Modernization: His Journals, 1863–1866*
156. George J. Tanabe, Jr., *Myōe the Dreamkeeper: Fantasy and Knowledge in Kamakura Buddhism*
157. William Wayne Farris, *Heavenly Warriors: The Evolution of Japan's Military, 500–1300*
158. Yu-ming Shaw, *An American Missionary in China: John Leighton Stuart and Chinese-American Relations*
159. James B. Palais, *Politics and Policy in Traditional Korea*
160. Douglas Reynolds, *China, 1898–1912: The Xinzheng Revolution and Japan*
161. Roger Thompson, *China's Local Councils in the Age of Constitutional Reform*
162. William Johnston, *The Modern Epidemic: History of Tuberculosis in Japan*
163. Constantine Nomikos Vaporis, *Breaking Barriers: Travel and the State in Early Modern Japan*
164. Irmela Hijiya-Kirschnereit, *Rituals of Self-Revelation: Shishōsetsu as Literary Genre and Socio-Cultural Phenomenon*
165. James C. Baxter, *The Meiji Unification through the Lens of Ishikawa Prefecture*
166. Thomas R. H. Havens, *Architects of Affluence: The Tsutsumi Family and the Seibu-Saison Enterprises in Twentieth-Century Japan*
167. Anthony Hood Chambers, *The Secret Window: Ideal Worlds in Tanizaki's Fiction*
168. Steven J. Ericson, *The Sound of the Whistle: Railroads and the State in Meiji Japan*
169. Andrew Edmund Goble, *Kenmu: Go-Daigo's Revolution*
170. Denise Potrzeba Lett, *In Pursuit of Status: The Making of South Korea's "New" Urban Middle Class*
171. Mimi Hall Yiengpruksawan, *Hiraizumi: Buddhist Art and Regional Politics in Twelfth-Century Japan*

172. Charles Shirō Inouye, *The Similitude of Blossoms: A Critical Biography of Izumi Kyōka (1873–1939), Japanese Novelist and Playwright*
173. Aviad E. Raz, *Riding the Black Ship: Japan and Tokyo Disneyland*
174. Deborah J. Milly, *Poverty, Equality, and Growth: The Politics of Economic Need in Postwar Japan*
175. See Heng Teow, *Japan's Cultural Policy Toward China, 1918–1931: A Comparative Perspective*
176. Michael A. Fuller, *An Introduction to Literary Chinese*
177. Frederick R. Dickinson, *War and National Reinvention: Japan in the Great War, 1914–1919*
178. John Solt, *Shredding the Tapestry of Meaning: The Poetry and Poetics of Kitasono Katue (1902–1978)*
179. Edward Pratt, *Japan's Protoindustrial Elite: The Economic Foundations of the Gōnō*
180. Atsuko Sakaki, *Recontextualizing Texts: Narrative Performance in Modern Japanese Fiction*
181. Soon-Won Park, *Colonial Industrialization and Labor in Korea: The Onoda Cement Factory*
182. JaHyun Kim Haboush and Martina Deuchler, *Culture and the State in Late Chosŏn Korea*
183. John W. Chaffee, *Branches of Heaven: A History of the Imperial Clan of Sung China*
184. Gi-Wook Shin and Michael Robinson, eds., *Colonial Modernity in Korea*
185. Nam-lin Hur, *Prayer and Play in Late Tokugawa Japan: Asakusa Sensōji and Edo Society*
186. Kristin Stapleton, *Civilizing Chengdu: Chinese Urban Reform, 1895–1937*
187. Hyung Il Pai, *Constructing "Korean" Origins: A Critical Review of Archaeology, Historiography, and Racial Myth in Korean State-Formation Theories*
188. Brian D. Ruppert, *Jewel in the Ashes: Buddha Relics and Power in Early Medieval Japan*
189. Susan Daruvala, *Zhou Zuoren and an Alternative Chinese Response to Modernity*
190. James Z. Lee, *The Political Economy of a Frontier: Southwest China, 1250–1850*
191. Kerry Smith, *A Time of Crisis: Japan, the Great Depression, and Rural Revitalization*
192. Michael Lewis, *Becoming Apart: National Power and Local Politics in Toyama, 1868–1945*
193. William C. Kirby, Man-houng Lin, James Chin Shih, and David A. Pietz, eds., *State and Economy in Republican China: A Handbook for Scholars*
194. Timothy S. George, *Minamata: Pollution and the Struggle for Democracy in PostwarJapan*
195. Billy K. L. So, *Prosperity, Region, and Institutions in Maritime China: The South Fukien Pattern, 946–1368*
196. Yoshihisa Tak Matsusaka, *The Making of Japanese Manchuria, 1904–1932*
197. Maram Epstein, *Competing Discourses: Orthodoxy, Authenticity, and Engendered Meanings in Late Imperial Chinese Fiction*